INTRODUCTION TO OPERATING SYSTEMS

William Stallings • William Murray
Chris Pappas • Abraham Silberschatz • Peter Baer Galvin
Selected by Bill Sinclair

UNIVERSITY OF PHOENIX
COLLEGE OF INFORMATION SYSTEMS AND TECHNOLOGY

Pearson Custom Publishing

Cover Illustration: "Circuitboard With Different Operating Systems,"
by IO Image/The Stock Illustration Source.

Printed in the United States of America

10 9 8 7 6 5 4 3

Please visit our website at www.pearsoncustom.com

ISBN 0–536–60175–5

BA 990578

PEARSON CUSTOM PUBLISHING
75 Arlington Street, Boston, MA 02116
A Pearson Education Company

CONTENTS

SECTION ONE: FUNDAMENTALS OF AN OPERATING SYSTEM (OS) 1

OPERATING SYSTEM OVERVIEW 3
- Operating System Objectives and Functions 3
- The Evolution of Operating Systems 7

MEMORY MANAGEMENT 15
- Memory Management Requirements 15
- Memory Partitioning 18
- Paging 18
- Basic Method 18
- Structure of the Page Table 23

VIRTUAL MEMORY 26
- Hardware and Control Structures 26
- Demand Paging 29
- Segmentation 31
- Combined Paging and Segmentation 32
- Segmentation with Paging 37
- Operating System Software 40

PROCESS DESCRIPTION AND CONTROL 44
- Process States 44
- Process Description 48
- Process Control 52

THREADS, SMP, AND MICROKERNELS 59
- Processes and Threads 59
- Symmetric Multiprocessing 66

UNIPROCESSOR SCHEDULING 69
- Types of Scheduling 69

MULTIPROCESSOR AND REAL-TIME SCHEDULING 72
- Multiprocessor Scheduling 72

I/O MANAGEMENT AND DISK SCHEDULING 74
- I/O Devices 75
- Organization of the I/O Function 76
- Operating System Design Issues 80

FILE MANAGEMENT 82
- Overview 82
- File Organization and Access 87
- File Directories 91
- File Sharing 95

DISTRIBUTED PROCESSING, CLIENT/SERVER, AND CLUSTERS 96

NOTES 97

SECTION TWO: PC OPERATING SYSTEMS 99
Understanding Windows Concepts and Terminology 101
Reasons for Developing Windows Applications 101
Key Elements of Windows 102
Getting Started 111
Windows 98 and NT Concepts and Terminology 111
Windows versus windows 112
Creating the "Look" 112
Object Classes to the Rescue 114
Using Object-Oriented Technology 114
Communication via Messages 117
Standard Windows Resources 120
Standard Windows Functions 120
A First Look at WINDOWS.H 120
Understanding the Style of Windows Code 121
The Seven Fundamental Steps for Developing Windows Programs 122

SECTION THREE: MAINFRAME OPERATING SYSTEMS 125
MVS History 127
MVS Description 128
MVS Tasks 130
Task-Related Control Structures 131
MVS Resource Allocation 133
ENQUE 133
Locks 134
Examples of Memory Management (System/370 and MVS) 134
Address Space Structure 134
Hardware and Control Structures 136
Operating-System Considerations 137
Multiprocessor and Real-Time Scheduling with MVS 138
I/O Management and Disk Scheduling with MVS 139

SECTION FOUR: UNIX AND LINUX 143
THE UNIX SYSTEM 145
History 145
Design Principles 149
Programmer Interface 150
File Manipulation 151
Process Control 153
Signals 155
Process Groups 156
Information Manipulation 156
Library Routines 156
User Interface 156
Shells and Commands 157
Standard I/O 158
Pipelines, Filters, and Shell Scripts 158

Process Management 159
Process Control Blocks 159
CPU Scheduling 161
Memory Management 162
Swapping 163
Paging 163
File System 165
Blocks and Fragments 165
Inodes 165
Directories 166
Mapping of a File Descriptor to an Inode 167
Disk Structures 168
Implementations 169
Layout and Allocation Policies 169
I/O System 171
Block Buffer Cache 172
Raw Device Interfaces 173
C-Lists 173
Interprocess Communication 174
Sockets 174
Network Support 176
Summary 178
THE LINUX SYSTEM 179
History 179
The Linux Kernel 180
The Linux System 181
Linux Distributions 181
Linux Licensing 182
Design Principles 182
Components of a Linux System 183
Kernel Modules 185
Module Management 185
Driver Registration 186
Conflict Resolution 186
Process Management 187
The Fork/Exec Process Model 187
Processes and Threads 189
Scheduling 190
Kernel Synchronization 190
Process Scheduling 192
Symmetric Multiprocessing 193
Memory Management 193
Management of Physical Memory 193
Virtual Memory 195
Execution and Loading of User Programs 197

File Systems 199
The Virtual File System 199
The Linux ext2fs File System 200
The Linux Proc File System 201
Input and Output 202
Block Devices 203
Character Devices 204
Interprocess Communication 205
Synchronization and Signals 205
Passing of Data Among Processes 206
Network Structure 206
Security 208
Authentication 208
Access Control 209
Summary 210
Bibliographical Notes 211

SECTION FIVE: WINDOWS NT 213
History 215
Design Principles 216
System Components 217
Hardware Abstraction Layer 217
Kernel 217
Executive 221
Environmental Subsystems 228
MS-DOS Environment 228
16-Bit Windows Environment 229
Win32 Environment 229
POSIX Subsystem 229
OS/2 Subsystem 229
Logon and Security Subsystems 230
File System 230
Internal Layout 230
Recovery 231
Security 232
Volume Management and Fault Tolerance 232
Compression 235
Networking 235
Protocols 235
Distributed-Processing Mechanisms 236
Redirectors and Servers 237
Domains 238
Name Resolution in TCP/IP Networks 238

Programmer Interface ... 239
Access to Kernel Objects ... 239
Process Management ... 241
Interprocess Communication ... 242
Memory Management ... 243
Summary ... 244

REFERENCES ... 245

INDEX ... 247

SECTION 1

FUNDAMENTALS OF AN OPERATING SYSTEM (OS)

OPERATING SYSTEM OVERVIEW

This chapter provides a brief history of operating systems. This history is interesting and also serves the purpose of providing an overview of operating system principles. We begin with a look at the objectives and functions of operating systems. Then we look at how operating systems have evolved from primitive batch systems to sophisticated multimode, multiuser systems.

Operating System Objectives and Functions

An operating system is a program that controls the execution of application programs and acts as an interface between the user of a computer and the computer hardware. It can be thought of as having three objectives:

- **Convenience:** An operating system makes a computer more convenient to use.
- **Efficiency:** An operating system allows the computer system resources to be used in an efficient manner.
- **Ability to evolve:** An operating system should be constructed in such a way as to permit the effective development, testing, and introduction of new system functions without interfering with service.

Let us examine these three aspects of an operating system in turn.

THE OPERATING SYSTEM AS A USER/COMPUTER INTERFACE The hardware and software used in providing applications to a user can be viewed in a layered or hierarchical fashion, as depicted in Figure 1-1. The user of those applications, the end user, generally is not concerned with the computer's architecture. Thus the end user views a computer system in terms of an application. That application can be expressed in a programming language and is developed by an application programmer. If one were to develop an application program as a set of machine instructions that is completely responsible for controlling the computer hardware, one would be faced with an overwhelmingly complex task. To ease this task, a set of system programs is provided. Some of these programs are referred to as utilities. These implement frequently used functions that assist in program creation, the management of files, and the control of I/O devices. A programmer will make use of these facilities in developing an application, and the application, while it is running, will invoke the utilities to perform certain functions. The most important system program is the operating system. The

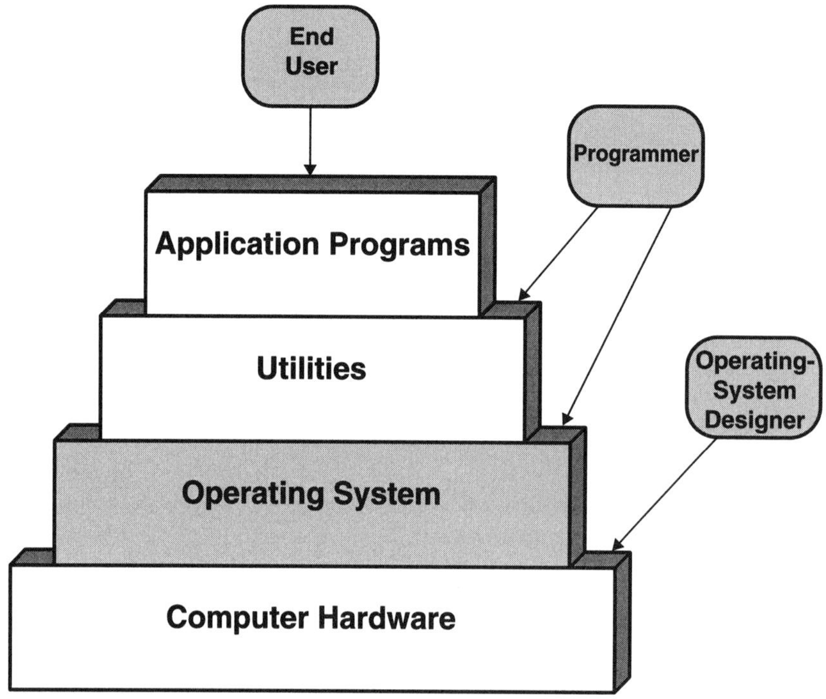

FIGURE 1-1 *Layers and Views of a Computer System*

operating system masks the details of the hardware from the programmer and provides the programmer with a convenient interface for using the system. It acts as mediator, making it easier for the programmer and for application programs to access and use those facilities and services.

Briefly, the operating system typically provides services in the following areas:

- **Program creation:** The operating system provides a variety of facilities and services, such as editors and debuggers, to assist the programmer in creating programs. Typically, these services are in the form of utility programs that are not actually part of the operating system but are accessible through the operating system.
- **Program execution:** A number of tasks need to be performed to execute a program. Instructions and data must be loaded into main memory, I/O devices and files must be initialized, and other resources must be prepared. The operating system handles all of this for the user.
- **Access to I/O devices:** Each I/O device requires its own peculiar set of instructions or control signals for operation. The operating system takes care of the details so that the programmer can think in terms of simple reads and writes.
- **Controlled access to files:** In the case of files, control must include an understanding of not only the nature of the I/O device (disk drive, tape drive) but also the file format on the storage medium. Again, the operating system worries about the details. Further, in the case of a system with multiple simultaneous users, the operating system can provide protection mechanisms to control access to the files.
- **System access:** In the case of a shared or public system, the operating system controls access to the system as a whole and to specific system resources. The access function must provide protection of resources and data from unauthorized users and must resolve conflicts for resource contention.

- **Error detection and response:** A variety of errors can occur while a computer system is running. These include internal and external hardware errors, such as a memory error or a device failure or malfunction; and various software errors, such as arithmetic overflow, attempt to access forbidden memory location, and inability of the operating system to grant the request of an application. In each case, the operating system must make the response that clears the error condition with the least impact on running applications. The response may range from ending the program that caused the error, to retrying the operation, to simply reporting the error to the application.
- **Accounting:** A good operating system will collect usage statistics for various resources and monitor performance parameters such as response time. On any system, this information is useful in anticipating the need for future enhancements and in tuning the system to improve performance. On a multiuser system, the information can be used for billing purposes.

THE OPERATING SYSTEM AS RESOURCE MANAGER A computer is a set of resources for the movement, storage, and processing of data and for the control of these functions. The operating system is responsible for managing these resources.

Can we say that it is the operating system that controls the movement, storage, and processing of data? From one point of view, the answer is yes: By managing the computer's resources, the operating system is in control of the computer's basic functions. But this control is exercised in a curious way. Normally, we think of a control mechanism as something external to that which is controlled, or at least as something that is a distinct and separate part of that which is controlled. (For example, a residential heating system is controlled by a thermostat, which is completely distinct from the heat-generation and heat-distribution apparatus.) This is not the case with the operating system, which as a control mechanism is unusual in two respects:

- The operating system functions in the same way as ordinary computer software; that is, it is a program executed by the processor.
- The operating system frequently relinquishes control and must depend on the processor to allow it to regain control.

The operating system is, in fact, nothing more than a computer program. Like other computer programs, it provides instructions for the processor. The key difference is in the intent of the program. The operating system directs the processor in the use of the other system resources and in the timing of its execution of other programs. But in order for the processor to do any of these things, it must cease executing the operating system program and execute other programs. Thus, the operating system relinquishes control for the processor to do some "useful" work and then resumes control long enough to prepare the processor to do the next piece of work. The mechanisms involved in all this should become clear as the chapter proceeds.

Figure 1-2 suggests the main resources that are managed by the operating system. A portion of the operating system is in main memory. This includes the *kernel*, or *nucleus*, which contains the most frequently used functions in the operating system and, at a given time, other portions of the operating system currently in use. The remainder of main memory contains other user programs and data. The allocation of this resource (main memory) is controlled jointly by the operating system and memory-management hardware in the processor, as we shall see. The operating system decides when an I/O device can be used by a program in execution and controls access to and use of files. The processor itself is a resource, and the operating system must determine how much processor time is to be devoted to the execution of a particular user program. In the case of a multiple-processor system, this decision must span all of the processors.

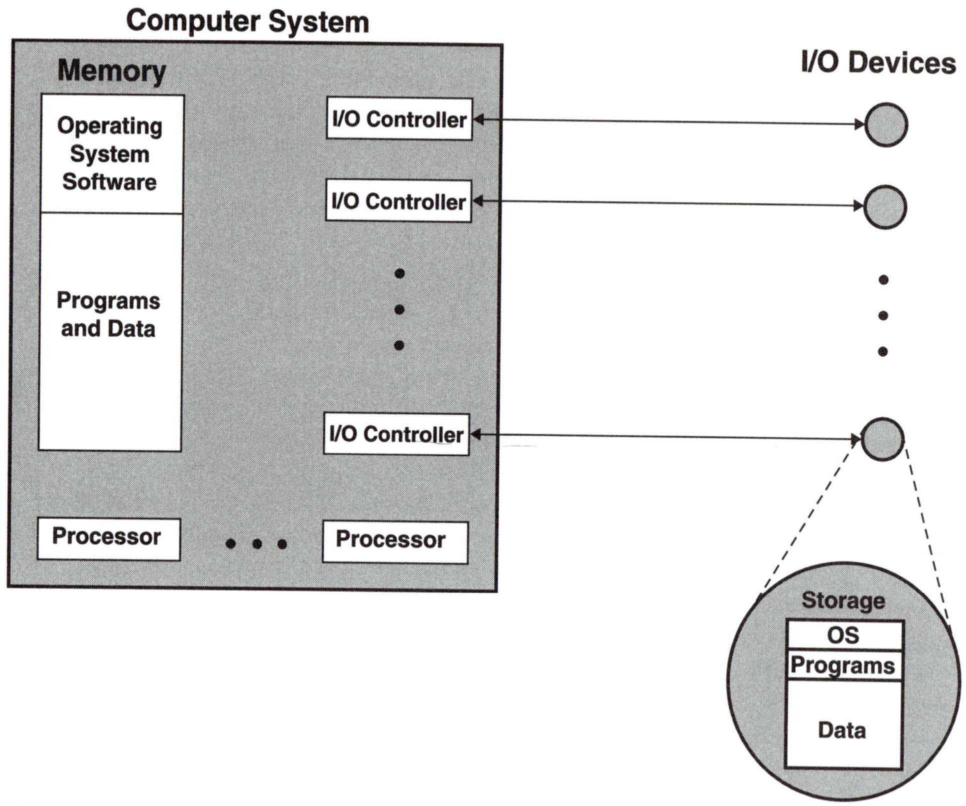

FIGURE 1-2 *The Operating System as a Resource Manager*

EASE OF EVOLUTION OF AN OPERATING SYSTEM A major operating system will evolve over time for a number of reasons:

- **Hardware upgrades plus new types of hardware:** For example, early versions of UNIX and OS/2 did not employ a paging mechanism because they were run on machines without paging hardware. More recent versions have been modified to exploit paging capabilities. Also, the use of graphics terminals and page-mode terminals instead of line-at-a-time scroll mode terminals may affect operating system design. For example, such a terminal may allow the user to view several applications at the same time through "windows" on the screen. This requires more sophisticated support in the operating system.
- **New services:** In response to user demand or in response to the needs of system managers, the operating system will expand to offer new services. For example, if it is found to be difficult to maintain good performance for users with existing tools, new measurement and control tools may be added to the operating system. Other examples include applications that require the use of windows on the display screen. This enhancement requires major upgrades to the operating system.
- **Fixes:** Any operating system has faults. These are discovered over the course of time and fixes are made. Of course, the fix may introduce new faults.

The need to change an operating system on a regular basis places certain requirements on its design. An obvious statement is that the system should be modular in construction, with clearly defined interfaces between the modules, and that it should be well documented. For large programs, such as the typical contemporary operating system, what might be referred to as straightforward modularization is inadequate (Denning 1980). That is, much more must be done than simply partitioning a program into subroutines.

The Evolution of Operating Systems

In attempting to understand the key requirements for an operating system and the significance of the major features of a contemporary operating system, it is useful to consider how operating systems have evolved over the years.

SERIAL PROCESSING With the earliest computers, from the late 1940s to the mid-1950s, the programmer interacted directly with the computer hardware; there was no operating system. These machines were run from a console, consisting of display lights, toggle switches, some form of input device, and a printer. Programs in machine code were loaded via the input device (e.g., a card reader). If an error halted the program, the error condition was indicated by the lights. The programmer could proceed to examine registers and main memory to determine the cause of the error. If the program proceeded to a normal completion, the output appeared on the printer.

These early systems presented two main problems:

- **Scheduling:** Most installations used a sign-up sheet to reserve machine time. Typically, a user could sign up for a block of time in multiples of a half hour or so. A user might sign up for an hour and finish in 45 minutes; this would result in wasted computer idle time. On the other hand, the user might run into problems, not finish in the allotted time, and be forced to stop before resolving the problem.
- **Setup time:** A single program, called a **job**, could involve loading the compiler plus the high-level language program (source program) into memory, saving the compiled program (object program), and then loading and linking together the object program and common functions. Each of these steps could involve mounting or dismounting tapes or setting up card decks. If an error occurred, the hapless user typically had to go back to the beginning of the setup sequence. Thus a considerable amount of time was spent just in setting up the program to run.

This mode of operation could be termed serial processing, reflecting the fact that users have access to the computer in series. Over time, various system software tools were developed to attempt to make serial processing more efficient. These included libraries of common functions, linkers, loaders, debuggers, and I/O driver routines that were available as common software for all users.

SIMPLE BATCH SYSTEMS Early machines were very expensive and therefore it was important to maximize machine utilization. The wasted time due to scheduling and setup time was unacceptable.

To improve utilization, the concept of a batch operating system was developed. It appears that the first batch operating system (and the first operating system of any kind) was developed in the mid-1950s by General Motors for use on an IBM 701 (Weizer 1981). The concept was subsequently refined and implemented on the IBM 704 by a number of IBM customers. By the early 1960s, a number of vendors had developed batch operating systems for their computer systems. IBSYS, the IBM operating system for the 7090/7094 computers, is particularly notable because of its widespread influence on other systems.

The central idea behind the simple batch processing scheme was the use of a piece of software known as the *monitor*. With the use of this type of operating system, the user no longer has direct access to the machine. Rather, the user submits the job on cards or tape to a computer operator, who *batches* the jobs together sequentially and places the entire batch on an input device for use by the monitor. Each program is constructed to branch back to the monitor when it completes processing, at which point the monitor would automatically begin loading the next program.

To understand how this scheme works, let us look at it from two points of view: that of the monitor and that of the processor. From the point of view of the monitor, it is the monitor that controls the sequence of events. For this to be so, much of the monitor must always be in main memory and available for execution (Figure 1-3). That portion is referred to as the

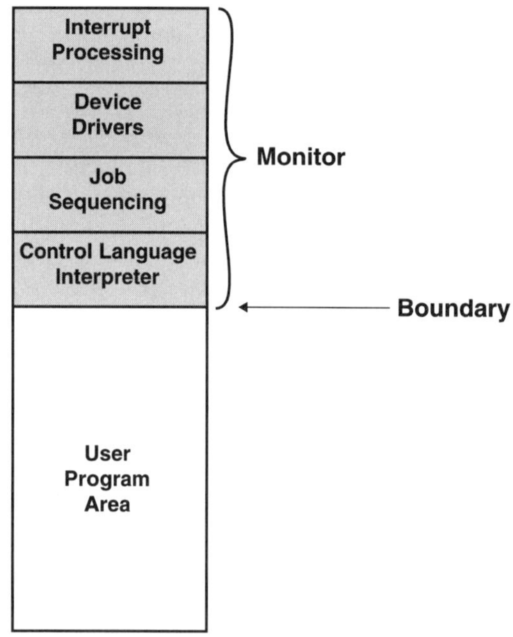

FIGURE 1-3 *Memory Layout for a Resident Monitor*

resident monitor. The rest of the monitor consists of utilities and common functions that are loaded as subroutines to the user program at the beginning of any job that requires them. The monitor reads in jobs one at a time from the input device (typically a card reader or magnetic tape drive). As it is read in, the current job is placed in the user program area, and control is passed to this job. When the job is completed, it returns control to the monitor, which immediately reads in the next job. The results of each job are printed out for delivery to the user.

Now let us consider this sequence from the point of view of the processor. At a certain point in time, the processor is executing instructions from the portion of main memory containing the monitor. These instructions cause the next job to be read in to another portion of main memory. Once a job has been read in, the processor will encounter in the monitor a branch instruction that instructs the processor to continue execution at the start of the user program. The processor will then execute the instructions in the user's program until it encounters an ending or error condition. Either event causes the processor to fetch its next instruction from the monitor program. Thus the phrase "control is passed to a job" simply means that the processor is now fetching and executing instructions in a user program, and "control is returned to the monitor" means that the processor is now fetching and executing instructions from the monitor program.

It should be clear that the monitor handles the scheduling problem. A batch of jobs is queued up, and jobs are executed as rapidly as possible, with no intervening idle time.

How about the job setup time? The monitor handles this as well. With each job, instructions are included in a primitive form of **job control language** (JCL). This is a special type of programming language used to provide instructions to the monitor. A simple example is that of a user submitting a program written in FORTRAN plus some data to be used by the program. Each FORTRAN instruction and each item of data is on a separate punched card or a separate record on tape. In addition to FORTRAN and data lines, the job includes job control instructions, which are denoted by '$' at the beginning. The overall format of the job looks like this:

```
$JOB
$FTN
•
•   FORTRAN instructions
•
$LOAD
$RUN
•
•   Data
•
$END
```

To execute this job, the monitor reads the $FTN line and loads the appropriate compiler from its mass storage (usually tape). The compiler translates the user's program into object code, which is stored in memory or mass storage. If it is stored in memory, the operation is referred to as "compile, load, and go." If it is stored on tape, then the $LOAD instruction is required. This instruction is read by the monitor, which regains control after the compile operation. The monitor invokes the loader, which loads the object program into memory in place of the compiler and transfers control to it. In this manner, a large segment of main memory can be shared among different subsystems, although only one such subsystem could be resident and executing at a time.

During the execution of the user program, any input instruction causes one line of data to be read. The input instruction in the user program causes an input routine that is part of the operating system to be invoked. The input routine checks to make sure that the program does not accidentally read in a JCL line. If this happens, an error occurs and control transfers to the monitor. At the successful or unsuccessful completion of the user job, the monitor will scan the input lines until it encounters the next JCL instruction. Thus, the system is protected against a program with too many or too few data lines.

We see that the monitor, or batch operating system, is simply a computer program. It relies on the ability of the processor to fetch instructions from various portions of main memory in order to seize and relinquish control alternately. Certain other hardware features are also desirable:

- **Memory protection:** While the user program is executing, it must not alter the memory area containing the monitor. If such an attempt is made, the processor hardware should detect an error and transfer control to the monitor. The monitor would then abort the job, print out an error message, and load in the next job.
- **Timer:** A timer is used to prevent a single job from monopolizing the system. The timer is set at the beginning of each job. If the timer expires, an interrupt occurs, and control returns to the monitor.
- **Privileged instructions:** Certain instructions are designated privileged and can be executed only by the monitor. If the processor encounters such an instruction while executing a user program, an error interrupt occurs. Among the privileged instructions are I/O instructions, so that the monitor retains control of all I/O devices. This prevents, for example, a user program from accidentally reading job control instructions from the next job. If a user program wishes to perform I/O, it must request that the monitor perform the operation for it. If a privileged instruction is encountered by the processor while it is executing a user program, the processor hardware considers this an error and transfers control to the monitor.
- **Interrupts:** Early computer models did not have this capability. This feature gives the operating system more flexibility in relinquishing control to and regaining control from user programs.

Of course, an operating system can be built without these features. But computer vendors quickly learned that the results are chaos, so even relatively primitive batch operating systems were provided with these hardware features.

With a batch operating system, machine time alternates between execution of user programs and execution of the monitor. There have been two sacrifices: Some main memory is now given over to the monitor and some machine time is consumed by the monitor. Both of these are forms of overhead. Even with this overhead, the simple batch system improves utilization of the computer.

MULTIPROGRAMMED BATCH SYSTEMS Even with the automatic job sequencing provided by a simple batch operating system, the processor is often idle. The problem is that I/O devices are slow compared to the processor. Figure 1-4 details a representative calculation.

Read one record	0.10015 seconds
Execute 100 instructions	0.0001 seconds
Write one record	0.0015 seconds
TOTAL	0.0031 seconds

$$\text{Percent CPU Utilization} = \frac{0.0001}{0.0031} = 0.032 = 3.2\%$$

FIGURE 1-4 *System Utilization Example*

The calculation concerns a program that processes a file of records and performs, on average, 100 machine instructions per record. In this example the computer spends over 96% of its time waiting for I/O devices to finish transferring data! Figure 1-5a illustrates this situation. The processor spends a certain amount of time executing, until it reaches an I/O instruction. It must then wait until that I/O instruction concludes before proceeding.

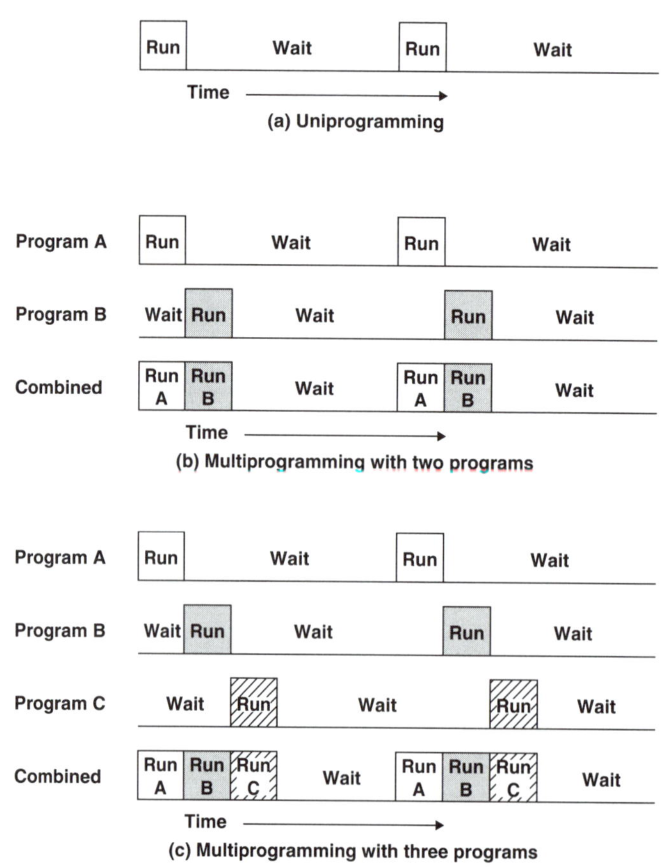

FIGURE 1-5 *Multiprogramming Example*

This inefficiency is not necessary. We know that there must be enough memory to hold the operating system (resident monitor) and one user program. Suppose that there is room for the operating system and two user programs. Now, when one job needs to wait for I/O, the processor can switch to the other job, which most likely is not waiting for I/O (Figure 1-5b). Furthermore, we might expand memory to hold three, four, or more programs and switch among all of them (Figure 1-5c). The process is known as **multiprogramming**, or **multitasking**. It is the central theme of modern operating systems.

To illustrate the benefit of multiprogramming, let us consider an example, based on one in (Turner 1986). Consider a computer with 256K words of available memory (not used by the operating system), a disk , a terminal, and a printer. Three programs, JOB1, JOB2, and JOB3, are submitted for execution at the same time, with the attributes listed in Table 1.1. We assume minimal processor requirements for JOB2 and JOB3 and continuous disk and printer use by JOB3. For a simple batch environment, these jobs will be executed in sequence. Thus, JOB1 completes in 5 minutes. JOB2 must wait until the 5 minutes is over, and then completes 15 minutes after that. JOB3 begins after 20 minutes and completes at 30 minutes from the time it was initially submitted. The average resource utilization, throughput, and response times are shown in the uniprogramming column of Table 1.2. Device-by-device utilization is illustrated in Figure 1-6. It is evident that there is gross underutilization for all resources when averaged over the required 30-minute time period.

TABLE 1.1
Sample Program Execution Attributes

	JOB 1	JOB 2	JOB 3
Type of job	Heavy compute	Heavy I/O	Heavy I/O
Duration	5 min	15 min	10 min
Memory required	50K	100K	80K
Need disk?	No	No	Yes
Need terminal?	No	Yes	No
Need printer?	No	No	Yes

TABLE 1.2
Effects of Multiprogramming on Resource Utilization

	Uniprogramming	Multiprogramming
Processor use	17%	33%
Memory use	30%	67%
Disk use	33%	67%
Printer use	33%	67%
Elapsed time	30 min	30 min
Throughput rate	6 jobs/h	6 jobs/h
Mean response time	18 min	18 min

Now suppose that the jobs are run concurrently under a multiprogramming operating system. Because there is little resource contention between the jobs, all three can run in nearly minimum time while coexisting with the others in the computer (assuming that JOB2 and JOB3 are allotted enough processor time to keep their input and output operations active). JOB1 will still require 5 minutes to complete, but at the end of that time, JOB2 will be one-

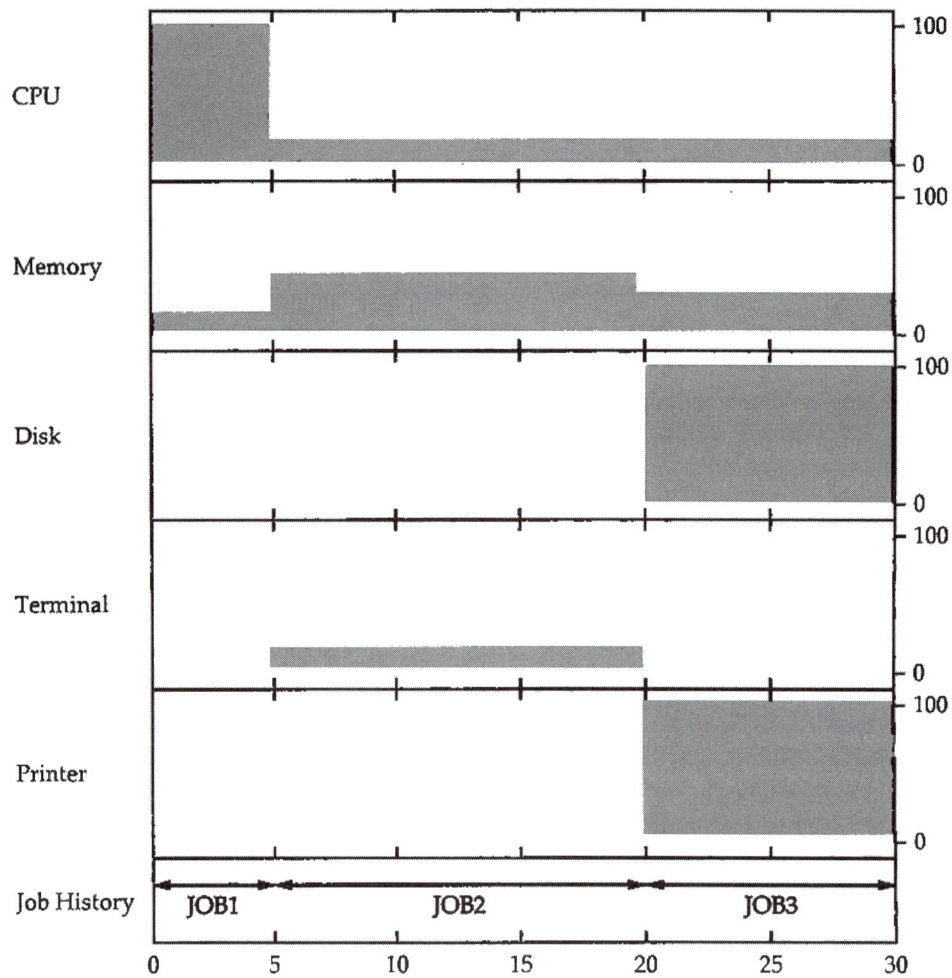

FIGURE 1-6 *Uniprogramming Utilization Histogram (Turner 1986)*

third finished and JOB3 half finished. All three jobs will have finished within 15 minutes. The improvement is evident when examining the multiprogramming column of Table 1.2, obtained from the histogram shown in Figure 1-7.

As with a simple batch system, a multiprogramming batch system must rely on certain computer hardware features. The most notable additional feature that is useful for multiprogramming is the hardware that supports I/O interrupts and DMA. With interrupt-driven I/O or DMA, the processor can issue an I/O command for one job and proceed with the execution of another job while the I/O is carried out by the device controller. When the I/O operation is complete, the processor is interrupted and control is passed to an interrupt-handling program in the operating system. The operating system will then pass control to another job.

Multiprogramming operating systems are fairly sophisticated compared to single-program, or **uniprogramming**, systems. To have several jobs ready to run, they must be kept in main memory, requiring some form of **memory management**. In addition, if several jobs are ready to run, the processor must decide which one to run, which requires some algorithm for scheduling. These concepts are discussed later in this chapter.

TIME-SHARING SYSTEMS With the use of multiprogramming, batch processing can be quite efficient. However, for many jobs, it is desirable to provide a mode in which the user

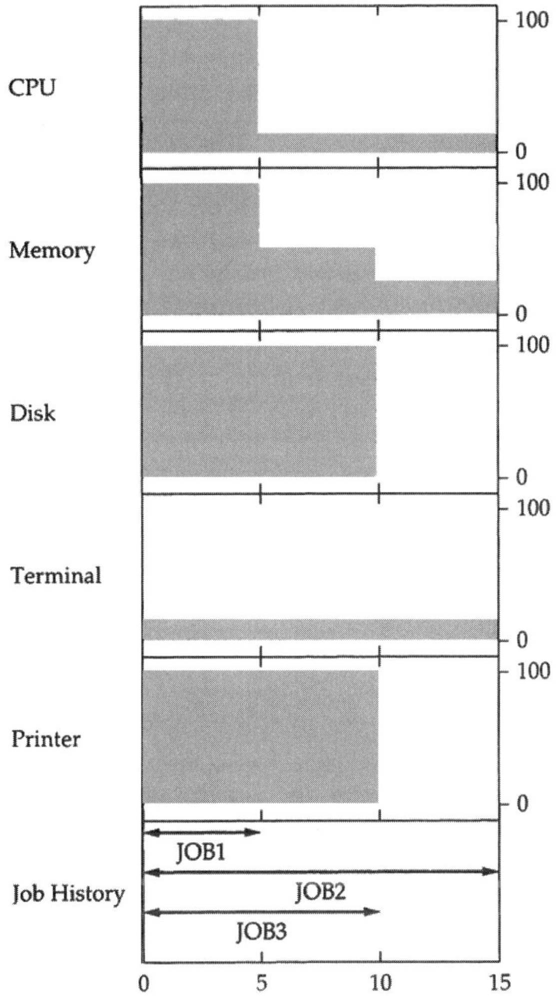

FIGURE 1-7 *Multiprogramming Utilization Histogram (Turner 1986)*

interacts directly with the computer. Indeed, for some jobs, such as transaction processing, an interactive mode is essential.

Today, the requirement for an interactive computing facility can be, and often is, met by the use of a dedicated microcomputer. That option was not available in the 1960s, when most computers were big and costly. Instead time sharing was developed.

Just as multiprogramming allows the processor to handle multiple batch jobs at a time, multiprogramming can be used to handle multiple interactive jobs. In this latter case, the technique is referred to as time sharing, because the processor's time is shared among multiple users. In a time-sharing system, multiple users simultaneously access the system through terminals, with the operating system interleaving the execution of each user program in a short burst or quantum of computation. Thus, if there are n users actively requesting service at one time, each user will only see on the average $1/n$ of the effective computer speed, not counting operating system overhead. However, given the relatively slow human reaction time, the response time on a properly designed system should be comparable to that on a dedicated computer.

Both batch multiprogramming and time sharing use multiprogramming. The key differences are listed in Table 1.3.

TABLE 1.3
Batch Multiprogramming versus Time Sharing

	Batch Multiprogramming	Time Sharing
Principal objective	Maximize processor use	Minimize response time
Source of instructions to operating system	Job control language instructions provided with the job	Commands entered at the terminal

One of the first time-sharing operating systems to be developed was the Compatible Time-Sharing System (CTSS) (Corbato 1962), developed at MIT by a group known as Project MAC (Machine-Aided Cognition, or Multiple-Access Computers). The system was first developed for the IBM 709 in 1961 and later transferred to an IBM 7094.

Compared to later systems, CTSS was quite primitive. The system ran on a machine with 32K 36-bit words of main memory, with the resident monitor consuming 5K of that. When control was to be assigned to an interactive user, the user's program and data were loaded into the remaining 27K of main memory. A system clock generated interrupts at a rate of approximately one every 0.2 seconds. At each clock interrupt, the operating system regained control and could assign the processor to another user. Thus, at regular time intervals, the current user would be preempted and another user loaded in. To preserve the old user's status for later resumption, the old user's programs and data were written out to disk before the new user's programs and data were read in. Subsequently, the old user's space would be restored when it was next given a turn.

To minimize disk traffic, user memory was only written out when the incoming program would overwrite it. This principle is illustrated in Figure 1-8. Assume that there are four interactive users with the following memory requirements:

- JOB1: 15K
- JOB2: 20K
- JOB3: 5K
- JOB4: 10K

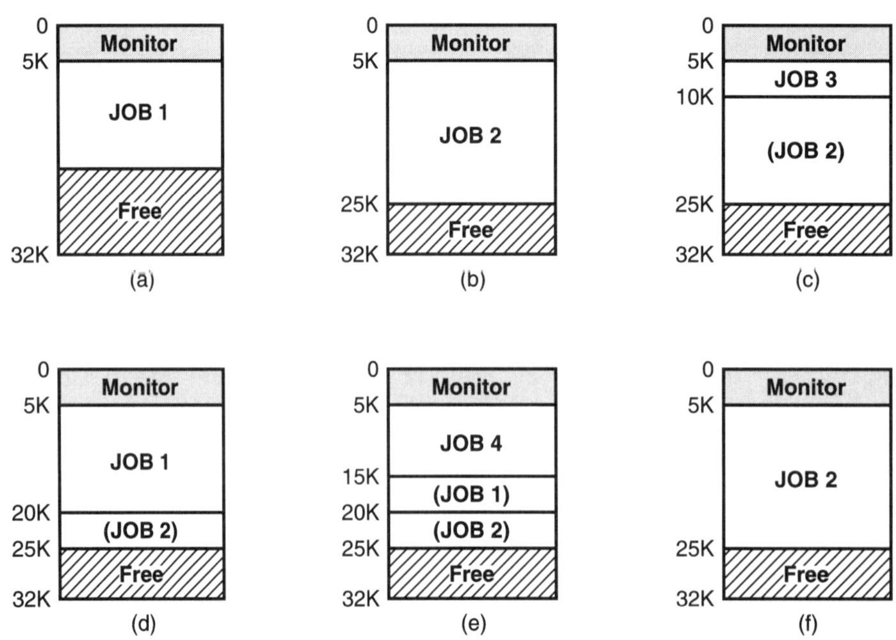

FIGURE 1-8 *CTSS Operation*

Initially, the monitor loads in JOB1 and transfers control to it (Figure 1-8a). Later, the monitor decides to transfer control to JOB2. Because JOB2 requires more memory than JOB1, JOB1 must be written out first, and then JOB2 can be loaded (Figure 1-8b). Next, JOB3 is loaded in to be run. However, because JOB3 is smaller than JOB2, a portion of JOB2 can remain in memory, reducing disk write time (Figure 1-8c). Later, the monitor decides to transfer control back to JOB1. An additional portion of JOB2 must be written out when JOB1 is loaded back into memory (Figure 1-8d). When JOB4 is loaded, part of JOB1 and the portion of JOB2 remaining in memory are retained (Figure 1-8e). At this point, if either JOB1 or JOB2 is activated, only a partial load will be required. In this example, it is JOB2 that runs next. This requires that JOB4 and the remaining resident portion of JOB1 be written out and that the missing portion of JOB2 be read in.

The CTSS approach is primitive compared to present-day time sharing, but it worked. It was extremely simple, which minimized the size of the monitor. Because a job was always loaded into the same locations in memory, there was no need for relocation techniques at load time (discussed later). The technique of only writing out what was necessary minimized disk activity. Running on the 7094, CTSS supported a maximum of 32 users.

Time sharing and multiprogramming raise a host of new problems for the operating system. If multiple jobs are in memory, then they must be protected from interfering with each other by, for example, modifying each other's data. With multiple interactive users, the file system must be protected so that only authorized users have access to a particular file. The contention for resources, such as printers and mass storage devices, must be handled.

MEMORY MANAGEMENT

In a uniprogramming system, main memory is divided into two parts: one part for the operating system (resident monitor, kernel) and one part for the program currently being executed. In a multiprogramming system, the "user" part of memory must be further subdivided to accommodate multiple processes. The task of subdivision is carried out dynamically by the operating system and is known as **memory management**.

Effective memory management is vital in a multiprogramming system. If only a few processes are in memory, then for much of the time all of the processes will be waiting for I/O and the processor will be idle. Thus memory needs to be allocated efficiently to pack as many processes into memory as possible.

We begin this section with a look at the requirements that memory management is intended to satisfy. Next, we approach the technology of memory management by looking at a variety of simple schemes that have been used. Our focus is the requirement that a program must be loaded into main memory in order to be executed. This discussion serves to introduce some of the fundamental principles of memory management.

Memory Management Requirements

While surveying the various mechanisms and policies associated with memory management, it is helpful to keep in mind the requirements that memory management is intended to satisfy. (Lister 1993) suggests five requirements:

- Relocation
- Protection
- Sharing
- Logical organization
- Physical organization

RELOCATION In a multiprogramming system, the available main memory is generally shared among a number of processes. Typically, it is not possible for the programmer to know in advance which other programs will be resident in main memory at the time of execution of his or her program. In addition, we would like to be able to swap active processes in and out of main memory to maximize processor utilization by providing a large pool of ready processes to execute. Once a program has been swapped out to disk, it would be quite limiting to declare that when it is next swapped back in, it must be placed in the same main-memory region as before.

Thus, we cannot know ahead of time where a program should be placed, and we must allow that the program may be moved about in main memory due to swapping. These facts raise some technical concerns related to addressing, as illustrated in Figure 1-9. The figure depicts a process image. For simplicity, let us assume that the process image occupies a contiguous region of main memory. Clearly, the operating system will need to know the location of process control information and of the execution stack, as well as the entry point to begin execution of the program for this process. Because the operating system is managing memory and is responsible for bringing this process into main memory, these addresses are easy to come by. In addition, however, the processor must deal with memory references within the program. Branch instructions contain an address to reference the instruction to be executed next. Data-reference instructions contain the address of the byte or word of data referenced. Somehow, the processor hardware and operating system software must be able to translate the memory references found in the code of the program into actual physical memory addresses, reflecting the current location of the program in main memory.

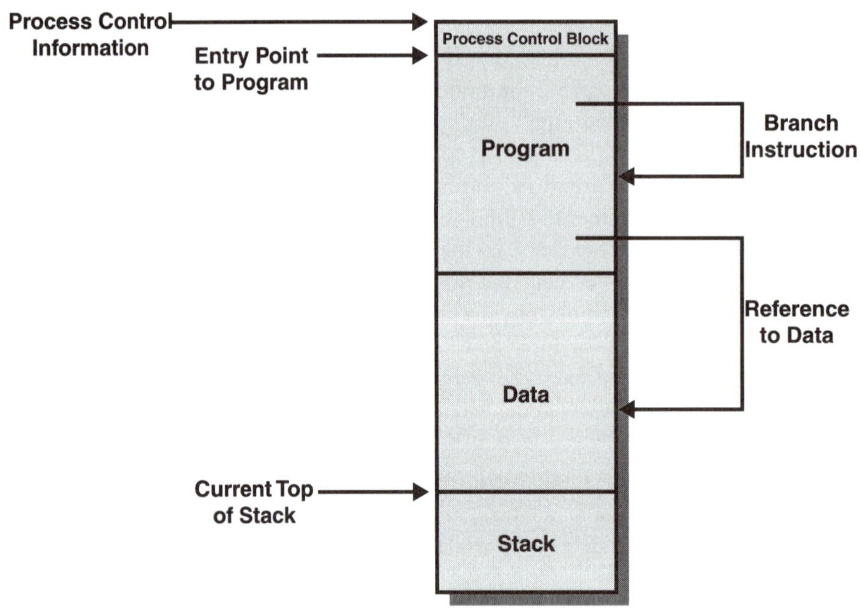

FIGURE 1-9 *Addressing Requirements for a Process*

PROTECTION Each process should be protected against unwanted interference by other processes, whether accidental or intentional. Thus, programs in other processes should not be able to reference memory locations in a process for reading or writing purposes without permission. In one sense, satisfaction of the relocation requirement increases the difficulty of satisfying the protection requirement. Because the location of a program in main memory is unknown, it is impossible to check absolute addresses at compile time to assure protection. Furthermore, most programming languages allow the dynamic calculation of addresses at run time (for example, by computing an array subscript or a pointer into a data structure). Hence all memory references generated by a process must be checked at run time to ensure that they refer only to the memory space allocated to that process. Fortunately, we shall see that mechanisms that support relocation also support protection requirement.

The process image layout of Figure 1-9 illustrates the protection requirement. Normally, a user process cannot access any portion of the operating system, either program or data. Again, usually a program in one process cannot branch to an instruction in another process. Without special arrangement, a program in one process cannot access the data area of another process. The processor must be able to abort such instructions at the point of execution.

Note that, in terms of our example, the memory protection requirement must be satisfied by the processor (hardware) rather than the operating system (software). This is because the operating system cannot anticipate all of the memory references that a program will make. Even if such anticipation were possible, it would be prohibitively time-consuming to screen each program in advance for possible memory-reference violations. Thus, it is only possible to assess the permissibility of a memory reference (data access or branch) at the time of execution of the instruction making the reference. To accomplish this, the processor hardware must have that capability.

SHARING Any protection mechanism must have the flexibility to allow several processes to access the same portion of main memory. For example, if a number of processes are executing the same program, it is advantageous to allow each process to access the same copy of the program rather than have its own separate copy. Processes that are cooperating on some task may need to share access to the same data structure. The memory-management system must therefore allow controlled access to shared areas of memory without compromising essential protection. Again, we will see that the mechanisms used to support relocation support sharing capabilities.

LOGICAL ORGANIZATION Almost invariably, main memory in a computer system is organized as a linear, or one-dimensional, address space, consisting of a sequence of bytes or words. Secondary memory, at its physical level, is similarly organized. While this organization closely mirrors the actual machine hardware, it does not correspond to the way in which programs are typically constructed. Most programs are organized into modules, some of which are unmodifiable (read only, execute only) and some of which contain data that may be modified. If the operating system and computer hardware can effectively deal with user programs and data in the form of modules of some sort, then a number of advantages can be realized:

1. Modules can be written and compiled independently, with all references from one module to another resolved by the system at run time.
2. With modest additional overhead, different degrees of protection (read only, execute only) can be given to different modules.
3. It is possible to introduce mechanisms by which modules can be shared among processes. The advantage of providing sharing on a module level is that this corresponds to the user's way of viewing the problem, and hence it is easy for the user to specify the sharing that is desired.

The tool that most readily satisfies these requirements is segmentation, which is one of the memory-management techniques explored here.

PHYSICAL ORGANIZATION Computer memory is organized into at least two levels, referred to as main memory and secondary memory. Main memory provides fast access at relatively high cost. In addition, main memory is volatile; that is, it does not provide permanent storage. Secondary memory is slower and cheaper than main memory and is usually not volatile. Thus secondary memory of large capacity can be provided to allow for long-term storage of programs and data, while a smaller main memory holds programs and data currently in use.

In this two-level scheme, the organization of the flow of information between main and secondary memory is a major system concern. The responsibility for this flow could be assigned to the individual programmer, but this is impractical and undesirable for two reasons:

1. The main memory available for a program plus its data may be insufficient. In that case, the programmer must engage in a practice known as overlaying, in which the program and data are organized in such a way that various modules can be assigned the same region of memory, with a main program responsible for switching the modules in and out as needed. Even with the aid of compiler tools, overlay programming wastes programmer time.
2. In a multiprogramming environment, the programmer does not know at the time of coding how much space will be available or where that space will be.

It is clear, then, that the task of moving information between the two levels of memory should be a system responsibility. This task is the essence of memory management.

Memory Partitioning

The principal operation of memory management is to bring programs into main memory for execution by the processor. In almost all modern multiprogramming systems, this involves a sophisticated scheme known as virtual memory. Virtual memory is, in turn, based on the use of one or both of two basic techniques: segmentation and paging. Before we can look at these virtual memory techniques, we must prepare the ground by looking at simpler techniques that do not involve virtual memory (Table 1.4). One of these techniques, partitioning, has been used in several variations in some now-obsolete operating systems. The other two techniques, simple paging and simple segmentation, are not used by themselves.

Paging

Suppose that main memory is partitioned into equal fixed-size chunks that are relatively small, and that each process is also divided into small fixed-size chunks of the same size. Then the chunks of a process, known as **pages**, could be assigned to available chunks of memory, known as **frames**, or page frames.

Another possible solution to the external fragmentation problem is to permit the logical address space of a process to be noncontiguous, thus allowing a process to be allocated physical memory wherever the latter is available. One way of implementing this solution is through the use of a **paging** scheme. Paging avoids the considerable problem of fitting the varying-sized memory chunks onto the backing store, from which most of the previous memory-management schemes suffered. When some code fragments or data residing in main memory need to be swapped out, space must be found on the backing store. The fragmentation problems discussed in connection with main memory are also prevalent with backing store, except that access is much slower, so compaction is impossible. Because of its advantages over the previous methods, paging in its various forms is commonly used in many operating systems.

Basic Method

Physical memory is broken into fixed-sized blocks called *frames*. Logical memory is also broken into blocks of the same size called *pages*. When a process is to be executed, its pages are loaded into any available memory frames from the backing store. The backing store is divided into fixed-sized blocks that are of the same size as the memory frames.

TABLE 1.4
Memory-Management Techniques

Technique	Description	Strengths	Weaknesses
Fixed Partitioning	Main memory is divided into a number of static partitions at system generation time. A process may be loaded into a partition of equal or greater size.	Simple to implement; little operating system overhead.	Inefficient use of memory due to internal fragmentation; number of active processes is fixed.
Dynamic Partitioning	Partitions are created dynamically, so that each process is loaded into a partition of exactly the same size as that process.	No internal fragmentation; more efficient use of main memory.	Inefficient use of processor due to the need for compaction to counter external fragmentation.
Simple Paging	Main memory is divided into a number of equal-size frames. Each process is divided into a number of equal-size pages of the same length as frames. A process is loaded by loading all of its pages into available, not necessarily contiguous, frames.	No external fragmentation.	A small amount of internal fragmentation.
Simple Segmentation	Each process is divided into a number of segments. A process is loaded by loading all of its segments into dynamic partitions that need not be contiguous.	No internal fragmentation.	Improved memory utilization and reduced overhead compared to dynamic partitioning.
Virtual-Memory Paging	As with simple paging, except that it is not necessary to load all of the pages of a process. Nonresident pages that are needed are brought in later automatically.	No external fragmentation; higher degree of multiprogramming; large virtual process space.	Overhead of complex memory management.
Virtual Memory Segmentation	As with simple segmentation, except that it is not necessary to load all of the segments of a process. Nonresident segments that are needed are brought in later automatically.	No internal fragmentation, higher degree of multiprogramming; large virtual address space; protection and sharing support.	Overhead of complex memory management.

The hardware support for paging is illustrated in Figure 1-10. Every address generated by the CPU is divided into two parts: a **page number (p)** and a **page offset (d)**. The page number is used as an index into a **page table**. The page table contains the base address of each page in physical memory. This base address is combined with the page offset to define the physical memory address that is sent to the memory unit. The paging model of memory is shown in Figure 1-11.

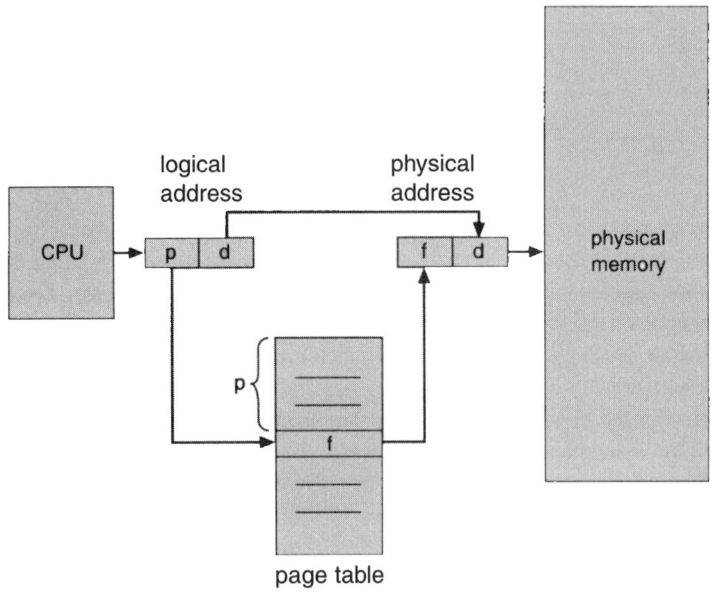

FIGURE 1-10 *Paging Hardware*

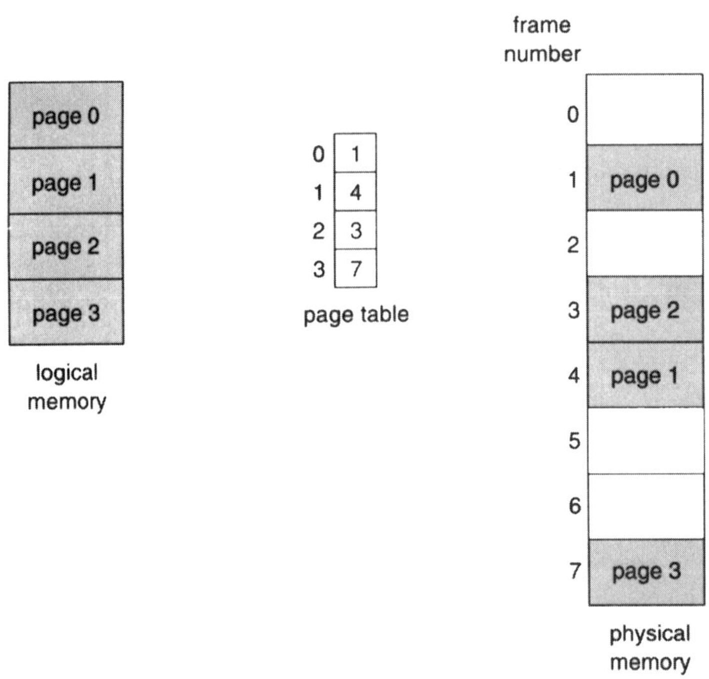

FIGURE 1-11 *Paging Model of Logical and Physical Memory*

The page size (like the frame size) is defined by the hardware. The size of a page is typically a power of 2 varying between 512 bytes and 16 megabytes per page, depending on the computer architecture. The selection of a power of 2 as a page size makes the translation of a logical address into a page number and page offset particularly easy. If the size of logical address space is 2^m, and a page size is 2^n addressing units (bytes or words), then the high-order $m–n$ bits of a logical address designate the page number, and the n low-order bits designate the page offset. Thus, the logical address is as follows:

page number	page offset
p	d
$m-n$	n

where p is an index into the page table and d is the displacement within the page.

For a concrete, although minuscule, example, consider the memory of Figure 1-12. Using a page size of 4 bytes and a physical memory of 32 bytes (8 pages), we show an example of how the user's view of memory can be mapped into physical memory. Logical address 0 is page 0, offset 0. Indexing into the page table, we find that page 0 is in frame 5. Thus, logical address 0 maps to physical address 20 (= (5 × 4) + 0). Logical address 3 (page offset 3) maps to physical address 23 (= (5 × 4) + 3). Logical address 4 is page offset 0; according to the page table, page 1 is mapped to frame 6. Thus, logical address 4 maps to physical address 24 (= (6 × 4) + 0). Logical address 13 maps to physical address 9.

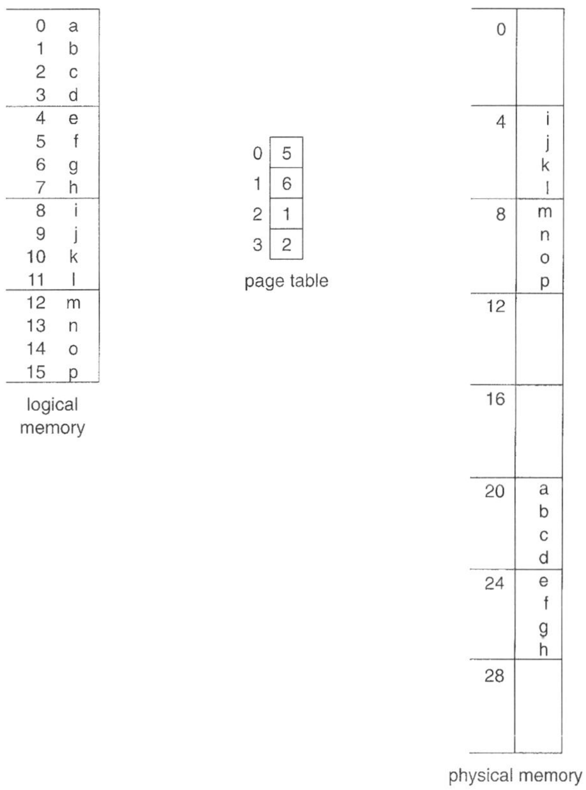

FIGURE 1-12 *Paging Example for a 32-byte Memory with 4-byte Pages*

Notice that paging itself is a form of dynamic relocation. Every logical address is bound by the paging hardware to some physical address. The observant reader will have realized that paging is similar to using a table of base (relocation) registers, one for each frame of memory.

When we use a paging scheme, we have no external fragmentation: *Any* free frame can be allocated to a process that needs it. However, we may have some internal fragmentation. Notice that frames are allocated as units. If the memory requirements of a process do not happen to fall on page boundaries, the *last* frame allocated may not be completely full. For example, if pages are 2048 bytes, a process of 72,766 bytes would need 35 pages plus 1086 bytes. It would be allocated 36 frames, resulting in an internal fragmentation of 2048 – 1086 = 962 bytes. In the worst case, a process would need n pages plus one byte. It would be allocated $n + 1$ frames, resulting in an internal fragmentation of almost an entire frame.

If process size is independent of page size, we expect internal fragmentation to average one-half page per process. This consideration suggests that small page sizes are desirable.

However, there is quite a bit of overhead involved in each page-table entry, and this overhead is reduced as the size of the pages increases. Also, disk I/O is more efficient when the number of data being transferred is larger. Generally, page sizes have grown over time as processes, data sets, and main memory have become larger. Today, pages typically are either 2 or 4 kilobytes.

When a process arrives in the system to be executed, its size, expressed in pages, is examined. Each page of the process needs one frame. Thus, if the process requires n pages, there must be at least n frames available in memory. If there are n frames available, they are allocated to this arriving process. The first page of the process is loaded into one of the allocated frames, and the frame number is put in the page table for this process. The next page is loaded into another frame, and its frame number is put into the page table, and so on (Figure 1-13).

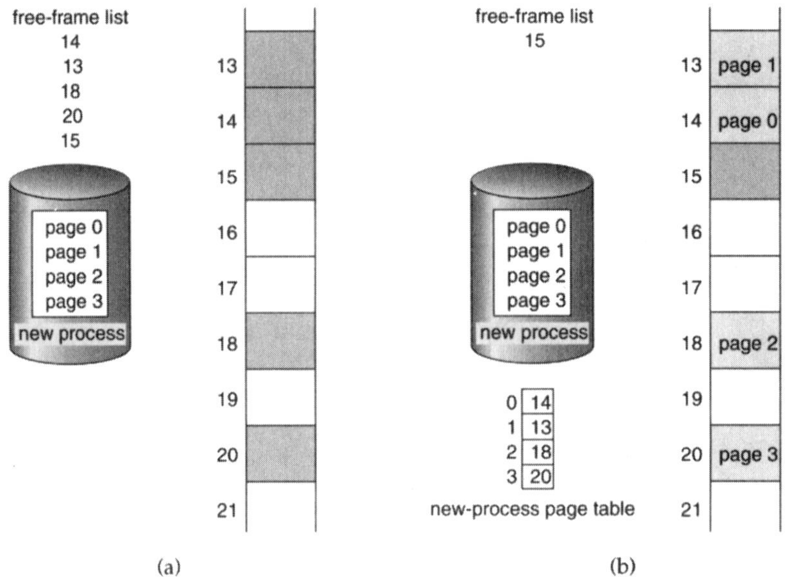

FIGURE 1-13 *Free Frames. (a) Before Allocation, and (b) After Allocation*

An important aspect of paging is the clear separation between the user's view of memory and the actual physical memory. The user program views that memory as one single contiguous space, containing only this one program. In fact, the user program is scattered throughout physical memory, which also holds other programs. The difference between the user's view of memory and the actual physical memory is reconciled by the address-translation hardware. The logical addresses are translated into physical addresses. This mapping is hidden from the user and is controlled by the operating system. Notice that the user process by definition is unable to access memory it does not own. It has no way of addressing memory outside of its page table, and the table includes only those pages that the process owns.

Since the operating system is managing physical memory, it must be aware of the allocation details of physical memory: which frames are allocated, which frames are available, how many total frames there are, and so on. This information is generally kept in a data structure called a **frame table**. The frame table has one entry for each physical page frame, indicating whether the latter is free or allocated and, if it is allocated, to which page of which process or processes.

In addition, the operating system must be aware that user processes operate in user space, and all logical addresses must be mapped to produce physical addresses. If a user makes a system call (to do I/O, for example) and provides an address as a parameter (a buffer, for instance), that address must be mapped to produce the correct physical address. The operating system maintains a copy of the page table for each process, just as it maintains a copy of the instruction counter and register contents. This copy is used to translate logical addresses to physical addresses whenever the operating system must map a logical address to a physical address manually. It is also used by the CPU dispatcher to define the hardware page table when a process is to be allocated the CPU. Paging therefore increases the context-switch time.

Structure of the Page Table

Each operating system has its own methods for storing page tables. Most allocate a page table for each process. A pointer to the page table is stored with the other register values (like the instruction counter) in the process control block. When the dispatcher is told to start a process, it must reload the user registers and define the correct hardware page-table values from the stored user page table.

HARDWARE SUPPORT The hardware implementation of the page table can be done in a number of different ways. In the simplest case, the page table is implemented as a set of dedicated **registers**. These registers should be built with very high-speed logic to make the paging address translation efficient. Every access to memory must go through the paging map, so efficiency is a major consideration. The CPU dispatcher reloads these registers, just as it reloads the other registers. Instructions to load or modify the page-table registers are, of course, privileged, so that only the operating system can change the memory map. The DEC PDP-11 is an example of such an architecture. The address consists of 16 bits, and the page size is 8K. The page table, thus, consists of eight entries that are kept in fast registers.

The use of registers for the page table is satisfactory if the page table is reasonably small (for example, 256 entries). Most contemporary computers, however, allow the page table to be very large (for example, 1 million entries). For these machines, the use of fast registers to implement the page table is not feasible. Rather, the page table is kept in main memory, and a **page-table base register (PTBR)** points to the page table. Changing page tables requires changing only this one register, substantially reducing context-switch time.

The problem with this approach is the time required to access a user memory location. If we want to access location *i*, we must first index into the page table, using the value in the PTBR offset by the page number for *i*. This task requires a memory access. It provides us with the frame number, which is combined with the page offset to produce the actual address. We can then access the desired place in memory. With this scheme, *two* memory accesses are needed to access a byte (one for the page-table entry, one for the byte). Thus, memory access is slowed by a factor of 2. This delay would be intolerable under most circumstances. We might as well resort to swapping!

The standard solution to this problem is to use a special, small, fast-lookup hardware cache, variously called **associative registers** or **translation look-aside buffers (TLBs)**. A set of associative registers is built of especially high-speed memory. Each register consists of two parts: a key and a value. When the associative registers are presented with an item, it is compared with all keys simultaneously. If the item is found, the corresponding value field is output. The search is fast; the hardware, however, is expensive. Typically, the number of entries in a TLB varies between 8 and 2048.

Associative registers are used with page tables in the following way. The associative registers contain only a few of the page-table entries. When a logical address is generated by the CPU, its page number is presented to a set of associative registers that contain page numbers and their corresponding frame numbers. If the page number is found in the associative registers, its frame number is immediately available and is used to access memory. The whole task may take less than 10 percent longer than it would were an unmapped memory reference used.

If the page number is not in the associative registers, a memory reference to the page table must be made. When the frame number is obtained, we can use it to access memory (Figure 1-14). In addition, we add the page number and frame number to the associative registers, so that they will be found quickly on the next reference. If the TLB is already full of entries, the operating system must select one for replacement. Unfortunately, every time a new page table is selected (for instance, each context switch), the TLB must be *flushed*

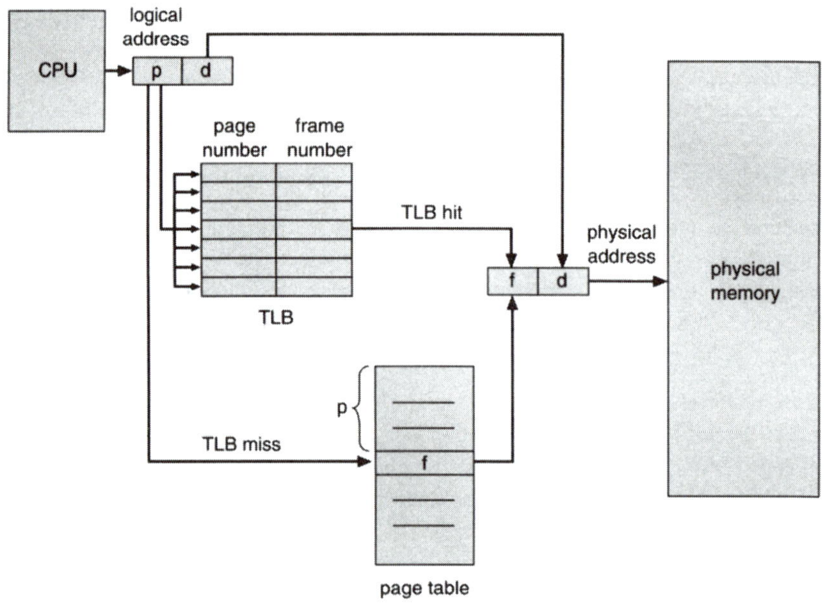

FIGURE 1-14 *Paging Hardware with TLB*

(erased) to ensure that the next executing process does not use the wrong translation information. Otherwise, there could be old entries in the TLB that contain valid virtual addresses but have incorrect or invalid physical addresses left over from the previous process.

The percentage of times that a page number is found in the associative registers is called the *hit ratio*. An 80-percent hit ratio means that we find the desired page number in the associative registers 80 percent of the time. If it takes 20 nanoseconds to search the associative registers, and 100 nanoseconds to access memory, then a mapped memory access takes 120 nanoseconds when the page number is in the associative registers. If we fail to find the page number in the associative registers (20 nanoseconds), then we must first access memory for the page table and frame number (100 nanoseconds), and then access the desired byte in memory (100 nanoseconds), for a total of 220 nanoseconds. To find the *effective memory-access time*, we must weigh each case by its probability:

$$\begin{aligned}\text{effective access time} &= 0.80 \times 120 + 0.20 \times 220\\ &= 140 \text{ nanoseconds.}\end{aligned}$$

In this example, we suffer a 40-percent slowdown in memory access time (from 100 to 140 nanoseconds).

For a 98-percent hit ratio, we have

$$\begin{aligned}\text{effective access time} &= 0.98 \times 120 + 0.02 \times 220\\ &= 122 \text{ nanoseconds.}\end{aligned}$$

This increased hit rate produces only a 22-percent slowdown in memory access time.

The hit ratio is clearly related to the number of associative registers. With the number of associative registers ranging between 16 and 512, a hit ratio of 80 to 98 percent can be obtained. The Motorola 68030 processor (used in Apple Macintosh systems) has a 22-entry TLB. The Intel 80486 CPU (found in some PCs) has 32 registers, and claims a 98-percent hit ratio.

PROTECTION Memory protection in a paged environment is accomplished by protection bits that are associated with each frame. Normally, these bits are kept in the page table. One bit can define a page to be read and write or read-only. Every reference to memory goes through the page table to find the correct frame number. At the same time that the physical address is being computed, the protection bits can be checked to verify that no writes are being made to a read-only page. An attempt to write to a read-only page causes a hardware trap to the operating system (memory-protection violation).

This approach to protection can be expanded easily to provide a finer level of protection. We can create hardware to provide read-only, read-write, or execute-only protection. Or, by providing separate protection bits for each kind of access, any combination of these accesses can be allowed, and illegal attempts will be trapped to the operating system.

One more bit is generally attached to each entry in the page table: a *valid-invalid* bit. When this bit is set to "valid," this value indicates that the associated page is in the process's logical address space, and is thus a legal (valid) page. If the bit is set to "invalid," this value indicates that the page is not in the process's logical address space. Illegal addresses are trapped by using the valid-invalid bit. The operating system sets this bit for each page to allow or disallow accesses to that page. For example, in a system with a 14-bit address space (0 to 16,383), we may have a program that should use only addresses 0 to 10,468. Given a page size of 2K, we get the situation shown in Figure 1-15. Addresses in pages 0, 1, 2, 3, 4, and 5 are mapped normally through the page table. Any attempt to generate an address in pages 6 or 7, however, finds that the valid-invalid bit is set to invalid, and the computer will trap to the operating system (invalid page reference).

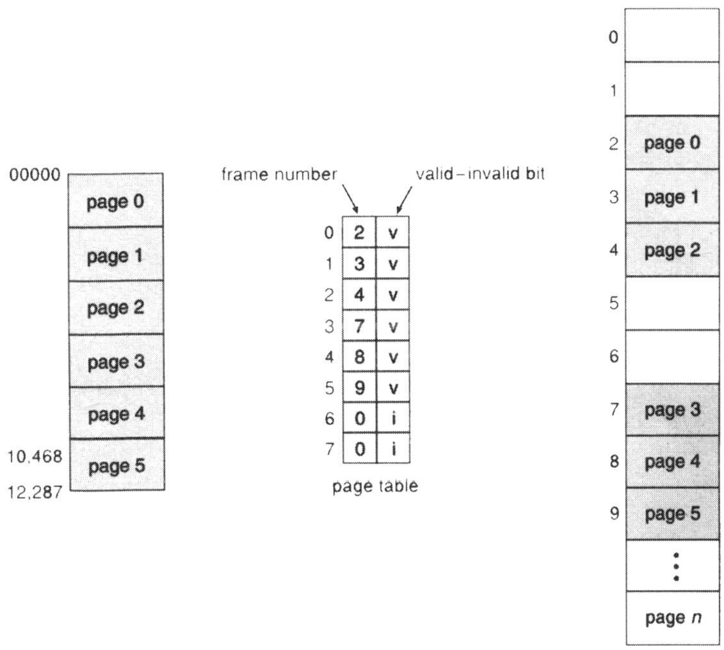

FIGURE 1-15 *Valid (v) or Invalid (i) Bit in a Page Table*

Notice that as the program extends only to address 10,468; any reference beyond that address is illegal. However, references to page 5 are classified as valid, so accesses to addresses up to 12,287 are valid. Only addresses from 12,288 to 16,383 are invalid. This problem is a result of the 2K page size and reflects the internal fragmentation of paging.

Rarely does a process use all of its address range. In fact, many processes use only a small fraction of the address space available to them. It would be wasteful in these cases to create a page table with entries for every page in the address range. Most of this table would be unused, but would take up valuable memory space. Some systems provide hardware, in the form of a **page-table length register (PTLR)**, to indicate the size of the page table. This value is checked against every logical address to verify that the address is in the valid range for the process. Failure of this test causes an error trap to the operating system.

VIRTUAL MEMORY

Comparing simple paging and simple segmentation, on the one hand, with fixed and dynamic partitioning, on the other, we see the foundation for a fundamental breakthrough in memory management.

HARDWARE AND CONTROL STRUCTURES

Two characteristics of paging and segmentation are the keys to this breakthrough:

1. All memory references within a process are logical addresses that are dynamically translated into physical addresses at run time. This means that a process may be swapped in and out of main memory such that it occupies different regions of main memory at different times during the course of execution.
2. A process may be broken up into a number of pieces (pages or segments) and these pieces need not be contiguously located in main memory during execution. The combination of dynamic run-time address translation and the use of a page or segment table permits this.

Now we come to the breakthrough. *If the preceding two characteristics are present, then it is not necessary that all of the pages or all of the segments of a process be in main memory during execution.* If the piece (segment or page) that holds the next instruction to be fetched and the piece that holds the next data location to be accessed are in main memory, then at least for a time execution may proceed.

Let us consider how this may be accomplished. For now, we can talk in general terms, and we will use the term *piece* refer to either page or segment, depending on whether paging or segmentation is employed. Suppose that it is time to bring a new process into memory. The operating system begins by bringing in only one or a few pieces, to include the piece that contains the start of the program. The portion of a process that is actually in main memory at any time is defined to be the **resident set** of the process. As the process executes, things proceed smoothly as long as all memory references are to locations that are in the resident set. Using the segment or page table, the processor always is able to determine whether this is so. If the processor encounters a logical address that is not in main memory, it generates an interrupt indicating a memory access fault. The operating system puts the interrupted process in a blocking state and takes control. For the execution of this process to proceed later, the operating system will need to bring into main memory the piece of the process that contains the logical address that caused the access fault. For this purpose, the operating system issues a disk I/O read request. After the I/O request has been issued, the operating system can dispatch another process to run while the disk I/O is performed. Once the desired piece has been brought into main memory, an I/O interrupt is issued, giving control back to the operating system, which places the affected process back into a Ready state.

It may immediately occur to you to question the efficiency of this maneuver, in which a process may be executing and have to be interrupted for no other reason than that you have failed to load in all of the needed pieces of the process. For now, let us defer consideration of this question with the assurance that efficiency is possible. Instead, let us ponder the implications of our new strategy. There are two implications, the second more startling than the first, and both lead to improved system utility:

1. More processes may be maintained in main memory. Because we are only going to load some of the pieces of any particular process, there is room for more processes. This leads to more efficient utilization of the processor, because it is more likely that at least one of the more numerous processes will be in a Ready state at any particular time.
2. It is possible for a process to be larger than all of main memory. One of the most fundamental restrictions in programming is lifted. Without the scheme we have been discussing, a programmer must be acutely aware of how much memory is

available. If the program being written is too large, the programmer must devise ways to structure the program into pieces that can be loaded separately in some sort of overlay strategy. With virtual memory based on paging or segmentation, that job is left to the operating system and the hardware. As far as the programmer is concerned, he or she is dealing with a huge memory, the size associated with disk storage. The operating system automatically loads pieces of a process into main memory as required.

Because a process executes only in main memory, that memory is referred to as **real memory**. But a programmer or user perceives a potentially much larger memory—that which is allocated on disk. This latter is referred to as **virtual memory** (see Figure 1-16). Virtual memory allows for very effective multiprogramming and relieves the user of the unnecessarily tight constraints of main memory. Table 1.5 summarizes characteristics of paging and segmentation, with and without the use of virtual memory.

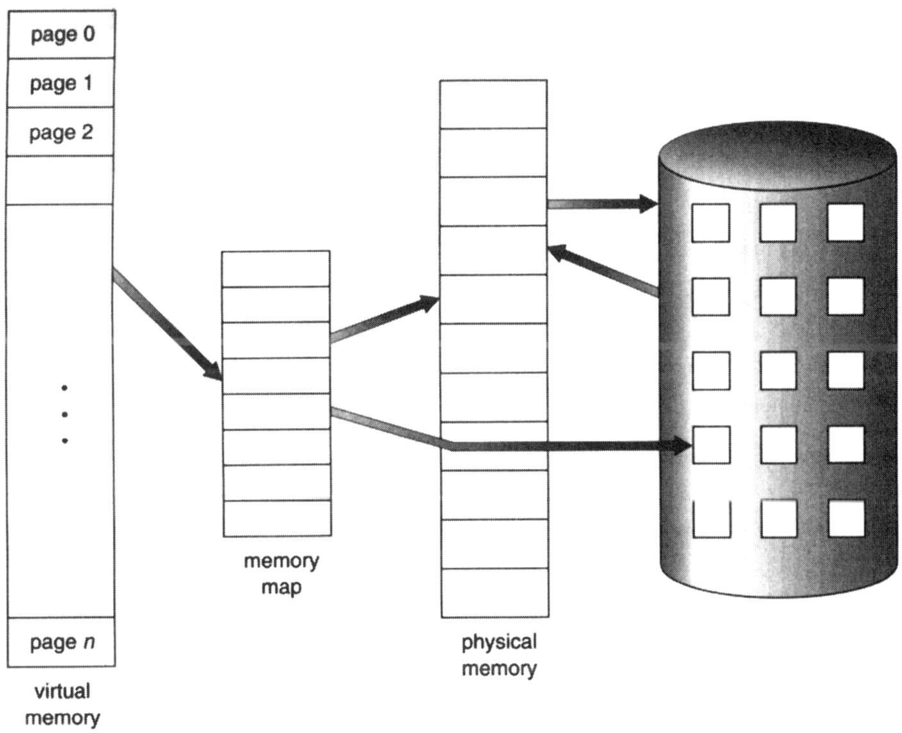

FIGURE 1-16 *Diagram Showing Virtual Memory Larger than Physical Memory*

At any one time, only a few pieces of any given process are in memory, and therefore more processes can be maintained in memory. Furthermore, time is saved because unused pieces are not swapped in and out of memory. However, the operating system must be clever about how it manages this scheme. In the steady state, practically all of main memory will be occupied with process pieces, so that the processor and operating system have direct access to as many processes as possible. Thus, when the operating system brings one piece in, it must throw another out. If it throws out a piece just before it is about to be used, then it will just have to go get that piece again almost immediately. Too much of this leads to a condition known as **thrashing**: The processor spends most of its time swapping pieces rather

TABLE 1.5
Characteristics of Paging and Segmentation

Simple Paging	Simple Segmentation	Virtual Memory Virtual Memory Paging	Segmentation
Main memory partitioned into small fixed-size chunks called frames	Main memory not partitioned	Main memory partitioned into small fixed-size chunks called frames	Main memory not partitioned
Program broken into pages by the compiler or memory management system	Program segments specified by the programmer to the compiler (i.e., the decision is made by the programmer)	Program broken into pages by the compiler or memory management system	Program segments specified by the programmer to the compiler (i.e., the decision is made by the programmer)
Internal fragmentation within frames	No internal fragmentation	Internal fragmentation within frames	No internal fragmentation
No external fragmentation	External fragmentation	No external fragmentation	External fragmentation
Operating system must maintain a page table for each process showing which frame each page is in.	Operating system must maintain a segment table for each process showing the load address and length of each segment.	Operating system must maintain a page table for each process showing which frame each page is in.	Operating system must maintain a segment table for each process showing the load address and length of each segment.
Operating system must maintain a free frame list.	Operating system must maintain a list of free holes in main memory.	Operating system must maintain a free frame list.	Operating system must maintain a list of free holes in main memory.
Processor uses page number, offset to calculate absolute address.	Processor uses segment number, offset to calculate absolute address.	Processor uses page number, offset to calculate absolute address.	Processor uses segment number, offset to calculate absolute address.
All the pages of a process must be in main memory for process to run, unless overlays are used.	All the segments of a process must be in main memory for process to run, unless overlays are used.	Not all pages of a process need be in main memory frames for the process to run. Pages may be read in as needed.	Not all segments of a process need be in main memory frames for the process to run. Segments may be read in as needed.
		Reading a page into main memory may require writing a page out to disk.	Reading a segment into main memory may require writing one or more segments out to disk.

than executing instructions. The avoidance of thrashing was a major research area in the 1970s and led to a variety of complex but effective algorithms. In essence, the operating system tries to guess, based on recent history, which pieces are least likely to be used in the near future.

Virtual memory is commonly implemented by **demand paging**. It can also be implemented in a segmentation system. Several systems provide a paged segmentation scheme, where segments are broken into pages. Thus, the user view is segmentation, but the operating system can implement this view with demand paging. **Demand segmentation** can also be used to provide virtual memory. Burroughs' computer systems have used demand segmentation. The IBM OS/2 operating system also uses demand segmentation. However, segment-replacement algorithms are more complex than are page-replacement algorithms because the segments have variable sizes.

Demand Paging

A demand-paging system is similar to a paging system with swapping (Figure 1-17). Processes reside on secondary memory (which is usually a disk). When we want to execute a process, we swap it into memory. Rather than swapping the entire process into memory, however, we use a **lazy** swapper. A lazy swapper never swaps a page into memory unless that page will be needed. Since we are now viewing a process as a sequence of pages, rather than one large contiguous address space, the use of the term *swap* is technically incorrect. A swapper manipulates entire processes, whereas a pager is concerned with the individual pages of a process. We shall thus use the term *pager*, rather than *swapper*, in connection with demand paging.

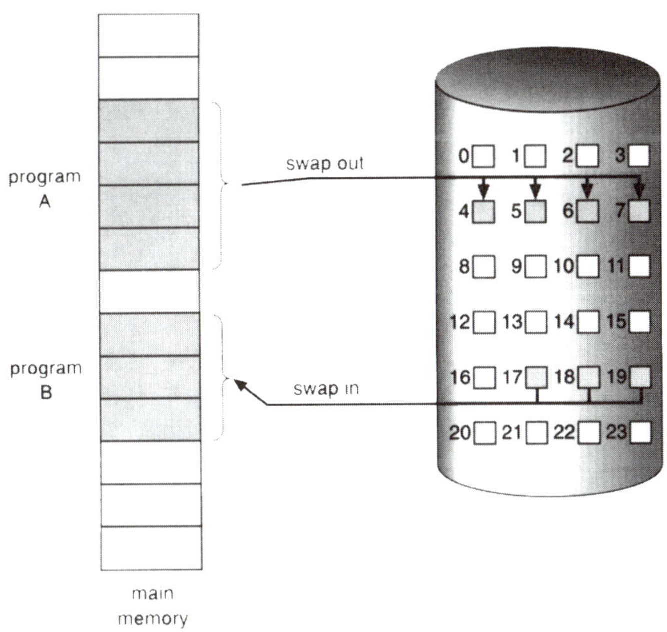

FIGURE 1-17 *Transfer of a Paged Memory to Contiguous Disk Space*

When a process is to be swapped in, the pager guesses which pages will be used before the process is swapped out again. Instead of swapping in a whole process, the pager brings only those necessary pages into memory. Thus, it avoids reading into memory pages that will not be used anyway, decreasing the swap time and the amount of physical memory needed.

With this scheme, we need some form of hardware support to distinguish between those pages that are in memory and those pages that are on the disk. The *valid-invalid* bit scheme can be used for this purpose. This time, however, when this bit is set to "valid," this value indicates that the associated page is both legal and in memory. If the bit is set to "invalid," this value indicates that the page either is not valid (that is, not in the logical address space of the process), or is valid but is currently on the disk. The page-table entry for a page that is brought into memory is set as usual, but the page-table entry for a page that is not currently in memory is simply marked invalid, or contains the address of the page on disk. This situation is depicted in Figure 1-18.

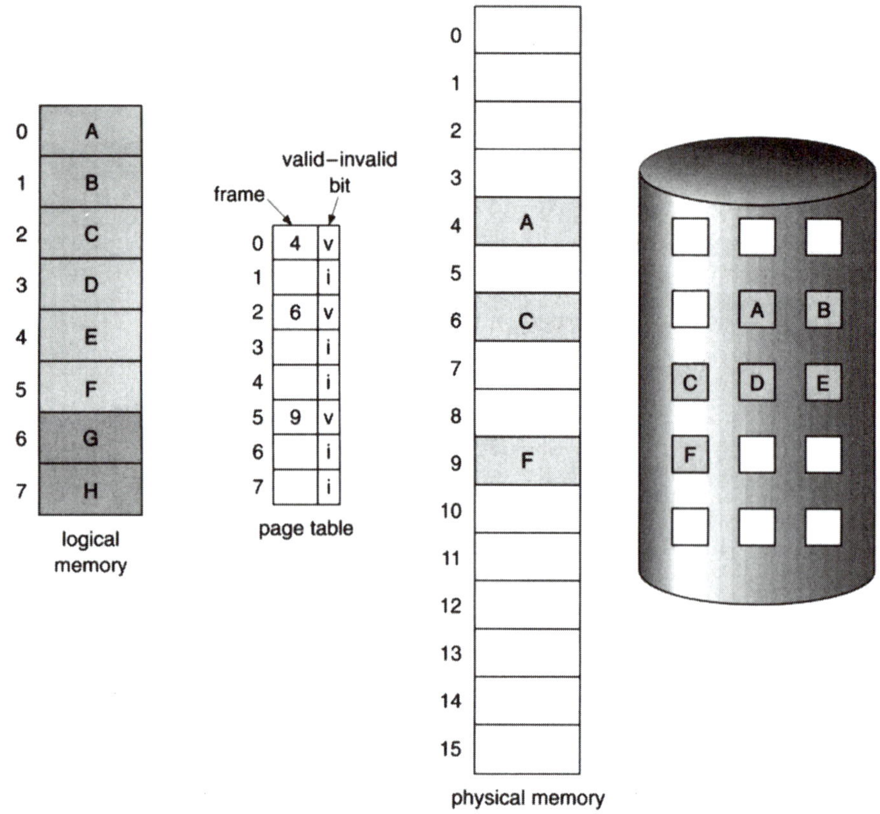

FIGURE 1-18 *Page Table When Some Pages Are Not in Main Memory*

Notice that marking a page invalid will have no effect if the process never attempts to access that page. Hence, if we guess right and page in all and only those pages that are actually needed, the process will run exactly as though we had brought in all pages. While the process executes and accesses pages that are *memory resident*, execution proceeds normally.

PAGE SIZE An important hardware design decision is the size of page to be used. There are several factors to consider. One is internal fragmentation. Clearly, the smaller the page size, the less the amount of internal fragmentation. To optimize the use of main memory, we would like to reduce internal fragmentation. On the other hand, the smaller the page, the greater the number of pages required per process. More pages per process means larger page tables. For large programs in a heavily multiprogrammed environment, this may mean that some portion of the page tables of active processes must be in virtual memory, not in main memory. Thus, there may be a double page fault for a single reference to memory: first to bring in the needed portion of the page table and second to bring in the process page. Another factor is that the physical characteristics of most secondary-memory devices, which are rotational, favor a larger page size for more efficient block transfer of data.

Table 1.6 indicates the page sizes used on some machines.

TABLE 1.6
Example Page Sizes

Computer	Page Size
Atlas	512 48-bit words
Honeywell-Multics	1,024 36-bit word
IBM 370/XA and 370/ESA	4 kilobytes
VAX family	512 bytes
IBM AS/400	512 bytes
DEC Alpha	8 kilobytes
Pentium	4 kilobytes or 4 megabytes
PowerPc	4 kilobytes

Finally, the design issue of page size is related to the size of physical main memory. Virtual memory implementations in most current systems were designed on the assumption that physical memory is not very large, typically in the range of 4 to 256 megabytes. However, we can expect to see even larger physical memory sizes on workstations and larger machines over the next few years.

At the same time that main memory is getting larger, the address space used by applications is also growing. The trend is most obvious on personal computers and workstations, where applications are becoming increasingly complex. Furthermore, contemporary programming techniques used in large programs tend to decrease the locality of references within a process (Huck 1993). For example,

- Object-oriented techniques encourage the use of many small program and data modules with references scattered over a relatively large number of objects over a relatively short period of time.
- Multithreaded applications result in abrupt changes in the instruction stream and in scattered memory references.

A number of designers have investigated the use of multiple page sizes (Talluri 1992, Khalidi 1993), and several microprocessor architectures support multiple pages sizes, including R4000, Alpha, SuperSPARC, and Pentium. For example, the R4000 supports seven page sizes (from 4K to 16 megabytes). Multiple page sizes provides the flexibility needed to use a TLB effectively. For example, large contiguous regions in the address space of a process, such as program instructions, may be mapped using a small number of large pages rather than a large number of small pages, while thread stacks may be mapped using the small page size.

SEGMENTATION

VIRTUAL MEMORY IMPLICATIONS Segmentation allows the programmer to view memory as consisting of multiple address spaces or segments. Segments may be of unequal, indeed dynamic, size. Memory references consist of a (segment number, offset) form of address.

This organization has a number of advantages to the programmer over a nonsegmented address space:

1. It simplifies the handling of growing data structures. If the programmer does not know ahead of time how large a particular data structure will become, it is necessary to guess unless dynamic segment sizes are allowed. With segmented virtual memory, the data structure can be assigned its own segment, and the operating system will expand or shrink the segment as needed. If a segment that needs to be expanded is in main memory and there is insufficient room, the

operating system may move the segment to a larger area of main memory, if available, or swap it out. In the latter case, the enlarged segment would be swapped back in at the next opportunity.

2. It allows programs to be altered and recompiled independently, without requiring the entire set of programs to be relinked and reloaded. Again, this is accomplished using multiple segments.
3. It lends itself to sharing among processes. A programmer can place a utility program or a useful table of data in a segment that can be referenced by other processes.
4. It lends itself to protection. Because a segment can be constructed to contain a well-defined set of programs or data, the programmer of system administrator can assign access privileges in a convenient fashion.

Combined Paging and Segmentation

Both paging and segmentation have their strengths. Paging, which is transparent to the programmer, eliminates external fragmentation and thus provides efficient use of main memory. In addition, because the pieces that are moved in and out of main memory are of fixed, equal size, it is possible to develop sophisticated memory-management algorithms that exploit the behavior of programs, as we shall see. Segmentation, which is visible to the programmer, has the strengths listed earlier, including the ability to handle growing data structures, modularity, and support for sharing and protection. To combine the advantages of both, some systems are equipped with processor hardware and operating system software to provide both.

In a combined paging/segmentation system, a user's address space is broken up into a number of segments, at the discretion of the programmer. Each segment is, in turn, broken up into a number of fixed-size pages, which are equal in length to a main-memory frame. If a segment has length less than that of a page, the segment occupies just one page. From the programmer's point of view, a logical address still consists of a segment number and a segment offset. From the system's point of view the segment offset is viewed as a page number and page offset for a page within the specified segment.

An important aspect of memory management that became unavoidable with paging is the separation of the user's view of memory and the actual physical memory. The user's view of memory is not the same as the actual physical memory. The user's view is mapped onto physical memory. The mapping allows differentiation between logical memory and physical memory.

BASIC METHOD What is the user's view of memory? Does the user think of memory as a linear array of bytes, some containing instructions and others containing data, or is there some other preferred memory view? There is general agreement that the user or programmer of a system does not think of memory as a linear array of bytes. Rather, the user prefers to view memory as a collection of variable-sized segments, with no necessary ordering among segments (Figure 1-19).

Consider how you think of a program when you are writing it. You think of it as a main program with a set of subroutines, procedures, functions, or modules. There may also be various data structures: tables, arrays, stacks, variables, and so on. Each of these modules or data elements is referred to by name. You talk about "the symbol table," "function *Sqrt*," "the main program," without caring what addresses in memory these elements occupy. You are not concerned with whether the symbol table is stored before or after the *Sqrt* function. Each of these segments is of variable length; the length is intrinsically defined by the purpose of the segment in the program. Elements within a segment are identified by their offset from the beginning of the segment: the first statement of the program, the seventeenth entry in the symbol table, the fifth instruction of the *Sqrt* function, and so on.

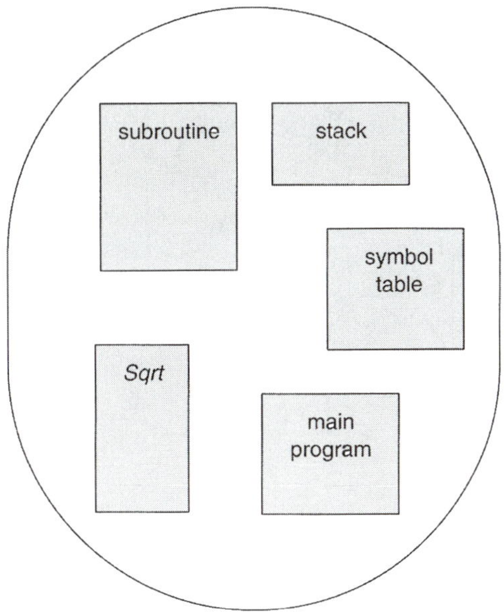

FIGURE 1-19 *User's View of a Program*

Segmentation is a memory-management scheme that supports this user view of memory. A logical address space is a collection of segments. Each segment has a name and a length. The addresses specify both the segment name and the offset within the segment. The user therefore specifies each address by two quantities: a segment name and an offset. (Contrast this scheme with the paging scheme, where the user specified only a single address, which was partitioned by the hardware into a page number and an offset, all invisible to the programmer.)

For simplicity of implementation, segments are numbered and are referred to by a segment number, rather than by a segment name. Thus, a logical address consists of a two tuple:

$$<\text{segment-number, offset}>$$

Normally, the user program is compiled, and the compiler automatically constructs segments reflecting the input program. A Pascal compiler might create separate segments for (1) the global variables; (2) the procedure call stack, to store parameters and return addresses; (3) the code portion of each procedure or function; and (4) the local variables of each procedure and function. A FORTRAN compiler might create a separate segment for each common block. Arrays might be assigned separate segments. The loader would take all these segments and assign them segment numbers.

HARDWARE Although the user can now refer to objects in the program by a two-dimensional address, the actual physical memory is still, of course, a one-dimensional sequence of bytes. Thus, we must define an implementation to map two-dimensional user-defined addresses into one-dimensional physical addresses. This mapping is effected by a **segment table**. Each entry of the segment table has a segment **base** and a segment **limit**. The segment base contains the starting physical address where the segment resides in memory, whereas the segment limit specifies the length of the segment.

The use of a segment table is illustrated in Figure 1-20. A logical address consists of two parts: a segment number, *s*, and an offset into that segment, *d*. The segment number is used as an index into the segment table. The offset *d* of the logical address must be between 0 and the segment limit. If it is not, we trap to the operating system (logical addressing attempt

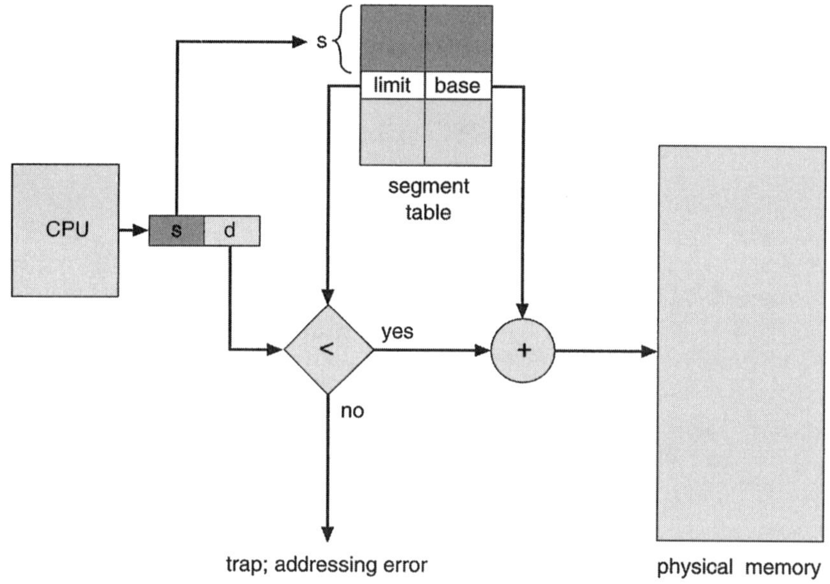

FIGURE 1-20 *Segmentation Hardware*

beyond end of segment). If this offset is legal, it is added to the segment base to produce the address in physical memory of the desired byte. The segment table is thus essentially an array of base-limit register pairs.

As an example, consider the situation shown in Figure 1-21. We have five segments numbered from 0 through 4. The segments are stored in physical memory as shown. The segment table has a separate entry for each segment, giving the beginning address of the segment in physical memory (the base) and the length of that segment (the limit). For exam-

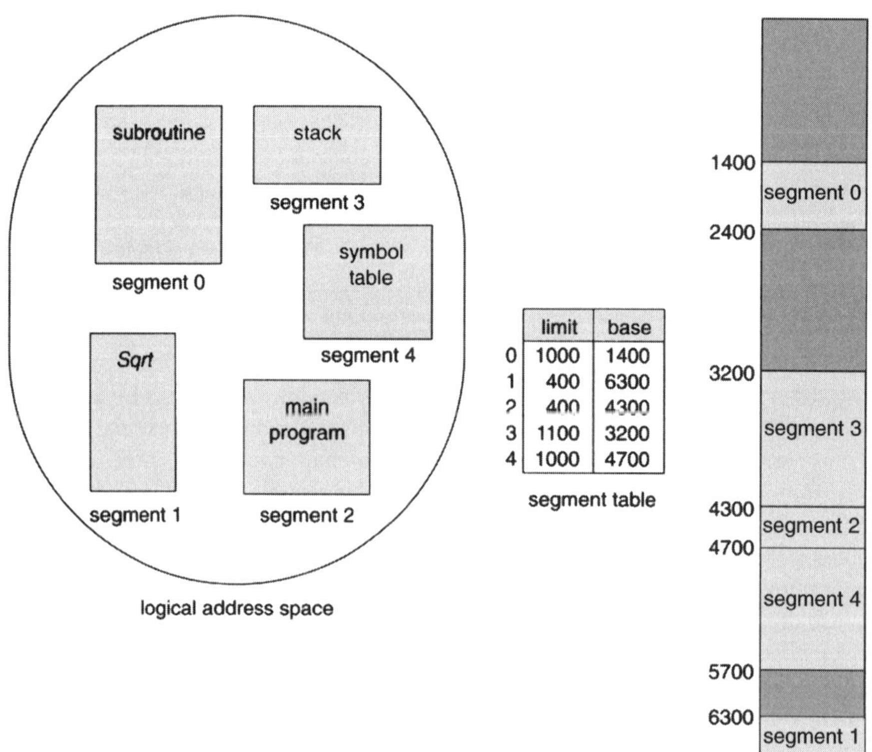

FIGURE 1-21 *Example of Segmentation*

ple, segment 2 is 400 bytes long, and begins at location 4300. Thus, a reference to byte 53 of segment 2 is mapped onto location 4300 + 53 = 4353. A reference to segment 3, byte 852, is mapped to 3200 (the base of segment 3) + 852 = 4052. A reference to byte 1222 of segment 0 would result in a trap to the operating system, as this segment is only 1000 bytes long.

IMPLEMENTATION OF SEGMENT TABLES Segmentation is closely related to the partition models of memory management presented earlier, the main difference being that one program may consist of several segments. Segmentation is a more complex concept, however, which is why we are describing it after discussing paging. Like the page table, the segment table can be put either in fast registers or in memory. A segment table kept in registers can be referenced quickly; the addition to the base and comparison with the limit can be done simultaneously to save time.

In the case where a program may consist of a large number of segments, it is not feasible to keep the segment table in registers, so we must keep it in memory. A **segment-table base register (STBR)** points to the segment table. Also, because the number of segments used by a program may vary widely, a **segment-table length register (STLR)** is used. For a logical address (s, d), we first check that the segment number s is legal (that is, $s <$ STLR). Then, we add the segment number to the STBR, resulting in the address (STBR + s) in memory of the segment-table entry. This entry is read from memory and we proceed as before: Check the offset against the segment length and compute the physical address of the desired byte as the sum of the segment base and offset.

As occurs with paging, this mapping requires two memory references per logical address, effectively slowing the computer system by a factor of 2, unless something is done. The normal solution is to use a set of associative registers to hold the most recently used segment-table entries. Again, a small set of associative registers can generally reduce the time required for memory accesses to no more than 10 or 15 percent slower than unmapped memory accesses.

PROTECTION AND SHARING A particular advantage of segmentation is the association of protection with the segments. Because the segments represent a semantically defined portion of the program, it is likely that all entries in the segment will be used the same way. Hence, we have some segments that are instructions, whereas other segments are data. In a modern architecture, instructions are non–self-modifying, so instruction segments can be defined as read-only or execute-only. The memory-mapping hardware will check the protection bits associated with each segment-table entry to prevent illegal accesses to memory, such as attempts to write into a read-only segment, or to use an execute-only segment as data. By placing an array in its own segment, the memory-management hardware will automatically check that array indexes are legal and do not stray outside the array boundaries. Thus, many common program errors will be detected by the hardware before they can cause serious damage.

Another advantage of segmentation involves the *sharing* of code or data. Each process has a segment table associated with it, which the dispatcher uses to define the hardware segment table when this process is given the CPU. Segments are shared when entries in the segment tables of two different processes point to the same physical location (Figure 1-22).

The sharing occurs at the segment level. Thus, any information can be shared if it is defined to be a segment. Several segments can be shared, so a program composed of several segments can be shared.

For example, consider the use of a text editor in a time-sharing system. A complete editor might be quite large, composed of many segments. These segments can be shared among all users, limiting the physical memory needed to support editing tasks. Rather than n copies of the editor, we need only one copy. For each user, we still need separate, unique segments to store local variables. These segments, of course, would not be shared.

It is also possible to share only parts of programs. For example, common subroutine packages can be shared among many users if they are defined as sharable, read-only segments. Two FORTRAN programs, for instance, may use the same *Sqrt* subroutine, but only one physical copy of the *Sqrt* routine would be needed.

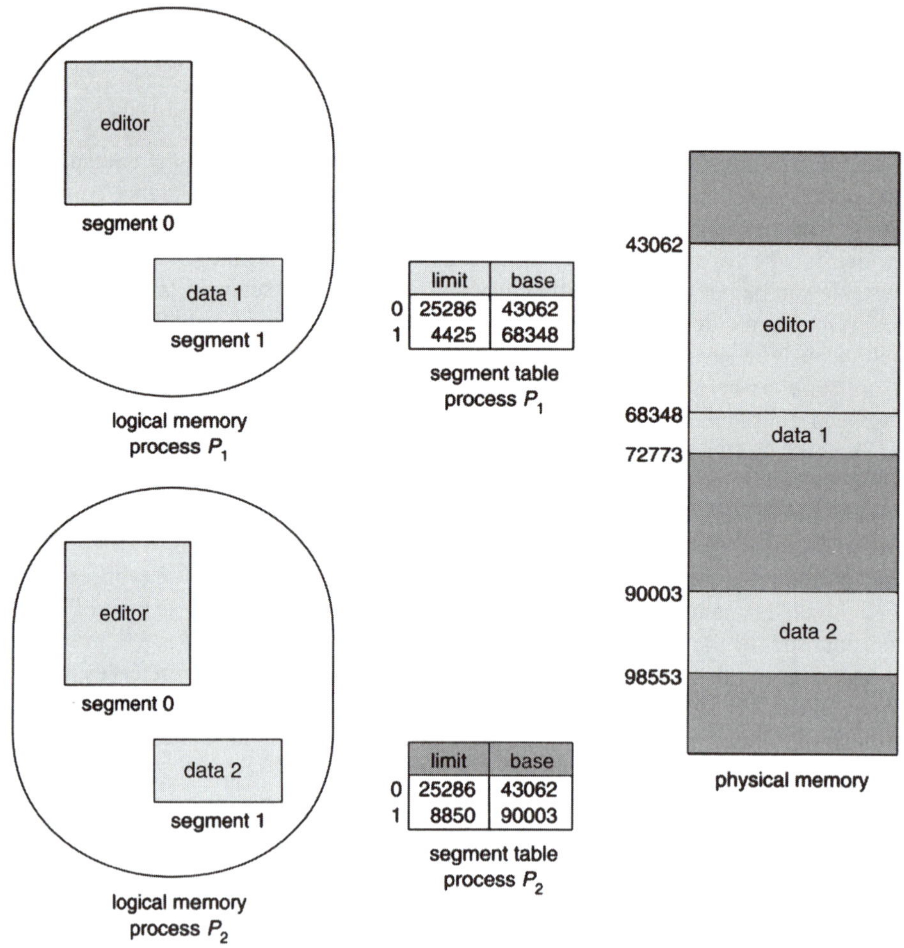

FIGURE 1-22 *Sharing of Segments in a Segmented Memory System*

Although this sharing appears simple, there are subtle considerations. Code segments typically contain references to themselves. For example, a conditional jump normally has a transfer address. The transfer address is a segment number and offset. The segment number of the transfer address will be the segment number of the code segment. If we try to share this segment, all sharing processes must define the shared code segment to have the same segment number.

For instance, if we want to share the *Sqrt* routine, and one process wants to make it segment 4 and another wants to make it segment 17, how should the *Sqrt* routine refer to itself? Because there is only one physical copy of *Sqrt*, it must refer to itself in the same way for both users—it must have a unique segment number. As the number of users sharing the segment increases, so does the difficulty of finding an acceptable segment number.

Read-only data segments that contain no physical pointers may be shared as different segment numbers, as may code segments that refer to themselves not directly, but rather only indirectly. For example, conditional branches that specify the branch address as an offset from the current program counter or relative to a register containing the current segment number would allow code to avoid direct reference to the current segment number.

FRAGMENTATION The long-term scheduler must find and allocate memory for all the segments of a user program. This situation is similar to paging *except* that the segments are of *variable* length; pages are all the same size. Thus, as with the variable-sized partition scheme, memory allocation is a dynamic storage-allocation problem, usually solved with a best-fit or first-fit algorithm.

Segmentation may then cause external fragmentation, when all blocks of free memory are too small to accommodate a segment. In this case, the process may simply have to wait until more memory (or at least a larger hole) becomes available, or compaction may be used to create a larger hole. Because segmentation is by its nature a dynamic relocation algorithm, we can compact memory whenever we want. If the CPU scheduler must wait for one process, due to a memory-allocation problem, it may (or may not) skip through the CPU queue looking for a smaller, lower-priority process to run.

How serious a problem is external fragmentation for a segmentation scheme? Would long-term scheduling with compaction help? The answers to these questions depend mainly on the average segment size. At one extreme, we could define each process to be one segment. This approach reduces to the variable-sized partition scheme. At the other extreme, every byte could be put in its own segment and relocated separately. This arrangement eliminates external fragmentation altogether; however, every byte would need a base register for its relocation, doubling memory use! Of course, the next logical step—fixed-sized, small segments—is paging. Generally, if the average segment size is small, external fragmentation will also be small. (By analogy, consider putting suitcases in the trunk of a car; they never quite seem to fit. However, if you open the suitcases and put the individual items in the trunk, everything fits.) Because the individual segments are smaller than the overall process, they are more likely to fit in the available memory blocks.

Segmentation with Paging

Both paging and segmentation have their advantages and disadvantages. In fact, of the two most popular microprocessors now being used, the Motorola 68000 line is designed based on a flat address space, whereas the Intel 80x86 family is based on segmentation. Both are merging memory models toward a mixture of paging and segmentation. It is possible to combine these two schemes to improve on each. This combination is best illustrated by two different architectures—the innovative but not widely used MULTICS system and the Intel 386.

MULTICS In the MULTICS system, a logical address is formed from an 18-bit segment number and a 16-bit offset. Although this scheme creates a 34-bit address space, the segment-table overhead is tolerable; we need only as many segment-table entries as we have segments, as there need not be empty segment-table entries.

However, with segments of 64K words, each of which consists of 36 bits, the average segment size could be large and external fragmentation could be a problem. Even if external fragmentation is not a problem, the search time to allocate a segment, using first-fit or best-fit, could be long. Thus, we may waste memory due to external fragmentation, or waste time due to lengthy searches, or both.

The solution adopted was to *page* the *segments*. Paging eliminates external fragmentation and makes the allocation problem trivial: any empty frame can be used for a desired page. Each page in MULTICS consists of 1K words. Thus, the segment offset (16 bits) is broken into a 6-bit page number and a 10-bit page offset. The page number indexes into the page table to give the frame number. Finally, the frame number is combined with the page offset to form a physical address. The translation scheme is shown in Figure 1-23. Notice that the difference between this solution and pure segmentation is that the segment table entry contains not the base address of the segment, but rather the base address of a *page table* for this segment.

We must now have a separate page table for each segment. However, because each segment is limited in length by its segment-table entry, the page table does not need to be full sized. It requires only as many entries as are actually needed. As with paging, the last page of each segment generally will not be completely full. Thus, we will have, on the average, one-half page of *internal* fragmentation per segment. Consequently, although we have eliminated external fragmentation, we have introduced internal fragmentation and increased table-space overhead.

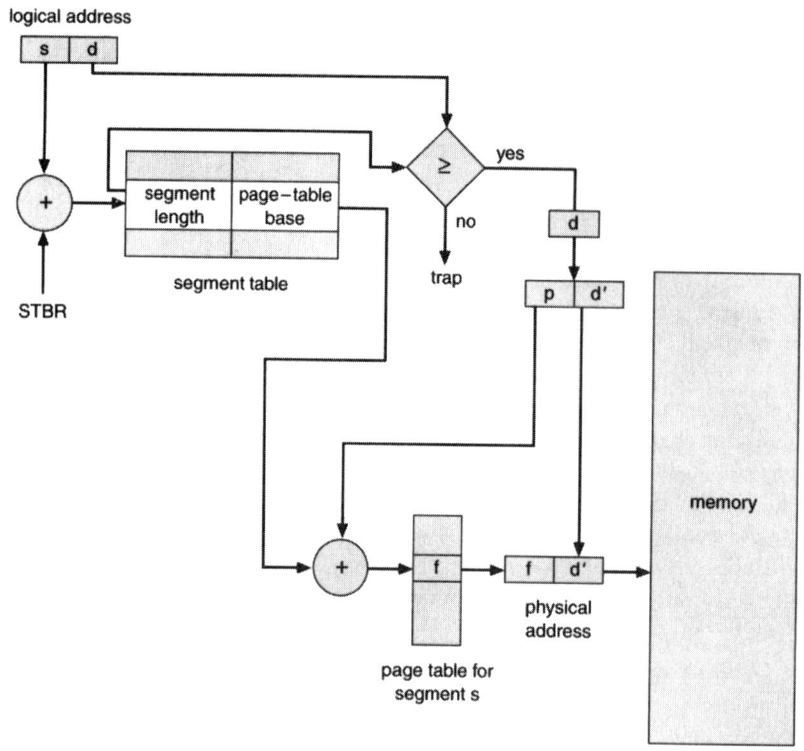

FIGURE 1-23 *Paged Segmentation on the GE 645 (MULTICS)*

In truth, even the paged-segmentation view of MULTICS just presented is simplistic. Because the segment number is an 18-bit quantity, we could have up to 262,144 segments, requiring an excessively large segment table. To ease this problem, MULTICS pages the segment table! The segment number (18 bits) is broken into an 8-bit page number and a 10-bit page offset. Hence, the segment table is represented by a page table consisting of up to 2^8 entries. Thus, in general, a logical address in MULTICS is as follows:

segment number		offset	
s_1	s_2	d_1	d_2
8	10	6	10

where s_1 is an index into the page table of the segment table and s_2 is the displacement within the page of the segment table. Now we have found the page containing the segment table we want. Then, d_1 is a displacement into the page table of the desired segment, and finally, d_2 is a displacement into the page containing the word to be accessed (see Figure 1-24).

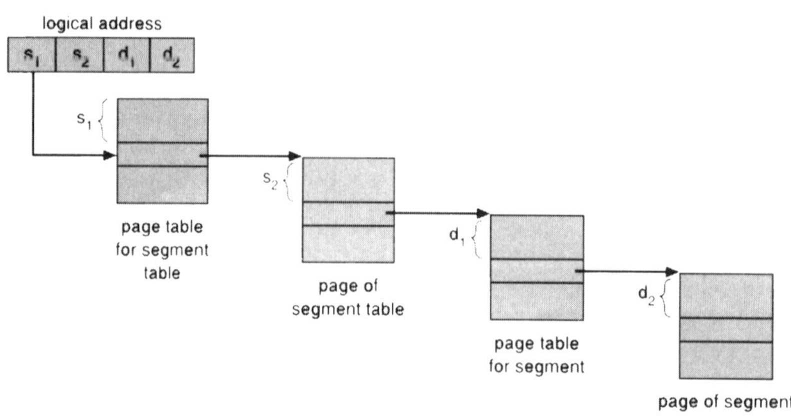

FIGURE 1-24 *Address Translation in MULTICS*

To ensure reasonable performance, 16 associative registers are available that contain the address of the 16 most recently referred pages. Each register consists of two parts: a key and a value. The key is a 24-bit field that is the concatenation of a segment number and a page number. The value is the frame number.

OS/2 32-BIT VERSION The IBM OS/2 32-bit version is an operating system running on top of the Intel 386 (and later) architecture. The 386 uses segmentation with paging for memory management. The maximum number of segments per process is 16K, and each segment can be as large as 4 gigabytes. The page size is 4K bytes. We shall not give a complete description of the memory-management structure of the 386 in this text. Rather, we shall present the major ideas.

The logical address space of a process is divided into two partitions. The first partition consists of up to 8K segments that are private to that process. The second partition consists of up to 8K segments that are shared among all the processes. Information about the first partition is kept in the **local descriptor table (LDT)**, information about the second partition is kept in the **global descriptor table (GDT)**. Each entry in the LDT and GDT table consists of 8 bytes, with detailed information about a particular segment including the base location and length of that segment.

The logical address is a pair (selector, offset), where the selector is a 16-bit number:

s	g	p
13	1	2

in which s designates the segment number, g indicates whether the segment is in the GDT or LDT, and p deals with protection. The offset is a 32-bit number specifying the location of the byte (word) within the segment in question.

The machine has six segment registers, allowing six segments to be addressed at any one time by a process. It has six 8-byte microprogram registers to hold the corresponding descriptors from either the LDT or GDT. This cache lets the 386 avoid having to read the descriptor from memory for every memory reference.

The physical address on the 386 is 32 bits long and is formed as follows. The segment register points to the appropriate entry in the LDT or GDT. The base and limit information about the segment in question are used to generate a *linear address*. First, the limit is used to check for address validity. If the address is not valid, a memory fault is generated, resulting in a trap to the operating system. If it is valid, then the value of the offset is added to the value of the base, resulting in a 32-bit linear address. This address is then translated into a physical address.

As pointed out previously, each segment is paged, and each page is 4K bytes. A page table may thus consist of up to 1 million entries. Because each entry consists of 4 bytes, each process may need up to 4 megabytes of physical address space for the page table alone. Clearly, we would not want to allocate the page table contiguously in main memory. The solution adopted in the 386 is to use a two-level paging scheme. The linear address is divided into a page number consisting of 20 bits, and a page offset consisting of 12 bits. Since we page the page table, the page number is further divided into a 10-bit page directory pointer and a 10-bit page table pointer. The logical address is as follows:

page number		page offset
p_1	p_2	d
10	10	12

So that the efficiency of physical-memory use can be improved, Intel 386 page tables can be swapped to disk. In this case, an invalid bit is used in the page-directory entry to indicate whether the table to which the entry is pointing is in memory or on disk. If the table is on disk, the operating system can use the other 31 bits to specify the disk location of the table; the table then can be brought into memory on demand.

Operating System Software

The design of the memory-management portion of an operating system depends on three fundamental areas of choice:

- Whether or not to use virtual memory techniques
- The use of paging or segmentation or both
- The algorithms employed for various aspects of memory management

The choices made in the first two areas depend on the hardware platform available. Thus, earlier UNIX implementations did not provide virtual memory because the processors on which the system ran did not support paging or segmentation. Neither of these techniques is practical without hardware support for address translation and other basic functions.

Two additional comments about the first two items in the preceding list are in order: First, with the exception of operating systems for some of the older personal computers, such as MS-DOS, and specialized systems, all important operating systems provide virtual memory. Second, pure segmentation systems are becoming increasingly rare. When segmentation is combined with paging, most of the memory-management issues confronting the operating system designer are in the area of paging. Thus, we can concentrate in this section on the issues associated with paging.

The choices in the third area are the domain of operating system software and are the subject of this section. Table 1.7 lists the key design elements that are examined. In each case, the key issue is one of performance: We would like to minimize the rate at which page faults occur, because page faults cause considerable software overhead. At a minimum, the operating system must make a decision concerning which resident page or pages to replace, and the I/O of exchanging pages is incurred. Then the operating system must schedule another process to run during the page I/O, causing a process switch. Accordingly, we would like to arrange matters so that, during the time that a process is executing, the probability of referencing a word on a missing page is minimized. In all of the areas referred to in Table 1.7, there is no definitive policy that works best. As we shall see, the task of memory management in a paging environment is fiendishly complex. Furthermore, the performance of any particular set of policies depends on main-memory size, the relative speed of main and secondary memory, the size and number of processes competing for resources, and the execution behavior of individual programs. This latter characteristic depends on the nature of the application, the programming language and compiler employed, the style of the programmer who wrote it, and, for an interactive program, the dynamic behavior of the user. Thus, the reader must expect no final answers here or anywhere. For smaller systems, the operating system designer should attempt to choose a set of policies that seems "good" over a wide range of conditions, based on the current state of knowledge. For larger systems, particularly

TABLE 1.7
Operating System Policies for Virtual Memory

Fetch Policy	**Resident Set Management**
Demand	Resident set size
Prepaging	Fixed
	Variable
Placement Policy	Replacement scope
	Global
Replacement Policy	Local
Basic algorithms	
Optimal	**Cleaning Policy**
Least recently used (LRU)	Demand
First in, first out (FIFO)	Precleaning
Clock	
Page buffering	**Load Control**
	Degree of multiprogramming

mainframes, the operating system should be equipped with monitoring and control tools that allow the site manager to tune the operating system to get "good" results based on site conditions.

FETCH POLICY The fetch policy determines when a page should be brought into main memory.

PLACEMENT POLICY The placement policy determines where in real memory a process piece is to reside.

REPLACEMENT POLICY In most operating system texts, the treatment of memory management includes a section entitled "replacement policy," which deals with the selection of a page in memory to be replaced when a new page must be brought in. This topic is sometimes difficult to explain because several interrelated concepts are involved:

- How many page frames are to be allocated to each active process
- Whether the set of pages to be considered for replacement should be limited to those of the process that caused the page fault or encompass all the page frames in main memory
- Among the set of pages considered, which particular page should be selected for replacement

We shall refer to the first two concepts as *resident set management*, which is dealt with in the next subsection, and reserve the term *replacement policy* for the third concept, which is discussed in this subsection.

The area of replacement policy is probably the most studied of any area of memory-management over the past 20 years. When all of the frames in main memory are occupied and it is necessary to bring in a new page to satisfy a page fault, the replacement policy determines which page currently in memory is to be replaced. All of the policies have as their objective that the page that is removed should be the page least likely to be referenced in the near future. Because of the principle of locality, there is a often a high correlation between recent referencing history and near-future referencing patterns. Thus, most policies try to predict future behavior on the basis of past behavior. One trade-off that must be considered is that the more elaborate and sophisticated the replacement policy, the greater the hardware and software overhead to implement it.

Frame Locking One restriction on replacement policy needs to be mentioned before looking at various algorithms: Some of the frames in main memory may be locked. When a frame is locked, the page currently stored in that frame may not be replaced. Much of the kernel of the operating system is held on locked frames, as well as key control structures. In addition, I/O buffers and other time-critical areas may be locked into main-memory frames. Locking is achieved by associating a lock bit with each frame. This bit may be kept in a frame table as well as being included in the current page table.

Basic Algorithms Regardless of the resident set management strategy (discussed in the next subsection), there are certain basic algorithms that are used for the selection of a page to replace. Replacement algorithms that have been considered in the literature include

- Optimal
- Least recently used (LRU)
- First-in, first-out (FIFO)
- Clock

The **optimal** policy selects for replacement that page for which the time to the next reference is the longest.

The **least-recently-used (LRU)** policy replaces the page in memory that has not been referenced for the longest time.

The **first-in, first-out (FIFO)** policy treats the page frames allocated to a process as a circular buffer, and pages are removed in round-robin style.

Whereas the LRU policy does nearly as well as an optimal policy, it is difficult to implement and imposes significant overhead. On the other hand, the FIFO policy is very simple to implement but performs relatively poorly. Over the years, operating system designers have tried a number of other algorithms to approximate the performance of LRU while imposing little overhead. Many of these algorithms are variants of a scheme referred to as the **clock policy**.

Page Buffering Although LRU and the clock policies are superior to FIFO, they both involve complexity and overhead not suffered with FIFO. In addition, there is the related issue that the cost of replacing a page that has been modified is greater than for one that has not, because the former must be written back out to secondary memory.

An interesting strategy that can improve paging performance and allow the use of a simpler page-replacement policy is page buffering. The VAX VMS approach is representative. VMS makes use of a variable-allocation, local-replacement strategy. The page-replacement algorithm is simple FIFO. To improve performance, a replaced page is not lost but rather is assigned to one of two lists: the free page list if the page has not been modified, or the modified page list if it has. Note that the page is not physically moved about in main memory; instead, the entry in the page table for this page is removed and placed in either the free or modified page list.

The free page list is a list of page frames available for reading in pages. VMS tries to keep some small number of frames free at all times. When a page is to be read in, the page frame at the head of the list is used; destroying the page that was there. When an unmodified page is to be replaced, it remains in memory and its page frame is added to the tail of the free page list. Similarly, when a modified page is to be written out and replaced, its page frame is added to the tail of the modified page list.

The important aspect of these maneuvers is that the page to be replaced remains in memory. Thus if the process references that page, it is returned to the resident set of that process at little cost. In effect, the free and modified page lists act as a cache of pages. The modified page list serves another useful function: Modified pages are written out in clusters rather than one at a time. This significantly reduces the number of I/O operations and therefore the amount of disk access time.

A simpler version of page buffering is implemented in the Mach operating system (Rashid 1988). In this case, no distinction is made between modified and unmodified pages.

Replacement Policy and Cache Size As was discussed earlier, main-memory size is getting larger and the locality of applications is decreasing. In compensation, cache sizes have been increasing. Large cache sizes, even multimegabyte ones, are now feasible design alternatives (Borg 1990). With a large cache, the replacement of virtual memory pages can have a performance impact. If the page frame selected for replacement is in the cache, then that cache block is lost as well as the page that it holds.

In systems that use some form of page buffering, it is possible to improve cache performance by supplementing the page replacement policy with a policy for page placement in the page buffer. Most operating systems place pages by selecting an arbitrary page frame from the page buffer; typically a first-in-first-out discipline is used. A study reported in (Kessler 1992) shows that a careful page placement strategy can result in 10 to 20% fewer cache misses than naive placement.

RESIDENT SET MANAGEMENT

Resident Set Size With paged virtual memory, it is not necessary and indeed may not be possible to bring all of the pages of a process into main memory to prepare it for execution. Thus, the operating system must decide how many pages to bring in—that is, how much main memory to allocate to a particular process. Several factors come into play:

- The smaller the amount of memory allocated to a process, the more processes that can reside in main memory at any one time. This increases the probability that the operating system will find at least one ready process at any given time, and hence reduces the time lost due to swapping.
- If a relatively small number of pages of a process are in main memory, then, despite the principle of locality, the rate of page faults will be rather high.
- Beyond a certain size, additional allocation of main memory to a particular process will have no noticeable effect on the page fault rate for that process because of the principle of locality.

With these factors in mind, two sorts of policies are to be found in contemporary operating systems. A **fixed-allocation** policy gives a process a fixed number of pages within which to execute. That number is decided at initial load time (process creation time) and may be determined based on the type of process (interactive, batch, type of application) or may be based on guidance from the programmer or system manager. With a fixed-allocation policy, whenever a page fault occurs in the execution of a process, one of the pages of that process must be replaced by the needed page.

A **variable-allocation** policy allows the number of page frames allocated to a process to be varied over the lifetime of the process. Ideally, a process that is suffering persistently high levels of page faults, indicating that the principle of locality only holds in a weak form for that process, will be given additional page frames to reduce the page fault rate; whereas a process with an exceptionally low page fault rate, indicating that the process is quite well-behaved from a locality point of view, will be given a reduced allocation, with the hope that this will not noticeably increase the page fault rate. The use of a variable-allocation policy relates to the concept of replacement scope, as explained in the next subsection.

The variable-allocation policy would appear to be the more powerful one. However, the difficulty with this approach is that it requires the operating system to assess the behavior of active processes. This inevitably requires software overhead in the operating system and is dependent on hardware mechanisms provided by the processor platform.

Replacement Scope The scope of a replacement strategy can be categorized as global or local. Both types of policies are activated by a page fault when there are no free page frames. A **local replacement policy** chooses only among the resident pages of the process that generated the page fault in selecting a page to replace. A **global replacement policy** considers all unlocked pages in main memory as candidates for replacement, regardless of which process owns a particular page. While it happens that local policies are easier to analyze, there is no convincing evidence that they perform better than global policies, which are attractive because of their simplicity of implementation and minimal overhead (Carr 1984, Maekawa 1987).

CLEANING POLICY A cleaning policy is the opposite of a fetch policy; it is concerned with determining when a modified page should be written out to secondary memory. Two common alternatives are demand cleaning and precleaning. With **demand cleaning**, a page is written out to secondary memory only when it has been selected for replacement. A **precleaning** policy writes modified pages before their page frames are needed so that pages can be written out in batches.

There is a danger in following either policy to the full. With precleaning, a page is written out but remains in main memory until the page-replacement algorithm dictates that it be removed. Precleaning allows the writing of pages in batches, but it makes little sense to write out hundreds or thousand of pages only to find that the majority of them have been modified again before they are replaced. The transfer capacity of secondary memory is limited and should not be wasted with unnecessary cleaning operations.

On the other hand, with demand cleaning, the writing of a dirty page is coupled to, and precedes, the reading in of a new page. This technique may minimize page writes but it means that a process that suffers a page fault may have to wait for two page transfers before it can be unblocked. This may decrease processor utilization.

A better approach incorporates page buffering. This allows the adoption of the following policy: Clean only pages that are replaceable, but decouple the cleaning and replacement operations. With page buffering, replaced pages can be placed on two lists: modified and unmodified. The pages on the modified list can periodically be written out in batches and moved to the unmodified list. A page on the unmodified list is either reclaimed if it is referenced, or lost when its frame is assigned to another page.

LOAD CONTROL Load control is concerned with determining the number of processes that will be resident in main memory, which has been referred to as the multiprogramming level. The load control policy is critical in effective memory management. If too few processes are resident at any one time, then there will be many occasions when all processes are blocked, and much time will be spent in swapping. On the other hand, if too many processes are resident, then, on average, the size of the resident set of each process will be inadequate and frequent faulting will occur. The result is thrashing.

PROCESS DESCRIPTION AND CONTROL

The design of an operating system must reflect the requirements it is intended to meet. All multiprogramming operating systems, from single-user systems such as Windows 95 to mainframe systems such as OS/390, which can support thousands of users, are built around the concept of the process. Thus, most requirements that the operating system must meet can be expressed with reference to processes:

- The operating system must interleave the execution of several processes to maximize processor utilization while providing reasonable response time.
- The operating system must allocate resources to processes in conformance with a specific policy (e.g., certain functions or applications are of higher priority) while at the same time avoiding deadlock.[1]
- The operating system may be required to support interprocess communication and user creation of processes, both of which may aid in the structuring of applications.

We begin our detailed study of operating systems with an examination of the way in which they represent and control processes. We first discuss process states, which characterize the behavior of processes. Then we look at the data structures that the operating system needs to represent the state of each process and other characteristics of processes that the operating system needs to achieve its objectives. Finally, process management in UNIX SVR4 is discussed.

PROCESS STATES

The principal function of a processor is to execute machine instructions residing in main memory. These instructions are provided in the form of programs. As explained in the preceding chapter, for reasons of efficiency and ease of programming, a processor may interleave the execution of a number of programs over time.

From the processor's point of view, it executes instructions from its repertoire in some sequence dictated by the changing values in the program counter register. Over time, the program counter may refer to code in different programs that are part of different applications.

From the point of view of an individual program, its execution involves a sequence of instructions within that program. The execution of an individual program is referred to as a process or task.

We can characterize the behavior of an individual process by listing the sequence of instructions that execute for that process. Such a listing is referred to as a *trace* of the process (see, for example, (Hoare 1985) for a rigorous treatment of traces). We can characterize behavior of the processor by showing how the traces of the various processes are interleaved.

THE CREATION AND TERMINATION OF PROCESSES Before attempting to refine our simple two-state model, it will be useful to discuss the creation and termination of processes; ultimately, and regardless of the model of process behavior that is used, the life of a process is bounded by its creation and termination.

Process Creation When a new process is to be added to those currently being managed, the operating system builds the data structures that are used to manage the process and allocates address space to the process. These actions constitute the creation of a new process.

Four common events lead to the creation of a process, as indicated in Table 1.8. In a batch environment, a process is created in response to the submission of a job. In an interactive environment, a process is created when a new user attempts to log on. In both cases, the operating system is responsible for the creation of the new process. An operating system may also create a process on behalf of an application. For example, if a user requests that a file be printed, the operating system can create a process that will manage the printing. The requesting process can thus proceed independently of the time required to complete the printing task.

TABLE 1.8
Reasons for Process Creation

New batch job	The operating system is provided with a batch job control stream, usually on tape or disk. When the operating system is prepared to take on new work, it will read the next sequence of job control commands.
Interactive logon	A user at a terminal logs on to the system.
Created by OS to provide a service	The operating system can create a process to perform a function on behalf of a user program, without the user having to wait (e.g., printing).
Spawned by existing process	For purposes of modularity or to exploit parallelism, a user program can dictate the creation of a number of processes.

Process Termination Table 1.9, based on (Pinkert 1989), summarizes typical reasons for process termination. Any computer system must provide a means for a process to indicate its completion. A batch job should include a Halt instruction or an explicit operating system service call for termination. In the former case, the Halt instruction will generate an interrupt to alert the operating system that a process has completed. For an interactive application, the action of the user will indicate when the process is completed. For example, in a time-sharing system, the process for a particular user is to be terminated when the user logs off or turns off his or her terminal. On a personal computer or workstation, a user may quit an application (e.g., word processing or spreadsheet). All of these actions ultimately result in a service request to the operating system to terminate the requesting process.

TABLE 1.9
Reasons for Process Termination

Normal completion	The process executes an OS service call to indicate that it has completed running.
Time limit exceeded	The process has run longer than the specified total time limit. There are a number of possibilities for the type of time that is measured. These include total elapsed time ("wall clock time"), amount of time spent executing, and, in the case of an interactive process, the amount of time since the user last provided any input.
Memory unavailable	The process requires more memory than the system can provide.
Bounds violation	The process tries to access a memory location that it is not allowed to access.
Protection error	The process attempts to use a resource or a file that it is not allowed to use, or it tries to use it in an improper fashion, such as writing to a read-only file.
Arithmetic error	The process tries a prohibited computation, such as division by zero, or tries to store numbers larger than the hardware can accommodate.
Time overrun	The process has waited longer than a specified maximum for a certain event to occur.
I/O failure	An error occurs during input or output, such as inability to find a file, failure to read or write after a specified maximum number of tries (when, for example, a defective area is encountered on a tape), or invalid operation (such as reading from the line printer).
Invalid instruction	The process attempts to execute a nonexistent instruction (often a result of branching into a data area and attempting to execute the data).
Privileged instruction	The process attempts to use an instruction reserved for the operating system.
Data misuse	A piece of data is of the wrong type, or is not initialized.
Operator or OS intervention	For some reason, the operator or the operating system has terminated the process (for example, if a deadlock exists).
Parent termination	When a parent terminates, the operating system may automatically terminate all of the offspring of that parent.
Parent request	A parent process typically has the authority to terminate any of its offspring.

Additionally, a number of error and fault conditions can lead to the termination of a process. Table 1.9 lists some of the more commonly recognized conditions.[2]

Finally, in some operating systems, a process may be terminated by the process that created it or when the parent process is itself terminated.

A FIVE-STATE MODEL A more natural way to handle this situation is to split the Not-running state into two states: Ready and Blocked. This is shown in Figure 1-25. For good measure, we have added two additional states that will prove useful. The five states are as follows:

- **Running:** The process that is currently being executed.
- **Ready:** A process that is prepared to execute when given the opportunity.
- **Blocked:** A process that cannot execute until some event occurs, such as the completion of an I/O operation.
- **New:** A process that has just been created but has not yet been admitted to the pool of executable processes by the operating system.
- **Exit:** A process that has been released from the pool of executable processes by the operating system, either because it halted or because it aborted for some reason.

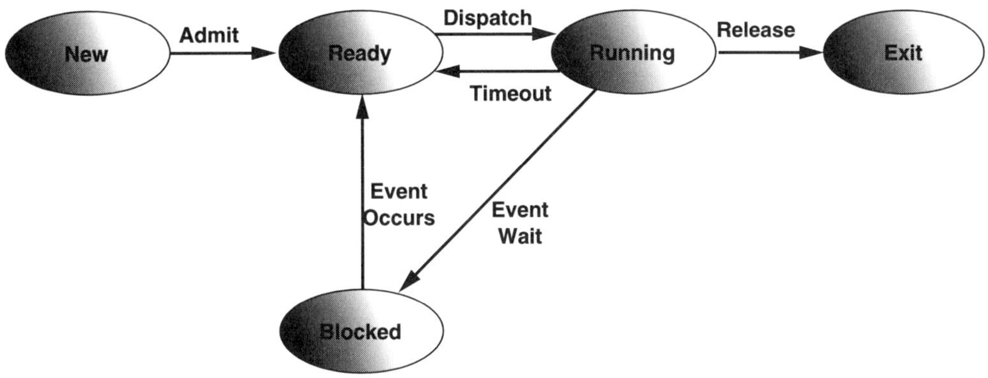

FIGURE 1-25 *Five-State Process Model*

Other Uses of Suspension Table 1.10 lists some reasons for the suspension of a process. One reason that we have discussed is the need to swap a process out to disk to enable a ready process to be brought in, or simply to relieve the pressure on the virtual memory system so that each remaining process has more main memory available to it. The operating system may have other motivations for suspending a process. For example, an auditing or tracing process may be employed to monitor activity on the system; the process may be used to record the level of utilization of various resources (processor, memory, channels) and the rate of progress of the user processes in the system. The operating system, under operator control, may turn this process on and off from time to time. If the operating system detects or suspects a problem, it may suspend a process. One example of this is deadlock. Another example: A problem is detected on a communications line, and the operator has the operating system suspend the process that is using the line while some tests are run.

TABLE 1.10
Reasons for Process Suspension

Swapping	The operating system needs to release sufficient main memory to bring in a process that is ready to execute.
Other OS reason	The operating system may suspend a background or utility process or a process that is suspected of causing a problem.
Interactive user of request	A user may wish to suspend execution of a program for purposes debugging or in connection with the use of a resource.
Timing	A process may be executed periodically (e.g., an accounting or system monitoring process) and may be suspended while waiting for the next time interval.
Parent process request	A parent process may wish to suspend execution of a descendent to examine or modify the suspended process, or to coordinate the activity of various descendents.

Another set of reasons concern the actions of an interactive user. For example, if a user suspects a flaw in the program, he or she may debug the program by suspending its execution, examining and modifying the program or data, and resuming execution. Or there may be a background process that is collecting trace or accounting statistics, which the user may wish to be able to turn on and off.

Timing considerations may also lead to a swapping decision. For example, if a process is to be activated periodically but is idle most of the time, then it should be swapped out between uses. A program that monitors utilization or user activity is an example.

Finally, a parent process may wish to suspend a descendent process. For example, process A may spawn process B to perform a file read. Subsequently, process B encounters an error in the file read procedure and reports this to process A. Process A suspends process B to investigate the cause.

In all of these cases, the activation of a suspended process is requested by the agent that initially requested the suspension.

PROCESS DESCRIPTION

The operating system controls events within the computer system. It schedules and dispatches processes for execution by the processor, allocates resources to processes, and responds to requests by user programs for basic services. Fundamentally, we can think of the operating system as that entity that manages the use of system resources by processes.

OPERATING SYSTEM CONTROL STRUCTURES If the operating system is to manage processes and resources, it must have information about the current status of each process and resource. The universal approach to providing this information is straightforward: The operating system constructs and maintains tables of information about each entity that it is managing. A general idea of the scope of this effort is indicated in Figure 1-26, which shows four different types of tables maintained by the operating system: memory, I/O, file, and process. Although the details will differ from one operating system to another, fundamentally, all operating systems maintain information in these four categories.

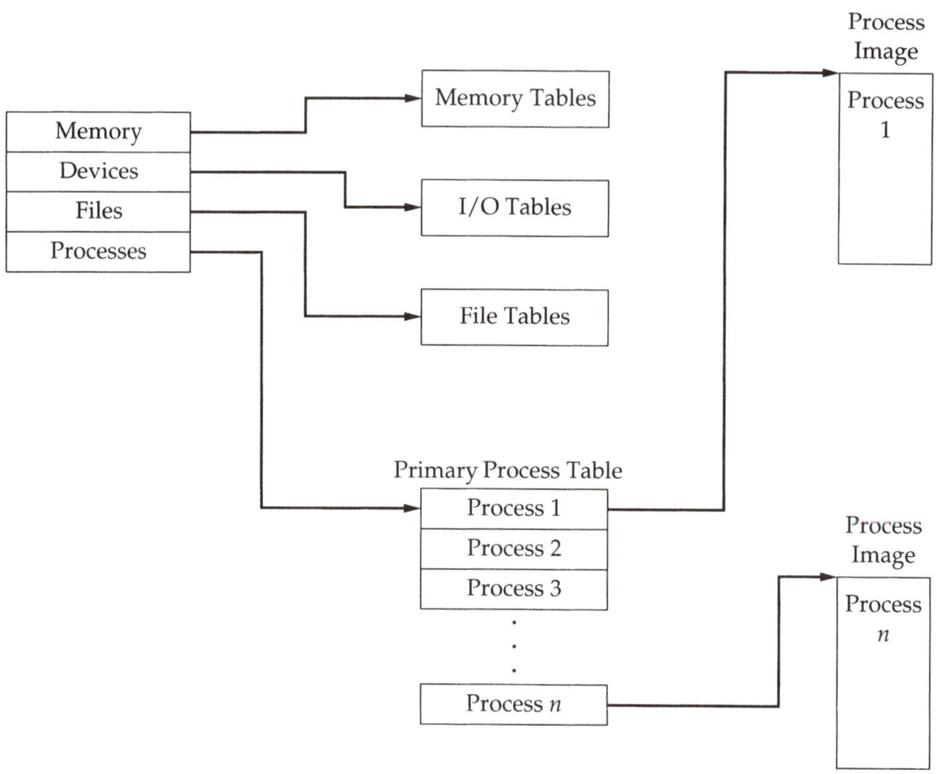

FIGURE 1-26 *General Structure of Operating System Control Tables*

Memory tables are used to keep track of both main (real) and secondary (virtual) memory. Some of main memory is reserved for use by the operating system; the remainder is available for use by processes. Processes are maintained on secondary memory using some sort of virtual memory or simple swapping mechanism. The memory tables must include the following information:

- The allocation of main memory to processes
- The allocation of secondary memory to processes
- Any protection attributes of segments of main or virtual memory, such as which processes may access certain shared memory regions
- Any information needed to manage virtual memory

I/O tables are used by the operating system to manage the I/O devices and channels of the computer system. At any given time, an I/O device may be available or assigned to a particular process. If an I/O operation is in progress, the operating system needs to know the status of the I/O operation and the location in main memory being used as the source or destination of the I/O transfer.

The operating system may also maintain **file tables**. These tables provide information about the existence of files, their location on secondary memory, their current status, and other attributes. Much, if not all, of this information may be maintained and used by a file management system, in which case the operating system has little or no knowledge of files. In other operating systems, much of the detail of file management is managed by the operating system itself.

Finally, the operating system must maintain process tables to manage processes. The remainder of this section is devoted to an examination of the required **process tables**. Before proceeding to this discussion, two additional points should be made. First, although Figure 1-26 shows four distinct sets of tables, it should be clear that these tables must be linked or cross-referenced in some fashion. Memory, I/O, and files are managed on behalf of processes, so there must be some reference to these resources, directly or indirectly, in the process tables. The files referred to in the file tables are accessible via an I/O device and will, at some times, be in main or virtual memory. The tables themselves must be accessible by the operating system and therefore are subject to memory management.

The second point refers to the earlier statement that the operating system creates and maintains these tables. The question of origin arises. How does the operating system know to create the tables in the first place? Clearly, the operating system must have some knowledge of the basic environment, such as how much main memory exists, what are the I/O devices and what are their identifiers, and so on. This is an issue of configuration. That is, when the operating system is initialized, it must have access to some configuration data that define the basic environment, and these data must be created outside the operating system, with human assistance.

PROCESS CONTROL STRUCTURES Consider what the operating system must know if it is to manage and control a process. First, it must know where the process is located, and second, it must know the attributes of the process that are necessary for its management.

Process Location Before we can deal with the questions of where a process is located or what its attributes are, we need to address an even more fundamental question: What is the physical manifestation of a process? At a minimum, a process must include a program or set of programs to be executed. Associated with these programs is a set of data locations for local and global variables and any defined constants. Thus, a process will consist of at least sufficient memory to hold the programs and data of that process. In addition, the execution of a program typically involves a stack that is used to keep track of procedure calls and parameter passing between procedures. Finally, each process has associated with it a number of attributes that are used by the operating system for process control. Typically, the collection of attributes is referred to as a **process control block.**[3] We can refer to this collection of program, data, stack, and attributes as the **process image** (Table 1.11).

TABLE 1.11
Typical Elements of a Process Image

User Data
The modifiable part of the user space. May include program data, a user stack area, and programs that may be modified.

User Program
The program to be executed.

System Stack
Each process has one or more last-in, first-out (LIFO) system stacks associated with it. A stack is used to store parameters and calling addresses for procedure and system calls.

Process Control Block
Data needed by the operating system to control the process (see Table 1.12).

The location of a process image will depend on the memory management scheme being used. In the simplest case, the process image is maintained as a contiguous block of memory. This block is maintained in secondary memory, usually disk. So that the operating system can manage the process, at least a small portion of its image must be maintained in main memory. To execute the process, the entire process image must be loaded into main memory or at least virtual memory. Thus, the operating system needs to know the location of each process on disk and, for each such process that is in main memory, the location of that process in main memory. We saw a slightly more complex variation on this scheme with the CTSS operating system. With CTSS, when a process is swapped out, part of the process image may remain in main memory. Thus, the operating system must keep track of which portions of the image of each process are still in main memory.

Most modern operating systems use a memory-management scheme in which a process image consists of a set of blocks that need not be stored contiguously. Depending on the scheme used, these blocks may be of variable length (called segments), or fixed length (called pages), or a combination. In any case, such schemes allow the operating system to bring in only a portion of any particular process. Thus at any given time, a portion of a process image may be in main memory, with the remainder in secondary memory.[4] Therefore, process tables maintained by the operating system must show the location of each segment and/or page of each process image.

Figure 1-26 depicts the structure of the location information in the following way. There is a primary process table with one entry for each process. Each entry contains, at least, a pointer to a process image. If the process image contains multiple blocks, this information is contained directly in the primary process table, or is available by cross-reference to entries in memory tables. Of course, this depiction is generic; a particular operating system will have its own way of organizing the location information.

Process Attributes A sophisticated multiprogramming system requires a great deal of information about each process. As was explained, this information can be considered to reside in a process control block. Different systems will organize this information in different ways. For now, let us simply explore the type of information that might be of use to an operating system, without considering in any detail how that information is organized.

Table 1.12 lists the typical categories of information required by the operating system for each process. You may be somewhat surprised at the quantity of information required. As you gain a greater appreciation of the responsibilities of the operating system, this list should appear more reasonable.

TABLE 1.12
Typical Elements of a Process Control Block

Process Identification

Identifiers

Numeric identifiers that may be stored with the process control block include

- Identifier of this process
- Identifier of the process that created this process (parent process)
- User identifier

Processor State Information

User-Visible Registers

A user-visible register is one that may be referenced by means of the machine language that the processor executes. Typically, there are from 8 to 32 of these registers, although some RISC implementations have over 100.

Control and Status Registers

These are a variety of processor registers that are employed to control the operation of the processor. These include

- *Program counter:* contains the address of the next instruction to be fetched
- *Condition codes:* result of the most recent arithmetic or logical operation (e.g., sign, zero, carry, equal, overflow)
- *Status information:* includes interrupt enabled/disabled flags, execution mode

Stack Pointers

Each process has one or more last-in, first-out (LIFO) system stacks associated with it. A stack is used to store parameters and calling addresses for procedure and system calls. The stack pointer points to the top of the stack.

Process Control Information

Scheduling and State Information

This is information that is needed by the operating system to perform its scheduling function. Typical items of information include

- *Process state:* defines the readiness of the process to be scheduled for execution (e.g., running, ready, waiting, halted).
- *Priority:* One or more fields may be used to describe the scheduling priority of the process. In some systems, several values are required (e.g., default, current, highest allowable).
- *Scheduling-related information:* this will depend on the scheduling algorithm used. Examples are the amount of time that the process has been waiting and the amount of time that the process executed the last time it was running.
- *Event:* identity of event the process is awaiting before it can be resumed.

Data Structuring

A process may be linked to other process in a queue, ring, or some other structure. For example, all processes in a waiting state for a particular priority level may be linked in a queue. A process may exhibit a parent-child (creator-created) relationship with another process. The process control block may contain pointers to other processes to support these structures.

Interprocess Communication

Various flags, signals, and messages may be associated with communication between two independent processes. Some or all of this information may be maintained in the process control block.

Process Privileges

Processes are granted privileges in terms of the memory that may be accessed and the types of instructions that may be executed. In addition, privileges may apply to the use of system utilities and services.

Memory Management

This section may include pointers to segment and/or page tables that describe the virtual memory assigned to this process.

Resource Ownership and Utilization

Resources controlled by the process may be indicated, such as opened files. A history of utilization of the processor or other resources may also be included; this information may be needed by the scheduler.

We can group the process control block information into three general categories:

- Process identification
- Processor state information
- Process control information

With respect to **process identification**, in virtually all operating systems, each process is assigned a unique numeric identifier, which may simply be an index into the primary process table (Figure 1-26); otherwise there must be a mapping that allows the operating system to locate the appropriate tables based on the process identifier. This identifier is useful in several ways. Many of the other tables controlled by the operating system may use process identifiers to cross-reference process tables. For example, the memory tables may be organized to provide a map of main memory with an indication of which process is assigned to each region. Similar references will appear in I/O and file tables. When processes communicate with one another, the process identifier informs the operating system of the destination of a particular communication. When processes are allowed to create other processes, identifiers indicate the parent and descendents of each process.

In addition to these process identifiers, a process may be assigned a user identifier that indicates the user responsible for the job.

Processor state information consists of the contents of processor registers. While a process is running, of course, the information is in the registers. When a process is interrupted, all of this register information must be saved so that it can be restored when the process resumes execution. The nature and number of registers involved depend on the design of the processor. Typically, the register set will include user-visible registers, control and status registers, and stack pointers.

Of particular note, all processor designs include a register or set of registers, often known as the program status word (PSW), that contains status information. The PSW typically contains condition codes plus other status information. A good example of a processor status word is that on Pentium machines, referred to as the EFLAGS register. This structure is used by any operating system (including UNIX and Windows NT) running on a Pentium computer.

The third major category of information in the process control block can be called, for want of a better name, **process control information**. This is the additional information needed by the operating system to control and coordinate the various active processes. The last part of Table 1.12 indicates the scope of this information. As we examine the details of operating system functionality, the need for the various items on this list should become clear.

As indicated in Table 1.12, the process control block may contain structuring information, including pointers that allow the linking of process control blocks. Thus, the queues that were described in the preceding section could be implemented as linked lists of process control blocks.

Process Control

MODES OF EXECUTION Before continuing with our discussion of the way in which the operating system manages processes, we need to distinguish between the mode of processor execution normally associated with the operating system and that normally associated with user programs. Most processors support at least two modes of execution. Certain instructions can only be executed in the more privileged mode. These would include reading or altering a control register, such as the program status word, primitive I/O instructions, and instructions that relate to memory management. In addition, certain regions of memory can only be accessed in the more privileged mode.

The less privileged mode is often referred to as the user mode, because user programs typically would execute in this mode. The more privileged mode is referred to as the system mode, control mode, or kernel mode. This last term refers to the kernel of the operating system, which is that portion of the operating system that encompasses the important system functions. Table 1.13 lists the functions typically found in the kernel of an operating system.

TABLE 1.13
Typical Functions of an Operating System Kernel

PROCESS MANAGEMENT

- Process creation and termination
- Process scheduling and dispatching
- Process switching
- Process synchronization and support for interprocess communication
- Management of process control blocks

MEMORY MANAGEMENT

- Allocation of address space to processes
- Swapping
- Page and segment management

I/O MANAGEMENT

- Buffer management
- Allocation of I/O channels and devices to processes

SUPPORT FUNCTIONS

- Interrupt handling
- Accounting
- Monitoring

The reason for using two modes should be clear. It is necessary to protect the operating system and key operating system tables, such as process control blocks, from interference by user programs. In the kernel mode, the software has complete control of the processor and all its instructions, registers, and memory. This level of control is not necessary and, for safety, is not desirable for user programs.

Two questions arise: How does the processor know in which mode it is to be executing, and how is the mode changed? Regarding the first question, typically there is a bit in the program status word (PSW) that indicates the mode of execution. This bit is changed in response to certain events. For example, when a user makes a call to an operating system service, the mode is set to the kernel mode. Typically, this is done by executing an instruction that changes the mode. An example of how this is done is the Change Mode (CHM) instruction on the VAX. When the user makes a system service call or when an interrupt transfers control to a system routine, the routine executes CHM to enter a more privileged mode and executes it again to enter a less privileged mode before returning control to the user process. If a user program attempts to execute a CHM, it will simply result in a call to the operating system, which will return an error unless the mode change is to be allowed.

PROCESS CREATION Earlier, we discussed the events that lead to the creation of a new process. Having discussed the data structures associated with a process, we are now in a position to describe briefly the steps involved in actually creating the process.

Once the operating system decides, for whatever reason (Table 1.8), to create a new process, it can proceed as follows:

1. Assign a unique process identifier to the new process. At this time, a new entry is added to the primary process table, which contains one entry per process.

2. Allocate space for the process. This includes all elements of the process image. Thus, the operating system must know how much space is needed for the private user address space (programs and data) and the user stack. These values can be assigned by default based on the type of process, or they can be set based on user request at job creation time. If a process is spawned by another process, the parent process can pass the needed values to the operating system as part of the process-creation request. If any existing address space is to be shared by this new process, the appropriate linkages must be set up. Finally, space for a process control block must be allocated.
3. The process control block must be initialized. The process identification portion contains the ID of this process plus other appropriate IDs, such as that of the parent process. The processor state information portion will typically be initialized with most entries as zero, except for the program counter (set to the program entry point) and system stack pointers (set to define the process stack boundaries). The process control information portion is initialized based on standard default values plus attributes that have been requested for this process. For example, the process state would typically be initialized to Ready or Ready, suspend. The priority may be set by default to the lowest priority unless an explicit request is made for a higher priority. Initially, the process may own no resources (I/O devices, files) unless there is an explicit request for these or unless they are inherited from the parent.
4. The appropriate linkages must be set. For example, if the operating system maintains each scheduling queue as a linked list, then the new process must be put in the Ready or Ready, suspend list.
5. There may be other data structures to be created or expanded. For example, the operating system may maintain an accounting file on each process to be used subsequently for billing and/or performance assessment purposes.

PROCESS SWITCHING On the face of it, the function of process switching would seem to be straightforward. At some time, a running process is interrupted and the operating system assigns another process to the Running state and turns control over to that process. However, several design issues are raised. First, what events trigger a process switch? Another issue is that we must recognize the distinction between mode switching and process switching. Finally, what must the operating system do to the various data structures under its control to achieve a process switch?

When to Switch Processes A process switch may occur any time that the operating system has gained control from the currently running process. Table 1.14 suggests the possible events that may give control to the operating system.

TABLE 1.14
Mechanisms for Interrupting the Execution of a Process

Mechanism	Cause	Use
Interrupt	External to the execution of the current instruction	Reaction to an asynchronous external event
Trap	Associated with the execution of the current instruction	Handling of an error or an exceptional condition
Supervisor call	Explicit request	Call to an operating system function

First, let us consider system interrupts. Actually, we can distinguish, as many systems do, two kinds of system interrupts, one of which is simply referred to as an interrupt, and the other as a trap. The former is due to some sort of event that is external to and independent of the currently running process, such as the completion of an I/O operation. The latter relates to an error or exception condition generated within the currently running process, such as an illegal file access attempt. With an ordinary **interrupt**, control is first transferred to an interrupt handler, which does some basic housekeeping and then branches to an operating system routine that is concerned with the particular type of interrupt that has occurred. Examples include the following:

- **Clock interrupt:** The operating system determines whether the currently running process has been executing for the maximum allowable time slice. If so, this process must be switched to a Ready state and another process dispatched.
- **I/O interrupt:** The operating system determines what I/O action has occurred. If the I/O action constitutes an event for which one or more processes are waiting, then the operating system moves all of the corresponding blocked processes to the Ready state (and Blocked, suspend processes to the Ready, suspend state). The operating system must then decide whether to resume execution of the process currently in the Running state or to preempt that process for a higher-priority Ready process.
- **Memory fault:** The processor encounters a virtual memory address reference for a word that is not in main memory. The operating system must bring in the block (page or segment) of memory containing the reference from secondary memory to main memory. After the I/O request is issued to bring in the block of memory, the operating system may perform a process switch to resume execution of another process; the process with the memory fault is placed in a blocked state. After the desired block is brought into memory, that process is placed in a ready state.

With a **trap**, the operating system determines whether or not the error is fatal. If so, then the currently running process is moved to the Exit state and a process switch occurs. If not, then the action of the operating system will depend on the nature of the error and the design of the operating system. It may attempt some recovery procedure or simply notify the user. It may do a process switch or resume the currently running process.

Finally, the operating system may be activated by a **supervisor call** from the program being executed. For example, a user process is running and an instruction is executed that requests an I/O operation, such as a file open. This call results in a transfer to a routine that is part of the operating system code. Generally, the use of a system call results in placing the user process in the Blocked state.

Mode Switching We discussed the inclusion of an interrupt cycle as part of the instruction cycle. Recall that, in the interrupt cycle, the processor checks to see if any interrupts have occurred, indicated by the presence of an interrupt signal. If no interrupts are pending, the processor proceeds to the fetch cycle and fetches the next instruction of the current program in the current process. If an interrupt is pending, the processor does the following:

1. It saves the context of the current program being executed.
2. It sets the program counter to the starting address of an *interrupt handler* program.
3. It switches from user mode to kernel mode so that the interrupt processing code may include privileged instructions.

The processor now proceeds to the fetch cycle and fetches the first instruction of the interrupt handler program, which will service the interrupt.

One question that may now occur to you is this: What constitutes the context that is saved? The answer is that it must include any information that may be altered by the execution of the interrupt handler and that will be needed to resume the program that was interrupted. Thus, the portion of the process control block that was referred to as processor state information must be saved. This includes the program counter, other processor registers, and stack information.

Does anything else need to be done? That depends on what happens next. The interrupt handler is typically a short program that performs a few basic tasks related to an interrupt. For example, it resets that flag or indicator that signals the presence of an interrupt. It may send an acknowledgment to the entity that issued the interrupt, such as an I/O module. And it may do some basic housekeeping relating to the effects of the event that caused the interrupt. For example, if the interrupt relates to an I/O event, the interrupt handler will check for an error condition. If an error has occurred, the interrupt handler may send a signal to the process that originally requested the I/O operation. If the interrupt is by the clock, then the handler will hand control over to the dispatcher, which will want to pass control to another process because the time slice allotted to the currently running process has expired.

What about the other information in the process control block? If this interrupt is to be followed by a switch to another process, than some work will need to be done. However, the key word in the previous sentence is *if*. In most operating systems, the occurrence of an interrupt does not necessarily mean a process switch. It is possible that, after the interrupt handler has executed, the currently running process will resume execution. In that case, all that is necessary is to save the processor state information when the interrupt occurs and restore that information when control is returned to the program that was in progress. Typically, the saving and restoring functions are performed in hardware.

Change of Process State It is clear, then, that the mode switch is a concept distinct from that of the process switch.[5] A mode switch may occur without changing the state of the process that is currently in the Running state. In that case, the context saving and subsequent restoral involve little overhead. However, if the currently running process is to be moved to another state (Ready, Blocked, etc.), then the operating system must make substantial changes in its environment. The steps involved in a full process switch are as follows:

1. Save the context of the processor, including program counter and other registers.
2. Update the process control block of the process that is currently in the Running state. This includes changing the state of the process to one of the other states (Ready; Blocked; Ready, suspend; or Exit). Other relevant fields must also be updated, including the reason for leaving the Running state and accounting information.
3. Move the process control block of this process to the appropriate queue (Ready; Blocked on Event i; Ready, suspend).
4. Select another process for execution; this topic is explored in Part Four.
5. Update the process control block of the process selected. This includes changing the state of this process to Running.
6. Update memory-management data structures. This may be required, depending on how address translation is managed.
7. Restore the context of the processor to that which existed at the time the selected process was last switched out of the Running state, by loading in the previous values of the program counter and other registers.

Thus, the process switch, which involves a state change, requires considerably more effort than a mode switch.

EXECUTION OF THE OPERATING SYSTEM We pointed out several intriguing facts about operating systems:

- The operating system functions in the same way as ordinary computer software; that is, it is a program executed by the processor.
- The operating system frequently relinquishes control and must depend on the processor to allow it to regain control.

If the operating system is just a collection of programs and if it is executed by the processor just like any other program, is the operating system a process? If so, how is it controlled? These interesting questions have received a number of answers from operating system designers. Figure 1-27 illustrates a range of approaches that are found in various contemporary operating systems.

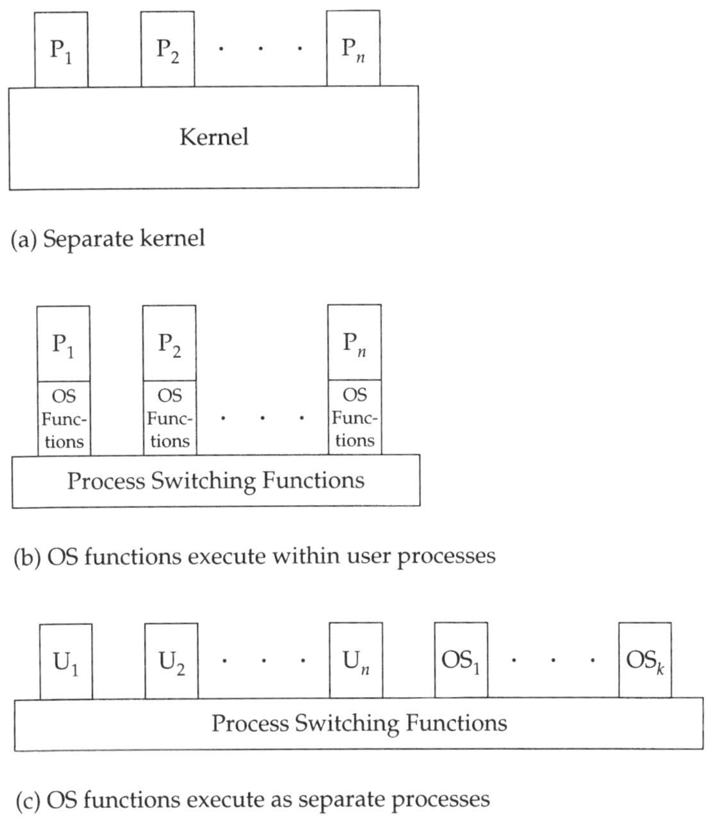

FIGURE 1-27 *Relationship Between Operating System and User Processes*

Nonprocess Kernel One approach, which is quite traditional and common on many older operating systems, is to execute the kernel of the operating system outside of any process (Figure 1-27a). With this approach, when the currently running process is interrupted or issues a supervisor call, the mode context of this process is saved and control is passed to the kernel. The operating system has its own region of memory to use and its own system stack for controlling procedure calls and returns. The operating system can perform any desired functions and restore the context of the interrupted process, which causes execution to resume in the interrupted user process. Alternatively, the operating system can complete the function of saving the environment of the process and proceed to schedule and dispatch another process. Whether this happens depends on the reason for the interruption and the circumstances at the time.

In any case, the key point here is that the concept of process is considered to apply only to user programs. The operating system code is executed as a separate entity that operates in privileged mode.

Execution within User Processes An alternative that is common with operating systems on smaller machines (minicomputers and microcomputers) is to execute virtually all operating system software in the context of a user process. The view is that the operating system is primarily a collection of routines that the user calls to perform various functions, executed within the environment of the user's process. This is illustrated in Figure 1-27b. At any given point, the operating system is managing *n* process images.

Figure 1-28 suggests a typical process image structure for this strategy. A separate kernel stack is used to manage calls/returns while the process is in kernel mode. Operating system code and data are in the shared address space and are shared by all user processes.

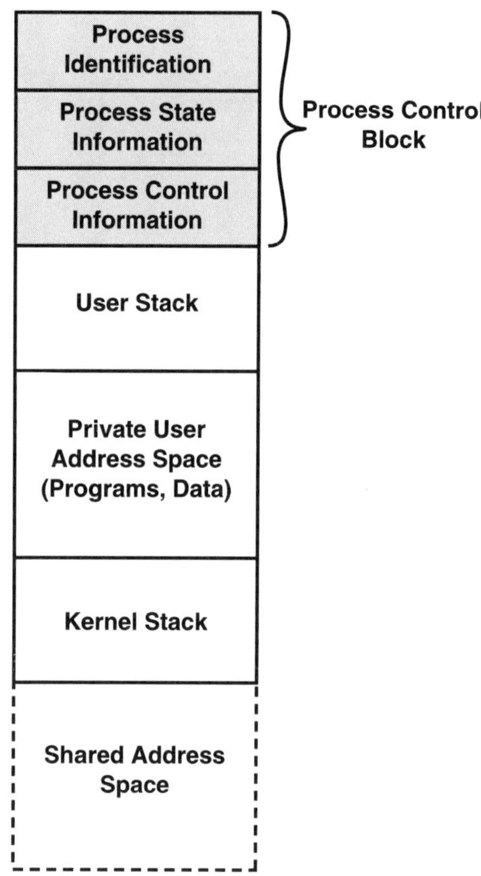

FIGURE 1-28 *Process Image: Operating System Executes within User Space*

When an interrupt, trap, or supervisor call occurs, the processor is placed in kernel mode and control is passed to the operating system. For this purpose, the mode context is saved and a mode switch takes place to an operating system routine. However, execution continues within the current user process. Thus, a process switch is not performed, just a mode switch within the same process.

If the operating system, upon completion of its work, determines that the current process should continue to run, then a mode switch resumes the interrupted program within the current process. This is one of the key advantages of this approach: A user program has been interrupted in order to employ some operating system routine, and then resumed, and all of this has occurred without incurring the penalty of two process switches. If, however, it is determined that a process switch is to occur rather than returning to the previously executing program, then control is passed to a process-switching routine. This routine may or may not execute in the current process, depending on system design. At some point, however, the current process has to be placed in a nonrunning state and another process designated as the running process. During this phase, it is logically most convenient to view execution as taking place outside of all processes.

In a way, this view of the operating system is quite remarkable. Simply put, at certain points in time, a process will save its state information, choose another process to run from among those that are ready, and relinquish control to that process. The reason this is not an arbitrary and indeed chaotic situation is that during the critical time, the code that is executed in the user process is shared operating system code and not user code. Because of the concept of user mode and kernel mode, the user cannot tamper with or interfere with the operating system routines, even though they are executing in the user's process environment. This further reminds us that there is a distinction between the concepts of process and program and that the relationship between the two is not one-to-one. Within a process, both a user program and operating system programs may execute, and the operating system programs that execute in the various user processes are identical.

Process-based Operating System Another alternative, illustrated in Figure 1-27c, is to implement the operating system as a collection of system processes. As in the other options, the software that is part of the kernel executes in a kernel mode. In this case, however, major kernel functions are organized as separate processes. Again, there may be a small amount of process-switching code that is executed outside of any process.

This approach has several advantages. It imposes a program design discipline that encourages the use of a modular operating system with minimal, clean interfaces between the modules. In addition, some noncritical operating system functions are conveniently implemented as separate processes. For example, we mentioned earlier a monitor program that records the level of utilization of various resources (processor, memory, channels) and the rate of progress of the user processes in the system. Because this program does not provide a particular service to any active process, it can only be invoked by the operating system. As a process, the function can run at an assigned priority level and be interleaved with other processes under dispatcher control. Finally, implementing the operating system as a set of processes is useful in a multiprocessor or multicomputer environment, in which some of the operating system services can be shipped out to dedicated processors, improving performance.

THREADS, SMP, AND MICROKERNELS

This chapter examines some more advanced concepts related to process management, which are found in a number of contemporary operating systems. First, we show that the concept of process is more complex and subtle than presented so far and in fact embodies two separate and potentially independent concepts: one relating to resource ownership and one relating to execution. This distinction has led to the development in some operating systems of a construct known as the *thread*. After examining threads, we look at symmetric multiprocessing (SMP). With SMP, the operating system must be able simultaneously to schedule different processes on multiple processors.

Processes and Threads

The discussion so far has presented the concept of a process as embodying two characteristics:

- **Unit of resource ownership:** A process is allocated a virtual address space to hold the process image, and from time to time may be assigned main memory plus control of other resources, such as I/O channels, I/O devices, and files.
- **Unit of dispatching:** A process is an execution path (trace) through one or more programs. This execution may be interleaved with that of other processes. Thus, a process has an execution state (Running, Ready, etc.) and a dispatching priority and is the entity that is scheduled and dispatched by the operating system.

In most operating systems, these two characteristics are indeed the essence of a process. However, some thought should convince the reader that these two characteristics are independent and could be treated independently by the operating system. This is done in a number of operating systems, particularly recently developed systems. To distinguish the two characteristics, the unit of dispatching is usually referred to as a **thread**, or **lightweight process**, while the unit of resource ownership is usually still referred to as a **process**, or **task**.[6]

MULTITHREADING Multithreading refers to the ability of an operating system to support multiple threads of execution within a single process. The traditional approach of a single thread of execution per process, in which the concept of a thread is not recognized, is referred to as a single-threaded approach. The two arrangements depicted in the left half of Figure 1-29 are single-threaded approaches. MS-DOS is an example of an operating system that supports a single user process and a single thread. Other operating systems, such as UNIX, support multiple user processes but only support one thread per process. The right half of Figure 1-29 depicts multithreaded approaches. A Java run-time engine is an example of a system of one process with multiple threads. Of interest in this section is the use of multiple processes, each of which support multiple threads. This approach is taken in Windows NT, Solaris, Mach, and OS/2, among others. In this section we give a general description of multithreading.

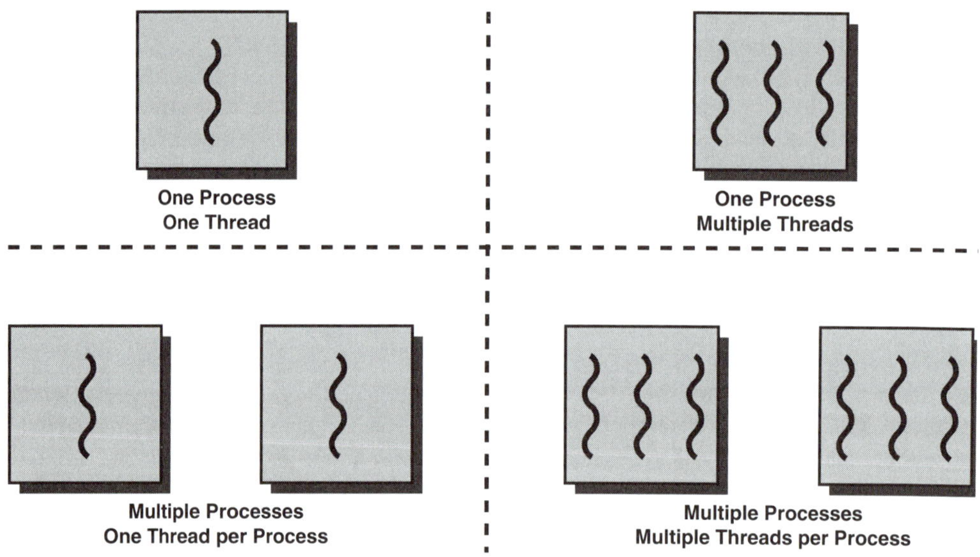

FIGURE 1-29 *Threads and Processes (Anderson 1997)*

In a multithreaded environment, a process is defined as the unit of protection and the unit of resource allocation. The following are associated with processes:

- A virtual address space that holds the process image
- Protected access to processors, other processes (for interprocess communication), files, and I/O resources (devices and channels)

Within a process, there may be one or more threads, each with the following:

- A thread execution state (Running, Ready, etc.)
- A saved thread context when not running; one way to view a thread is as an independent program counter operating within a process

- An execution stack
- Some per-thread static storage for local variables
- Access to the memory and resources of its process, shared with all other threads in that process

Figure 1-30 illustrates the distinction between threads and processes from the point of view of process management. In a single-threaded process model (i.e., there is no distinct concept of thread), the representation of a process includes its process control block and user address space, as well as user and kernel stacks to manage the call/return behavior of the execution of the process. While the process is running, processor registers are controlled by that process, and the contents of these registers are saved when the process is not running. In a multithreaded environment, there is still a single process control block and user address space associated with the process, but now there are separate stacks for each thread, as well as a separate control block for each thread containing register image, priority, and other thread-related state information.

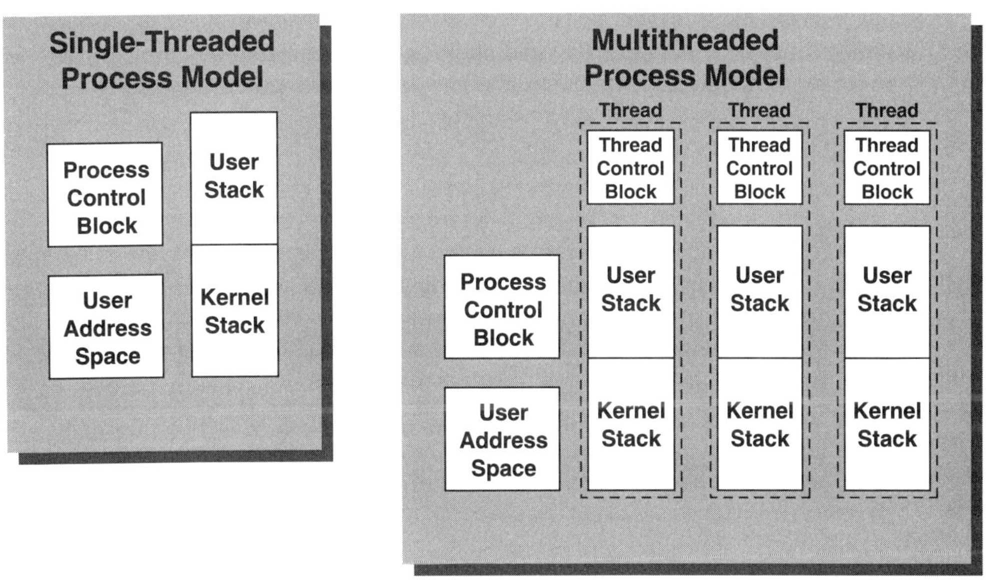

FIGURE 1-30 *Single-Threaded and Multithreaded Process Models*

Thus, all of the threads of a process share the state and resources of that process. They reside in the same address space and have access to the same data. When one thread alters an item of data in memory, other threads see the results if and when they access that item. If one thread opens a file with read privileges, other threads in the same process can also read from that file.

The key benefits of threads derive from the performance implications: It takes far less time to create a new thread in an existing process than to create a brand-new process, less time to terminate a thread, and less time to switch between two threads within the same process. Thus, if there is an application or function that should be implemented as a set of related units of execution, it is far more efficient to do so as a collection of threads rather than a collection of separate processes. Studies done by the Mach developers show that the speed-up in process creation compared to a comparable UNIX implementation, which does not use threads, is a factor of 10 (Tevanian 1987).

An example of an application that could make use of threads is a server, such as a file server on a local area network. As each new file request comes in, a new thread can be spawned for the file management program. Because a server will handle many requests, many threads will be created and destroyed in a short period. If the server is a multiprocessor, then multiple threads within the same process can be executing simultaneously on different processors. The thread construct is also sometimes useful on a single processor to simplify the structure of a program that is logically doing several different functions.

Threads also enhance efficiency in communication between different executing programs. In most operating systems, communication between independent processes requires the intervention of the kernel to provide protection and the mechanisms needed for communication. However, because threads within the same process share memory and files, they can communicate with each other without invoking the kernel.

(Letwin 1988) gives four examples of the uses of threads in a single-user multiprocessing system:

- **Foreground and background work:** For example, in a spreadsheet program, one thread could display menus and read user input, while another thread executes user commands and updates the spreadsheet. This arrangement often increases the perceived speed of the application by allowing the program to prompt for the next command before the previous command is complete.
- **Asynchronous processing:** Asynchronous elements in the program can be implemented as threads. For example, as a protection against power failure, one can design a word processor to write its RAM buffer to disk once every minute. A thread can be created whose sole job is periodic backup and that schedules itself directly with the operating system; there is no need for fancy code in the main program to provide for time checks or to coordinate input and output.
- **Speed execution:** A multithreaded process can compute one batch of data while reading the next batch from a device. On a multiprocessing system, multiple threads from the same process will actually be able to execute simultaneously.
- **Organizing programs:** Programs that involve a variety of activities or a variety of sources and destinations of input and output may be easier to design and implement using threads.

Scheduling and dispatching is done on a thread basis; hence most of the state information dealing with execution is maintained in thread-level data structures. There are, however, several actions that affect all of the threads in a process and that the operating system must manage at the process level. Suspension involves swapping the address space out of main memory. Because all threads in a process share the same address space, all threads must enter a suspend state at the same time. Similarly, termination of a process terminates all threads within that process.

THREAD FUNCTIONALITY Like processes, threads have execution states and may synchronize with one another.

Thread States As with processes, the key states for a thread are Running, Ready, and Blocked. Generally, it does not make sense to associate suspend states with threads because such states are process-level concepts. In particular, if a process is swapped out, all of its threads are necessarily swapped out because they all share the address space of the process.

There are four basic thread operations associated with a change in thread state (Anderson 1997):

- **Spawn:** Typically, when a new process is spawned, a thread for that process is also spawned. Subsequently, a thread within a process may spawn another thread within the same process, providing an instruction pointer and arguments for the new thread. The new thread is provided with its own register context and stack space and placed on the ready list.

- **Block:** When a thread needs to wait for an event, it will block (saving its user registers, program counter, and stack pointers). The processor may now turn to the execution of another ready thread.
- **Unblock:** When the event for which a thread is blocked occurs, the thread is moved to the ready state.
- **Finish:** When a thread completes, its register context and stacks are deallocated.

A significant issue is whether the blocking of a thread results in the blocking of the entire process. In other words, if one thread in a process is blocked, does this prevent the running of any other thread in the same process even if that other thread is in a ready state? Clearly, some of the flexibility and power of threads is lost if the one blocked thread blocks an entire process.

USER-LEVEL AND KERNEL-LEVEL THREADS There are two broad categories of thread implementation: user-level threads (ULTs) and kernel-level threads (KLTs).[7] The latter are also referred to in the literature as kernel-supported threads or lightweight processes.

User-level Threads In a pure ULT facility, all of the work of thread management is done by the application and the kernel is not aware of the existence of threads. Figure 1-31a depicts the pure ULT approach. Any application can be programmed to be multithreaded by using a threads library, which is a package of routines for ULT management. The threads library contains code for creating and destroying threads, for passing messages and data between threads, for scheduling thread execution, and for saving and restoring thread contexts.

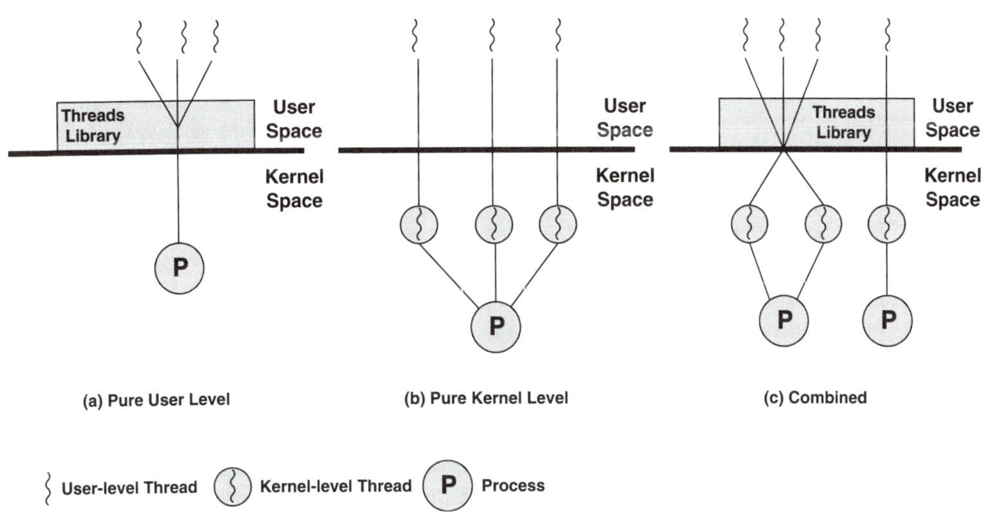

FIGURE 1-31 *User-Level and Kernel-Level Threads*

By default, an application begins with a single thread and begins running in that thread. This application and its thread are allocated to a single process managed by the kernel. At any time that the application is running (the process is in the Running state), the application may spawn a new thread to run within the same process. Spawning is done by invoking the spawn utility in the threads library. Control is passed to that utility by a procedure call. The threads library creates a data structure for the new thread and then passes control to one of the threads within this process that is in the Ready state, using some scheduling algorithm. When control is passed to the library, the context of the current thread is saved, and when control is passed from the library to a thread, the context of that thread is restored. The context essentially consists of the contents of user registers, the program counter, and stack pointers.

All of the activity described in the preceding paragraph takes place in user space and within a single process. The kernel is unaware of this activity. The kernel continues to schedule the process as a unit and assigns a single execution state (Ready, Running, Blocked, etc.) to that process. The following examples should clarify the relationship between thread scheduling and process scheduling. Suppose that process B is executing in its thread 3. Each of the following are possible occurrences:

1. The application executing in thread 3 makes a system call that blocks B. For example, an I/O call is made. This causes control to transfer to the kernel. The kernel invokes the I/O action, places process B in the blocked state, and switches to another process. Meanwhile, according to the data structure maintained by the threads library, thread 3 of process B is still in the running state. It is important to note that thread 3 is not actually running in the sense of being executed on a processor; but it is perceived as being in the Running state by the threads library.
2. A clock interrupt passes control to the kernel and the kernel determines that the currently running process (B) has exhausted its time slice. The kernel places process B in the Ready state and switches to another process. Meanwhile, according to the data structure maintained by the threads library, thread 3 of process B is still in the Running state.

In both of the preceding cases, when the kernel switches control back to process B, execution resumes in thread 3. Also note that a process can be interrupted, either by exhausting its time slice or by being preempted by a higher-priority process, while it is executing code in the threads library. Thus, a process may be in the midst of a thread switch from one thread to another when interrupted. When that process is resumed, execution continues within the threads library, which completes the thread switch and transfers control to a new thread within that process.

There are a number of advantages to the use of ULTs instead of KLTs:

1. Thread switching does not require kernel mode privileges because all of the thread management data structures are within the user address space of a single process. Therefore, the process does not switch to the kernel mode to do thread management. This saves the overhead of two mode switches (user to kernel; kernel back to user).
2. Scheduling can be application specific. One application may benefit most from a simple round-robin scheduling algorithm, while another might benefit from a priority-based scheduling algorithm. The scheduling algorithm can be tailored to the application without disturbing the underlying OS scheduler.
3. ULTs can run on any operating system. No changes are required to the underlying kernel to support ULTs. The threads library is a set of application-level utilities shared by all applications.

There are two distinct disadvantages of ULTs compared to KLTs:

1. In a typical operating system, most system calls are blocking. Thus, when a thread executes a system call, not only is that thread blocked, but all of the threads within the process are blocked.
2. In a pure ULT strategy, a multithreaded application cannot take advantage of multiprocessing. A kernel assigns one process to only one processor at a time. Therefore, only a single thread within a process can execute at a time. In effect, we have application-level multiprogramming within a single process. While this multiprogramming can result in a significant speedup of the application, there

are applications that would benefit from the ability to execute portions of code concurrently.

There are ways to work around these two problems. For example, both problems can be overcome by writing an application as multiple processes rather than multiple threads. But this approach eliminates the main advantage of threads: Each switch becomes a process switch rather than a thread switch, resulting in much greater overhead.

Another way to overcome the problem of blocking threads is to use a technique referred to as *jacketing*. The purpose of jacketing is to convert a blocking system call into a non-blocking system call. For example, instead of directly calling a system I/O routine, a thread calls an application-level I/O jacket routine. Within this jacket routine is code that checks to determine if the I/O device is busy. If it is, the thread enters the Ready state and passes control (through the threads library) to another thread. When this thread later is given control again, it checks the I/O device again.

Kernel-level Threads In a pure KLT facility, all of the work of thread management is done by the kernel. There is no thread management code in the application area, simply an application programming interface (API) to the kernel thread facility. Windows NT and OS/2 are examples of this approach.

Figure 1-31b depicts the pure KLT approach. Any application can be programmed to be multithreaded. All of the threads within an application are supported within a single process. The kernel maintains context information for the process as a whole and for individual threads within the process. Scheduling by the kernel is done on a thread basis. This approach overcomes the two principal drawbacks of the ULT approach. First, the kernel can simultaneously schedule multiple threads from the same process on multiple processors. Second, if one thread in a process is blocked, the kernel can schedule another thread of the same process. Another advantage of the KLT approach is that kernel routines themselves can be multithreaded.

The principal disadvantage of the KLT approach compared to the ULT approach is that the transfer of control from one thread to another within the same process requires a mode switch to the kernel. To illustrate the differences, Table 1.15 shows the results of measurements taken on a uniprocessor VAX machine running a UNIX-like operating system. The two benchmarks are Null Fork, the time to create, schedule, execute, and complete a process/thread that invokes the null procedure (i.e., the overhead of forking a process/thread); and Signal-Wait, the time for a process/thread to signal a waiting process/thread and then wait on a condition (i.e., the overhead of synchronizing two processes/threads together). To put these numbers in perspective, a procedure call on the VAX used in this study takes about 7 ms, while a kernel trap takes about 17 ms. We see that there is an order of magnitude or more of difference between ULTs and KLTs and similarly between KLTs and processes.

TABLE 1.15
Thread Operation Latencies (μs) (Anderson 1992)

Operation	User-level Threads	Kernel-level Threads	Processes
Null Fork	34	948	11,300
Signal-Wait	37	441	1,840

Thus, on the face of it, while there is a significant speedup by using KLT multithreading compared to single-threaded processes, there is an additional significant speedup by using ULTs. However, whether or not the additional speedup is realized depends on the nature of the applications involved. If most of the thread switches in an application require kernel mode access, then a ULT based scheme may not perform much better than a KLT-based scheme.

Combined Approaches Some operating systems provide a combined ULT/KLT facility (Figure 1-31c). Solaris is the principal example of this. In a combined system, thread creation is done completely in user space as is the bulk of the scheduling and synchronization of threads within an application. The multiple ULTs from a single application are mapped onto some (smaller or equal) number of KLTs. The programmer may adjust the number of KLTs for a particular application and machine to achieve the best overall results.

In a combined approach, multiple threads within the same application can run in parallel on multiple processors and a blocking system call need not block the entire process. If properly designed, this approach should combine the advantages of the pure ULT and KLT approaches while minimizing the disadvantages.

SYMMETRIC MULTIPROCESSING

Traditionally, the computer has been viewed as a sequential machine. Most computer programming languages require the programmer to specify algorithms as sequences of instructions. A processor executes programs by executing machine instructions in a sequence and one at a time. Each instruction is executed in a sequence of operations (fetch instruction, fetch operands, perform operation, store results).

This view of the computer has never been entirely true. At the microoperation level, multiple control signals are generated at the same time. Instruction pipelining, at least to the extent of overlapping fetch and execute operations, has been around for a long time. Both of these are examples of performing functions in parallel.

As computer technology has evolved and as the cost of computer hardware has dropped, computer designers have sought more and more opportunities for parallelism, usually to improve performance and, in some cases, to improve reliability. We will examine the two most popular approaches to providing parallelism by replicating processors: symmetric multiprocessors (SMPs) and clusters. SMPs are discussed in this section.

SMP ARCHITECTURE It is useful to see where SMP architectures fit into the overall category of parallel processors. A taxonomy that highlights parallel processor systems first introduced by Flynn (Flynn 1972) is still the most common way of categorizing such systems. Flynn proposed the following categories of computer systems:

- **Single Instruction Single Data (SISD) stream:** A single processor executes a single instruction stream to operate on data stored in a single memory.
- **Single Instruction Multiple Data (SIMD) stream:** A single machine instruction controls the simultaneous execution of a number of processing elements on a lockstep basis. Each processing element has an associated data memory, so that each instruction is executed on a different set of data by the different processors. Vector and array processors fall into this category.
- **Multiple Instruction Single Data (MISD) stream:** A sequence of data is transmitted to a set of processors, each of which executes a different instruction sequence. This structure has never been implemented.
- **Multiple Instruction Multiple Data (MIMD) stream:** A set of processors simultaneously execute different instruction sequences on different data sets.

With the MIMD organization, the processors are general purpose because they must be able to process all of the instructions necessary to perform the appropriate data transformation. MIMDs can be further subdivided by the means in which the processors communicate (Figure 1-32). If the processors each have a dedicated memory, then each processing element is a self-contained computer. Communication among the computers is either via fixed paths or via some network facility. Such a system is known as a **cluster**, or multicomputer. If the processors share a common memory, then each processor accesses programs and data stored in the shared memory, and processors communicate with each other via that memory; such a system is known as a **shared memory multiprocessor**.

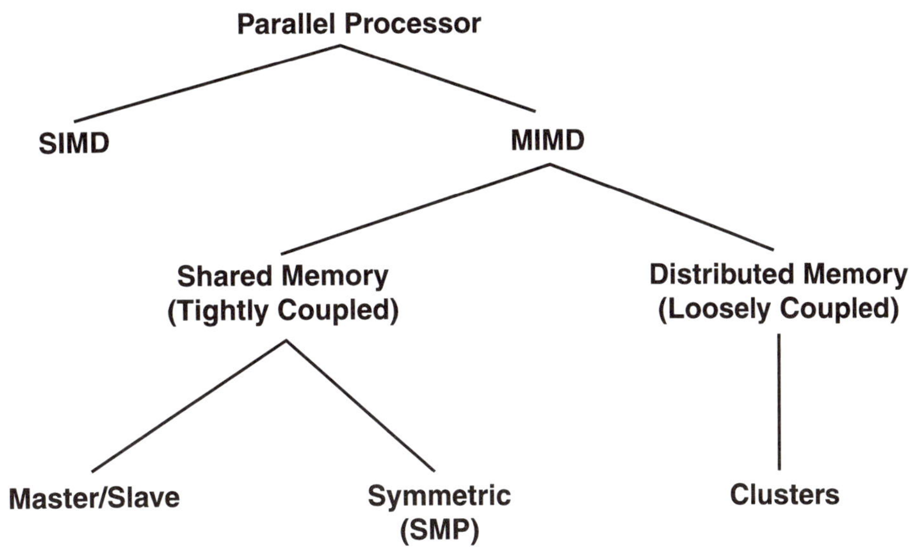

FIGURE 1-32 *Parallel Processor Architectures*

One general classification of shared memory multiprocessors is based on how processes are assigned to processors. The two fundamental approaches are master/slave and symmetric. With a **master/slave** architecture, the operating system kernel always runs on a particular processor. The other processors may only execute user programs and perhaps operating system utilities. The master is responsible for scheduling processes or threads. Once a process/thread is active, if the slave needs service (e.g., an I/O call), it must send a request to the master and wait for the service to be performed. This approach is quite simple and requires little enhancement to a uniprocessor multiprogramming operating system. Conflict resolution is simplified since one processor has control of all memory and I/O resources. The disadvantages of this approach are as follows: (1) A failure of the master brings down the whole system, and (2) the master can become a performance bottleneck because it alone must do all scheduling and process management. In a **symmetric multiprocessor**, the kernel can execute on any processor, and typically each processor does self-scheduling from the pool of available processes or threads. The kernel can be constructed as multiple processes or multiple threads, allowing portions of the kernel to execute in parallel. The SMP approach complicates the operating system. It must ensure that two processors do not choose the same process and that processes are not somehow lost from the queue. Techniques must be employed to resolve and synchronize claims to resources.

The design of both SMPs and clusters is complex, involving issues relating to physical organization, interconnection structures, interprocessor communication, operating system design, and application software techniques. Our concern here is primarily with operating system design issues, although we touch briefly on organization.

SMP ORGANIZATION Figure 1-33 depicts the general organization of an SMP. There are multiple processors, each of which contains its own control unit, arithmetic-logic unit, and registers. Each processor has access to a shared main memory and the I/O devices through some form of interconnection mechanism; a shared bus is a common facility. The processors can communicate with each other through memory (messages and status information left in shared address spaces). It may also be possible for processors to exchange signals directly. The memory is often organized so that multiple simultaneous accesses to separate blocks of memory are possible.

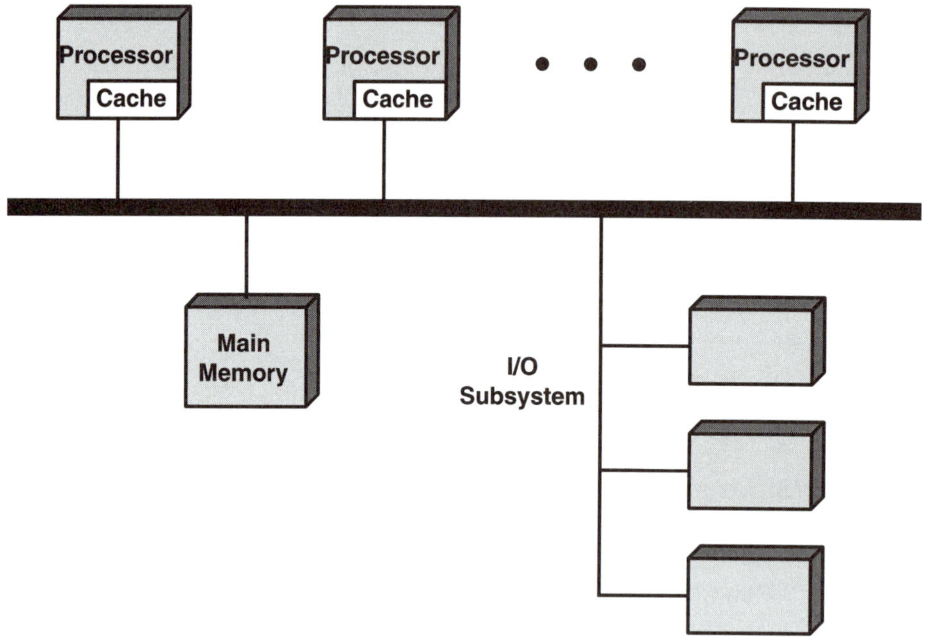

FIGURE 1-33 *Symmetric Multiprocessor Organization*

In modern machines, processors generally have at least one level of cache memory that is private to the processor. This use of cache introduces some new design considerations. Because each local cache contains an image of a portion of main memory, if a word is altered in one cache, it could conceivably invalidate a word in another cache. To prevent this, the other processors must be alerted that an update has taken place. This problem is known as the *cache coherence* problem and is typically addressed in hardware rather than by the operating system.[8]

MULTIPROCESSOR OPERATING SYSTEM DESIGN CONSIDERATIONS An SMP operating system manages processor and other computer resources so that the user may view the system in the same fashion as a multiprogramming uniprocessor system. A user may construct applications that use multiple processes or multiple threads within processes without regard to whether a single processor or multiple processors will be available. Thus a multiprocessor operating system must provide all the functionality of a multiprogramming system plus additional features to accommodate multiple processors. Among the key design issues are the following:

- **Simultaneous concurrent processes or threads:** Kernel routines need to be reentrant to allow several processors to execute the same kernel code simultaneously. With multiple processors executing the same or different parts of the kernel, kernel tables and management structures must be managed properly to avoid deadlock or invalid operations.
- **Scheduling:** Scheduling may be performed by any processor, so conflicts must be avoided. If kernel-level multithreading is used, then the opportunity exists to schedule multiple threads from the same process simultaneously on multiple processors.
- **Synchronization:** With multiple active processes having potential access to shared address spaces or shared I/O resources, care must be taken to provide effective synchronization. Synchronization is a facility that enforces mutual exclusion and event ordering. A common synchronization mechanism used in multiprocessor operating systems is locks.

- **Memory management:** Memory management on a multiprocessor must deal with all of the issues found on uniprocessor machines. In addition, the operating system needs to exploit the available hardware parallelism, such as multiported memories, to achieve the best performance. The paging mechanisms on different processors must be coordinated to enforce consistency when several processors share a page or segment and to decide on page replacement.
- **Reliability and fault tolerance:** The operating system should provide graceful degradation in the face of processor failure. The scheduler and other portions of the operating system must recognize the loss of a processor and restructure management tables accordingly.

Because multiprocessor operating system design issues generally involve extensions to solutions to multiprogramming uniprocessor design problems, we do not treat multiprocessor operating systems separately. Rather, specific multiprocessor issues are addressed in the proper context throughout this book.

UNIPROCESSOR SCHEDULING

In a multiprogramming system, multiple processes are maintained in main memory. Each process alternates between using a processor and waiting for I/O to be performed or for some other event to occur. The processor or processors are kept busy by executing one process while the others wait.

The key to multiprogramming is scheduling. In fact, four types of scheduling are typically involved (Table 1.16). The remaining three types of scheduling, which are types of processor scheduling, are addressed throughout this book.

TABLE 1.16
Types of Scheduling

Long-term scheduling	The decision to add to the pool of processes to be executed
Medium-term scheduling	The decision to add to the number of processes that are partially or fully in main memory
Short-term scheduling	The decision as to which available process will be executed by the processor
I/O scheduling	The decision as to which process's pending I/O request shall be handled by an available I/O device

The section begins with an examination of the three types of processor scheduling, showing the way in which they are related. We see that long-term scheduling and medium-term scheduling are driven primarily by performance concerns related to the degree of multiprogramming. Thus, the remainder of this section concentrates on short-term scheduling and is limited to a consideration of scheduling on a single-processor system. Because the use of multiple processors adds additional complexity, it is best to focus on the uniprocessor case first, so that the differences among scheduling algorithms can be clearly seen.

TYPES OF SCHEDULING

The aim of processor scheduling is to assign processes to be executed by the processor or processors over time, in a way that meets system objectives, such as response time, throughput, and processor efficiency. In many systems, this scheduling activity is broken down into three separate functions: long-, medium-, and short-term scheduling. The names suggest the relative frequency with which these functions are performed.

Figure 1-34 relates the scheduling functions to the process state transition diagram. Long-term scheduling is performed when a new process is created. This is a decision to add a new process to the set of processes that are currently active. Medium-term scheduling is a part of the swapping function. This is a decision to add a process to those that are at least partially in main memory and therefore available for execution. Short-term scheduling is the actual decision of which ready process to execute next. Figure 1-35 reorganizes the state transition diagram to suggest the nesting of scheduling functions.

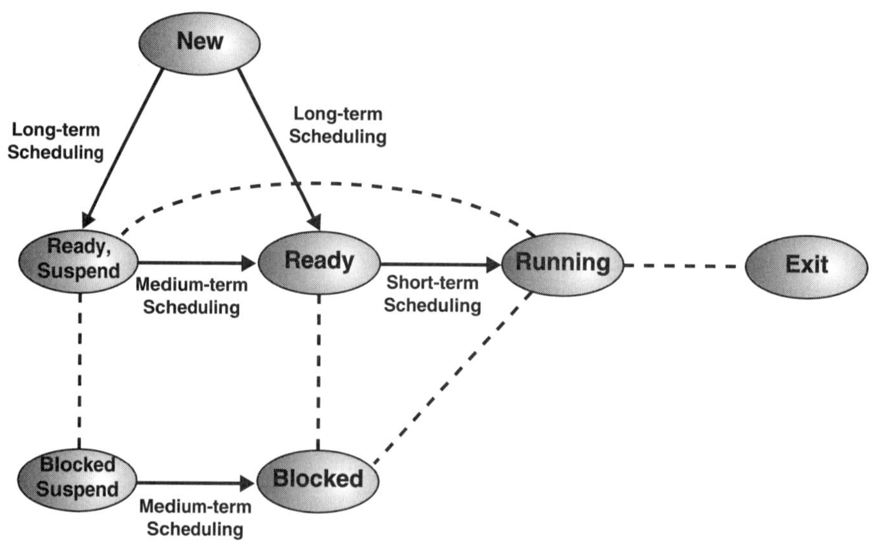

FIGURE 1-34 *Scheduling and Process State Transitions*

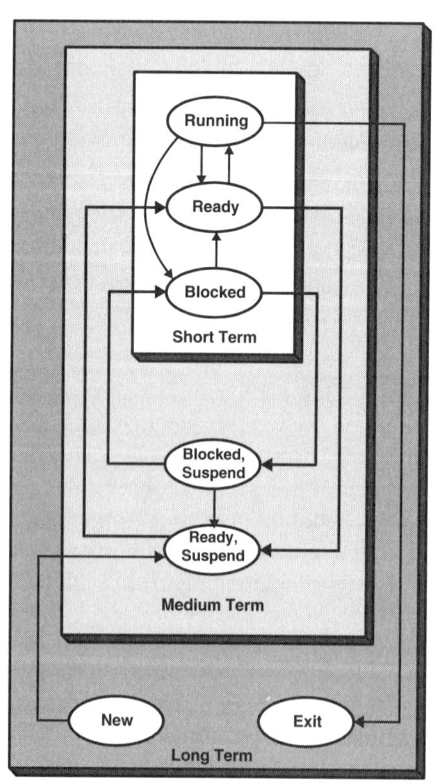

FIGURE 1-35 *Levels of Scheduling*

Scheduling affects the performance of the system because it determines which processes will wait and which will progress. This point of view is presented in Figure 1-36, which shows the queues involved in the state transitions of a process. Fundamentally, scheduling is a matter of managing queues to minimize queuing delay and to optimize performance in a queuing environment.

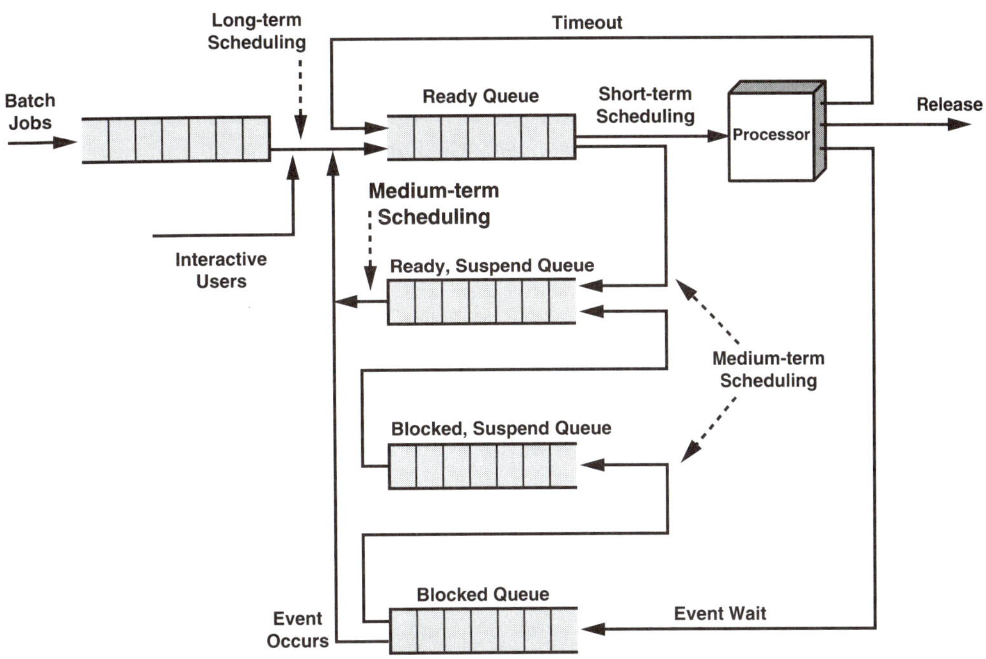

FIGURE 1-36 *Queuing Diagram for Scheduling*

LONG-TERM SCHEDULING The long-term scheduler determines which programs are admitted to the system for processing. Thus, it controls the degree of multiprogramming. Once admitted, a job or user program becomes a process and is added to the queue for the short-term scheduler. In some systems, a newly created process begins in a swapped-out condition, in which case it is added to a queue for the medium-term scheduler.

In a batch system, or for the batch portion of a general-purpose operating system, newly submitted jobs are routed to disk and held in a batch queue. The long-term scheduler creates processes from the queue when it can. There are two decisions involved here. First, the scheduler must decide that the operating system can take on one or more additional processes. Second, the scheduler must decide which job or jobs to accept and turn into processes. Let us briefly consider these two decisions.

The decision as to when to create a new process is generally driven by the desired degree of multiprogramming. The more processes that are created, the smaller is the percentage of time that each process can be executed (i.e., more processes are competing for the same amount of processor time). Thus, the long-term scheduler may limit the degree of multiprogramming to provide satisfactory service to the current set of processes. Each time a job terminates, the scheduler may make the decision to add one or more new jobs. Additionally, if the fraction of time that the processor is idle exceeds a certain threshold, the long-term scheduler may be invoked.

The decision as to which job to admit next can be on a simple first-come-first-served basis, or it can be a tool to manage system performance. The criteria used may include priority, expected execution time, and I/O requirements. For example, if the information is available, the scheduler may attempt to keep a mix of processor-bound and I/O-bound processes.[9] Also, the decision may be made depending on which I/O resources are to be requested, in an attempt to balance I/O usage.

For interactive programs in a time-sharing system, a process request is generated by the act of a user attempting to connect to the system. Time-sharing users are not simply queued up and kept waiting until the system can accept them. Rather, the operating system will accept all authorized comers until the system is saturated, using some predefined measure of saturation. At that point, a connection request is met with a message indicating that the system is full and the user should try again later.

MEDIUM-TERM SCHEDULING Medium-term scheduling is part of the swapping function. Typically, the swapping-in decision is based on the need to manage the degree of multiprogramming. On a system that does not use virtual memory, memory management is also an issue. Thus, the swapping-in decision will consider the memory requirements of the swapped-out processes.

SHORT-TERM SCHEDULING In terms of frequency of execution, the long-term scheduler executes relatively infrequently and makes the coarse-grained decision of whether or not to take on a new process, and which one to take. The medium-term scheduler is executed somewhat more frequently to make a swapping decision. The short-term scheduler, also known as the dispatcher, executes most frequently and makes the fine-grained decision of which process to execute next.

The short-term scheduler is invoked whenever an event occurs that may lead to the suspension of the current process or that may provide an opportunity to preempt a currently running process in favor of another. Examples of such events include the following:

- Clock interrupts
- I/O interrupts
- Operating system calls
- Signals

MULTIPROCESSOR AND REAL-TIME SCHEDULING

This section continues our survey of process scheduling. We begin with an examination of issues raised by the availability of more than one processor. A number of design issues are explored.

Multiprocessor Scheduling

When a computer system contains more than a single processor, several new issues are introduced into the design of the scheduling function. We begin with a brief overview of multiprocessors and then look at the rather different considerations when scheduling is done at the process level and the thread level.

We can classify multiprocessor systems as follows:

- **Loosely coupled multiprocessor, or cluster:** Consists of a collection of relatively autonomous systems, each processor having its own main memory and I/O channels.
- **Functionally specialized processors:** Such as an I/O processor. In this case, there is a master, general-purpose processor; specialized processors are controlled by the master processor and provide services to it.

- **Tightly coupled multiprocessing:** Consists of a set of processors that share a common main memory and are under the integrated control of an operating system.

Our concern in this section is with the last category, and specifically with issues relating to scheduling.

GRANULARITY A good way of characterizing multiprocessors and placing them in context with other architectures is to consider the synchronization granularity, or frequency of synchronization, between processes in a system. We can distinguish five categories of parallelism that differ in the degree of granularity. These are summarized in Table 1.17, which is adapted from (Gehringer 1987) and (Woodbury 1989).

TABLE 1.17
Synchronization Granularity and Processes

Grain Size	Description	Synchronization Interval (Instructions)
Fine	Parallelism inherent in a single instruction stream	<20
Medium	Parallel processing or multitasking within a single application	20–200
Coarse	Multiprocessing of concurrent processes in a multiprogramming environment	200–2000
Very Coarse	Distributed processing across network nodes to form a single computing environment	2,000–1M
Independent	Multiple unrelated processes	(N/A)

DESIGN ISSUES Scheduling on a multiprocessor involves three interrelated issues:

- The assignment of processes to processors
- The use of multiprogramming on individual processors
- The actual dispatching of a process.

In looking at these three issues, it is important to keep in mind that the approach taken will depend, in general, on the degree of granularity of the applications and on the number of processors available.

PROCESS SCHEDULING In most traditional multiprocessor systems, processes are not dedicated to processors. Rather there is a single queue for all processors, or if some sort of priority scheme is used, there are multiple queues based on priority, all feeding in to the common pool of processors. In any case, we can view the system as being a multiserver queuing architecture.

THREAD SCHEDULING As we have seen, with threads, the concept of execution is separated from the rest of the definition of a process. An application can be implemented as a set of threads, which cooperate and execute concurrently in the same address space.

On a uniprocessor, threads can be used as a program structuring aid and to overlap I/O with processing. Because of the minimal penalty in doing a thread switch compared to a process switch, these benefits are realized with little cost. However, the full power of threads becomes evident in a multiprocessor system. In this environment, threads can be used to exploit true parallelism in an application. If the various threads of an application are simultaneously run on separate processors, dramatic gains in performance are possible. However, it can be shown that for applications that require significant interaction among threads (medium-grain parallelism), small differences in thread management and scheduling can have a significant performance impact (Anderson 1989). The area of thread scheduling on multiprocessors is one of active research; the discussion here provides an overview of key issues and approaches.

Among the many proposals for multiprocessor thread scheduling and processor assignment, four general approaches stand out:

- **Load sharing:** Processes are not assigned to a particular processor. A global queue of ready threads is maintained, and each processor, when idle, selects a thread from the queue. The term *load sharing* is used to distinguish this strategy from load-balancing schemes in which work is allocated on a more permanent basis (e.g., see (Feitelson 1990)).[10]
- **Gang scheduling:** A set of related threads is scheduled to run on a set of processors at the same time, on a one-to-one basis.
- **Dedicated processor assignment:** This is the opposite of the load-sharing approach and provides implicit scheduling defined by the assignment of threads to processors. Each program is allocated a number of processors equal to the number of threads in the program, for the duration of the program execution. When the program terminates, the processors return to the general pool for possible allocation to another program.
- **Dynamic scheduling:** The number of threads in a program can be altered during the course of execution.

Load Sharing Load sharing is perhaps the simplest approach and the one that carries over most directly from a uniprocessor environment. It has several advantages:

- The load is distributed evenly across the processors, assuring that no processor is idle while work is available to do.
- No centralized scheduler is required; when a processor is available, the scheduling routine of the operating system is run on that processor to select the next thread.
- The global queue can be organized and accessed using priority-based schemes and schemes that consider execution history or anticipated processing demands,

(Leutenegger 1990) analyzes three different versions of load sharing:

- **First come first served (FCFS):** When a job arrives, each of its threads is placed consecutively at the end of the shared queue. When a processor becomes idle, it picks the next ready thread, which it executes until completion or blocking.
- **Smallest number of threads first:** The shared ready queue is organized as a priority queue, with highest priority given to threads from jobs with the smallest number of unscheduled threads. Jobs of equal priority are ordered according to which job arrives first. As with FCFS, a scheduled thread is run to completion or blocking.
- **Preemptive smallest number of threads first:** Highest priority is given to jobs with the smallest number of incomplete threads. An arriving job with a smaller number of threads than an executing job will preempt threads belonging to the scheduled job.

I/O MANAGEMENT AND DISK SCHEDULING

Perhaps the messiest aspect of operating system design is input/output. Because there is such a wide variety of devices and applications of those devices, it is difficult to develop a general, consistent solution.

We begin this section with a brief discussion of I/O devices and the organization of the I/O functions. These topics, which generally come within the scope of computer architecture, set the stage for an examination of I/O from the point of view of the operating system.

We also examine operating system design issues, including design objectives, and the way in which the I/O function can be structured. One of the basic I/O services provided by the operating system is a buffering function, which improves overall performance.

I/O Devices

As was mentioned, external devices that engage in I/O with computer systems can be roughly grouped into three categories:

- **Human readable:** Suitable for communicating with the computer user. Examples include video display terminals, consisting of display, keyboard, and perhaps other devices such as a mouse; and printers.
- **Machine readable:** Suitable for communicating with electronic equipment. Examples are disk and tape drives, sensors, controllers, and actuators.
- **Communication:** Suitable for communicating with remote devices. Examples are digital line drivers and modems.

There are great differences across classes and even substantial differences within each class. Among the key differences are the following:

- **Data rate:** There may be differences of several orders of magnitude between the data transfer rates. Table 1.18 gives some examples.

TABLE 1.18
Examples of I/O Devices Categorized by Purpose, Partner, and Data Rate (Hennessey 1990)

Device	Purpose	Partner	Data Rate (kilobytes/s)
Keyboard	Input	Human	0.01
Mouse	Input	Human	0.02
Voice input	Input	Human	0.02
Scanner	Input	Human	200
Voice output	Output	Human	0.6
Line printer	Output	Human	1
Laser printer	Output	Human	100
Graphics display	Output	Human	30,000
CPU to frame buffer	Output	Human	200
Network—terminal	Input or output	Machine	0.05
Network—LAN	Input or output	Machine	200
Optical disk	Storage	Machine	500
Magnetic tape	Storage	Machine	2,000
Magnetic disk	Storage	Machine	2,000

- **Application:** The use to which a device is put has an influence on the software and policies in the operating system and supporting utilities. For example, a disk used for files requires the support of file management software. A disk used as a backing store for pages in a virtual memory scheme depends on the use of virtual memory hardware and software. Furthermore, these applications have an impact on disk scheduling algorithms. As another example, a terminal may be used by an ordinary user or a system administrator. These uses imply different privilege levels and perhaps different priorities in the operating system.
- **Complexity of control:** A printer requires a relatively simple control interface. A disk is much more complex. The effect of these differences on the operating system is filtered to some extent by the complexity of the I/O module that controls the device.
- **Unit of transfer:** Data may be transferred as a stream of bytes or characters (e.g., terminal I/O) or in larger blocks (e.g., disk I/O).
- **Data representation:** Different data encoding schemes are used by different devices, including differences in character code and parity conventions.
- **Error conditions:** The nature of errors, the way in which they are reported, their consequences, and the available range of responses differ widely from one device to another.

This diversity makes a uniform and consistent approach to I/O, both from the point of view of the operating system and from the point of view of user processes, difficult to achieve.

Organization of the I/O Function

Three techniques for performing I/O:

- **Programmed I/O:** The processor issues an I/O command, on behalf of a process, to an I/O module; that process then busy-waits for the operation to be complete before proceeding.
- **Interrupt-driven I/O:** The processor issues an I/O command on behalf of a process, continues to execute subsequent instructions, and is interrupted by the I/O module when the latter has completed its work. The subsequent instructions may be in the same process, if it is not necessary for that process to wait for the completion of the I/O. Otherwise, the process is suspended pending the interrupt and other work is performed.
- **Direct memory access (DMA):** A DMA module controls the exchange of data between main memory and an I/O module. The processor sends a request for the transfer of a block of data to the DMA module and is interrupted only after the entire block has been transferred.

Table 1.19 indicates the relationship among these three techniques. In most computer systems, DMA is the dominant form of transfer that must be supported by the operating system.

TABLE 1.19 I/O Techniques

	No Interrupts	Use of Interrupts
I/O-to-memory transfer through processor	Programmed I/O	Interrupt-driven I/O
Direct I/O-to-memory transfer		Direct memory access (DMA)

THE EVOLUTION OF THE I/O FUNCTION As computer systems have evolved, there has been a pattern of increasing complexity and sophistication of individual components. Nowhere is this more evident than in the I/O function. The evolutionary steps can be summarized as follows:

1. The processor directly controls a peripheral device. This is seen in simple microprocessor-controlled devices.
2. A controller or I/O module is added. The processor uses programmed I/O without interrupts. With this step, the processor becomes somewhat divorced from the specific details of external device interfaces.
3. The same configuration as step 2 is used, but now interrupts are employed. The processor need not spend time waiting for an I/O operation to be performed, thus increasing efficiency.
4. The I/O module is given direct control of memory via DMA. It can now move a block of data to or from memory without involving the processor, except at the beginning and end of the transfer.
5. The I/O module is enhanced to become a separate processor, with a specialized instruction set tailored for I/O. The central processing unit (CPU) directs the I/O processor to execute an I/O program in main memory. The I/O processor fetches and executes these instructions without processor intervention. This allows the processor to specify a sequence of I/O activities and to be interrupted only when the entire sequence has been performed.
6. The I/O module has a local memory of its own and is, in fact, a computer in its own right. With this architecture, a large set of I/O devices can be controlled, with minimal processor involvement. A common use for such an architecture has been to control communications with interactive terminals. The I/O processor takes care of most of the tasks involved in controlling the terminals.

As one proceeds along this evolutionary path, more and more of the I/O function is performed without processor involvement. The central processor is increasingly relieved of I/O-related tasks, improving performance. With the last two steps (5–6), a major change occurs with the introduction of the concept of an I/O module capable of executing a program.

A note about terminology: For all of the modules described in steps 4 through 6, the term *direct memory access* (DMA) is appropriate, because all of these types involve direct control of main memory by the I/O module. Also, the I/O module in step 5 is often referred to as an **I/O channel**, and that in step 6 as an **I/O processor**; however, each term is, on occasion, applied to both situations. In the latter part of this section, we will use the term I/O *channel* to refer to both types of I/O modules.

DIRECT MEMORY ACCESS Figure 1-37 indicates, in general terms, the DMA logic. The DMA unit is capable of mimicking the processor and, indeed, of taking over control of the system from the processor. It needs to do this to transfer data to and from memory over the system bus. Typically, the DMA module must use the bus only when the processor does not need it, or it must force the processor to suspend operation temporarily. The latter technique is more common and is referred to as cycle stealing, because the DMA unit in effect steals a bus cycle.

The DMA technique works as follows. When the processor wishes to read or write a block of data, it issues a command to the DMA module by sending to the DMA module the following information:

- Whether a read or write is requested, using the read or write control line between the processor and the DMA module
- The address of the I/O device involved, communicated on the data lines

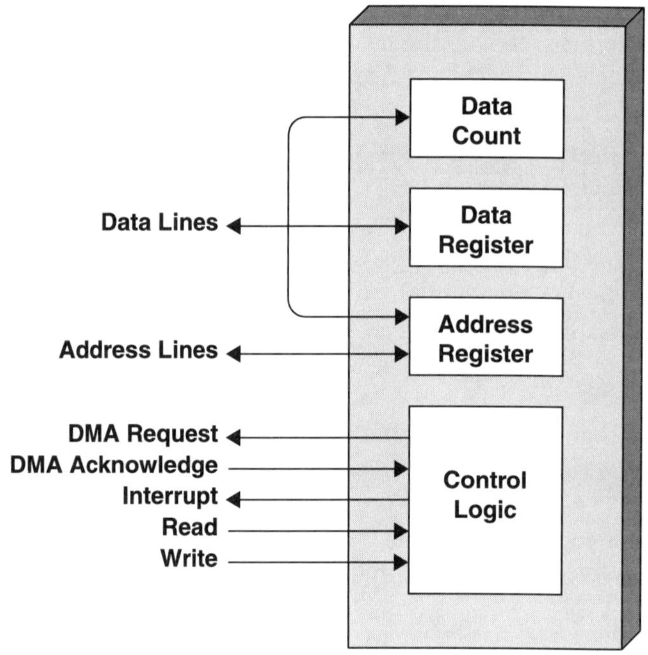

FIGURE 1-37 *Typical DMA Block Diagram*

- The starting location in memory to read from or write to, communicated on the data lines and stored by the DMA module in its address register
- The number of words to be read or written, again communicated via the data lines and stored in the data count register

The processor then continues with other work. It has delegated this I/O operation to the DMA module. The DMA module transfers the entire block of data, one word at a time, directly to or from memory, without going through the processor. When the transfer is complete, the DMA module sends an interrupt signal to the processor. Thus, the processor is involved only at the beginning and end of the transfer.

Figure 1-38 shows where in the instruction cycle the processor may be suspended. In each case, the processor is suspended just before it needs to use the bus. The DMA unit then

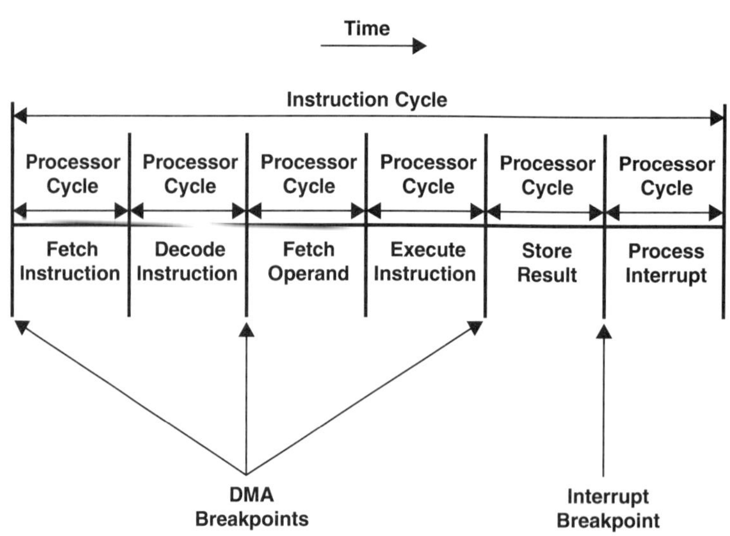

FIGURE 1-38 *DMA and Interrupt Breakpoints During an Instruction Cycle*

transfers one word and returns control to the processor. Note that this is not an interrupt; the processor does not save a context and do something else. Rather, the processor pauses for one bus cycle. The overall effect is to cause the processor to execute more slowly. Nevertheless, for a multiple-word I/O transfer, DMA is far more efficient than interrupt-driven or programmed I/O.

The DMA mechanism can be configured in a variety of ways. Some possibilities are shown in Figure 1-39. In the first example, all modules share the same system bus. The DMA module, acting as a surrogate processor, uses programmed I/O to exchange data between memory and an I/.O module through the DMA module. This configuration, while it may be inexpensive, is clearly inefficient: As with processor-controlled programmed I/O, each transfer of a word consume two bus cycles.

The number of required bus cycles can be cut substantially by integrating the DMA and I/O functions. As Figure 1-39b indicates, this means that there is a path between the DMA module and one or more I/O modules that does not include the system bus. The DMA logic may actually be a part of an I/O module, or it may be a separate module that controls one or more I/O modules. This concept can be taken one step further by connecting I/O modules to the DMA module using an I/O bus (Figure 1-39c). This reduces the number of I/O interfaces in the DMA module to one and provides for an easily expandable configuration. In all of these cases (Figures 1-39b and 1-39c), the system bus that the DMA module shares with the processor and main memory is used by the DMA module only to exchange data with memory and to exchange control signals with the processor. The exchange of data between the DMA and I/O modules takes place off the system bus.

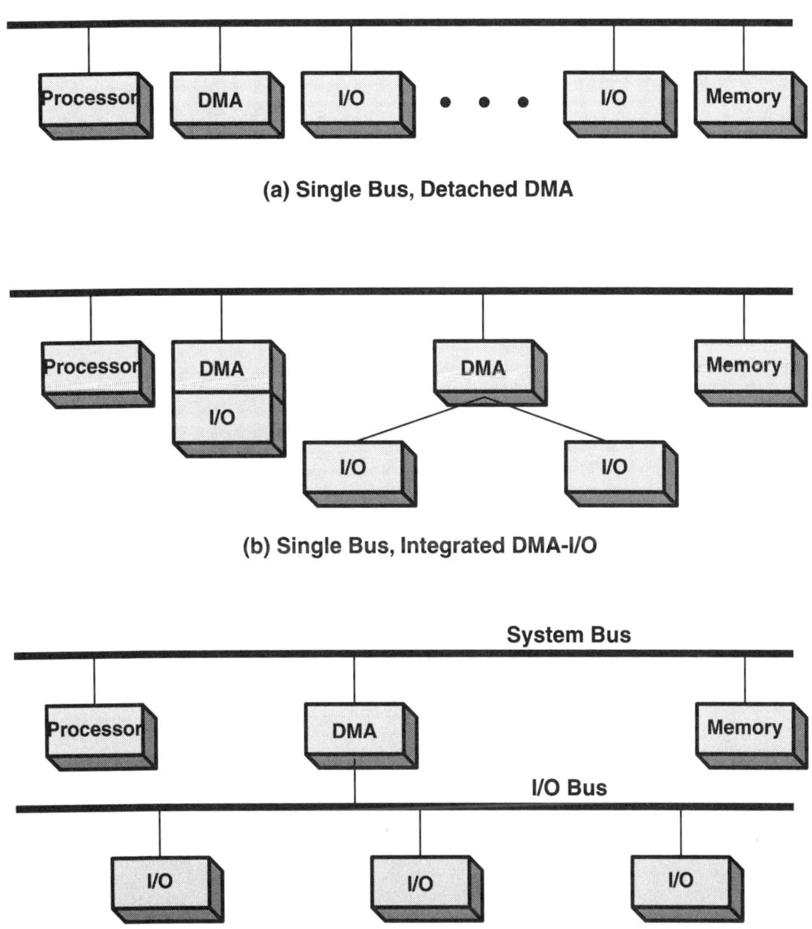

FIGURE 1-39 *Alternative DMA Configurations*

Operating System Design Issues

DESIGN OBJECTIVES Two objectives are paramount in designing the I/O facility: efficiency and generality. **Efficiency** is important because I/O operations often form a bottleneck in a computing system. Looking again at Table 1.17, we see that most I/O devices are extremely slow compared with main memory and the processor. One way to tackle this problem is multiprogramming, which, as we have seen, allows some processes to be waiting on I/O operations while another process is executing. However, even with the vast size of main memory in today's machines, it will still often be the case that I/O is not keeping up with the activities of the processor. Swapping is used to bring in additional ready processes to keep the processor busy, but this in itself is an I/O operation. Thus, a major effort in I/O design has been schemes for improving the efficiency of the I/O. The area that has received the most attention, because of its importance, is disk I/O, and much of this chapter will be devoted to a study of disk I/O efficiency.

The other major objective is **generality**. In the interests of simplicity and freedom from error, it is desirable to handle all devices in a uniform manner. This statement applies both to the way in which processes view I/O devices and the way in which the operating system manages I/O devices and operations. Because of the diversity of device characteristics, it is difficult in practice to achieve true generality. What can be done is to use a hierarchical, modular approach to the design of the I/O function. This approach hides most of the details of device I/O in lower-level routines so that processes and upper levels of the operating system see devices in terms of general functions, such as read, write, open, close, lock, unlock. We turn now to a discussion of this approach.

LOGICAL STRUCTURE OF THE I/O FUNCTION In the discussion of system structure, we emphasized the hierarchical nature of modern operating systems. The hierarchical philosophy is that the functions of the operating system should be separated according to their complexity, their characteristic time scale, and their level of abstraction. Following this approach leads to an organization of the operating system into a series of levels. Each level performs a related subset of the functions required of the operating system. It relies on the next lower level to perform more primitive functions and to conceal the details of those functions. It provides services to the next higher layer. Ideally, the levels should be defined so that changes in one level do not require changes in other levels. Thus we have decomposed one problem into a number of more manageable subproblems.

In general, lower layers deal with a far shorter time scale. Some parts of the operating system must interact directly with the computer hardware, where events can have a time scale as brief as a few billionths of a second. At the other end of the spectrum, parts of the operating system communicate with the user, who issues commands at a much more leisurely pace, perhaps one every few seconds. The use of a set of levels conforms nicely to this environment.

Applying this philosophy specifically to the I/O facility leads to the type of organization suggested by Figure 1-40. The details of the organization will depend on the type of device and the application. The three most important logical structures are presented in the figure. Of course, a particular operating system may not conform exactly to these structures. However, the general principles are valid and most operating systems approach I/O in approximately this way.

Let us consider the simplest case first, that of a local peripheral device that communicates in a simple fashion, such as a stream of bytes or records (Figure 1-40a). The levels involved are as follows:

- **Logical I/O:** The logical I/O module deals with the device as a logical resource and is not concerned with the details of actually controlling the device. The logical I/O module is concerned with managing general I/O functions on behalf of user processes, allowing them to deal with the device in terms of a device identifier and simple commands such as open, close, read, write.

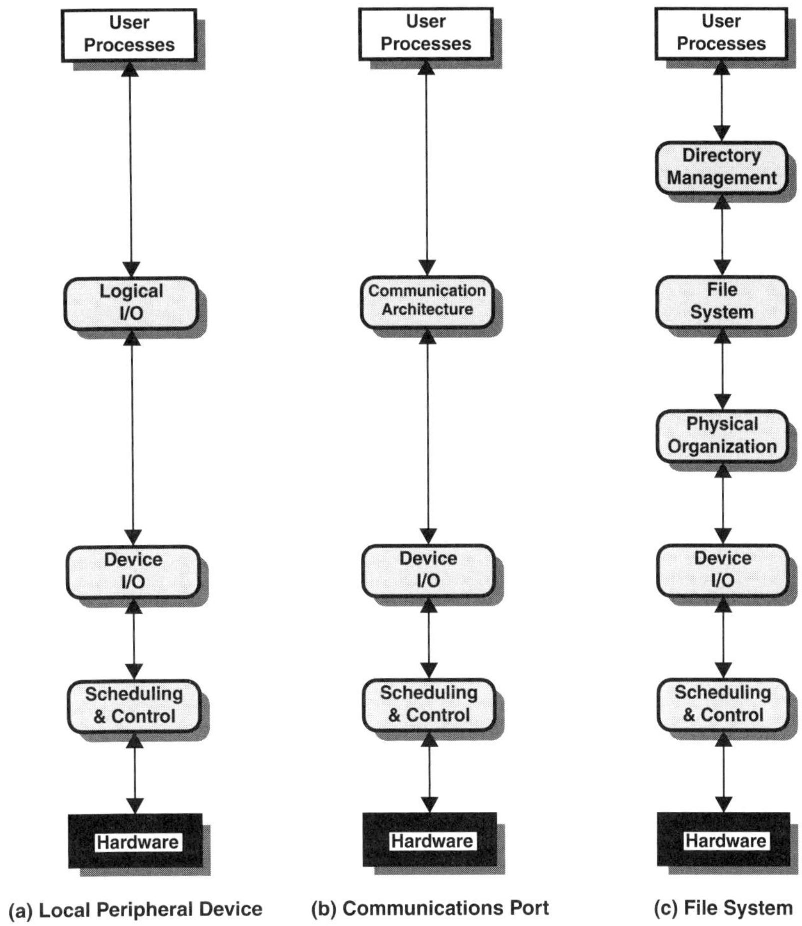

FIGURE 1-40 *A Model of I/O Organization*

- **Device I/O:** The requested operations and data (buffered characters, records, etc.) are converted into appropriate sequences of I/O instructions, channel commands, and controller orders. Buffering techniques may be used to improve utilization.
- **Scheduling and control:** The actual queuing and scheduling of I/O operations occurs at this level, as well as the control of the operations. Thus, interrupts are handled at this level and I/O status is collected and reported. This is the level of software that actually interacts with the I/O module and hence the device hardware.

For a communications device, the I/O structure (Figure 1-40b) looks much the same as that just described. The principal difference is that the logical I/O module is replaced by a communications architecture, which may itself consist of a number of layers. For example, the well-known open-system interconnection (OSI) architecture consists of seven layers.

Figure 1-40c shows a representative structure for managing I/O on a secondary storage device that supports a file system. The three levels not previously discussed are as follows:

- **Directory management:** At this level, symbolic file names are converted to identifiers that either reference the file directly or indirectly through a file descriptor or index table. This level is also concerned with user operations that affect the directory of files, such as add, delete, reorganize.
- **File system:** This level deals with the logical structure of files and with the operations that can be specified by users, such as open, close, read, write. Access rights are also managed at this level.

- **Physical organization:** Just as virtual memory addresses must be converted into physical main-memory addresses, taking into account the segmentation and paging structure, logical references to files and records must be converted to physical secondary storage addresses, taking into account the physical track and sector structure of the file. Allocation of secondary storage space and main storage buffers is generally treated at this level as well.

Because of the importance of the file system, we will spend some time in looking at its various components.

FILE MANAGEMENT

In most applications, the file is the central element. Whatever the objective of the application, it involves the generation and use of information. With the exception of real-time applications and some other specialized applications, the input to the application is by means of a file, and in virtually all applications, output is saved in a file for long-term storage and for later access by the user and by other programs.

Files have a life outside of any individual application that uses them for input and/or output. Users wish to be able to access files, save them, and maintain the integrity of their contents. To aid in these objectives, virtually all computer systems provide separate file management systems. Typically, such a system consists of system utility programs that run as privileged applications. However, at the very least, a file management system needs special services from the operating system; at the most, the entire file management system is considered part of the operating system. Thus, it is appropriate to consider at least the basic elements of file management in this book.

We begin with an overview, followed by a look at alternative organizations of files. Although file organization is generally beyond the scope of the operating system, it is essential to have a general understanding of the alternatives in order to appreciate some of the design tradeoffs involved in file management.

OVERVIEW

FILES Four terms are in common use when discussing files:

- Field
- Record
- File
- Database

A **field** is the basic element of data. An individual field contains a single value, such as an employee's last name, a date, or the value of a sensor reading. It is characterized by its length and data type (e.g., ASCII string, decimal). Depending on the file design, fields may be fixed length or variable length. In the latter case, the field often consists of two or three subfields: the actual value to be stored, the name of the field, and, in some cases, the length of the field. In other cases of variable-length fields, the length of the field is indicated by the use of special demarcation symbols between fields.

A **record** is a collection of related fields that can be treated as a unit by some application programs. For example, an employee record would contain such fields as name, social security number, job classification, date of hire, and so on. Again, depending on design, records may be of fixed length or variable length. A record will be of variable length if some of its fields are of variable length or if the number of fields may vary. In the latter case, each field is usually accompanied by a field name. In either case, the entire record usually includes a length field.

A **file** is a collection of similar records. The file is treated as a single entity by users and applications and may be referenced by name. Files have unique file names and may be created and deleted. Access control restrictions usually apply at the file level. That is, in a shared system, users and programs are granted or denied access to entire files. In some more sophisticated systems, such controls are enforced at the record or even the field level.

A **database** is a collection of related data. The essential aspects of a database are that the relationships that exist among elements of data are explicit and that the database is designed for use by a number of different applications. A database may contain all of the information related to an organization or project, such as a business or a scientific study. The database itself consists of one or more types of files. Usually, there is a separate database management system, although that system may make use of some file management programs.

Users and applications wish to make use of files. Typical operations that must be supported include the following (Livadas 1990):

- **Retrieve_All:** Retrieve all the records of a file. This will be required for an application that must process all of the information in the file at one time. For example, an application that produces a summary of the information in the file would need to retrieve all records. This operation is often equated with the term *sequential processing*, because all of the records are accessed in sequence.
- **Retrieve_One:** This requires the retrieval of just a single record. Interactive, transaction-oriented applications need this operation.
- **Retrieve_Next:** This requires the retrieval of the record that is "next" in some logical sequence to the most recently retrieved record. Some interactive applications, such as filling in forms, may require such an operation. A program that is performing a search may also use this operation.
- **Retrieve_Previous:** Similar to retrieve next, but in this case the record that is "previous" to the currently accessed record is retrieved.
- **Insert_One:** Insert a new record into the file. It may be necessary that the new record fit into a particular position to preserve a sequencing of the file.
- **Delete_One:** Delete an existing record. Certain linkages or other data structures may need to be updated to preserve the sequencing of the file.
- **Update_One:** Retrieve a record, update one or more of its fields, and rewrite the updated record back into the file. Again, it may be necessary to preserve sequencing with this operation. If the length of the record has changed, the update operation is generally more difficult than if length is preserved.
- **Retrieve_Few:** Retrieve a number of records. For example, an application or user may wish to retrieve all records that satisfy a certain set of criteria.

The nature of the operations that are most commonly performed on a file will influence the way the file is organized.

FILE MANAGEMENT SYSTEMS A file management system is that set of system software that provides services to users and applications in the use of files. Typically, the only way that a user or application may access files is through the file management system. This relieves the user or programmer of the necessity of developing special-purpose software for each application and provides the system with a means of controlling its most important asset. (Grosshans 1986) suggests the following objectives for a file management system:

- To meet the data management needs and requirements of the user, which include storage of data and the ability to perform the operations in the preceding list
- To guarantee, to the extent possible, that the data in the file are valid
- To optimize performance, both from the system point of view in terms of overall throughput and from the user's point of view in terms of response time
- To provide I/O support for a variety of storage device types

- To minimize or eliminate the potential for lost or destroyed data
- To provide a standardized set of I/O interface routines
- To provide I/O support for multiple users, in the case of multiple-user systems

With respect to the first point, meeting user requirements, the extent of those requirements depends on the variety of applications and the environment in which the computer system will be used. For an interactive, general-purpose system, the following constitute a minimal set of requirements:

1. Each user should be able to create, delete, and change files.
2. Each user may have controlled access to other users' files.
3. Each user may control what type of accesses are allowed to the user's files.
4. Each user should be able to restructure the user's files in a form appropriate to the problem.
5. Each user should be able to move data between files.
6. Each user should be able to back up and recover the user's files in case of damage.
7. Each user should be able to access the user's files by a symbolic name.

These objectives and requirements should be kept in mind throughout our discussion of file management systems.

File System Architecture One way of getting a feel for the scope of file management is to look at a depiction of a typical software organization, as suggested in Figure 1-41. Of course, different systems will be organized differently, but this organization is reasonably representative. At the lowest level, device drivers communicate directly with peripheral devices or their controllers or channels. A **device driver** is responsible for starting I/O operations on a device and processing the completion of an I/O request. For file operations, the typical devices controlled are disk and tape drives. Device drivers are usually considered to be part of the operating system.

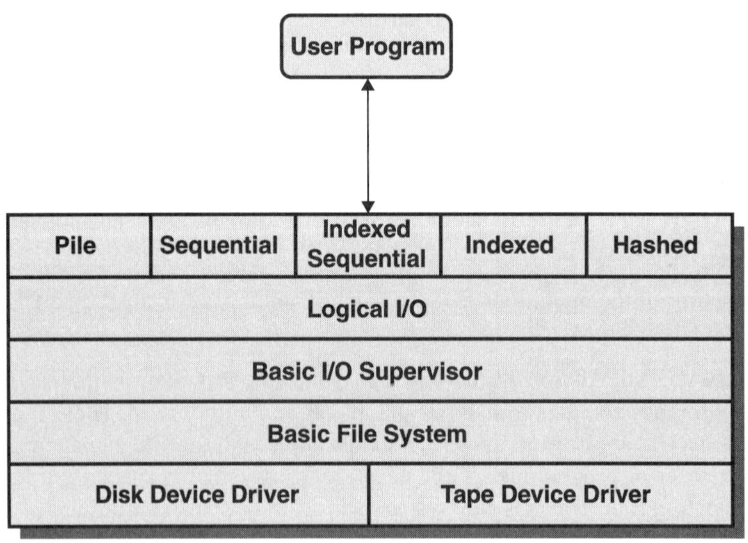

FIGURE 1-41 *File System Software Architecture (Grosshans 1986)*

The next level is referred to as the **basic file system**, or the **physical I/O** level. This is the primary interface with the environment outside of the computer system. It deals with blocks of data that are exchanged with disk or tape systems. Thus, it is concerned with the placement of those blocks on the secondary storage device and on the buffering of those blocks in main memory. It does not understand the content of the data or the structure of the files involved. The basic file system is often considered part of the operating system.

The **basic I/O supervisor** is responsible for all file I/O initiation and termination. At this level, control structures are maintained that deal with device I/O, scheduling, and file status. The basic I/O supervisor is concerned with the selection of the device on which file I/O is to be performed, on the basis of which file has been selected. It is also concerned with scheduling disk and tape accesses to optimize performance. I/O buffers are assigned and secondary memory is allocated at this level. The basic I/O supervisor is part of the operating system.

Logical I/O enables users and applications to access records. Thus, whereas the basic file system deals with blocks of data, the logical I/O module deals with file records. Logical I/O provides a general-purpose record I/O capability and maintains basic data about files.

The level of the file system closest to the user is usually termed the **access method**. It provides a standard interface between applications and the file systems and devices that hold the data. Different access methods reflect different file structures and different ways of accessing and processing the data. Some of the most common access methods are shown in Figure 1-41.

File Management Functions Another way of viewing the functions of a file system is shown in Figure 1-42. Let us follow this diagram from left to right. Users and application programs interact with the file system by means of commands for creating and deleting files and for performing operations on files. Before performing any operation, the file system must identify and locate the selected file. This requires the use of some sort of directory that serves to describe the location of all files, plus their attributes. In addition, most shared systems enforce user access control: Only authorized users are allowed to access particular files in particular ways. The basic operations that a user or application may perform on a file are performed at the record level. The user or application views the file as having some structure that organizes the records, such as a sequential structure (e.g., personnel records are stored alphabetically by last name). Thus, to translate user commands into specific file manipulation commands, the access method appropriate to this file structure must be employed.

Whereas users and applications are concerned with records, I/O is done on a block basis. Thus, the records of a file must be blocked for output and unblocked after input. To support block I/O of files, several functions are needed. The secondary storage must be managed. This involves allocating files to free blocks on secondary storage and managing free storage so as to know what blocks are available for new files and growth in existing files. In addition, individual block I/O requests must be scheduled. Both disk scheduling and file allocation are concerned with optimizing performance. As might be expected, these functions therefore need to be considered together. Furthermore, the optimization will depend on the structure of the files and the access patterns. Accordingly, developing an optimum file management system from the point of view of performance is an exceedingly complicated task.

Figure 1-42 suggests a division between what might be considered the concerns of the file management system as a separate system utility and the concerns of the operating system, with the point of intersection being record processing. This division is arbitrary; various approaches are taken in various systems.

In the remainder of this chapter, we look at some of the design issues suggested in Figure 1-42. We begin with a discussion of file organizations and access methods. Although this topic is beyond the scope of what is usually considered the concerns of the operating system, it is impossible to assess the other file-related design issues without an appreciation of file organization and access.

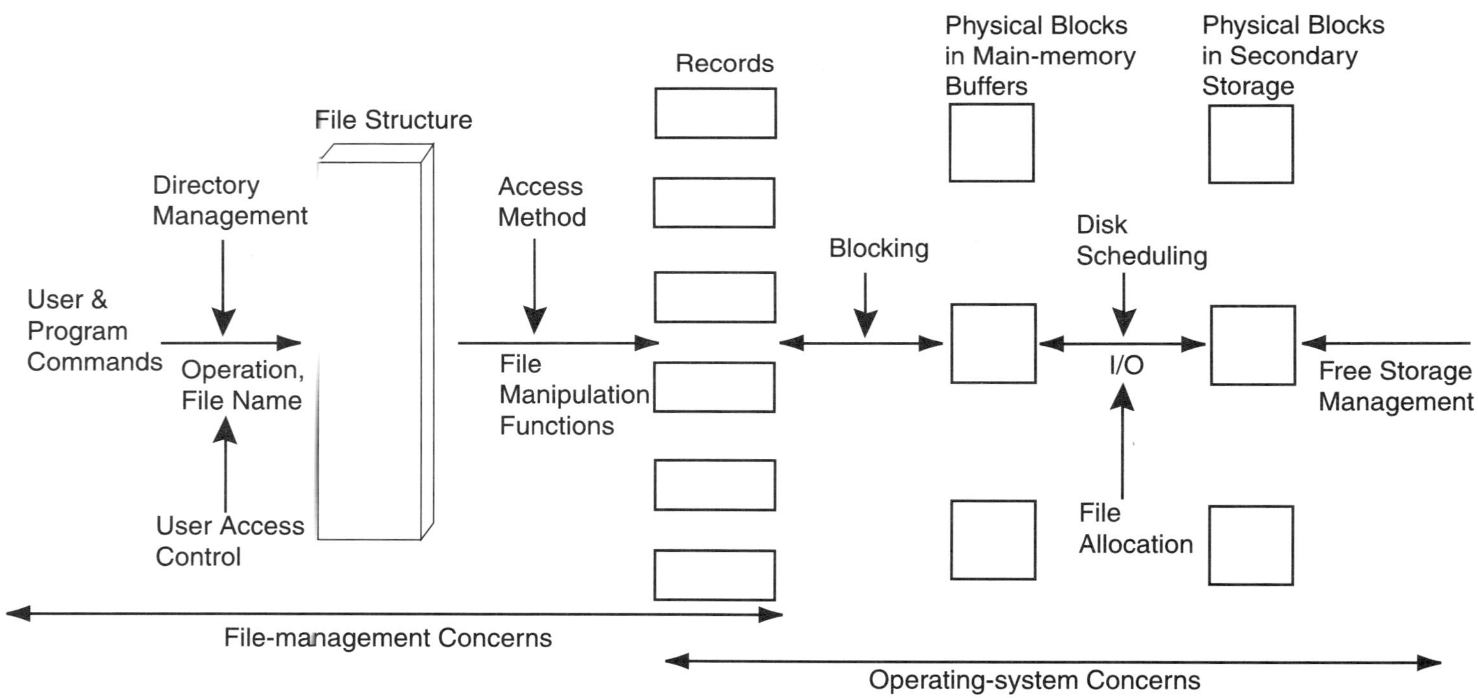

FIGURE 1-42 *Elements of File Management*

File Organization and Access

In this section, we use the term *file organization* to refer to the logical structuring of the records as determined by the way in which they are accessed. The physical organization of the file on secondary storage depends on the blocking strategy and the file allocation strategy.

In choosing a file organization, several criteria are important:

- Rapid access
- Ease of update
- Economy of storage
- Simple maintenance
- Reliability

The relative priority of these criteria will depend on the applications that will use the file. For example, if a file is only to be processed in batch mode, with all of the records accessed every time, then rapid access for retrieval of a single record is of minimal concern. A file stored on CD-ROM will never be updated, and so ease of update is not an issue.

These criteria may conflict. For example, for economy of storage, there should be minimum redundancy in the data. On the other hand, redundancy is the primary means of increasing the speed of access to data. An example of this is the use of indexes.

The number of alternative file organizations that have been implemented or just proposed is unmanageably large, even for a book devoted to file systems. In this brief survey, we will outline five fundamental organizations. Most structures used in actual systems either fall into one of these categories or can be implemented with a combination of these organizations. The five organizations, depicted in Figure 1-43, are as follows:

- The pile
- The sequential file
- The indexed sequential file
- The indexed file
- The direct, or hashed, file

Table 1.20 summarizes relative performance aspects of these five organizations.

THE PILE The least-complicated form of file organization may be termed the pile. Data are collected in the order in which they arrive. Each record consists of one burst of data. The purpose of the pile is simply to accumulate the mass of data and save it. Records may have different fields, or similar fields in different orders. Thus, each field should be self-describing, including a field name as well as a value. The length of each field must be implicitly indicated by delimiters, explicitly included as a subfield, or known as default for that field type.

Because there is no structure to the pile file, record access is by exhaustive search. That is, if we wish to find a record that contains a particular field with a particular value, it is necessary to examine each record in the pile until the desired record is found or the entire file has been searched. If we wish to find all records that contain a particular field or contain that field with a particular value, then the entire file must be searched.

Pile files are encountered when data is collected and stored prior to processing or when data are not easy to organize. This type of file uses space well when the stored data vary in size and structure, is perfectly adequate for exhaustive searches, and is easy to update. However, beyond these limited uses, this type of file is unsuitable for most applications.

THE SEQUENTIAL FILE The most common form of file structure is the sequential file. In this type of file, a fixed format is used for records. All records are of the same length, consisting of the same number of fixed-length fields in a particular order. Because the length and position of each field is known, only the values of fields need to be stored; the field name and length for each field are attributes of the file structure.

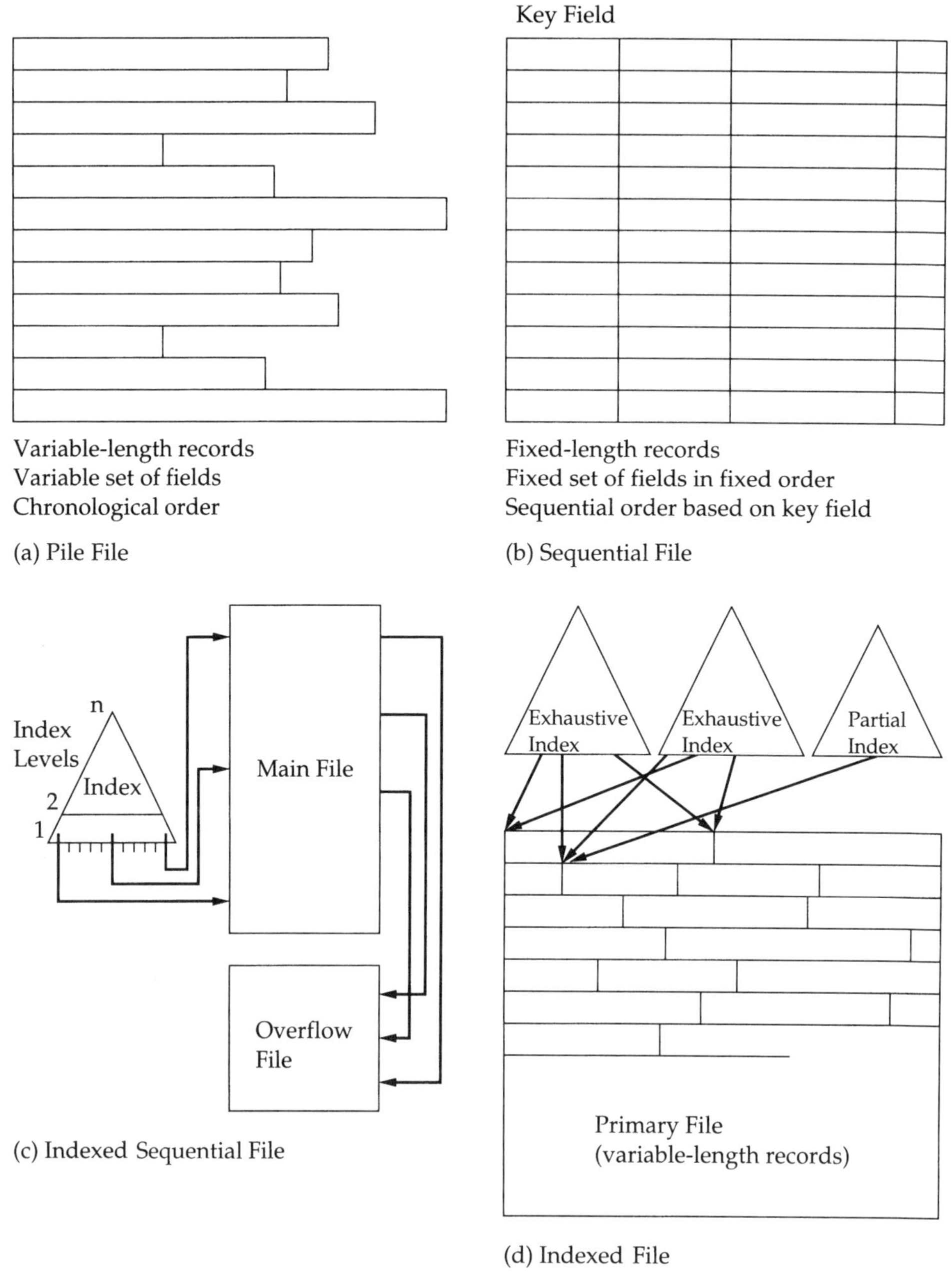

FIGURE 1-43 *Common File Organization*

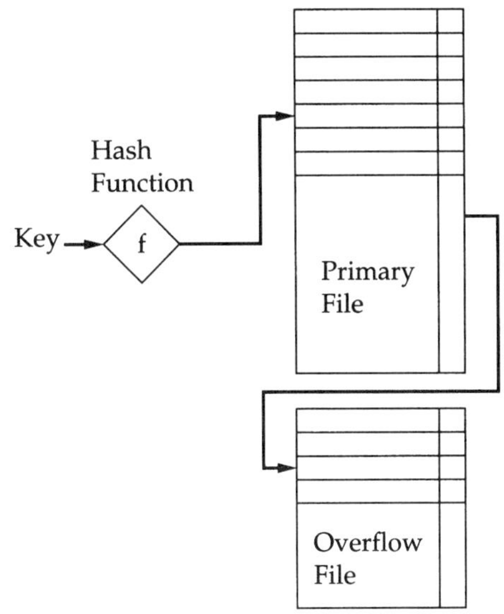

(e) Hash file

FIGURE 1-43 *Common File Organization* (continued)

TABLE 1.20
Grades of Performance for Five Basic File Organizations (Wiederhold 1987)

	Space		**Update**		**Retrieval**		
File Method	Attributes Variable	Fixed	Record Size Equal	Greater	Single record	Subset	Exhaustive
Pile	A	B	A	E	E	D	B
Sequential	F	A	D	F	F	D	A
Indexed sequential	F	B	B	D	B	D	B
Indexed	B	C	C	C	A	B	D
Hashed	F	B	B	F	B	F	E

A	=	Excellent, well suited to this purpose	$\approx O(r)$
B	=	Good	$\approx O(o \times r)$
C	=	Adequate	$\approx O(r \log n)$
D	=	Requires some extra effort	$\approx O(n)$
E	=	Possible with extreme effort	$\approx O(r \times n)$
F	=	Not reasonable for this purpose	$\approx O(n^{>1})$

where

r	=	size of the result
o	=	number of records that overflow
n	=	number of records in file

One particular field, usually the first field in each record, is referred to as the **key field.** The key field uniquely identifies the record; thus key values for different records are always different. Further, the records are stored in key sequence: alphabetical order for a text key, and numerical order for a numerical key.

Sequential files are typically used in batch applications and are generally optimum for such applications if they involve the processing of all the records (e.g., a billing or payroll application). The sequential file organization is the only one that is easily stored on tape as well as disk.

For interactive applications that involve queries and/or updates of individual records, the sequential file provides poor performance. Access requires the sequential search of the file for a key match. If the entire file, or a large portion of the file, can be brought into main memory at one time, more efficient search techniques are possible. Nevertheless, considerable processing and delay are encountered to access a record in a large sequential file. Additions to the file also present problems. Typically, a sequential file is stored in simple sequential ordering of the records within blocks. That is, the physical organization of the file on tape or disk directly matches the logical organization of the file. In this case, the usual procedure is to place new records in a separate pile file, called a log file or transaction file. Periodically, a batch update is performed that merges the log file with the master file to produce a new file in correct key sequence.

An alternative is to organize the sequential file physically as a linked list. One or more records are stored in each physical block. Each block on disk contains a pointer to the next block. The insertion of new records involves pointer manipulation but does not require that the new records occupy a particular physical block position. Thus, some added convenience is obtained at the cost of additional processing and overhead.

THE INDEXED SEQUENTIAL FILE A popular approach to overcoming the disadvantages of the sequential file is the indexed sequential file. The indexed sequential file maintains the key characteristic of the sequential file: Records are organized in sequence based on a key field. Two features are added: an index to the file to support random access, and an overflow file. The index provides a lookup capability to reach quickly the vicinity of a desired record. The overflow file is similar to the log file used with a sequential file, but is integrated so that records in the overflow file are located by following a pointer from their predecessor record.

In the simplest indexed sequential structure, a single level of indexing is used. The index in this case is a simple sequential file. Each record in the index file consists of two fields: a key field, which is the same as the key field in the main file, and a pointer into the main file. To find a specific field, the index is searched to find the highest key value that is equal to or precedes the desired key value. The search continues in the main file at the location indicated by the pointer.

To see the effectiveness of this approach, consider a sequential file with 1 million records. To search for a particular key value will require on average one-half million record accesses. Now suppose that an index containing 1,000 entries is constructed, with the keys in the index more or less evenly distributed over the main file. Now it will take on average 500 accesses to the index file followed by 500 accesses to the main file to find the record. The average search length is reduced from 500,000 to 1,000.

Additions to the file are handled in the following manner: Each record in the main file contains an additional field not visible to the application, which is a pointer to the overflow file. When a new record is to be inserted into the file, it is added to the overflow file. The record in the main file that immediately precedes the new record in logical sequence is updated to contain a pointer to the new record in the overflow file. If the immediately preceding record is itself in the overflow file, then the pointer in that record is updated. As with the sequential file, the indexed sequential file is occasionally merged with the overflow file in batch mode.

The indexed sequential file greatly reduces the time required to access a single record, without sacrificing the sequential nature of the file. To process the entire file sequentially, the records of the main file are processed in sequence until a pointer to the overflow file is found, then accessing continues in the overflow file until a null pointer is encountered, at which time accessing of the main file is resumed where it left off.

To provide even greater efficiency in access, multiple levels of indexing can be used. Thus the lowest level of index file is treated as a sequential file and a higher-level index file is created for that file. Consider again a file with 1 million records. A lower-level index with 10,000 entries is constructed. A higher-level index into the lower level index of 100 entries can then be constructed. The search begins at the higher-level index (average length = 50 accesses) to find an entry point into the lower-level index. This index is then searched (average length = 50) to find an entry point into the main file, which is then searched (average length = 50). Thus the average length of search has been reduced from 500,000 to 1,000 to 150.

THE INDEXED FILE The indexed sequential file retains one limitation of the sequential file: effective processing is limited to that which is based on a single field of the file. When it is necessary to search for a record on the basis of some other attribute than the key field, both forms of sequential file are inadequate. In some applications, this flexibility is desirable.

To achieve this flexibility, a structure is needed that employs multiple indexes, one for each type of field that may be the subject of a search. In the general indexed file, the concept of sequentiality and a single key are abandoned. Records are accessed only through their indexes. The result is that there is now no restriction on the placement of records as long as a pointer in at least one index refers to that record. Furthermore, variable-length records can be employed.

Two types of indexes are used. An exhaustive index contains one entry for every record in the main file. The index itself is organized as a sequential file for ease of searching. A partial index contains entries to records where the field of interest exists. With variable-length records, some records will not contain all fields. When a new record is added to the main file, all of the index files must be updated.

Indexed files are used mostly in applications where timeliness of information is critical and where data are rarely processed exhaustively. Examples are airline reservation systems and inventory control systems.

THE DIRECT OR HASHED FILE The direct, or hashed, file exploits the capability found on disks to access directly any block of a known address. As with sequential and indexed sequential files, a key field is required in each record. However, there is no concept of sequential ordering here.

Direct files are often used where very rapid access is required, where fixed-length records are used, and where records are always accessed one at a time. Examples are directories, pricing tables, schedules, and name lists.

File Directories

CONTENTS Associated with any file management system and collection of files is a file directory. The directory contains information about the files, including attributes, location, and ownership. Much of this information, especially that concerned with storage, is managed by the operating system. The directory is itself a file, owned by the operating system and accessible by various file management routines. Although some of the information in directories is available to users and applications, this is generally provided indirectly by system routines. Thus, users cannot directly access the directory even in read-only mode.

Table 1.21 suggests the information typically stored in the directory for each file in the system. From the user's point of view, the directory provides a mapping between file names, known to users and applications, and the files themselves. Thus, each file entry includes the name of the file. Virtually all systems deal with different types of files and different file organizations, and this information is also provided. An important category of information about each file concerns its storage, including its location and size. In shared systems, it is also important to provide information that is used to control access to the file. Typically, one

TABLE 1.21
Information Elements of a File Directory

	Basic Information
File Name	Name as chosen by creator (user or program). Must be unique within a specific directory.
File Type	For example: text, binary, load module, etc.
File Organization	For systems that support different organizations
	Address Information
Volume	Indicates device on which file is stored
Starting Address	Starting physical address on secondary storage (e.g., cylinder, track, and block number on disk)
Size Used	Current size of the file in bytes, words, or blocks
Size Allocated	The maximum size of the file
	Access Control Information
Owner	User who is assigned control of this file. The owner may be able to grant/deny access to other users and to change these privileges.
Access Information	A simple version of this element would include the user's name and password for each authorized user.
Permitted Actions	Controls reading, writing, executing, transmitting over a network
	Usage Information
Date Created	When file was first placed in directory
Identity of Creator	Usually but not necessarily the current owner
Date Last Read Access	Date of the last time a record was read
Identity of Last Reader	User who did the reading
Date Last Modified	Date of the last update, insertion, or deletion
Identity of Last Modifier	User who did the modifying
Date of Last Backup	Date of the last time the file was backed up on another storage medium
Current Usage	Information about current activity on the file, such as process or processes that have the file open, whether it is locked by a process, and whether the file has been updated in main memory but not yet on disk

user is the owner of the file and may grant certain access privileges to other users. Finally, usage information is needed to manage the current use of the file and to record the history of its usage.

STRUCTURE The way in which the information of Table 1.21 is stored differs widely among various systems. Some of the information may be stored in a header record associated with the file; this reduces the amount of storage required for the directory, making it easier to keep all or much of the directory in main memory to improve speed. Some key elements, of course, must be in the directory; typically, these include the name, address, size, and organization.

The simplest form of structure for a directory is that of a list of entries, one for each file. This structure could be represented by a simple sequential file, with the name of the file serving as the key. In some earlier single-user systems, this technique has been used. However, it is inadequate when multiple users share a system and even for single users with many files.

To understand the requirements for a file structure, it is helpful to consider the types of operations that may be performed on the directory:

- **Search:** When a user or application references a file, the directory must be searched to find the entry corresponding to that file.
- **Create file:** When a new file is created, an entry must be added to the directory.
- **Delete file:** When a file is deleted, an entry must be removed from the directory.
- **List directory:** All or a portion of the directory may be requested. Generally, this request is made by a user and results in a listing of all files owned by that user, plus some of the attributes of each file (e.g., type, access control information, usage information).

The simple list is not suited to supporting these operations. Consider the needs of a single user. The user may have many types of files, including word-processing text files, graphic files, spreadsheets, and so on. The user may like to have these organized by project, by type, or in some other convenient way. If the directory is a simple sequential list, it provides no help in organizing the files and forces the user to be careful not to use the same name for two different types of files. The problem is much worse in a shared system. Unique naming becomes a serious problem. Furthermore, it is difficult to conceal portions of the overall directory from users when there is no inherent structure in the directory.

A start in solving these problems would be to go to a two-level scheme. In this case, there is one directory for each user, and a master directory. The master directory has an entry for each user directory, providing address and access control information. Each user directory is a simple list of the files of that user. This arrangement means that names must be unique only within the collection of files of a single user, and that the file system can easily enforce access restriction on directories. However, it still provides users with no help in structuring collections of files.

A more powerful and flexible approach, and one that is almost universally adopted, is the hierarchical, or tree-structure, approach (Figure 1-44). As before, there is a master directory, which has under it a number of user directories. Each of these user directories, in turn, may have subdirectories and files as entries. This is true at any level: That is, at any level, a directory may consist of entries for subdirectories and/or entries for files.

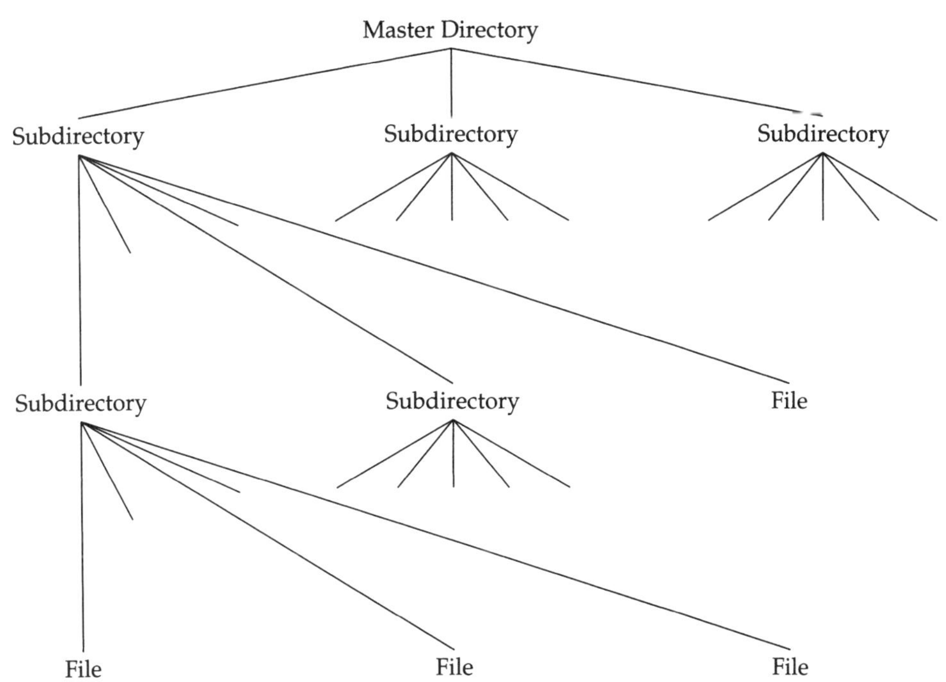

FIGURE 1-44 *Tree-Structured Directory*

It remains to say how each directory and subdirectory is organized. The simplest approach, of course, is to store each directory as a sequential file. When directories may contain a very large number of entries, such an organization may lead to unnecessarily long search times. In that case, a hashed structure is to be preferred.

NAMING Users need to be able to refer to a file by a symbolic name. Clearly, each file in the system must have a unique name in order that file references be unambiguous. On the other hand, it is an unacceptable burden on users to require that they provide unique names, especially in a shared system.

The use of a tree-structured directory minimizes the difficulty in assigning unique names. Any file in the system can be located by following a path from the root or master directory down various branches until the file is reached. The series of directory names, culminating in the file name itself, constitute a **pathname** for the file. As an example, the file in the lower left-hand corner of Figure 1-45 has the pathname /User B/Word/UnitA/ABC. The slash is used to delimit names in the sequence. The name of the master directory is implicit, because all paths start at that directory. Note that it is perfectly acceptable to have

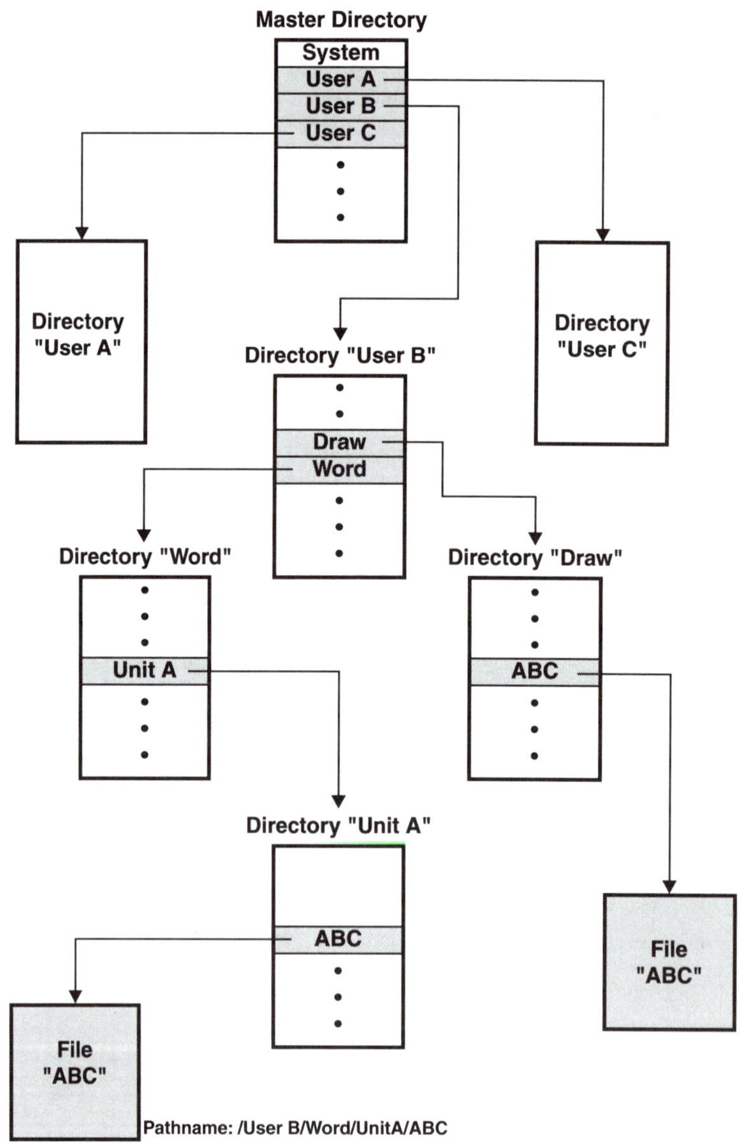

FIGURE 1-45 *Example of Tree-Structured Directory*

several files with the same file name, as long as they have unique pathnames. Thus, there is another file in the system with the file name ABC, but that has the pathname/User B/Draw/ABC.

Although the pathname facilitates the selection of file names, it would be awkward for a user to have to spell out the entire pathname every time a reference is made to a file. Typically, an interactive user or a process has associated with it a current directory, often referred to as the **working directory**. Files are then referenced relative to the working directory. For example, if the working directory for user B is "Word," then the pathname UnitA/ABC is sufficient to identify the file in the lower left-hand corner of Figure 1-45. When an interactive user logs on, or when a process is created, the default for the working directory is the user directory. During execution, the user can navigate up or down in the tree to define a different working directory.

File Sharing

In a multiuser system, there is almost always a requirement for allowing files to be shared among a number of users. Two issues arise: access rights and the management of simultaneous access.

ACCESS RIGHTS The file system should provide a flexible tool for allowing extensive file sharing among users. The file system should provide a number of options so that the way in which a particular file is accessed can be controlled. Typically, users or groups of users are granted certain access rights to a file. A wide range of access rights have been used. The following list is representative of access rights that can be assigned to a particular user for a particular file:

- **None:** The user may not even learn of the existence of the file, much less access it. To enforce this restriction, the user would not be allowed to read the user directory that includes this file.
- **Knowledge:** The user can determine that the file exists and who its owner is. The user is then able to petition the owner for additional access rights.
- **Execution:** The user can load and execute a program, but cannot copy it. Proprietary programs are often made accessible with this restriction.
- **Reading:** The user can read the file for any purpose, including copying and execution. Some systems are able to enforce a distinction between viewing and copying. In the former case, the contents of the file can be displayed to the user, but the user has no means for making a copy.
- **Appending:** The user can read add data to the file, often only at the end, but cannot modify or delete any of the file's contents. This right is useful in collecting data from a number of sources.
- **Updating:** The user can modify, delete, and add to the file's data. This normally includes writing the file initially, rewriting it completely or in part, and removing all or a portion of the data. Some systems distinguish among different degrees of updating.
- **Changing protection:** The user can change the access rights granted to other users. Typically, this right is held only by the owner of the file. In some systems, the owner can extend this right to others. To prevent abuse of this mechanism, the file owner will typically be able to specify which rights can be changed by the holder of this right.
- **Deletion:** The user can delete the file from the file system.

These rights can be considered to constitute a hierarchy, with each right implying those that precede it. Thus, if a particular user is granted the updating right for a particular file, then that user is also granted the following rights: knowledge, execution, reading, and appending.

One user is designated as owner of a given file, usually the person who initially created it. The owner has all of the access rights listed previously, and may grant rights to others. Access can be provided to different classes of users:

- **Specific user:** Individual users who are designated by user ID.
- **User groups:** A set of users who are not individually defined. The system must have some way of keeping track of the membership of user groups.
- **All:** All users who have access to this system. These are public files.

SIMULTANEOUS ACCESS When access is granted to append or update a file to more than one user, the operating system or file management system must enforce discipline. A brute-force approach is to allow a user to lock the entire file when it is to be updated. A finer grain of control is to lock individual records during update. Essentially, this is the readers/writers problem. Issues of mutual exclusion and deadlock must be addressed in designing the shared access capability.

DISTRIBUTED PROCESSING, CLIENT/SERVER, AND CLUSTERS

With the increasing availability of inexpensive yet powerful personal computers and servers, there has been an increasing trend toward distributed data processing (DDP), in which processors, data, and other aspects of a data processing system may be dispersed within an organization. A DDP system involves a partitioning of the computing function and may also involve a distributed organization of databases, device control, and interaction (network) control.

In many organizations, there is heavy reliance on personal computers coupled with servers. Personal computers are used to support a variety of user-friendly applications, such as word processing, spreadsheet, and presentation graphics. The servers house the corporate database plus sophisticated database management and information systems software. Linkages are needed among the personal computers and between each personal computer and the server. Various approaches are in common use, ranging from treating the personal computer as a simple terminal to a high degree of integration between personal computer applications and the server database.

These application trends have been supported by the evolution of distributed capabilities in the operating system and support utilities. A spectrum of capabilities have been explored:

- **Communications architecture:** This is software that supports a network of independent computers. It provides support for distributed applications, such as electronic mail, file transfer, and remote terminal access. However, the computers retain a distinct identity to the user and to the applications, which must communicate with other computers by explicit reference. Each computer has its own separate operating system, and a heterogeneous mix of computers and operating systems is possible, as long as all machines support the same communications architecture.
- **Network operating system:** This is a configuration in which there is a network of application machines, usually single-user workstations and one or more "server" machines. The server machines provide networkwide services or applications, such as file storage and printer management. Each computer has its own private operating system. The network operating system is simply an adjunct to the local operating system that allows application machines to interact with server machines. The user is aware that there are multiple independent computers and must deal with them explicitly. Typically, a common communications architecture is used to support these network applications.
- **Distributed operating system:** A common operating system shared by a network of computers. It looks to its users like an ordinary centralized operating

system but provides the user with transparent access to the resources of a number of machines. A distributed operating system may rely on a communications architecture for basic communications functions; more commonly, a stripped-down set of communications functions is incorporated into the operating system to provide efficiency.

The technology of the communications architecture is well developed and is supported by all vendors. The most widely used communications architecture is the TCP/IP protocol suite. Network operating systems are a much more recent phenomenon, but a number of commercial products exist. The leading edge of research and development for distributed systems is in the area of distributed operating systems.

NOTES

1 Deadlock occurs if two processes need the same two resources to continue and each has ownership of one. Each process will wait indefinitely for the missing resource.

2 A forgiving operating system might, in some cases, allow the user to recover from a fault without terminating the process. For example, if a user requests access to a file and that access is denied, the operating system might simply inform the user that access is denied and allow the process to proceed.

3 Other commonly used names for this data structure are task control block, process descriptor, and task descriptor.

4 This brief discussion slides over some details. In particular, all of the process image for an active process is always in secondary memory. When a portion of the image is loaded into main memory, it is copied rather than moved. Thus the secondary memory retains a copy of all segments and/or pages. However if the main-memory portion of the image is modified, the secondary copy will be out of date until the main memory portion is copied back onto the disk.

5 The term *context switch* is often found in OS literature and textbooks. Unfortunately, although most of the literature uses this term to mean what is here called a process switch, other sources use it to mean a mode switch or even a thread switch.

6 Alas, even this degree of consistency cannot be maintained. In OS/390, the concepts of address space and task, respectively, correspond roughly to the concepts of process and thread that we describe in this section. Also, the term *lightweight process* is used as (1) equivalent to the term *thread*, (2) a particular type of thread known as a kernel-level thread, or (3) in the case of Solaris, an entity that maps user-level threads to kernel-level threads.

7 The acronyms ULT and KLT are unique to this book and introduced for conciseness.

8 A description of hardware-based cache coherency schemes is provided in (Stallings 1996).

9 A process is regarded as processor bound if it mainly performs computational work and occasionally uses I/O devices. A process is regarded as I/O bound if it spends more time using I/O devices than using the processor.

10 Some of the literature on this topic refers to this approach as *self-scheduling*, since each processor schedules itself without regard to other processors. However, this term is also used in the literature to refer to programs written in a language that allows the programmer to specify the scheduling (e.g., see (Foster 1991).

SECTION 2

PC OPERATING SYSTEMS

UNDERSTANDING WINDOWS CONCEPTS AND TERMINOLOGY

Except for niche environments, words like UNIX and OS/2 are quickly fading under the all-consuming evolution of Microsoft Windows 95/98 and Windows NT. In today's development environment, it is impossible to avoid coding for, or interacting with, some form of Microsoft Windows. The truth of this statement is why you are reading this!

This is designed to help you master Windows in all its forms, from the historic 16-bit Windows 2.x and 3.x underpinnings to the user-friendly Windows 95 and its tweaked 98 counterpart to the "Big Brother" of all Microsoft OSs—Windows NT.

Whether you are an experienced Windows 98 developer already or you want to upgrade your programming skills, you'll find accurate and thorough explanations of all Windows concepts, terms, and programming fundamentals right here at your fingertips.

Reasons for Developing Windows Applications

Imagine a future of information interchange that is language-independent, hardware- and software-indifferent, and file-format-transparent. Imagine a future where universal knowledge is virtually at your fingertips; a future free of cryptic protocols, translation algorithms, and inaccessible domains. The operating system of the future will be able to:

- Access information from any source
- Communicate with others
- Easily store, retrieve, and browse information
- Integrate various kinds of information
- Automate everyday business procedures

This almost unbelievable scenario is the goal of the visionary software engineers at Microsoft. Windows 98 already includes many of these features in its document-centric approach, and the next release of Windows NT will include even more. We are on the evolutionary migration path toward tapping vast storehouses of universal knowledge.

OBJECTS ARE EVERYTHING The goals for "information at your fingertips" include the creation, use, organization, and finding of information, regardless of what or where it is. This requires a consistent object model representation for application or system information. This scalable, easy-to-use object model gives the user a personal work space that can be customized, controlled, and extremely flexible.

Objects provide a consistent look to all of the controls for the visual interface, regardless of the data source: CD, camcorder, VCR, CD-ROM, or DVD. The object-model representation of information will take into consideration what kind or class of data is being represented. It will also consider where the information is found (the context), independent of the implementation (or provider). For example, a faxed message has certain common characteristics, regardless of whether the fax was simply received over the phone or transferred from an internal message center. However, the object-model would differentiate unique features, or the quality of the service. Design emphasis will shift totally to that of an object-based philosophy, where there will be one model for all interactions, regardless of type (users, processes, documents, or devices).

To fully understand and appreciate Windows, you must start with each product's goals and target audiences. From the user's viewpoint, Windows 98, with its new user interface, is the most updated version of Windows yet! Windows was designed to be a document-centric environment. A document-centric environment means that programs open the applications (type the name of a word processor program and that program will start the word processor automatically), not the more common way of opening Microsoft Word and searching for the file to edit.

Under Windows, the emphasis is on creating, editing, manipulating, storing, and retrieving data. The Windows NT operating system was designed as a 32-bit, high-end, secure computing platform. Windows NT is targeted for the developer, power end user, corporate MIS manager, multihardware platform, and network server implementor.

Current Windows OSs are 32-bit preemptive multitasking OSs that combine the ease of use and proven productivity of the older 16-bit nonpreemptive version of Windows (3.1) with the power and advanced capabilities of a new high-end operating system. Windows also unlocks the potential of a wide range of advanced PC hardware as it runs on Intel-based 80x86 microprocessors and RISC architectures, and it supports symmetric multiprocessing (MIPS). Thus, Windows extends your investment in hardware but not at the expense of previous investments in software. Both Windows run all carefully developed 16-bit applications written for MS-DOS and Windows 3.1. Carefully developed programs are those that follow Microsoft's rules for program development.

Upward compatibility makes Windows a safe platform for future application development. Windows 98 offers the advantages of Plug-and-Play, which frees the user from having to configure applicable hardware items such as modems, printers, pointers, etc. The Windows NT hardware interface enables it to take advantage of all current I/O technologies, from CD audio to real-time video, and to evolve with future developments. The real success for all of the generations of Microsoft Windows can be summed up in one sentence: "It makes people more productive than ever before."

Key Elements of Windows

Many users are so profoundly happy with their Windows 3.x version, that they can't understand the hoopla about Windows 98 or Windows NT. As good as Windows 3.x was, there was still a lot of room for improvement. The following discussion explains the features that make Windows the platform for development well into the next century.

BEGINNINGS: WINDOWS The Windows NT development group began laying their foundations back in the late 1980s and the Windows 95 development group began in the early 1990s. The Windows NT development team was headed by Dave Cutler and included expert software engineers with experience in designing Windows, UNIX, VMS, and OS/2. The first successful boot of Windows NT took place in late 1989 on an Intel i860. In early 1990, Microsoft made the decision to base the Windows operating systems on a Windows-based 32-bit application program interface (API). Microsoft then focused its design around the Intel and RISC architectures.

WINDOWS AS OPERATING SYSTEMS Compared to the conventional 16-bit MS-DOS operating system with Windows 3.1, the Windows 98 and NT operating systems offer considerable advantages to both users and programmers. Individually, the three primary capabilities (graphics-oriented user interface, multitasking, and hardware independence) are not new. What is innovative is attempting to combine all three of them into a single microcomputer operating system! Windows NT still retains the "look" of earlier versions of Windows, such as Windows 3.x. Windows 98, however, presents an entirely new user interface.

Common User Interface The most obvious capability provided by Windows is the standardized graphics-oriented user interface. This consistent user interface uses pictures, or icons, to represent drives, files, subdirectories, and many of the operating system commands and actions. Most Windows applications make use of both the keyboard and mouse interfaces. Although most functions of Windows applications can be controlled through the keyboard, using the mouse is often easier for many tasks. With a common interface, the user will no longer have to spend long hours learning to use a new application program as all Windows applications have an intuitive feel. This consistent user interface is achieved by using subroutines built directly into Windows to construct menus and dialog boxes. For example, all menus have the same keyboard and mouse interface because Windows, not the application itself, handles the job.

Preemptive Multitasking A multitasking operating system allows the user to have several applications, or several instances of the same application, running concurrently. At any time, the user can move the windows on the screen, change their size, switch between applications, and exchange information among Windows. One of the main differences between Windows 3.1 (Win32s) and Windows (Win32) is true preemptive multitasking. Though the visual interface between all Windows versions may appear similar, what is going on in the background is completely different.

With the 16-bit version of Windows 3.1, you could have several applications loaded, but only one of them could actually use the processor at any given time. The distinction between a task that was processing and one that was merely running was important. Under Windows, the processor automatically switches between applications and does not have to wait for the currently executing program to release control of the processor. This is true preemptive multitasking.

Windows also provides a third state called *active*. An active application is the one receiving the user's attention or focus. Just as only one application can be processing at any given instant, so too can only one application be active at a time. However, there can be any number of concurrently running tasks. Partitioning up the microprocessor's time is the responsibility of Windows. It controls the sharing of the microprocessor by using queued input and messages.

Before the advent of true multitasking operating systems, application programs had exclusive control of all the computer's resources, including the input and output devices, memory, video display, and even the CPU itself. Under Windows, however, all of these valuable resources must be shared. For example, a standard C/C++ program no longer has access to all the memory not used by the system or the program itself.

Greatly Improved Memory Management Next to the microprocessor itself, memory is the second most important shared resource under Windows. With more than one application running at the same time, the applications must cooperate to share memory in order not to exhaust the resource. Additionally, as new programs are started up and old ones are terminated, memory can become fragmented. Windows is capable of consolidating free memory space by moving blocks of code and data in memory. Windows permits applications to "overcommit" memory. That is, an application can contain more code than will actually fit into memory at one time. Windows can discard code from memory and later reload the code from the program's executable (.exe) file.

In addition, Windows allows the user to have several instances, or copies, of the same program running concurrently. To conserve space, Windows shares the same code. Programs running under Windows can even share routines located in other .exe files. The files that contain these shared routines are called *dynamic link libraries (DLLs)*. Windows includes the mechanism to link the program with the routines in the DLLs at run time.

Queue-Based Input Under Windows, an application does not make explicit calls to read from the keyboard or mouse input device. Instead, keyboard and mouse input are treated as a shared resource under Windows. No longer can a C/C++ program read directly from the keyboard by means of a **getchar()** function call. Windows itself receives all input from the keyboard, mouse, and timer in the *system queue*. It is the queue's responsibility to redirect the input to the appropriate application by copying it from the system queue into the application queue. When the application is ready to process any input, it reads from its queue and dispatches a message to the appropriate window. This input is provided in a uniform format called an *input message*. All input messages specify the system time, the state of the keyboard, the scan code of any depressed key, the position of the mouse, which mouse button has been pressed (if any), and information specifying which device generated the message.

The good news is that all keyboard, mouse, and timer messages have identical formats and are all processed in the same manner. Additionally, with each message, Windows provides a device-independent virtual key code that identifies the key (it doesn't matter which type of keyboard is used), the device-dependent scan code generated by the keyboard, and the status of other keys on the keyboard, such as NUM LOCK, ALT, SHIFT, and CTRL. Because the keyboard and mouse are a shared resource, one keyboard and one mouse must supply all the input for each program running under Windows. With the keyboard, all input messages go directly to the currently active window. However, mouse messages are handled differently; they are sent to the window that is immediately beneath the mouse cursor.

Windows allows a program to set a timer so that one of its windows receives a message at periodic intervals. Timer messages are very similar to keyboard and mouse messages, in that they go directly into the program's message queue. There are also other messages that get into a program's message queue as a result of the program calling certain Windows functions. These functions will be discussed individually as they occur in example programs.

Message-Based Communication Windows uses what is called a *message system* to disseminate information in a multitasking environment. From the application's viewpoint, a message can be seen as a notification that some event of interest has occurred, which may or may not require a specific action. These events may be initiated by the user, such as clicking or moving the mouse, changing the size of a window, or making a menu selection. The signaled event, however, could also be generated by the application. For example, Microsoft Excel could have finished a recalculation, resulting in a need to update a displayed bar chart. In this case, Excel would send itself an "update window" message. It is also possible for Windows to generate messages, as in the case of a "close session" message. In this example, Windows must inform each application of the intent to shut down.

One last major message source could be an instrument monitoring program, such as one indicating that a critical nuclear process had reached the specified pressure. Regardless of the source of the message, your program must take the appropriate action. There are two major points to keep in mind when thinking about the role of messages in Windows.

First, it is through the message system that Windows achieves its multitasking capabilities. The message system makes it possible for Windows to share the processor among different applications. Each time Windows sends a message to the application program, it also grants processor time.

Secondly, the role of messages under Windows is to enable an application to respond to events in the environment, whether these events are generated by the application itself, by other concurrently running applications, by the user, or by Windows. Each time an event occurs, Windows makes a note of it and distributes an appropriate message to the interested applications. Thus, at the simplest level, the most important task for all versions of Windows is to process messages!

Hardware Independence Historically, hardware devices change at a much faster rate than do operating systems. Consider, for example, the number of new printers introduced each year. Another advantage provided by Windows is hardware device independence. This section will concentrate on a discussion on how device independence is accomplished.

Windows frees the programmer from having to account for every possible variety of monitor, printer, input device, and CPU available! Currently, a non-Windows application must be written to include drivers for every possible device that it uses. This has always been one of the major inefficiencies in software development. For example, to make an application capable of printing on any printer, the developer must furnish a different driver for each printer type that may be encountered. This requires many software companies to write essentially the same device driver over and over. For instance, essentially the same Hewlett-Packard LaserJet 5 driver would be needed for WordPerfect, Microsoft Word, AutoCad, and so on. Under DOS, each software company would have to develop its own driver.

All Windows versions allow each device driver—for a video display, printer, keyboard, or mouse—to be written only once. Instead of each software company writing its own complete set, the hardware company writes one driver for the Windows environment. Microsoft includes many drivers with Windows, and others are available from the hardware or software manufacturer. One of the enhancements available with Windows is external support for font cartridges. This capability has been incorporated into the Hewlett-Packard Laserjet driver, for example. When Windows is installed, it includes one driver for each device in the current system. Whenever a command to print or draw is sent from an application, Windows feeds the output through the appropriate driver. Incorporating the necessary drivers directly into the system eliminates a great deal of redundant programming effort.

Because applications interact directly with Windows rather than with any specific device driver, from the programmer's perspective, application development has become easier. When a command is sent from the application to draw a filled rectangle, Windows will automatically carry out the task. By the same token, each device driver works with every Windows application. Developers save time, and users no longer have to worry whether each new application will support their favorite generic-brand digitizer pad. Windows achieves this device independence by specifying the capabilities the hardware must have in conjunction with the software development and/or device-driver kits.

Every routine, regardless of its complexity, is capable of breaking itself down into a minimal set of operations required for a device. For example, not every plotter is capable of drawing an ellipse. As an application developer, however, you can still use the kit routines to draw an ellipse, even if the plotter has no specific ellipse capabilities. Because every plotter connected to Windows must be minimally capable of drawing a line, Windows can break the ellipse routine down into a series of small lines.

In terms of input, Windows is also able to specify a set of minimum capabilities to ensure that your application will receive only valid, predefined input. Windows has predefined a set of legal keystrokes. In other words, Windows predefines all the keystrokes that a Windows application can possibly receive. The valid keystroke set is very similar to that produced by the keyboard. Should a manufacturer produce a keyboard containing keys that do not exist in the Windows list of acceptable keys, the manufacturer would also have to supply additional software that would translate these "illegal" keystrokes into Windows legal keystrokes. This predefined input covers all input devices, including the mouse. Therefore, even if someone should develop a six-button mouse, you won't have to worry about compatibility issues. The manufacturer would again have to supply the software necessary to convert all mouse input to Windows predefined possibilities of mouse-button clicks.

Plug-and-Play Windows 98 supports a feature called *Plug-and-Play*. Plug-and-Play will allow hardware devices designed for Windows 98 to be inserted into computers with no additional hardware or software adjustments. Imagine plugging in a serial port, parallel port, sound card, or modem and doing nothing else!

Reusable Dynamic Link Libraries Just about all of Microsoft Windows' capabilities come from a set of DLLs that enhance the base operating system and provide a powerful and flexible graphics user interface (GUI). Dynamic link libraries contain predefined functions that are linked with an application program when it is loaded (dynamically) instead of when the .exe file is generated (statically). Windows did not originate the idea of linking libraries to application code, however. The C/C++ language depends heavily on libraries to implement standard functions for different systems. For example, the linker copies C/C++ run-time library functions, such as **getchar()** and **printf()**, into a program's .exe file.

This collection of routines saves a programmer from having to recreate a new procedure for a common operation, such as reading in a character or formatting output. Programmers can build their own libraries to include additional capabilities, such as changing a font and justifying text. The new function can then be made available as a general tool, eliminating redundant design. As mentioned earlier, Windows libraries are dynamically linked. With DLLs, the linker does not copy the library functions into the program's .exe file. Instead, while the program is executing, it makes calls to the functions in the library. An immediate advantage to this technique is memory conservation. No matter how many applications are running, there is only one copy of the library in the computer's RAM memory at a time.

Microsoft's new library format for Windows DLLs is more versatile. Though they have retained the same format as any other DOS .exe file (although they cannot themselves be executed), they can hold anything programs hold. In addition to functions, DLLs can also encode data and even incorporate graphics resources, such as cursor shapes and bitmaps. Windows DLLs expand the range of shared resources and save programmers even more time. Technically, when an application makes a call to a Windows function, the compiler must generate machine code for a call to the function that is located in one of the Windows DLLs. This presents a problem, because until the program is actually running under Windows, the address of the Windows function is unknown.

The solution to this problem is called *delayed binding* or *dynamic linking*. New linkers allow a program to have calls to functions that cannot be fully resolved at link time. Only when the program is loaded into memory to be run are the far function calls resolved. Windows allows your compiler to take advantage of "import libraries" that are used to properly prepare a Windows program for dynamic linking. These import libraries contain a record for each Windows function that your application can call. This record defines the Windows module that contains this function and, in many cases, an ordinal value (a numeric value) that corresponds to the function in the module.

For example, a Windows application could make a call to the Windows **PostMessage()** function. When you link the program, the linker finds the **PostMessage()** function listed in the library. The linker obtains the ordinal number for the function and embeds this information in the program's .exe file. When the program is run, Windows then links the call the program makes with the actual **PostMessage()** function.

WIN16 VERSUS WIN32 Technically speaking, Windows 3.x is a sophisticated application that requires MS-DOS. It is not, although it may appear to be, a full-fledged operating system. Windows 3.x is optimized for x86 machines and uses only a small amount of system resources. For example, Windows 3.x operates very well with just 4 MB of RAM memory. By its very nature, Windows 3.x is a nonpreemptive operating environment that is very DOS-dependent. Windows operating systems are *not* based on 16-bit MS-DOS, although several DOS components have been "discovered" in Windows 98.

Both Windows 98 and NT are 32-bit operating systems. Windows 98 works well with 6–8 MB of RAM memory and Windows NT works best with 16 MB of RAM memory. Windows NT also operates on multiple hardware platforms with multiple processors. For example, you may have a server running Windows NT that uses four RISC microprocessors! Both Windows run 16-bit and 32-bit applications. This feature allows upward compatibility with older MS-DOS and Windows 3.x applications. The following discussion highlights several new components of the Windows operating systems.

Platform Independence One of Microsoft's major goals for Windows NT was system portability. They have succeeded. Windows NT applications are portable across several of the most popular architectures. *Hardware portability* enables code to be moved from one microprocessor to another with as little rewriting as possible. This portability allows developers and end users alike to benefit from being able to have the same operating system run on different systems. As a result, with Windows NT, a salesperson in the field can use a Windows interface on a pen-based system that matches the ones on a portable computer, on the networked microcomputer at the office, and on the minicomputer in the development lab.

For the end user, there is only one set of commands to learn. For the developer, there is only one product to design, both are happy. Financially, there is also only one initial outlay for a cross-system interface. Portability is a matter of degree. The real question is not whether software will port, but how difficult it is to port. Windows NT excels in portability. First, Windows NT is not written in a hardware-restrictive assembly language but in portable C, a programming language available on all target architectures.

Second, Windows NT minimizes the amount of code that interacts directly with the hardware. Third, because it is impossible to avoid hardware-dependent code, these routines have been localized. By not spreading hardware-dependent algorithms throughout the entire operating system, Windows NT makes porting easy. Each target environment need replace only those code sections specific to their architecture. Specifically, Windows NT encapsulates hardware-dependent code inside a DLL known as the *hardware abstraction layer* (HAL). The HAL intercepts hardware interaction, such as I/O interrupts and memory access, with a layer of software. The HAL takes care of the communication between the standard Windows NT operation and the hardware-dependent implementation. This allows the core of Windows NT to remain unchanged from architecture to architecture.

All Platform Compatibility with Win32s With the tremendous cost of software development, designing one application that runs on multiple software platforms offers money and time savings advantages. It is extremely easy to write one Windows application that can be compiled to run under Windows 3.x, Windows 98, or Windows NT. This software portability does not exist between DOS, Windows, OS/2, and the UNIX operating systems. The success of this software portability between Windows 3.x and Windows 98 or NT lies in the Win32s and Win32 APIs. Table 2.1 lists the Win32s enhancements to Windows 3.1.

TABLE 2.1
Improvements of Win32s over Win16

Feature	Description
32-bit addressing	Win32 processes access a flat, 32-bit address space instead of the segmented address space of Win16.
32-bit heap	Win32 heap allocation routines, such as HeapAlloc() and HeapFree(), are supported.
Exception handling	The Win32s API also provides this Win32 capability.
Shared memory	Win32s provides some of the interprocess memory sharing support of Win32.
Virtual memory	Win32s allows control over a program's address space. For example, some Win32 virtual memory functions and features are provided in Win32s.
File I/O	Win32s provides its own file I/O functions, replacing the MS-DOS functions used by Win16 programs but incompatible with Win32 applications.
Universal thunks	Win32s allows a Win32 application to call Win16 DLLs.

Specifically, Windows NT takes full advantage of all Win32 API features and offers access to multiple processors, distributed processing, networking, and security. Windows NT has full access to all Win32 functions and features, including **AngleLine()** and 32-bit world coordinate features. Windows 98 also uses the 32-bit Win32 API but is currently restricted in its access to multiple processors and security features. Additionally, Windows 98 does not have access to all Win32 functions and features.

For example, Windows 98 uses a 16-bit world coordinate system and does not allow access to certain functions, such as **AngleLine()**. The official word from Microsoft is that Windows 98 will support all functions that are supported in both Win32 and Win32s—in 32-bit mode! Table 2.2 lists those features exclusive to Win32 and *not* supported by Win32s.

TABLE 2.2
Win32 Features Not Supported by Win32s

Feature	Description
GDI improvements	The 32-bit GDI is capable of drawing paths and bezier curves, and of rotating bitmaps.
Multithread support	Unlike Windows 3.1, which is a single-threaded environment, Win32 supports multithreads and processes.
Network API	Win32 provides mail slots and named pipes.
Security	Win32 provides user security to Windows NT, which is not available under Win16 or Win32s, and is not currently supported by Windows 98.
Tape backup	Win32 provides tape backup support.
Remote procedure call (RPC)	Win32 allows the control of an application from a different computer via network communication.
Console API	Character-based application development is not supported under Win32s.

Windows 3.x can use a limited set of Win32 functions. However, these functions must be accessed through the 16-bit Win32s API.

Multiprocessing Very soon you are going to see a proliferation of microcomputers containing more than one microprocessor. It seems that one high-speed Pentium just isn't enough! For those high-end users, Windows NT can take advantage of multiprocessor architectures. Each additional processor added to the system delivers a linear increase in performance. A Windows NT application can allocate each thread (subtask or procedure) of the program to its own processor. Windows NT can even dedicate individual processors to system-level tasks. With this design, both the application and the operating system receive the benefits of multiprocessing. All of this is accomplished without any modifications to the application. Windows NT automatically takes full advantage of symmetric multiprocessing whenever available. Therefore, the user immediately benefits from improved performance through this transparent conversion.

Scalability *Scalability* is a term that refers to an operating system's ability to run on different platforms. Windows NT runs on computers ranging from notebooks to superservers, Intel-based systems, MIPS-based systems, Alpha systems, and symmetric multiprocessing machines.

Distributed Computing One of the design goals behind Windows involved information sharing. The workplace has evolved from a company having one large mainframe computer to the proliferation of smaller and cheaper microcomputers. As a result of this hardware metamorphosis, there has come a need for these isolated microcomputer systems to communicate with one another. Windows solves this software and hardware handshaking by directly incorporating networking capabilities into the operating systems.

Security Today, more than ever, data security is an issue that more and more individuals and corporations are becoming increasingly aware of. When data storage and retrieval moved from one large mainframe to networked microcomputers, MIS managers began worrying seriously about data security. Naturally, this was not a concern of just the individual corporation, but was also an even more serious matter for our government. The government saw the need to secure one user's resources from another and to prevent any one user from garnering all of the system resources at any moment in time. Although not currently a part of Windows 98, Windows NT targets the United States Department of Defenses Class C2 security level.

This standard defines what is known as a *discretionary*, or *need-to-know*, level of protection. It also defines a set of standards that allows privilege-level audit capabilities. Basically, a C2-compliant operating system allows the owner of a system resource to decide who can access it. A system monitor keeps track of who is accessing the data and at what time. The U.S. government standard encompasses security levels from D (lowest security level) through A (highest security level). The fundamental structure of Windows NT will allow its security rating to migrate to the higher security levels.

Windows Open Systems Architecture Through the use of its Windows Open Systems Architecture (WOSA), Microsoft has defined an open set of network interface standards for file sharing, print sharing, database access, electronic mail, and system configuration and administration. WOSA allows end users of Windows to access multivendor information services.

Crash Management Under Windows 98 or Windows NT, the system crashes experienced under Windows 3.x are a thing of the past. These are robust platforms with proven stability and integrity. They prevent business critical applications from experiencing any data corruption through advanced memory protection schemes. No single process—or the operating system—can bring a program down, as each is given its own unique memory space. Windows also protects from system crashes by isolating each application from direct hardware access. Windows checks each request for validity and correct privilege level. Finally, new file systems for Windows provide many file fixes, such as a full recovery system, to quickly restore file integrity. The new file systems maintain a transaction log that insures the integrity of the disk structure, even if there is a system shutdown.

Virtual Memory Windows takes advantage of a flat or linear programming platform, as opposed to the segmented platforms of the past. Both users and developers alike can benefit by applications that demand large amounts of RAM for peak performance. These full 32-bit operating systems, combined with a 64-bit address capability, essentially eliminate all architectural limits for your applications. One of the major goals for Windows was the operating system's ability to run MS-DOS and 16-bit Windows applications as is. This is quite an undertaking, as each environment views physical memory in a unique manner.

Microsoft's solution was to allow each of Windows environment subsystems to view memory in a manner corresponding to what each 16-bit application expects. By using a 32-bit flat address virtual memory system, an application's virtual address space represents a set of addresses available to a process and any of its threads. At runtime, the virtual memory manager translates or maps each virtual address into an actual physical address. Because the operating system is doing a validation between virtual addresses and physical addresses, it prevents individual processes from bumping into each other.

Many systems running Windows do not have access to large quantities of physical memory. Instead, when the virtual memory manager detects a shortage of physical memory, it automatically transfers (or pages) some of the physical memory's contents to disk. Paged data frees up the store of available physical memory. This allows needed code or data to be moved into memory. Whenever a virtual address maps to paged information, these operating systems automatically load or reload the needed data. Windows is sophisticated enough to customize itself to whatever physical RAM is available. It does this by dynamically balancing physical RAM between paged memory and a file cache.

COMPARISON OF WINDOWS The list of features that each version of Windows provides is indeed confusing. Table 2.3 provides, in tabular form, a summary of features for each version of Windows.

TABLE 2.3
Features of Windows

Feature	Windows Version 3.1	98	NT
Features 32-bit preemptive multitasking		*	*
Has auto hardware detection		*	*
Has automatic recovery from a system failure			*
Has C-2 security level			*
Has crash protection between Win16 apps			*
Has data protection			*
Has desktop user profiles		*	*
Fully exploits 386 to Pentium platforms		*	*
Features LAN connectivity and peer-to-peer networking		*	*
Has new interface		*	*
Has open networking architecture		*	*
Has open system management architecture		*	*
Has plug-and-play technology		*	*
Has remote access services		*	*
Runs IBM Presentation Manager			*
Runs on PowerPC, MIPS, Alpha RISC systems			*
Runs Win16 device drivers	*	*	
Has secure user profiles			*
Supports disk compression	*	*	*
Supports MS-DOS	*	*	many
Supports multiple file systems + FAT		*	*
Supports multiple processors			*
Supports OpenGL		*	*
Supports SNMP and DMI standards		*	*
Supports Win16 applications	*	*	*
Supports Win32 applications		*	*
Uses Win32 APIs		*	*
Uses Win32s APIs	*	*	*

If we are to believe the rumors that abound concerning these operating systems, the next version of Windows NT will incorporate even more Windows 98 features. This version of Windows NT, Windows 2000, is already in Beta. Eventually, however, Windows 98 will merge into Windows NT as Microsoft's single operating system! Do you believe it?

SUPPORT FOR NEW TECHNOLOGIES One area that may prove to be of interest to application developers is support for the Universal Serial Bus (USB). This is a new standard designed to replace the present device dependence on a limited number of hardware interrupts. Existing systems have seen ever-increasing competition by peripherals—modems, pointers, sound cards, and the like—for the limited resources represented by the 16 available hardware interrupts. The USB is designed to offer a virtually unlimited number of connections for existing and newer devices, while providing effective throughput speed orders of magnitude higher than the speed of existing channels.

Windows 98 includes support for AGP (accelerated graphics port) video cards, MMX processors, and DVD-ROM drives. In addition, you can now even connect multiple displays (using multiple display cards). Likewise, the new multilink channel aggregation (MCA) technology allows you to boost bandwidth by combining two or more communication lines.

NEW WIZARDS AND UTILITIES Included in Windows 98 is the Update Wizard, which allows you to connect to Microsoft's Web site to download the latest patches, drivers, and enhancements—automatically! A Tune-Up Wizard is included to defragment drives and delete unnecessary files. The System File Checker examines critical .DLL, .COM, .VXD, and other files, testing for corruption and/or modification. This utility will restore the original files if necessary. Though none of the features have any immediate impact on how you design applications for Windows, they may offer opportunities and perhaps a few suggestions for the directions of your own development projects.

Getting Started

The intent of this section is to help moderately experienced C/C++ programmers make the transition to writing applications that use the Microsoft Windows APIs. This section covers how to use popular Windows functions, messages, and data structures to carry out useful tasks common to Windows applications.

The C/C++ programming language is the preferred development language for Windows applications. Many of the programming features of Windows were designed with the C/C++ programmer in mind. Windows applications can also be developed in Microsoft's Visual Basic and in Borland's Delphi and assembly language, but these languages present additional challenges and/or limitations that are typically avoided when writing applications in C/C++.

REQUIRED SOFTWARE For Windows application development, you will need:

- A 32-bit C/C++ compiler. Again, we recommend either the Microsoft or Borland compilers.
- Either Windows 98 or Windows NT running on your system.
- Access to the Win32 API (usually provided by the compiler manufacturer).

SYSTEM REQUIREMENTS All versions of Windows will work with 80386 or higher processors and at least 100-MB hard drives. Windows 3.x will work well with 4 MB of RAM memory. We feel that 6–8 MB of RAM memory is required for good performance under Windows 98 and 12–16 MB of RAM memory when using Windows NT.

For optimal performance for developers, we recommend the following system configuration for the best overall performance and ease of use:

• Audio board	Microsoft or Sound Blaster
• CD-ROM	4x or 6x speed CD-ROM drive
• Floppy disk type	1.44 MB 3.5"
• Hard disk	1 GB (minimum)
• Main system	Pentium running at 200 MHZ (or greater)
• Mouse	Microsoft mouse
• RAM memory	16 MB of RAM
• Video	32-bit local video bus graphics adapter

Windows 98 and NT Concepts and Terminology

Before you can begin programming a Windows application, you need to understand those concepts and terms specific to multitasking GUI applications. These new concepts and terms can be broken down into two distinct areas, visual and behind-the-scenes. Visual features include standard Windows items such as title bars, icons, radio buttons, push buttons, menus, and scroll bars. Behind-the-scenes features include invoking functions and recognizing and responding to messages.

Just like any technical area of study, for example, digital logic, knowing the correct terminology is important for correctly communicating with others. For this reason, each of the Windows features have been given a name and an associated usage. This section will introduce you to the basic vocabulary that will enable you to confidently discuss and develop Windows applications.

WINDOWS VERSUS WINDOWS

To begin, Windows refers to the two Microsoft operating systems, Windows 98 and NT. The term *window* refers specifically to a rectangular portion of the screen representing a program, with an application-independent format. To the end user, this window is the visual interface between them and the application generating the window. To the application, this window is the rectangular area of the screen under the control of the application. How the application was written determines this window's shape, size, and screen location. In Windows, whenever the user launches an application, a new window is created. Whenever the user selects a window control or option, the program responds. One of the ways to terminate an application is simply to close this window.

As you have just seen, a window represents much more than a simple rectangle appearing on the screen. This visual interface also relates directly to specific application features, such as terminating the program. In this sense, a window represents the fundamental substructure of the Windows system and is just as important as this visual user-application information exchange. For example, though the window itself represents the graphics-oriented user interface, it is also the visible manifestation of a multitasking and hardware-independent environment. The visible overlap of applications conveys to the user the true multitasking capabilities of Windows. Because the screen is partitioned into different windows, the user can direct input to a specific application within the multitasking environment by using the keyboard or mouse to select one of the concurrently running applications. Windows then intercepts the user's input and allocates any necessary resources (such as the processor or memory) as needed.

With each window representing an individually executing application, you can easily see how this window metaphor highlights the hardware-independent substructure of Windows. From each application's viewpoint, its window is the screen. However, because Windows does not permit applications to access the physical screen directly, all interaction must be performed through the window. Because of the intervention by Windows, it doesn't matter to the application that the window may be only a portion of the entire display; to the application, the window is the entire display. It is Windows itself that sits between each application and any interaction between specific devices, such as the keyboard, monitor, printer, and so on, making all necessary translations.

CREATING THE "LOOK"

One of the main objectives to Windows was making every new application you purchase as easy as possible to learn. One way Windows accomplishes this is by requiring every Windows application to behave in a certain manner and to contain common, recognizable features. A brief list of shared characteristics might include: the Help menu and related capabilities, control boxes, About boxes, and so on. These commonalities give Windows a comforting predictability from application to application. The discussion that follows describes each of these components in detail.

THE WINDOW BORDER Working from the outside in, all windows are bordered. The border consists of the lines that frame a window. To the newcomer, the border may appear only to delineate one application window from another. However, by moving the mouse pointer over a border and holding down the left mouse button, the user can alter a window's size and shape.

THE WINDOW TITLE BAR In a multitasking environment, knowing which concurrently executing application you are using is important. For this reason, all application windows contain, in the top physical position, a title bar displaying the application's name. The title bar and the associated title are centered in Windows NT and placed just to the right of the applications icon under Windows 98. The title is printed left-justified in this area. Writing the code necessary to title your application is as simple as passing its title string, for example, "My Program," to the **CreateWindow()** function. **CreateWindow()** assigns this string to the main window object's title data member (data members are functionally the same as an older high-level language's record fields).

THE CONTROL BOX The upper-left corner of all title bars contains a control box. Under Windows NT, the control box is drawn as a small square box with a flat, shadowed rectangle. Under Windows 98, the control box is usually an application-supplied and visually related icon.

THE SYSTEM MENU When the user clicks on an application's control box, they see displayed a drop-down system menu. The system menu lists several standard options, such as Restore, Move, Size, Minimize, Maximize, and Close (Windows NT includes a Switch To option).

THE MINIMIZE BOX The window's minimize box appears in the upper-right hand corner of the window. Under Windows NT 2.1, this is a small, downward-pointing arrow that causes the window to shrink to a small picture, or icon. Windows 98 uses an underscore symbol to represent a collapsed window.

THE MAXIMIZE BOX The upper-right hand corner of a window also houses the maximize box. Under Windows NT, this is a small, upward-pointing arrow that causes the window to expand to full size. Windows 98 uses a small rectangle with a heavy bar at the top to represent an expanded window and title bar area. When the window is maximized, this image changes to either a downward-pointing arrow or two overlapped rectangles, representing the option to return the application back to original proportions.

THE TERMINATE BOX Windows 98 also includes one additional icon in the upper-right hand corner of the window, representing the terminate box. This is a small rectangle with a heavy "X" drawn in it, used to terminate an application whenever the user clicks the mouse over the icon.

THE VERTICAL SCROLL BAR Scroll bars, in general, are not required window features. However, so many programs use them that they almost appear to be a standard window control. Windows demands that Vertical scroll bars be drawn vertically on the righthand side of the client area. Vertical scroll bars have arrows at either end, pointing in opposite directions, a colored band, and a transparent window block, sometimes called the *thumb*. The thumb shows the position of the currently displayed contents in relation to the document as a whole, which is represented visually by the colored band.

A program uses the vertical scroll bar to select which page of a multiple-page file to display to the window. Clicking either arrow shifts the display one line at a time. Clicking the thumb below the upward arrow and dragging it causes screen output to move rapidly to any portion of the application's screen output. One of the best uses for the vertical scroll bar is for moving through a multiple-page word processing document.

THE HORIZONTAL SCROLL BAR Just like vertical scroll bars, horizontal scroll bars are optional window controls. If an application uses a horizontal scroll bar, it appears at the bottom of the window and runs the extent of the client area. It has arrows at its extremes that point in opposite directions, a colored band, and a transparent window block, or thumb. The thumb shows the position of the currently displayed contents in relation to the document as a whole, which is represented by the colored band.

Typically, horizontal scroll bars are used to shift the display left or right, choosing which set of multiple columns of information to be displayed. Clicking either arrow causes the screen image to shift one column at a time. Clicking the thumb to the right of the left-pointing arrow and dragging the thumb causes the screen output to shift rapidly horizontally to any portion of the application's screen output. One of the best uses for the horizontal scroll bar is to move through multiple columns of a spreadsheet application in which not all of the columns of information can't fit into one window's width.

THE MENU BAR All Windows applications have a menu bar immediately below the title bar. The menu bar is used for making menu and submenu selections (menu items are always left-justified within the menu bar). These selections can be made by pointing and clicking the menu command or, alternatively, by using a "hot-key" combination. Hot-key combinations often use the ALT key in conjunction with a letter shown in bold and underlined.

THE CLIENT OR WORK AREA The largest portion of a window, occupying the most screen real estate, is the client area. The client area is the application's primary location for output. It is the application's responsibility to manage the client area of the window, and only the application can output to the client area.

Object Classes to the Rescue

At this point, you are familiar with the most common components and features of a standard Windows window. From a programming perspective, the good news is that you do not have to write the bare-bones code to create each one of them. Instead you use off-the-shelf, reusable windows objects. There may even be an occasion when you will want to create two windows with a similar appearance and behavior. An excellent example of this involves the Windows Paint program. Paint allows users to clip or copy a portion of a graphics image by running two instances (or copies) of Paint. The information is copied from one instance of Paint to the other. Therefore, it is logical that each instance of Paint look and behave as its counterpart. Therefore, each instance of Paint must have its own window with an identical "look and feel."

Windows accomplishes this commonality by creating new applications based on existing window classes. Windows allows a programmer to create windows with a wide variety of characteristics. They may be of different sizes, placed on different areas of the display, have different text in the caption bars, have different display colors, or use different mouse cursors. Every window that you create in a Windows application must be based on a window class. Five of these window classes have already been registered by Windows during its initialization phase. You can also have your application register its own classes.

Windows specifies some of a window's characteristics as parameters to the **CreateWindow()** function. Other parameters are specified in a separate window class structure. To allow several windows to be created and based on the same window class, a window class needs to be registered. Once registered, the class becomes available to all programs running under Windows. Windows of similar appearance and behavior can be grouped into classes to reduce the amount of information that needs to be maintained.

Each window class has its own shareable window class structure, so there is no needless replication of the window class parameters. Also, because two windows of the same class use the same functions and any associated subroutines, classes save time and storage because there is no code duplication. The most important characteristic to shared classes, however, is that they all share the same "look and feel."

Using Object-Oriented Technology

One of the most important goals to any GUI interface deals with the common look and familiar modes of operation between different applications. If the coding for this look and user interaction were left up to the individual programmer, two things would happen. First, there would be no common look. Every programmer would have a different idea of how to draw and place an object and how it should interface with the user. Second, hardly any programs would ever get written. This later problem deals with the coding complexity involved in doing grounds-up GUI design. Fortunately, we are in the age of object-oriented programming. When you are programming for Windows, you are actually using object-oriented programming. Instead of writing the GUI code yourself, you merely use a previously written object. These objects provide the "look and feel" that end users anticipate.

By definition, in object-oriented programming, an object is an abstract data type that consists of a data structure and various functions that act on the data structure. Additionally, objects receive messages that can cause them to change. For example, a graphics object, like a vertical scroll bar, is a collection of data that can be manipulated as a single entity and is presented to the user as part of the visual interface. In particular, a graphics object represents both the data and the functions dealing with the presentation of the data. Some examples of graphics objects include menus, title bars, control boxes, and scroll bars. The next section describes several new graphics objects that affect the user's view of an application.

ICON OBJECTS A familiar proverb says that one picture is worth a thousand words; accordingly, icons can be very powerful. They attract the user's attention. Icons relate to program actions in the same way that assembly language mnemonics are translated into machine-code instructions. Icons and mnemonics are visual symbols associated with some sort of action. In the case of a mnemonic, this is a readable abbreviation for some action. In the case of an icon, you have a small symbol used to remind the user of a particular operation, idea, or product. For example, when a spreadsheet application is minimized, it could display a very small histogram icon to remind the user the application is still running. Clicking the histogram would cause Windows to bring the application to active status. Windows provides several stock icons, including a question mark, exclamation point, asterisk, and upturned palm. Using various Windows tools, users can create their own device-independent color icon designs. The function **DrawIcon()** allows an application to easily place an icon within the client area.

CURSOR OBJECTS A Windows cursor is a graphic symbol, unlike the blinking underscore of DOS. The graphic symbol changes according to the placement of the pointing device; this helps to show the operations currently available. The best example of this would be the change from the standard Windows arrow cursor to the small hourglass cursor that indicates a pause while a selected command is being executed. Incorporated into Windows are several stock cursors: the original diagonal arrow, a vertical arrow, an hourglass, crosshairs, an I-beam, and several others. Using the Windows tools, your application can also create its own unique cursors.

CARET OBJECTS Unlike a cursor object, a caret is a graphic symbol used to show the user where input will be received. Though a typical Windows window contains many graphic markers, only the caret blinks. Most of the time, mouse input is associated with a cursor and keyboard input with a caret. However, the mouse can move or change the input emphasis of a caret. To help clarify the difference between a cursor and a caret, remember that Windows carets behave most like the standard DOS cursor. An example is the I-beam caret provided for you automatically in dialog boxes. Unlike icons and cursors, an application must create its own carets by using the **CreateCaret()** and **ShowCaret()** functions. Except for the automatic I-beam dialog box caret, there are no stock carets.

MESSAGE BOX OBJECTS There will be many occasions on which a program will want to inform the user of a particular action. For these purposes, there are message box objects. A message box is a pop-up window that contains a title, an icon, and a message.

Programs easily generate message boxes with a simple call to the function **MessageBox()**. **MessageBox()** creates, displays, and receives the user's response from the message box. In a syntax similar to assigning data items to a structure member, your program needs only to supply the message title; the message itself; instructions on which stock icon to use (if any); and, if applicable, the stock response to use (such as OK). Other stock user responses include Yes/No, Yes/No/Cancel, OK/Cancel, Retry/Cancel. Your program can also access standard icons such as IconExclamation, IconAsterisk, IconQuestion, and IconHandand.

DIALOG BOX OBJECTS Dialog boxes are very similar to message boxes, except that they receive more complex types of user responses than do simple selections of fixed options. Dialog boxes are also pop-up windows; however, dialog boxes are primarily used to receive input from the user.

A dialog box allows an application to receive information, one field or box of information at a time, rather than one character at a time. The graphic design of a dialog box is created for you automatically by Windows. Dialog boxes are considered program resources because their contents are specific to a particular application. You use your C/C++ compiler's resource editor to define dialog box objects.

FONT OBJECTS If you understand the simple definition of an object, meaning the syntactic combination of data members (remember, a member is no different than a record field), bundled with all of the function members that make the object do something, you'll understand why even fonts are considered objects. Long gone are the days when the characters displayed on your monitor came from a single character ROM built into your system. On the contrary, today's applications seem to have unlimited font capabilities, from typefaces to point sizes to the standard bold, italics, and underline.

Your programs use font objects, or resources, to define a complete set of characters from one typeface, all with a certain size and style. Fonts can be manipulated to give text a variety of appearances. By using built-in routines, Windows allows for the dynamic modification of a typeface, including boldface or italic, underlining, or changing the font size. Windows provides all of the necessary functions for displaying text anywhere within the client area and, even better, due to Windows device independence, an application's output will have a consistent appearance from one output device to the next.

BITMAP OBJECTS You can think of a bitmap object as a small picture. There are two basic uses for bitmaps. First, bitmaps are used to draw pictures on the display. For example, Windows uses many small bitmaps to draw arrows in scroll bars; to display check marks when the user selects pull-down menu options; and to draw the system menu box, the size box, and many others. Bitmaps are also used for creating brushes, which will be covered shortly. These pixel pictures are stored in memory. Bitmaps are used whenever an application wants to display a graphics image quickly. Because the object is being transferred directly from memory, it can be displayed faster than the code necessary to recreate the image that can be executed.

For all of their display speed characteristics, bitmaps do have their disadvantages. First, depending on their size, bitmaps can occupy an unpredictably large portion of memory. For each pixel being displayed, there has to be an equivalent representation in memory. Displaying the same bitmap in color versus a monochrome rendering requires much more memory. In a monochrome bitmap, one bit can define a pixel as on or off. However, a color bitmap using 16 colors requires that each pixel be represented by 4 bits. In computer work, a nibble is 4 bits. Thus, as the resolution of the graphics image increases, so does the memory requirement—and what about today's 64-bit graphics devices!

A less serious disadvantage, because there are ways of coding around this, is that a bitmap is a composite picture, meaning that you cannot break apart its individual components. Take, for example, a bitmap of a personal computer. The user cannot go into this bitmap and click only on the image of the monitor to select it separately from the entire system. However, if the bitmap had been constructed from a series of routines, an application would be able to change the data supplied to these routines and modify the picture. For example, an application could modify the personal computer drawing routine to include a monitor, system unit, keyboard, and so on.

PEN OBJECTS You might not realize that all Windows applications use pen objects to draw lines and outline shapes. Pen objects have three basic characteristics: line width, style (dotted, dashed, solid, and so on), and color. Under Windows, a pen for drawing black lines and one for drawing white lines are always available to each application. The black pen is the default pen. Of course, you can always create your own pens. One good example of an alternate pen style is the dashed line that many spreadsheet applications use to highlight user-selected groups of cells.

BRUSH OBJECTS Many graphics applications use a small picture of a tipped paint can dribbling paint to represent a flood-fill type operation. In Windows, brushes are used to paint colors and to flood fill areas with predefined patterns. A Windows brush has a minimum size of 8 x 8 pixels and, like pens, have three basic characteristics: size, pattern, and color. With their 8 x 8 pixel minimum, brushes are said to have a pattern—not a style, as pens do. A brush's appearance may come from a compiler-supplied definition, such as a solid color to hatched to diagonal, or from an application-supplied bit-pattern.

Communication via Messages

Because the term *multitasking* does not mean "multihardware," something has to take control of directing I/O from each concurrently running application down to the one system that all applications are sharing. Windows takes charge of the single system's keyboard, video display, mouse, parallel and serial ports, memory, and program execution. It is important to realize that Windows accomplishes all that it does because of its hardware dominance. For example, it is only by taking control of the hardware that Windows can partition the display screen into separate windows.

By managing the hardware, Windows can intercept all user input and distribute that input as messages to the appropriate applications. Finally, it is only through the total control of the hardware that Windows can ensure that an application can interface with a variety of output devices, thereby creating a "virtual machine." Under Windows, an application does not write directly to the screen, process any hardware interrupts, or output directly to the printer. Instead, the application uses the appropriate Windows functions or it waits for an appropriate message to be delivered. Applications development under Windows must now incorporate the processing of the application and the user's view of the application through Windows.

From an applications viewpoint, a message is a notification that some event of interest has occurred—an event that may or may not require a specific action. These events may have been initiated by the user by clicking, moving the mouse, changing the size of a window, or making a menu selection. However, the signaled event could have been generated by the application. The net effect of all of this is that applications must now be totally oriented toward processing messages. Applications must be capable of awakening, determining the appropriate action based on the type of message received, taking that action to completion, and returning to sleep. As a result of this new communication, Windows applications are significantly different from their older DOS counterparts. Under Windows 3.1, over 2,300 function calls were available. Windows has access to even more.

Windows divides message processing into three general layers, called EXECUTIVE, GDI (graphics device interface), and USER. The EXECUTIVE module is responsible for memory management, loading and running an application, and scheduling. The GDI contains all of the routines to create and display graphics.The USER module takes care of all other application requirements.

STANDARD MESSAGE FORMATS In this next section, you will take a closer look at the message system, examining the format and sources of messages, several common message types, and the ways in which both Windows and your application go about processing messages. The purpose of a message is to notify your program that an event of interest has occurred. Technically, a message is not of interest just to the application, but to a specific window within that application. Therefore, every message is addressed to a window.

There are actually two categories of message queues, the Windows system message queue and each concurrently running program's message queue. Each message in the system message queue must eventually be transferred to a program's message queue. The program's message queue stores all messages for all the windows in that program. The following four parameters are associated with all messages: a window handle (identifying which window is receiving the message), a message type, an 1Param value, and a wParam value. Under Windows 3.x, handles are 16 bits, messages are 16 bits, LPARAM is 32 bits, and WPARAM is 16 bits. Under Windows 98 and NT, handles are 32 bits, messages are 32 bits, LPARAM is 32 bits and WPARAM is now 32 bits (because the parameter types are defined as symbolic constants LPARAM and WPARAM instead of standard data types, their specific meaning can be easily redefined for each target platform).

The window handle in an object-oriented programming environment is simply an identifier of an object, which for the current syntax is the identifier of the particular window to which the message is addressed. Frequently, this handle will reference an object (defined in the form of a data structure) that is located in a movable portion of memory. It is important to realize that, even though the portion of memory can be moved, the handle remains the same. This allows Windows to manage memory efficiently while leaving the relocation invisible to the application. Because multiple windows can be created based on the same window class, a single window function could process messages for more than one window within a single program. Under these circumstances, the application would use the handle to determine which window is receiving the message.

The message type obtains its meaning from one of several symbolic constants defined in the standard windows.h header file, discussed later in this chapter. Under Windows, each message type is represented by a two-character mnemonic, followed by the underscore character and, finally, a descriptor to complete the message. The most common message types include WM_CREATE, WM_PAINT, WM_CLOSE, WM_COPY, and WM_PASTE. Other message types include control window messages BM_xxxxxxxxxx, edit control messages EM_xxxxxxxxxx, and list box messages LB_xxxxxxxxxx (where xxxxxxxxxx represents different message types within the same category). If this list is not sufficient, your application can create and register its own types. Application-specific message types are not shared by other applications and are one way of generating private message types.

The contents of these last two parameters, LPARAM and WPARAM, provide any additional information necessary to interpret the message and vary, depending on the message type. Examples of the types of information that would be passed include which key was just struck, the position of the vertical or horizontal scroll bar elevators, the selected pop-up menu item, the position of the mouse, and even the status of the mouse buttons.

WHO SENDS MESSAGES? Basically, there are four sources for a message. An application can receive a message from the user, from Windows itself, from the application program itself, or from another application. It is through the underlying structure of messages that Windows is capable of multitasking. Therefore, all messages must be processed by Windows.

Typical, user-input messages include keystroke information, mouse movements, point-and-click coordinates, menu selections, the location of scroll bar elevators, and so on. Your application program will devote a great deal of time to processing user messages.

When Windows itself is posting an application-specific message, Windows is usually signaling a state change—for example, when the user clicks an application's icon to make that application active. In this case, Windows tells the application that its main window is being opened, that its size and location are being modified, and so forth. Windows-originated messages can be either responded to or ignored, depending on the current state of an application.

To facilitate application-to-application message posting, Microsoft has developed the dynamic data exchange (DDE) protocol. Currently, most applications written for Windows do not take full advantage of the fourth type of message source, intertask communication. However, this category will become increasingly important as more and more applications use this integration capability.

PROCESSING MESSAGES Application-specific processing of recognized message types is usually performed by functions. A Windows application will have a procedure for processing each type of message that is of interest to any of its windows. However, different windows may respond differently to messages of the same type. For example, one application may have two windows that respond in different ways to the press of the mouse button.

The first window may respond by changing the background color; the second window may respond by placing cross-hatching on a spreadsheet. Because the same message can be interpreted differently by different windows, you can understand why Windows addresses each message to a specific window within an application. Not only will the application have a different procedure to handle each message type, it will need a procedure to handle each message type for each window. The window procedure is used to group together all the message-type procedures for a Windows application.

THE STANDARD MESSAGE LOOP All of the stand-alone functions your program uses to process messages are triggered by what is called the Windows application *message processing loop*. Each application will contain procedures to create and initialize windows, which are followed by the message processing loop and, finally, by some required closing code. The message loop is responsible for processing a message delivered by Windows to the main body of the program. Here the program acknowledges the message and requests Windows to send it to the appropriate window procedure for processing. Then the window procedure executes the desired action.

As you have already seen, messages can be sent from one of two queues, either the system queue or the application's message queue. The message queue and dispatching priority are two factors that can influence the sequence in which a message is processed. Messages are first placed in the system queue. When a message reaches the front of the queue, it is sent over to the appropriate application's message queue. This dual mode allows Windows to keep track of all messages while allowing each application to track only those messages that pertain to it. Most messages go into these queues as you would expect, in first-in-first-out order (FIFO). These are called *synchronous messages*. Most Windows applications use this type of dispatching method.

However, there are occasions when Windows will push a message to the end of the queue, thereby preventing it from being dispatched. Messages of this type are called *asynchronous messages*. Care must be taken when sending an asynchronous message that overrides the application's normal sequence of processing. There are three types of asynchronous messages: paint, timer, and quit. A timer message, for example, causes a certain action to take effect at a specified time, regardless of the messages to be processed at that moment. Therefore, a timer message will cause all other messages in the queue to be pushed farther from the queue front.

Windows also has asynchronous messages that can be sent to other applications. This scenario is unique, in that the receiving application doesn't put the message into its queue. Instead, the message immediately calls the receiving application's appropriate window procedure, where the message then executes.

How does Windows dispatch messages that are pending for several applications at once? Windows settles this issue in one of two ways. One method of message processing is called *dispatching* priority. Each time Windows loads an application, it sets the application's priority to one of the following four levels:

- HIGH_PRIORITY_CLASS
- IDLE_PRIORITY_CLASS
- NORMAL_PRIORITY_CLASS
- REALTIME_PRIORITY_CLASS

However, an application can change its priority. All things being equal, Windows would then settle any dispatching contention by sending messages to the highest-priority application. A data communications application is an example of a program that might need to raise its priority level. If your system were connected to a distant host computer, you would want to process the information being sent long distance as soon as possible.

Normally, an application with a properly chosen priority level won't need to change a message's priority. Because tampering with an application's priority level is very uncommon, Windows must have another method for dispatching messages to concurrent applications with the same priority level. Besides processing the messages in the queue, whenever Windows sees that a particular application has a backlog of unprocessed messages, it hangs on to any new messages for that application while continuing to dispatch other messages to other applications.

Standard Windows Resources

In general, a resource represents data that is included in a program's .exe file, although, technically speaking, it does not reside in a program's normal data segment. The graphics objects described earlier included icons, cursors, carets, message boxes, dialog boxes, fonts, bitmaps, pens, and brushes. These are all examples of Windows resources. When Windows loads a program into memory for execution, very often it will leave all of the resources on the disk. One example of this is when the user first requests to see an application's About dialog box. Before Windows can display the About box, it must first access the disk to copy this information from the program's .exe file into memory.

To make the most efficient reuse of memory possible, an application typically defines its resources as read-only and discardable. This allows Windows to discard the resource whenever more memory is required. Under Windows 3.x, resources are essentially unowned, and should the resource be requested again, Windows simply reads the disk and reloads the data into memory. Thus, multiple instances of the same application running concurrently (for instance, a word processor), will not only share the application's program code, but its resource definitions as well. Under Win32, resources are owned by the application and are not sharable.

Standard Windows Functions

The following list contains some of the most frequently used message processing functions: **RegisterWindowMessage()**, **PostMessage()**, and **DispatchMessage()**. Officially called the *API*, parameters are passed via the stack to the various modules that make up Windows. Under Windows 3.x, Windows functions returned 16-bit integer addresses. However, under Windows these addresses are now 32 bits as they are no longer the shorter 2-byte integer-offset addresses, but instead a full 4-byte integer-linear address.

CALLING CONVENTION As just discussed, parameters to all Windows functions are passed via the stack. In a C/C++ program, for example, function parameters are first pushed onto the stack and then the function is called. Normally, the parameters are pushed starting from the right-most parameter and going to the left-most parameter. Upon return from the function, the calling procedure must adjust the stack pointer to a value equal to the number of bytes originally pushed onto the stack. In Windows, however, things look slightly different.

One of the most frequently observed function modifiers seen in Windows applications is the WINAPI modifier. The WINAPI modifier instructs the C/C++ compiler to push parameters from left to right, with the called function having the responsibility to adjust the stack before the return. It is no longer the job of the calling procedure to adjust the stack.

Windows uses this calling convention because it turns out to be more space-efficient. Therefore, the Microsoft C/C++ compiler understands that any function declared with the symbolic constant WINAPI is to use the more efficient calling convention. However, the efficiency of using the WINAPI calling convention comes with its own set of problems. This calling sequence makes coding functions with a variable number of parameters more difficult. For this reason, the Windows C/C++ compiler still uses **_cded** when prototyping variable argument functions.

A First Look at WINDOWS.H

Many Windows functions work with their own specified data types and variables, which your program can access. These variables and types are defined in previously mentioned header files. To use certain functions, you must include the header file in which they are defined. This is accomplished by placing an #include statement in your source program. Technically, the #define statements found in these header files associate a numeric constant with a text identifier, for example:

```
#define WM_CREATE 0x0001
```

The C/C++ compiler will use the hexadecimal constant 0x0001 as a replacement for WM_CREATE during preprocessing. Other typedef statements may appear a bit unusual, for example:

```
typedef int    INT
typedef float  FLOAT
```

In Microsoft C/C++, both int and float are reserved words. Your applications should use the uppercase INT and FLOAT for one very good reason: Should you decide to port your application over to another C/C++ compiler, it would certainly be much easier to change the typedef statements within the header file than to change all the occurrences of a particular identifier.

You may be interested to know that the original version of windows.h contained Windows-specific constants, type, and function prototypes, and occupied a mere 110 kilobytes. However, with the advent of Win32 and the introduction of Windows, this file became too unwieldy. The information contained in this header file increased from 110 kilobytes to over 567 kilobytes. Currently, windows.h simply points to more than 28 separate #include files containing this information. These files now contain over 350 constant declarations, the typedef declarations, and over 2,000 Windows function declarations. This explains just one of the reasons it takes so long to compile a Windows application.

Understanding the Style of Windows Code

Even if you already know how to code in C or C++, you may initially find Windows source code a little confusing. Not only does this new code contain never-before-seen functions, but how things are defined appears to be unique. The name for this style of coding is known as *Hungarian style*. Officially, this Hungarian style of notation can be credited to the Microsoft programmer Charles Simonyi. In Hungarian notation, variable names begin with a lowercase letter or letters that describe the data type of the variable. This variable name prefix is then followed by the name of the variable, which is represented by a meaningful use of upper- and lowercase letters. This approach allows each variable to have attached a mnemonic representing the variable's data type. For example:

```
LONG LPARAM
unsigned int UINT
```

By prefacing each identifier with a reminder of its data type (L for Long-PARAM and U for UnsignedINT), you can actually avoid some very common mistakes before compiling your program. The following statement looks harmless but is incorrect and may go unchecked.

```
Variable1 = Variable2;
```

However, using Hungarian notation, you would undoubtedly catch the following mistake:

```
Lvariable1 = Uvariable2;
```

Hopefully, the following list will bring you "on board" as quickly as possible to the more frequently used Windows type prefixes:

Prefix	Data Type Represented
a	atom
b	BOOL (integer)
by	BYTE (unsigned character)
c	character (ANSI ASCII 8-bit)
dw	DWORD (unsigned long)
fn	function
h	HANDLE (unsigned integer)
hDC	HANDLE to a device context
i	integer (16 bits in Windows 3.x, 32 bits under Windows 98 and NT)
id	integral id value
l	LONG (long)
lp	long (far) pointer
lpsz	long pointer to null-terminated string
n	short integer
np	near (short) pointer
p	pointer
pfn	function pointer
pst	pointer to a structure
psz	pointer to null-terminated string
pv	pointer to void
s	string
sz	NULL (/0) terminated string
u	unsigned
v	void
w	WORD (unsigned 16-bit value)
w	character (UNICODE 16-bit)
x	short (when used as the X coordinate)
y	short (when used as the Y coordinate)

The Seven Fundamental Steps for Developing Windows Programs

All programming languages have a systematized set of steps required to build the majority of applications. Under Windows, these common steps involve:

1. A call to **WinMain()**, where program execution begins, along with any additional Windows/C/C++ functions.
2. Application-specific menu creation and menu descriptions stored in a resource script file.
3. Optional creation of the application's dialog boxes.
4. Optional creation of icons, cursors, and bitmaps.
5. Defining the project.
6. Compiling and linking all related files.
7. Debugging.

As you can quickly see, creating an actual Windows application will require the use of several project development tools.

THE VISUAL C/C++ COMPILER When developing a Windows application, the project file and its associated options control how the application will be built.

THE RESOURCE EDITOR You use your C/C++ compiler's resource editors to create application-specific menus, dialog boxes, icons, cursors, and bitmaps. The use of these editors is almost intuitive, but on-line help is provided, should you run into a problem.

THE RESOURCE COMPILER Frequently, a Windows application will use its own resources, such as menus, icons, and dialog boxes. Each of these resources must be predefined in a file called a *resource script file*. The resource compiler does pretty much what its name suggests—it compiles the resource—and the additional information is added to the application's final .exe file by the project utility. This approach allows Windows to load and use the resources from the .exe file.

USING THE LINKER All Windows applications can be linked with the C/C++ linker under the management of the project utility, which resolves all external references.

SECTION 3

MAINFRAME OPERATING SYSTEMS

MVS HISTORY

By 1964, IBM had a firm grip on the computer market with its 7000 series of machines. In that year, IBM announced the System/360, a new family of computer products. Although the announcement itself was no surprise, it contained some unpleasant news for current IBM customers: The 360 product line was incompatible with older IBM machines. Thus, the transition to the 360 would be difficult for the current customer base. This was a bold step by IBM but one they felt was necessary to break out of some of the constraints of the 7000 architecture and to produce a system capable of evolving with the new integrated circuit technology. The strategy paid off both financially and technically. The 360 was the success of the decade and cemented IBM as the overwhelmingly dominant computer vendor with a market share above 70%. And, with some modifications and extensions, the architecture of the 360 remains to this day, more than a quarter of a century later, the architecture of IBM's large computers.

Although the operating-system software for IBM's mainframes has changed beyond recognition from that of the initial 360 offering, its origins can be traced back to those early days. The System/360 was the industry's first planned family of computers. The family covered a wide range of performance and cost. The various models were compatible in that a program written for one model was capable of being executed by another model in the family with only a difference in the time needed to execute. Thus, the first announced operating system for the new machines, OS/360, was intended to be a single operating system that could operate on all machines in the family. However, the widening spectrum of the 360 family and the diversity of user needs forced IBM to introduce a variety of operating systems. Here, we concentrate on the line of development that led to MVS.

The original OS/360 was a multiprogramming batch system and remained so for some time. Its most complete version, MVT (Multiprogramming with a Variable number of Tasks) was released in 1969 and was the most flexible of the OS/360 variants. The memory allocation for a job was variable and need not be decided until run time. It became the most popular operating system on IBM's large 360s and early large 370s. MVT was missing some of the features present in the more advanced of its competitors' offerings, such as the ability to support multiple processors, virtual storage, and source-level debugging, but it did provide a more complete set of facilities and supporting utilities than any other contemporary operating system. In such areas as job scheduling, peripheral support, number of different systems supported, and conversion support from older systems, OS/360 was unequaled (Weizer 1981).

MVT allowed only 15 jobs to run concurrently. OS/SVS (Single Virtual Storage) was introduced in 1972 as an interim operating system to take advantage of the IBM/370 architecture. The most noteworthy addition was support for virtual memory. With SVS, a virtual address space of 16MB was established. However, this address space had to be shared among the operating system and all active jobs. Soon, even this amount of memory appeared inadequate.

In response to growing memory needs of application programmers, IBM introduced MVS. As with SVS, and as dictated by the 370 architecture, virtual addresses were limited to 24 bits, and hence 16MB. However, with MVS, the limit is 16MB *per job*. That is, each job has its own dedicated virtual memory of 16MB. The operating system maps blocks of virtual memory into real main memory and is able to keep track of the separate virtual memories for each job. Actually, each job typically gets something less than half of its assigned virtual memory; the rest is available for use by the operating system.

The 24-bit address space, even with separate virtual memories for each job, quickly became inadequate for some users. IBM extended its underlying processor to handle 31-bit addresses, a facility known as *extended addressing* (XA). To take advantage of this new hardware, a new version of MVS, known as MVS/XA, was introduced in 1983. With MVS/XA, the per-job address space grew to a maximum of 2GB (gigabytes). This, believe it or not, is still not considered adequate for some environments and some applications. Accordingly, in what may represent the last major extension of the 370 (really the 360) architecture, IBM developed the Enterprise System Architecture (ESA) and the enhanced operating system, MVS/ESA. The same 2GB address space per job that was available in MVS/XA is also available for programs and data. What is new is that there are up to 15 additional 2GB address spaces for data available only to a specific job. Thus, the maximum addressable virtual memory per job is 32GB.

MVS DESCRIPTION

MVS is probably the largest and most complex operating system ever developed. It requires a minimum of 2MB of resident storage. A more realistic configuration would require 6MB for the operating system The four most important factors that have determined the design of MVS are the following:

- Support of batch and interactive jobs
- Virtual storage of up to 32GB per job or user
- Tightly coupled multiprocessing; this architecture consists of a number of processors that share the same main memory.
- Sophisticated resource allocation and monitoring facilities to achieve efficient use of the system's large memory, multiple processors, and complex I/O channel structure.

The need to deal with multiple processors is a requirement not faced in OS/2 and UNIX System V. When there are multiple processors, each of which may execute any process, and when communication among processes running on different processors is supported, the complexity of the operating system can be significantly greater than for a single-processor machine.

Figure 3-1 gives a simplified view of the major building blocks. An outer shell contains services and interfaces visible to users and to system operators responsible for maintaining and tuning the system. In addition to a collection of programs needed for program creation and compilation, there is a job-management subsystem with the following functions:

- Interpret operator commands (from an operator console) and route appropriate messages.
- Read job input data from and write job output data to peripheral devices.
- Allocate I/O devices to a job and notify the operator of any physical data units (e.g., tape reel, disk pack) that have to be mounted prior to the execution of a job.
- Convert the job into tasks that can be processed by task management.

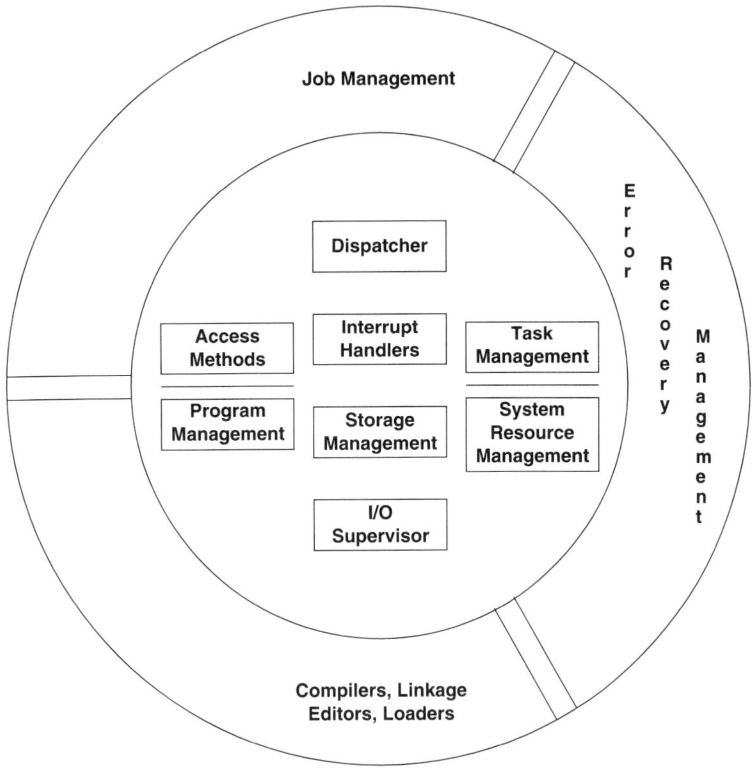

FIGURE 3-1 *Simplified View of Building Blocks of the MVS Operating System (Prasad 1981)*

Finally, the outer shell includes an elaborate management subsystem for error recovery that assures that job faults are isolated so as to not interfere with the rest of the operation and so that the fault can be diagnosed. If possible, the job or jobs affected by the error will be enabled to continue execution.

The core of the operating system consists of a set of major modules or subsystems that interact with each other, the hardware, and the outer shell. These include the following:

- *Dispatcher:* The dispatcher can be regarded as the manager of the processors. Its function is to scan the queue of ready tasks and to schedule one for execution.
- *Interrupt handlers:* The System/370 architecture supports a wide variety of interrupts. Any interrupt causes the current process to be suspended and control to pass to the appropriate handler routine.
- *Task management:* A task is essentially a process, as we have used that latter term. Task management is responsible for the creation and deletion of tasks, the control of their priorities, the management of task queues for serially reusable resources (e.g., I/O devices), and the synchronization of events.
- *Program management:* This module is responsible for linking together the necessary steps involved in the execution of a program. This module can be driven by JCL commands or in response to user requests to compile and execute a program.
- *Storage management:* This module is responsible for managing virtual and real memory.
- *System resource management:* This module is responsible for the allocation of resources among address spaces (processes).
- *Access methods:* An application program usually employs an access method in performing an I/O operation. An access method is an interface between an application program and the I/O supervisor. An access method relieves the application

program from the burden of writing channel programs, building various control blocks required by the I/O supervisor, and handling termination conditions.

- *I/O supervisor:* The I/O supervisor performs initiation and completion of the I/O operation at a hardware level. It issues the Start I/O instruction, which causes an I/O channel processor to execute an I/O program from main memory, and it also handles the interrupt arising from completion of I/O operations.

It is worth saying a few words here about the system resources manager (SRM). The SRM gives MVS a degree of sophistication unique among operating systems. No other mainframe operating system, and certainly no other type of operating system, can match the functions performed by SRM.

The concept of resource includes processor, real memory, and I/O channels. In performing resource allocation, SRM accumulates statistics pertaining to the use of processor, channel, and various key data structures. Its purpose is to provide optimum performance based on performance monitoring and analysis. The installation sets forth various performance objectives, and these serve as guidance to the SRM, which dynamically modifies installation and job performance characteristics based on system use. In turn, the SRM provides reports that enable the trained operator to refine the configuration and parameter settings to improve service to the user.

One example will give the flavor of SRM activity. Real memory is divided into equal-sized blocks called *frames*, of which there may be many thousands. Each frame can hold a block of virtual memory, which is referred to as a *page*. SRM receives control approximately 20 times per second and inspects each and every page frame. If the page has not been referenced or changed, a counter is incremented by 1. Over a period, SRM averages these numbers to determine the average number of seconds that a page frame in the system goes untouched. The system operator can review this quantity to determine the degree of "stress" on the system. By reducing the number of active jobs allowed on the system, this average can be kept high. One useful guideline is that this average should be kept above 2 minutes to avoid major performance problems (Johnson 1989). That may sound like a lot, but it isn't.

MVS TASKS

The MVS operating system makes use of a highly structured process environment. In MVS, virtual memory is broken up into large regions called *address spaces*. Roughly speaking, a single address space corresponds to a single application. Within that address space, a number of tasks may be generated. It is the MVS task that is the unit of dispatching.

Typically, a hundred or more address spaces exist concurrently, each of which may have many tasks. Thus, MVS is capable of, and often is, managing thousands of tasks concurrently.

Figure 3-2, based on a figure in Leban and Arnold (Leban 1984), gives an example of the way in which multiple tasks are generated within an address space. The application supports inquiry transactions from a number of terminals. The program is broken up into four modules: a main program, and three programs for the three types of inquiry: customer, order, and product. When the application is loaded into the system, the address space starts out with some memory devoted to MVS, and the main program loaded (Figure 3-2a). Then, a terminal user enters a customer inquiry. As a result, Main issues a request to create a new task to execute the customer module, and this is loaded in to the address space (Figure 3-2b). While this transaction is in progress, a second terminal issues an order request, and that module is loaded in as a separate task (Figure 3-2c). Next, while both transactions are still in progress, a third terminal issues an order inquiry. The code for the order module is already in the address space

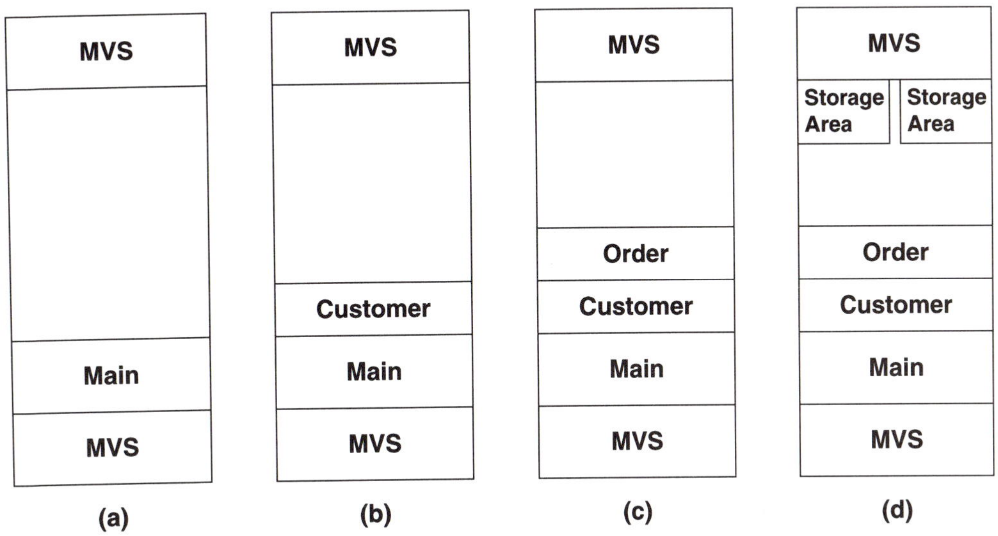

FIGURE 3-2 *Address Space Layout for an MVS Application*

and can be used by more than one task. However, each task will need its own private region of memory for local variables and stack processing, as illustrated in Figure 3-2d.

Explicitly, MVS makes use of only three task states: Ready, Active (running), and Waiting. However, an entire address space may be swapped out to secondary storage. Thus, all the tasks of that address space are suspended, as we have used that term.

Each task is represented by a task control block (TCB). In addition, there is another type of dispatchable entity, the service request. The *service request* is a "system task," of which there are two kinds. Some system tasks provide services to a specific application and are executed in the address space of that application; others are involved in interaddress space operations and do not execute in any user address space but, rather, in the system's reserved address space. These system tasks, collectively, can be considered the kernel of the MVS operating system. Each system task has its own service request block (SRB), and the dispatcher chooses among all ready SRBs and TCBs when it is time to dispatch the next task.

Thus, two apparently modern concepts, that of threads within a process and that of the operating system as a set of processes are found, in their own way, in MVS.

Task-Related Control Structures

Table 3.1 lists the major control structures that MVS uses to manage user tasks and system tasks. These structures collectively encompass much of what we have referred to as process control blocks. Global service request blocks are used to manage system tasks that do not execute within a user address space. The remaining structures are all concerned with address space management. The address space control block (ASCB) and address space extension block (ASXB) contain information about address spaces. The distinction is that the ASCB information is needed by MVS when it is executing in the system's reserved address space, whereas the ASXB contains additional information that is needed only when MVS is dealing

TABLE 3.1
MVS Process Control Structures

Global Service Request Block (SRB)	Represents a system task that is independent of any user address space. Includes: • Address of the ASCB to which the routine will be dispatched • Entry point to routine • Address of a parameter list to be passed to routine • Priority level
Address Space Control Block (ASCB)	Contains system-wide information about an address space. That is, this is information about an address space that is needed by MVS when not executing within a particular user address space. Information includes: • Pointers to create queues of ASCBs • Whether the address space is swapped-out • Dispatching priority • Real and virtual memory allocated to this address space • Number of Ready TCBs in this address space • Pointer to ASXB
Address Space Extension Block (ASXB)	Contains information about an address space not of global interest. Includes: • Number of TCBs in this address space • Pointer to TCB dispatching queue for this address space • Pointer to local SRB dispatching queue for this address space • Pointer to interrupt handler save area
Local Service Request Block (SRB)	Represents a system task that is executed within a particular user address space. Includes: • Address of the ASCB to which the routine will be dispatched • Entry point to routine • Address of a parameter list to be passed to routine • Priority level
Task Control Block (TCB)	Represents a user program in execution. Contains information needed for managing a task within an address space. Includes: • Processor status information • Pointers to programs that are part of this task

with and executing in a specific user address space. Finally, local SRBs and TCBs contain information about dispatchable entities within an address space.

Figure 3-3 shows how these structures are organized and suggests the dispatching discipline observed by MVS. Global SRBs are maintained in a queue of descending priority in the system queue area, which is a region of main memory that cannot be swapped. Thus, global SRBs are always available in main memory. When a processor is available, MVS first searches this queue for a Ready SRB. If none are found, MVS then looks for an address space that has at least one Ready TCB or SRB. For this purpose, a queue of ASCBs is maintained in the system queue area. Each address space is assigned an overall priority level; hence, the ASCBs can be arranged in descending priority.

Once an address space is selected, MVS can work with the structures in that address space, referred to as the local system queue area. MVS selects the highest-priority SRB, or failing that, the highest-priority TCB to dispatch. In this example, the TCB queue structure for a batch job is shown. It consists of the following tasks:

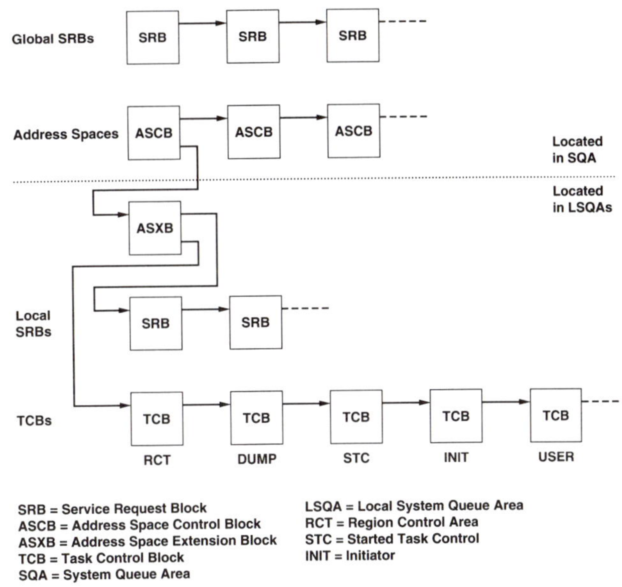

FIGURE 3-3 *MVS Dispatcher Queues (Paans 1986)*

- *Region control task:* Responsible for managing this address space on behalf of all the tasks executing in it.
- *Dump:* Responsible for dumping the address space if the address space terminates abnormally.
- *Started control task:* The TCB for the program that starts the address space.
- *Initiator:* Responsible for loading a stream of batch jobs.
- *User task:* The application itself consists of one or more user tasks.

The advantage of splitting the control information into global and local is that as much information as possible about an address space can be swapped out with the address space, thus conserving main memory.

MVS RESOURCE ALLOCATION

MVS provides two facilities for enforcing mutual exclusion with respect to the use of resources: enqueing and locking. Enqueing is concerned with user-controlled resources such as files, whereas locking is concerned with MVS system resources.

ENQUE

The ENQUE facility is used to regulate access to shared data resources. The requested resource may be an entire disk volume, one or more files, records within a file, program control blocks, or any work areas within main storage. A process (an address space) requests shared control if the resource is to be read only, and exclusive control if the data might be modified. Table 3.2 indicates the rules used by MVS to determine the action when an ENQUE request is issued. In essence, the scheme conforms to the readers/writers model, giving priority to writers.

TABLE 3.2 Decision Table for MVS ENQUE Facility

	Resource Status at Time of Request		
Request Type	Free	Shared	Exclusive
Shared	Honored	Honored unless exclusive request is queued	Queued
Exclusive	Honored	Queued	Queued

In addition to an outright request for access, the user may specify that the availability of the resource is to be tested but that control of the resource is not requested, or the user may specify that control of the resource is to be assigned to the requester only if the resource is immediately available. These options may be used to prevent deadlock or to notify the operator that there is a problem.

Locks

Locks enforce mutual exclusion for access to system resources by MVS routines. A lock is simply an area in common virtual storage, and is usually kept permanently in main memory. It contains bits to indicate whether the lock is in use and, if so, who owns the resource. Locks come in two classes and two types. The classes are:

- *Global:* Across all address spaces
- *Local:* Across all tasks in a single address space

The types are:

- *Spin:* The processor executes a test-and-set type of instruction waiting for the lock; this is busy-waiting.
- *Suspend:* The task waiting is suspended.

Spin locks are used for critical sections that run for only a short time. A suspend lock implies a long critical section and the profitability of suspending a denied process and then dispatching another process. Local locks are always suspend locks, whereas there are both spin and suspend global locks.

To prevent deadlocks, locks are arranged in a hierarchy; this is the strategy discussed earlier to prevent the circular-wait condition. A processor may request only locks higher in the hierarchy than locks it currently holds.

A detailed, though somewhat dated, discussion of MVS locks can be found in (Katzan 1984).

EXAMPLES OF MEMORY MANAGEMENT (SYSTEM/370 AND MVS)

Address Space Structure

The IBM System/370 architecture uses a two level memory structure and refers to the two levels as segments and pages, although the segmentation approach lacks many of the features described earlier. For the basic 370 architecture, the page size may be either 2KB or 4KB, and the segment size is fixed at either 64KB or 1MB. For the 370/XA and 370/ESA architectures, the page size is 4KB and the segment size is 1MB. In this discussion, we refer primarily to the XA-ESA structure.

Figure 3-4a depicts the format for a virtual address. The byte index specifies one of 4KB within a page; the page index specifies one of 256 pages within a segment; and the segment index identifies one of 2048 user-visible segments. Thus, the user sees a virtual address space of 2^{31} bytes (2GB) of virtual storage.

Figure 3-5 shows the evolution of address space structures for the 370 architecture. The original 370 family, which supported the original MVS operating system, employed 24-bit

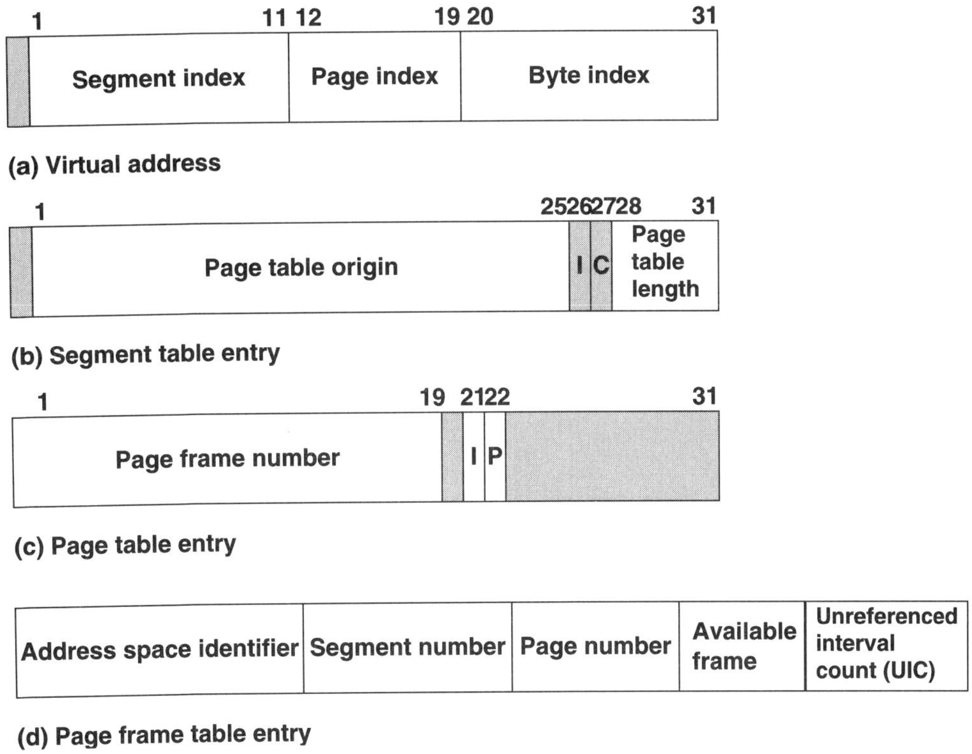

FIGURE 3-4 *IBM System 370/XA and 370/ESA Memory Management Formats*

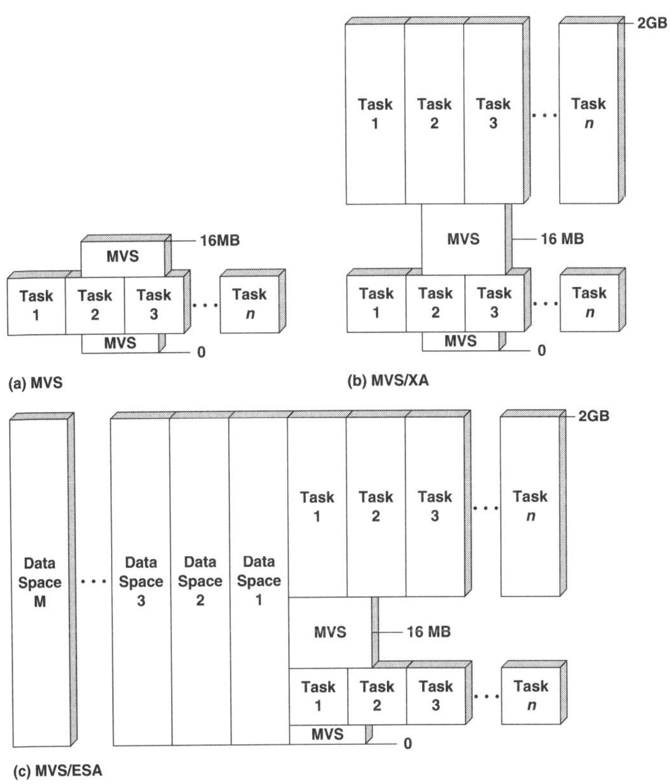

FIGURE 3-5 *MVS Address Space Structure*

addresses, allowing a virtual address space of 16MB. Any job or application could be assigned up to the 16MB of virtual memory. Part of the address space is reserved for MVS programs and data structures. Within a given address space, one or more tasks may be activated. As we mentioned earlier, this corresponds to the concept of multiple threads within a single process.

Eventually, IBM discovered that for two reasons the 24-bit address structure was inadequate for many customers and applications. First, applications were becoming more complex and involved the use of larger data structures. And second, the growth in MVS was such that it came to occupy anywhere from one-half to three-fourths of the user's virtual address space.[1] The result was that available virtual address space was shrinking as user requirements were expanding! Thus, IBM modified the basic architecture to provide extended addressing (XA). The resulting architecture is called System 370/XA, which supports MVS/XA. This architecture supports the 31-bit address scheme depicted in Figure 3-4a. Each application or job now has 2GB of virtual address space available. This space is divided into two regions divided by the 16MB line. Below this line, the space dedicated to MVS remains, and the remainder is available for one or more programs. Above this line, some additional space is also reserved for MVS, with the remainder available for programs whose requirements exceed the amount available below the line. Thus, a single task may employ user space above and below the line.

The latest version of the System 370 architecture and the corresponding MVS are referred to as Enterprise System Architecture (ESA) (Plambeck 1989), which represents a further step by IBM to satisfy the seemingly insatiable need for virtual storage by large-scale applications. System 370/ESA employs the same addressing structure as XA by allowing an address space of 2GB for MVS support programs and data, and for user programs. In addition, a program may address up to 15 additional 2GB address spaces for data only, giving a total virtual address space for a single application of 16 terabytes (TB) (244 bytes).

Hardware and Control Structures

To manage storage, segment and page tables are used. There is one segment table for each virtual address space. Thus, each virtual address space contains a number of segments, with one entry in the segment table per segment.

The format for a segment table entry is shown in Figure 3-4b. The 25-bit page table origin points to the page table for that segment; six 0 bits are appended to the 25-bit field to form a 31-bit real address. The page table length indicates the number of entries in the page table (= 16 × PTL). The segment-invalid (I) bit is set when some malfunction or unrecoverable error occurs and indicates that the segment is unavailable. The common (C) bit indicates whether this segment is private to an address space or is shared by several address spaces. In the latter case, segment and page table entries relating to this segment may remain in the translation lookaside buffer after this address space is swapped out.

Each page table entry (Figure 3-4c) includes an invalid (I) bit that indicates whether the corresponding page is in real memory. If it is, the page frame number gives the location of the page; 12 bits are appended to the right of this number to form the real address. The protection (P) bit, when set, prevents Writes but allows Reads to the corresponding page.

For 370/XA, address translation proceeds. In addition, a translation lookaside buffer holds recently referenced segment and page table entries.

For 370/ESA, additional logic is needed. In the 370 machine instruction set, virtual memory references are made through the general-purpose registers (GPR). Associated with each of the 370's 16 general-purpose 32-bit registers is an access register (AR). When a GPR is used as a base register for an operand location, the corresponding AR specifies the address space in which the operand is located. Thus, it is possible for a different virtual address space to be associated with each GPR. By changing the contents of an AR, many different virtual address spaces may be accessed.

The ESA option is activated by a bit in the program status word. When it is in use, two sorts of translation are needed to calculate a real address. Figure 3-6 illustrates the mechanism. The example makes use of a 370 instruction type that is used for indexing. The first operand is a register. The second operand is a virtual location referenced by the sum of a 12-bit displacement plus the contents of a base register and an index register, both of which are from the pool of general-purpose registers. The 4-bit base register designation (B2) is also used to refer to one of 16 address space registers. The contents of that address space register is used as input to a translation process involving several tables that results in the real address of the segment table for a particular address space. This table, plus the virtual address, serve as input to the dynamic address translation mechanism that ultimately yields the real address.

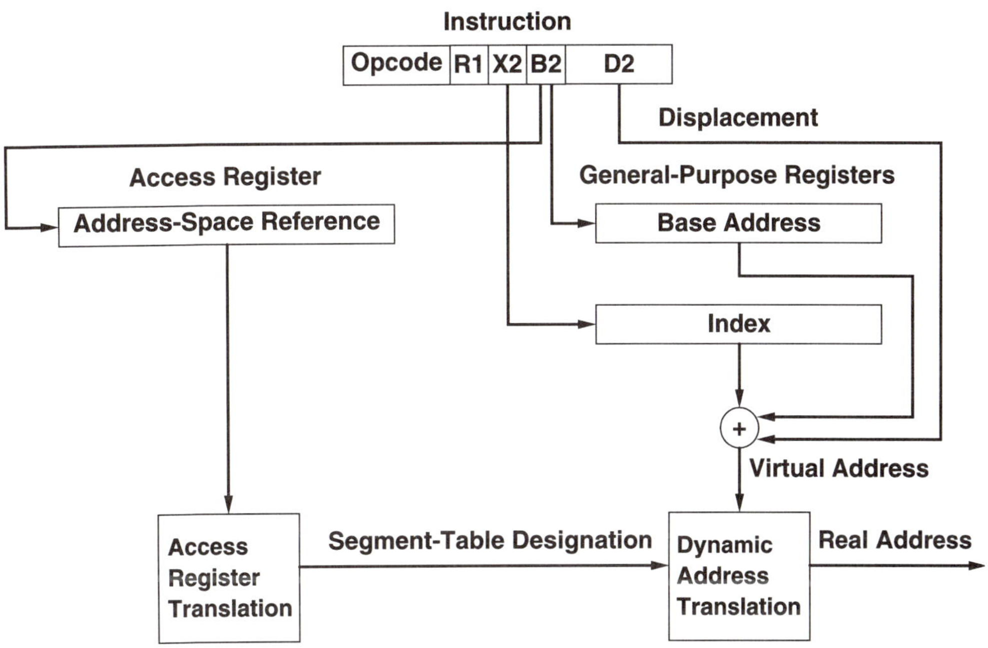

FIGURE 3-6 *370/ESA Address Translation (Plambeck 1989)*

Operating-System Considerations

MVS makes use of the hardware features just described for memory management. MVS employs a global page replacement strategy. The system maintains a list of page frames that are available. When a new page must be brought in, a page frame from this list is used. When the number of available frames drops below a certain threshold, the operating system performs a page-stealing operation by converting a number of active pages to available pages. The decision to steal a particular page is based on the activity history of each page currently residing in a real storage frame. Pages that have not been accessed for a relatively long time are good candidates for page stealing. In essence, a least-recently-used policy is followed.

To implement this policy, MVS makes use of two sources of information: a storage key associated with each frame, and a page frame table. The storage key is a control field associated with each frame of real memory. Two bits of that key that are relevant for page replacement are the reference bit and the change bit. The reference bit is set to 1 when any address within the frame is accessed for Read or Write, and it is set to 0 when a new page is loaded into the frame. The change bit is set to 1 when a Write operation is performed on any location within the frame. The page frame table contains an entry for each frame of real memory. Each entry contains the following fields (Figure 3-4d):

- *Address space identifier:* Identifies the owner address space for that frame.
- *Segment number, page number:* Virtual page occupying this frame.
- *Available frame:* Indicates whether the frame is available or occupied.
- *Unreferenced interval count (UIC):* Indicates how long it has been since a program referenced this frame.

Once per second, MVS checks the reference bit for every single frame in real memory. If the reference bit is not on (the frame has not been referenced), the system increments the UIC for that frame. If the reference bit is on, MVS resets the reference bit and sets UIC to 0. When it is necessary to steal pages, MVS selects those frames with the longest UIC for replacement. This replacement policy can be modified by a technique known as *storage isolation*, which requires that each address space maintain a specified minimum number of pages. Thus, a page frame may not be stolen from an address space if stealing it causes the number of its pages to fall below the minimum for that address space.

MULTIPROCESSOR AND REAL-TIME SCHEDULING WITH MVS

Recall that the process environment of MVS consists of the following controllable entities (see Figure 3-3):

- *Global-service request block (global SRB):* Used to manage a system task that does not execute within a user address space. A global SRB represents a system task involved in interaddress space operations.
- *Address space control block (ASCB) and address space extension block (ASXB):* Used to manage an address space that corresponds roughly to a single application or job. The work within each address space consists of a set of system tasks and users' tasks.
- *Service request block (SRB):* Used to manage a system task that does execute within a user address space, which corresponds to a service request issued by one of the tasks in the address space.
- *Task control block (TCB):* Represents one of the tasks within an address space.

Tasks represented by SRBs are nonpreemptive; if such a task is interrupted, it receives control after the interruption has been processed. In contrast, a task controlled by a TCB is preemptive. If it is interrupted, control passes to the dispatcher when the interruption handling completes; the dispatcher may then select some other task to run.

Global SRBs are maintained in a queue of descending priority in the system queue area, which is a region of main memory that cannot be swapped. Thus, global SRBs are always available in main memory. When a processor is available, MVS first searches this queue for a ready SRB. If none are found, MVS then looks for an address space that has at least one ready TCB or SRB. For this purpose, a queue of ASCBs is maintained in the system queue area. Each address space is assigned an overall priority level; hence, the ASCBs can be arranged in descending priority. Once an address space is selected, MVS can work with the structures in that address space, which is referred to as the local system queue area. MVS selects the highest-priority SRB, or failing that, the highest-priority TCB to dispatch.

Dispatching priorities in MVS exist at 256 levels, and GSRBs are dispatched above the highest defined level. Within a given dispatching priority level, address spaces are in a FCFS queue. Dispatching priorities are organized into sets, or bands, of 16 levels each. Typically, an address space is assigned to a band and stays within that band. Within each band, the upper 6 levels are individually specifiable as *fixed priorities*, and the lower 10 levels form a *mean-time-to-wait (MTTW) group*. Within the MTTW group, address space priorities are determined by the average time between waits in each address space. Those waits of shorter intervals (usually for I/O completion) have higher priorities; those with long stretches of CPU use without intervening I/O activity have lower priorities.

When an address space is created, it is assigned to a *performance group*, which dictates the priority that that address space will enjoy. An address space in a performance group is considered to go through a sequence of *performance periods*. Performance periods allow a transaction, or any job, to be managed differently as it ages. The measure of that aging is accumulated service, and the means of changing management parameters is the passage from one performance period to the next. When a performance group is defined, one or more performance periods can be specified. Each performance period is characterized by a duration and a priority. An address space begins in period 1 and remains at the priority level specified for that period until it has exhausted the processing time for that period. Then it moves to a lower priority in period 2 for the duration of that period. The duration in each performance period is specified in terms of service units. A service unit is an interval of CPU time differing by basic CPU model, number of processors, and operating-system environment; it ranges between 1 and 11 msec of processor time.

Thus, the overall workload is broken down into performance groups—first, on the basis of similar types (transaction, batch, subsystem) or address spaces, and second, according to priorities established for the various workload constituents. Then, within an address space, a breakdown is established on the basis of expected duration of transactions. For example, a time-sharing address space might be defined as follows:

- Period 1: Highest priority and a duration of 1000 service units
- Period 2: Next highest priority and a duration of 4000 service units
- Period 3: Lowest priority and unlimited duration

With this structure, we would expect trivial commands to complete within period 1, giving the best service with highest probability of access to the system. Longer commands would exhaust the allocation in period 1 and run to completion in period 2, still giving reasonably good service. The commands in this category would be somewhat more complex than the shortest commands and fewer of these commands would be running concurrently. Finally, the longest commands, which might trigger a compile or an application program, would run at still lower service.

I/O MANAGEMENT AND DISK SCHEDULING WITH MVS

MVS is designed to provide a layered I/O facility that allows programmers to ignore the many details of I/O operations or to bypass or add to some phases of the I/O operation. Figure 3-7 illustrates the logical structure of I/O within MVS. A typical I/O sequence involves the following steps:

1. The user program begins an I/O operation by issuing an OPEN macro instruction for a target I/O device and then requesting input or output by using a macro such as GET, PUT, READ, or WRITE. An I/O macro instruction invokes an operating-system service known as an **access method**. The access method interprets the command and determines which system resources are required. The user could bypass the access method, but this would require the user program to deal with the I/O operation in much greater detail and at a finer-grained level of control.

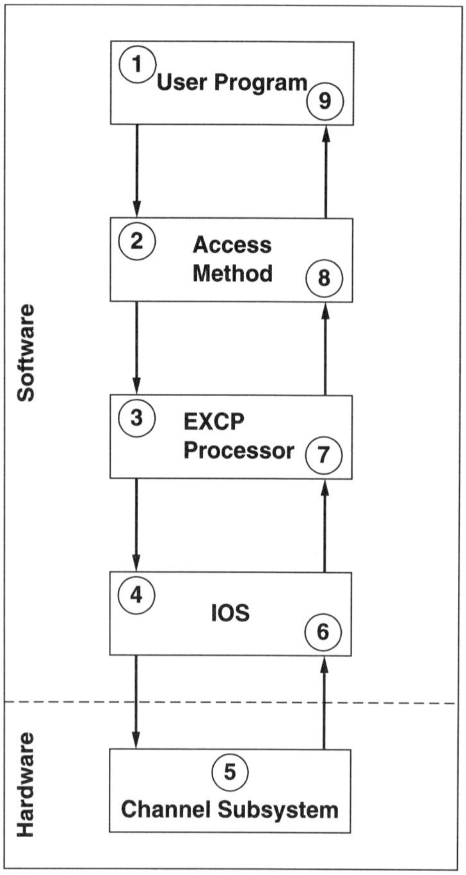

FIGURE 3-7 *MVS I/O Services*

2. MVS access methods fall into three categories: conventional access methods, telecommunications access methods, and the virtual storage access method (VSAM). Table 3.3 summarizes the access methods available with MVS. With an access method, the program is insulated from I/O details and need be concerned only with using the proper access method to meet its needs.
3. To request the movement of data, either the access method or the user program presents information about the operation to the EXCP (execute channel program) processor. EXCP translates this information into a format understandable to the channel subsystem and invokes the I/O supervisor (IOS). Essentially, EXCP is a program that creates an I/O supervisor block (IOSB) for use by the IOS. The IOSB contains the instructions to the IOS and the main memory addresses involved in the transfer.
4. IOS places the request for I/O on the queue for the chosen I/O device and initiates the channel subsystem. The channel subsystem is initiated by issuing a start I/O command that references the channel program in main memory. The CPU is now free to do other work until the channel subsystem indicates that the I/O operation has completed.
5. The channel subsystem is a separate processor that can read and execute channel commands, or instructions, in main memory. It selects the best channel path for data transmission between main memory and the device, and controls the movement of data. When I/O is completed, the subsystem issues an interrupt to the CPU.

TABLE 3.3
MVS Access Methods

Conventional Access Methods

Basic Sequential Access Method (BSAM)
Records in a file are sequentially organized. BSAM provides the ability to read and write only physical records and only in sequence.

Queued Sequential Access Method (QSAM)
Records in a file are sequentially organized. With QSAM, logical records can be grouped together and stored in larger physical records (blocks). QSAM handles the blocking and deblocking of logical records and performs buffered I/O.

Basic Direct Access Method (BDAM)
BDAM allows input and output of individual blocks by specifying the physical track and record number.

Indexed Sequential Access Method (ISAM)
One or more fields, called keys, in a record uniquely identify that record. Records can be accessed either directly, by supplying a key, or sequentially in key order.

Basic Partitioned Access Method (BPAM)
The file is grouped into independent collections of records, called members. All the records in a member have the same attributes, such as logical record length and block size. A directory holds the name and location of each member. BPAM maintains and accesses the directory. Once a member is located by using BPAM, records are accessed by using BSAM or QSAM.

Virtual Storage Access Methods

Virtual Storage Access Method (VSAM)
This access method is specifically designed to take advantage of the virtual memory hardware and MVS virtual memory software. It supports both direct and sequential access and provides greater performance and flexibility than other file access methods.

Telecommunication Access Methods

Basic Telecommunication Access Method (BTAM)
BTAM provides a simple capability for transmitting data in the form of messages to and from remote terminals.

Telecommunication Access Method (TCAM)
Supports a wider variety of terminals than BTAM. Allows an application to perform its own message routing, message editing, and error checking.

Virtual Telecommunication Access Method (VTAM)
VTAM is the access method used to support the system network architecture (SNA). It provides a powerful terminal-handling capacity in the context of a full communications architecture.

6. IOS evaluates the interrupt and returns control to EXCP.
7. EXCP updates various tables to indicate the result of the I/O operation and passes control to the dispatcher.
8. The dispatcher reactivates the access method to respond to the completion of the I/O request.
9. The access method returns control to the user program, together with any required status information.

Much of the I/O activity involves only the channel subsystem and not the main processor. Thus, the MVS I/O architecture provides a facility that is both powerful and efficient.

Notes

[1] This was so even though much of MVS is not located in the user's virtual address space

SECTION

4

UNIX AND LINUX

The UNIX System

Although operating-system concepts can be considered in purely theoretical terms, it is often useful to see how they are implemented in practice. This chapter presents an in-depth examination of the 4.3BSD operating system, a version of UNIX, as an example of the various concepts presented in this book. By examining a complete, real system, we can see how the various concepts discussed in this book relate both to one another and to practice. We consider first a brief history of UNIX, and present the system's user and programmer interfaces. Then, we discuss the internal data structures and algorithms used by the UNIX kernel to support the user-programmer interface.

HISTORY

The first version of UNIX was developed in 1969 by Ken Thompson of the Research Group at Bell Laboratories to use an otherwise idle PDP-7. He was soon joined by Dennis Ritchie. Thompson, Ritchie, and other members of the Research Group produced the early versions of UNIX.

Ritchie had previously worked on the MULTICS project, and MULTICS had a strong influence on the newer operating system. Even the name *UNIX* is merely a pun on *MULTICS*. The basic organization of the file system, the idea of the command interpreter (the shell) as a user process, the use of a separate process for each command, the original line-editing characters (# to erase the last character and @ to erase the entire line), and numerous other features came directly from MULTICS. Ideas from various other operating systems, such as from MIT's CTSS and the XDS-940 system, were also used.

Ritchie and Thompson worked quietly on UNIX for many years. Their work on the first version allowed them to move it to a PDP-11/20, for a second version. A third version resulted from their rewriting most of the operating system in the systems-programming language C, instead of the previously used assembly language. C was developed at Bell Laboratories to support UNIX. UNIX was also moved to larger PDP-11 models, such as the 11/45 and 11/70. Multiprogramming and other enhancements were added when it was rewritten in C and moved to systems (such as the 11/45) that had hardware support for multiprogramming.

As UNIX developed, it became widely used within Bell Laboratories and gradually spread to a few universities. The first version widely available outside Bell Laboratories was

Version 6, released in 1976. (The version number for early UNIX systems corresponds to the edition number of the *UNIX Programmer's Manual* that was current when the distribution was made; the code and the manuals were revised independently.)

In 1978, Version 7 was distributed. This UNIX system ran on the PDP-11/70 and the Interdata 8/32, and is the ancestor of most modern UNIX systems. In particular, it was soon ported to other PDP-11 models and to the VAX computer line. The version available on the VAX was known as 32V. Research has continued since then.

After the distribution of Version 7 in 1978, the UNIX Support Group (USG) assumed administrative control and responsibility from the Research Group for distributions of UNIX within AT&T, the parent organization for Bell Laboratories. UNIX was becoming a product, rather than simply a research tool. The Research Group has continued to develop their own version of UNIX, however, to support their own internal computing. Next came Version 8, which included a facility called the *stream I/O system* that allows flexible configuration of kernel IPC modules. It also contained RFS, a remote file system similar to Sun's NFS. Next came Versions 9 and 10 (the latter version, released in 1989, is available only within Bell Laboratories).

USG mainly provided support for UNIX within AT&T. The first external distribution from USG was System III, in 1982. System III incorporated features of Version 7, and 32V, and also of several UNIX systems developed by groups other than Research. Features of UNIX/RT, a real-time UNIX system, as well as numerous portions of the Programmer's Work Bench (PWB) software tools package were included in System III.

USG released System V in 1983; it is largely derived from System III. The divestiture of the various Bell operating companies from AT&T has left AT&T in a position to market System V aggressively. USG was restructured as the UNIX System Development Laboratory (USDL), which released UNIX System V Release 2 (V.2) in 1984. UNIX System V Release 2, Version 4 (V.2.4) added a new implementation of virtual memory with copy-on-write paging and shared memory. USDL was in turn replaced by AT&T Information Systems (ATTIS), which distributed System V Release 3 (V.3) in 1987. V.3 adapts the V8 implementation of the stream I/O system and makes it available as *STREAMS*. It also includes RFS, an NFS-like remote file system.

The small size, modularity, and clean design of early UNIX systems led to UNIX-based work at numerous other computer-science organizations, such as at Rand, BBN, the University of Illinois, Harvard, Purdue, and even DEC. The most influential of the non-Bell Laboratories and non-AT&T UNIX development groups, however, has been the University of California at Berkeley.

The first Berkeley VAX UNIX work was the addition in 1978 of virtual memory, demand paging, and page replacement to 32V; this work was done by Bill Joy and Ozalp Babaoglu to produce 3BSD UNIX. This version was the first implementation of any of these facilities on any UNIX system. The large virtual-memory space of 3BSD allowed the development of very large programs, such as Berkeley's own Franz LISP. The memory-management work convinced the Defense Advanced Research Projects Agency (DARPA) to fund Berkeley for the development of a standard UNIX system for government use; 4BSD UNIX was the result.

The 4BSD work for DARPA was guided by a steering committee that included many notable people from the UNIX and networking communities. One of the goals of this project was to provide support for the DARPA Internet networking protocols (TCP/IP). This support was provided in a general manner. It is possible in 4.2BSD to communicate uniformly among diverse network facilities, including local-area networks (such as Ethernets and token rings) and wide-area networks (such as NSFNET). This implementation was the most important reason for the current popularity of these protocols. It was used as the basis for the implementations of many vendors of UNIX computer systems, and even other operating systems. It permitted the Internet to grow from 60 connected networks in 1984 to more than 8000 networks and an estimated 10 million users in 1993.

In addition, Berkeley adapted many features from contemporary operating systems to improve the design and implementation of UNIX. Many of the terminal line-editing functions of the TENEX (TOPS-20) operating system were provided by a new terminal driver. A new user interface (the C Shell), a new text editor (ex/vi), compilers for Pascal and LISP, and many new systems programs were written at Berkeley. For 4.2BSD, certain efficiency improvements were inspired by the VMS operating system.

UNIX software from Berkeley is released in *Berkeley Software Distributions*. It is convenient to refer to the Berkeley VAX UNIX systems following 3BSD as 4BSD, although there were actually several specific releases, most notably 4.1BSD and 4.2BSD. The generic numbers BSD and 4BSD are used for the PDP-11 and VAX distributions of Berkeley UNIX. 4.2BSD, first distributed in 1983, was the culmination of the original Berkeley DARPA UNIX project. 2.9BSD is the equivalent version for PDP-11 systems.

In 1986, 4.3BSD was released. It was so similar to 4.2BSD that its manuals described 4.2BSD more comprehensively than the 4.2BSD manuals did. It did include numerous internal changes, however, including bug fixes and performance improvements. Some new facilities also were added, including support for the Xerox Network System protocols.

4.3BSD Tahoe was the next version, released in 1988. It included various new developments, such as improved networking congestion control and TCP/IP performance. Also, disk configurations were separated from the device drivers, and are now read off the disks themselves. Expanded time-zone support is also included. 4.3BSD Tahoe was actually developed on and for the CCI Tahoe system (Computer Console, Inc., Power 6 computer), rather than for the usual VAX base. The corresponding PDP-11 release is 2.10.lBSD, which is distributed by the USENIX Association, which also publishes the 4.3BSD manuals. The 4.32BSD Reno release saw the inclusion of an implementation of ISO/OSI networking.

The last Berkeley release, 4.4BSD, was finalized in June of 1993. It includes new X.25 networking support, and POSIX standard compliance. It also has a radically new file system organization, with a new virtual file system interface and support for *stackable* file systems, allowing file systems to be layered on top of each other for easy inclusion of new features. An implementation of NFS is also included in the release, as is a new log-based file system. The 4.4BSD virtual memory system is derived from Mach. Several other changes, such as enhanced security and improved kernel structure, are also included. With the release of version 4.4, Berkeley has halted its research efforts.

4BSD was the operating system of choice for VAXes from its initial release (1979) until the release of Ultrix, DEC's BSD implementation. 4BSD is still the best choice for many research and networking installations. Many organizations would buy a 32V license and order 4BSD from Berkeley without even bothering to get a 32V tape.

The current set of UNIX operating systems is not limited to those by Bell Laboratories and Berkeley, however. Sun Microsystems helped popularize the BSD flavor of UNIX by shipping it on their workstations. As UNIX has grown in popularity, it has been moved to many different computers and computer systems. A wide variety of UNIX, and UNIX-like, operating systems have been created. DEC supports its UNIX (called Ultrix) on its workstations and is replacing Ultrix with another UNIX-derived operating system, OSF/1; Microsoft rewrote UNIX for the Intel 8088 family and called it XENIX, and its new Windows NT operating system is heavily influenced by UNIX; IBM has UNIX (AIX) on its PCs, workstations, and mainframes. In fact, UNIX is available on almost all general-purpose computers; it runs on personal computers, workstations, minicomputers, mainframes, and supercomputers, from Apple Macintosh IIs to Cray IIs. Because of its wide availability, it is used in environments ranging from academic to military to manufacturing process control. Most of these systems are based on Version 7, System III, 4.2BSD, or System V.

The wide popularity of UNIX with computer vendors has made UNIX the most portable of operating systems, and has made it possible for users to expect a UNIX environment independent of any specific computer manufacturer. But the large number of implementations of the system has led to remarkable variation in the programming and user interfaces distributed by the vendors. For true vendor independence, application-program developers need consistent interfaces. Such interfaces would allow all "UNIX" applications to run on all UNIX systems, which is certainly not the current situation. This issue has become important as UNIX has become the preferred program-development platform for applications ranging from databases to graphics and networking, and has led to a strong market demand for UNIX standards.

There are several standardization projects underway, starting with the */usr/group 1984 Standard* sponsored by the UniForum industry user's group. Since then, many official standards bodies have continued the effort, including IEEE and ISO (the POSIX standard). The X/Open Group international consortium completed XPG3, a Common Application Environment, which subsumes the IEEE interface standard. Unfortunately, XPG3 is based on a draft of the ANSI C standard, rather than the final specification, and therefore needs to be redone. The XPG4 is due out in 1993. In 1989, the ANSI standards body standardized the C programming language, producing an ANSI C specification that vendors were quick to adopt. As these projects continue, the variant flavors of UNIX will converge and there will be one programming interface to UNIX, allowing UNIX to become even more popular. There are in fact two separate sets of powerful UNIX vendors working on this problem: the AT&T-guided UNIX International (UI) and the Open Software Foundation (OSF) have both agreed to follow the POSIX standard. Recently, many of the vendors involved in those two groups have agreed on further standardization (the COSE agreement) on the Motif window environment, and ONC+ (which includes Sun RPC and NFS) and DCE network facilities (which includes AFS and an RPC package).

AT&T replaced its ATTIS group in 1989 with the UNIX Software Organization (USO), which shipped the first merged UNIX, System V Release 4. This system combines features from System V, 4.3BSD, and Sun's SunOS, including long file names, the Berkeley file system, virtual memory management, symbolic links, multiple access groups, job control, and reliable signals; it also conforms to the published POSIX standard, POSIX.1. After USO produced SVR4, it became an independent AT&T subsidiary named Unix System Laboratories (USL); in 1993, it was purchased by Novell, Inc.

Figure 4-1 summarizes the relationships among the various versions of UNIX.

The UNIX system has grown from a personal project of two Bell Laboratories employees to an operating system being defined by multinational standardization bodies. Yet this system is still of interest to academia. We believe that UNIX has become and will remain an important part of operating-system theory and practice. UNIX is an excellent vehicle for academic study. For example, the Tunis operating system, the Xinu operating system, and the Minix operating system are based on the concepts of UNIX, but were developed explicitly for classroom study. There is a plethora of ongoing UNIX-related research systems, including Mach, Chorus, Comandos, and Roisin. The original developers, Ritchie and Thompson, were honored in 1983 by the Association for Computing Machinery Turing award for their work on UNIX

The specific UNIX version used in this chapter is the VAX version of 4.3BSD. This system is used because it implements many interesting operating-system concepts, such as demand paging with clustering, and networking. It has also been influential in other UNIX systems, in standards, and in networking developments. The VAX implementation is used because 4.3BSD was developed on the VAX and that machine still represents a convenient point of reference, despite the recent proliferation of implementations on other hardware (such as the Motorola 68040 and 88000, the Intel i486, the Sun SPARC, DEC Alpha, HP Precision, and the MIPS R4000 CPUs).

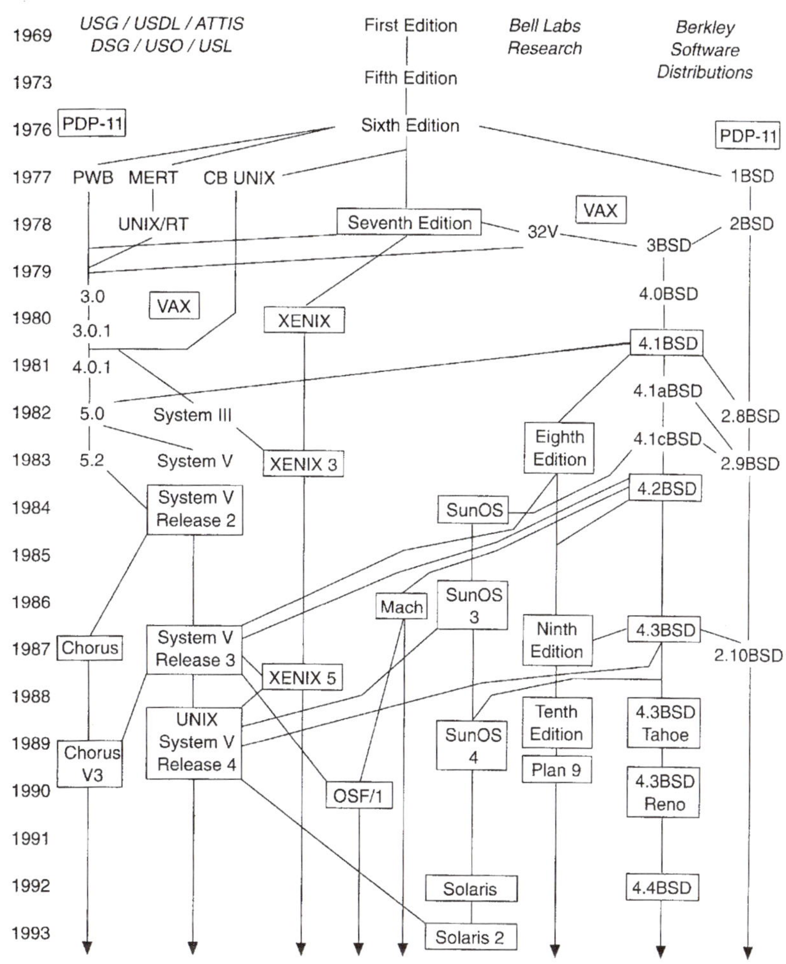

FIGURE 4-1 *History of UNIX Versions*

DESIGN PRINCIPLES

UNIX was designed to be a time-sharing system. The standard user interface (the shell) is simple and can be replaced by another, if desired. The file system is a multilevel tree, which allows users to create their own subdirectories. Each user data file is simply a sequence of bytes.

Disk files and I/O devices are treated as similarly as possible. Thus, device dependencies and peculiarities are kept in the kernel as much as possible; even in the kernel, most of them are confined to the device drivers.

UNIX supports multiple processes. A process can easily create new processes. CPU scheduling is a simple priority algorithm. 4.3BSD uses demand paging as a mechanism to support memory-management and CPU-scheduling decisions. Swapping is used if a system is suffering from excess paging.

Because UNIX was originated first by one programmer, Ken Thompson, and then by another, Dennis Ritchie, as a system for their own convenience, it was small enough to understand. Most of the algorithms were selected for *simplicity*, not for speed or sophistication. The intent was to have the kernel and libraries provide a small set of facilities that was sufficiently powerful to allow a person to build a more complex system if one were needed. UNIX's clean design has resulted in many imitations and modifications.

Although the designers of UNIX had a significant amount of knowledge about other operating systems, UNIX had no elaborate design spelled out before its implementation. This flexibility appears to have been one of the key factors in the development of the system. Some design principles were involved, however, even though they were not made explicit at the outset.

The UNIX system was designed by programmers for programmers. Thus, it has always been interactive, and facilities for program development have always been a high priority. Such facilities include the program *make* (which can be used to check to see which of a collection of source files for a program need to be compiled, and then to do the compiling) and the *Source Code Control System (SCCS)* (which is used to keep successive versions of files available without having to store the entire contents of each step).

The operating system is written mostly in C, which was developed to support UNIX, since neither Thompson nor Ritchie enjoyed programming in assembly language. The avoidance of assembly language was also necessary because of the uncertainty about the machine or machines on which UNIX would be run. It has greatly simplified the problems of moving UNIX from one hardware system to another.

From the beginning, UNIX development systems have had all the UNIX sources available on-line, and the developers have used the systems under development as their primary systems. This pattern of development has greatly facilitated the discovery of deficiencies and their fixes, as well as of new possibilities and their implementations. It has also encouraged the plethora of UNIX variants existing today, but the benefits have outweighed the disadvantages: if something is broken, it can be fixed at a local site; there is no need to wait for the next release of the system. Such fixes, as well as new facilities, may be incorporated into later distributions.

The size constraints of the PDP-11 (and earlier computers used for UNIX) have forced a certain elegance. Where other systems have elaborate algorithms for dealing with pathological conditions, UNIX just does a controlled crash called *panic*. Instead of attempting to cure such conditions, UNIX tries to prevent them. Where other systems would use brute force or macro-expansion, UNIX mostly has had to develop more subtle, or at least simpler, approaches.

These early strengths of UNIX produced much of its popularity, which in turn produced new demands that challenged those strengths. UNIX was used for tasks such as networking, graphics, and real-time operation, which did not always fit into its original text-oriented model. Thus, changes were made to certain internal facilities and new programming interfaces were added. These new facilities, and others—particularly window interfaces—required large amounts of code to support them, radically increasing the size of the system. For instance, networking and windowing both doubled the size of the system. This pattern in turn pointed out the continued strength of UNIX—whenever a new development occurred in the industry, UNIX could usually absorb it, but still remain UNIX.

PROGRAMMER INTERFACE

As do most operating systems, UNIX consists of two separable parts: the kernel and the systems programs. We can view the UNIX operating system as being layered, as shown in Figure 4-2. Everything below the system-call interface and above the physical hardware is the *kernel*. The kernel provides the file system, CPU scheduling, memory management, and other operating-system functions through system calls. Systems programs use the kernel-supported system calls to provide useful functions, such as compilation and file manipulation.

System calls define the *programmer interface* to UNIX; the set of systems programs commonly available defines the *user interface*. The programmer and user interface define the context that the kernel must support.

System calls in VAX 4.2BSD are made by a trap to location 40 of the VAX interrupt vectors. Parameters are passed to the kernel on the hardware stack; the kernel returns values in registers R0 and R1. Register R0 may also return an error code. The carry bit distinguishes a normal return from an error return.

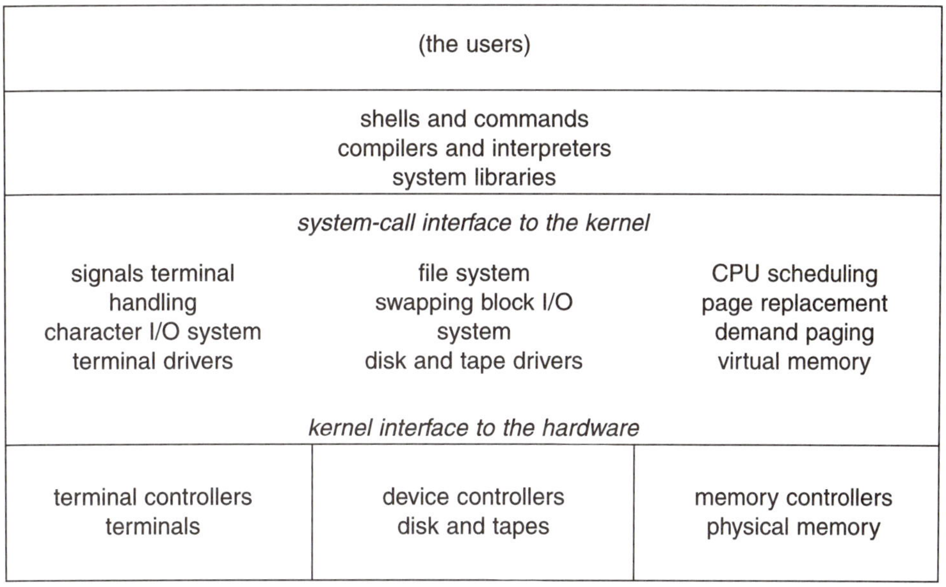

FIGURE 4-2 *4.3BSD Layer Structure*

This level of detail is seldom seen by a UNIX programmer, fortunately. Most systems programs are written in C, and the *UNIX Programmer's Manual* presents all system calls as C functions. A system program written in C for 4.3BSD on the VAX can generally be moved to another 4.3BSD system and simply recompiled, even though the two systems may be quite different. The details of system calls are known only to the compiler. This feature is a major reason for the portability of UNIX programs.

System calls for UNIX can be roughly grouped into three categories: file manipulation, process control, and information manipulation. We listed a fourth category, device manipulation, but since devices in UNIX are treated as (special) files, the same system calls support both files and devices (although there is an extra system call for setting device parameters).

File Manipulation

A *file* in UNIX is a sequence of bytes. Different programs expect various levels of structure, but the kernel does not impose a structure on files. For instance, the convention for text files is lines of ASCII characters separated by a single newline character (which is the linefeed character in ASCII), but the kernel knows nothing of this convention.

Files are organized in tree-structured *directories*. Directories are themselves files that contain information on how to find other files. A *path name* to a file is a text string that identifies a file by specifying a path through the directory structure to the file. Syntactically, it consists of individual file-name elements separated by the slash character. For example, in */usr/local/font*, the first slash indicates the root of the directory tree, called the *root* directory. The next element, *usr*, is a subdirectory of the root, *local* is a subdirectory of *usr*, and *font* is a file or directory in the directory *local*. Whether *font* is an ordinary file or a directory cannot be determined from the path-name syntax.

The UNIX file system has both *absolute path names* and *relative path names*. Absolute path names start at the root of the file system and are distinguished by a slash at the beginning of the path name; */usr/local/font* is an absolute path name. Relative path names start at the *current directory*, which is an attribute of the process accessing the path name. Thus, *local/font* indicates a file or directory named *font* in the directory *local* in the current directory, which might or might not be */usr*.

A file may be known by more than one name in one or more directories. Such multiple names are known as *links*, and all links are treated equally by the operating system. 4.3BSD also supports *symbolic links*, which are files containing the path name of another file. The two kinds of links are also known as *hard links* and *soft links*. Soft (symbolic) links, unlike hard links, may point to directories and may cross file-system boundaries.

The file name "." in a directory is a hard link to the directory itself. The file name ".." is a hard link to the parent directory. Thus, if the current directory is */user/jlp/programs*, then *../bin/wdf* refers to */user/jlp/bin/wdf*.

Hardware devices have names in the file system. These *device special files* or *special files* are known to the kernel as device interfaces, but are nonetheless accessed by the user by much the same system calls as are other files.

Figure 4-3 shows a typical UNIX file system. The root (/) normally contains a small number of directories as well as */vmunix*, the binary boot image of the operating system; */dev* contains the device special files, such as */dev/console*, */dev/lp0, /dev/mt0*, and so on; */bin*

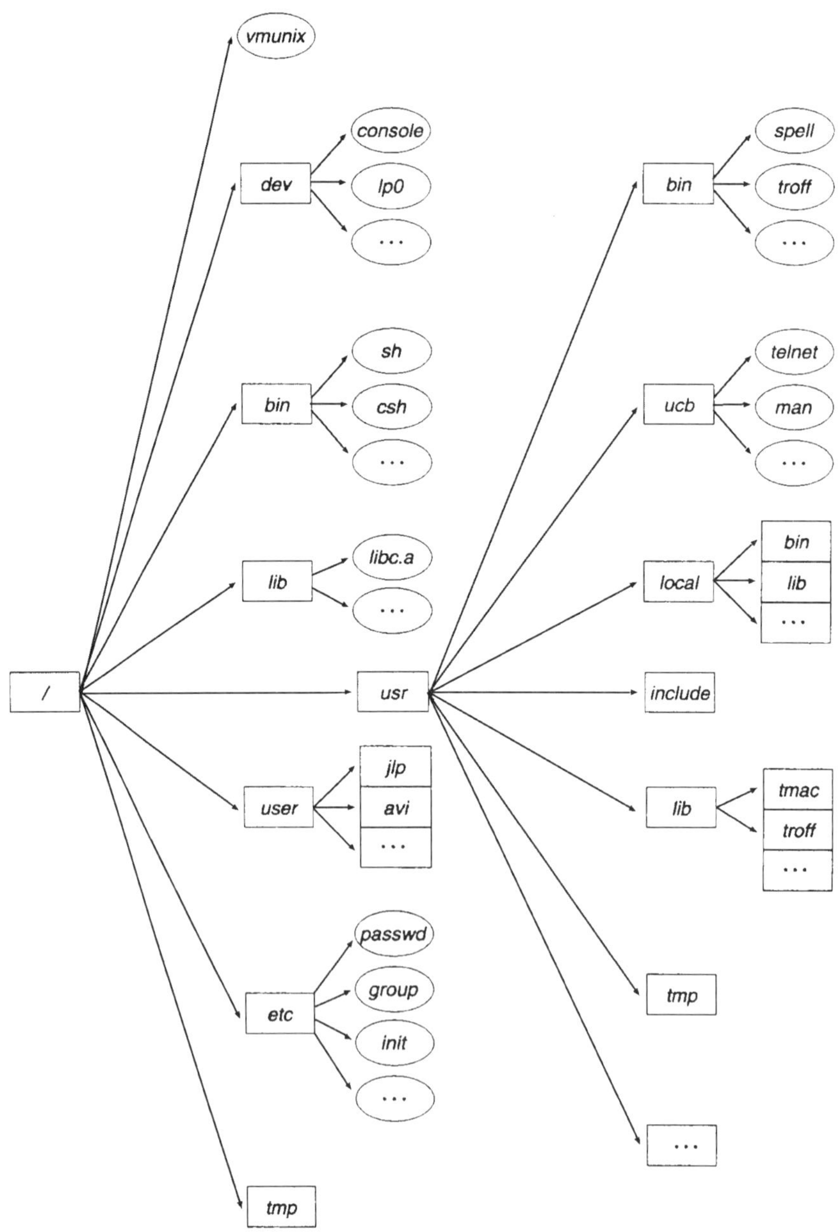

FIGURE 4-3 *Typical UNIX Directory Structure*

contains the binaries of the essential UNIX systems programs. Other binaries may be in */usr/bin* (for applications systems programs, such as text formatters), */usr/ucb* (for systems programs written by Berkeley rather than by AT&T), or */usr/local/bin* (for systems programs written at the local site). Library files—such as the C, Pascal, and FORTRAN subroutine libraries—are kept in */lib* (or */usr/lib* or */usr/local/lib*).

The files of users themselves are stored in a separate directory for each user, typically in */user*. Thus, the user directory for *carol* would normally be in */user/carol*. For a large system, these directories may be further grouped to ease administration, creating a file structure with */user/prof/avi* and */user/staff/carol*. Administrative files and programs, such as the password file, are kept in */etc*. Temporary files can be put in */tmp*, which is normally erased during system boot, or in */usr/tmp*.

Each of these directories may have considerably more structure. For example, the font-description tables for the troff formatter for the Merganthaler 202 typesetter are kept in */usr/lib/troff/dev202*. All the conventions concerning the location of specific files and directories have been defined by programmers and their programs; the operating-system kernel needs only */etc/init*, which is used to initialize terminal processes, to be operable.

System calls for basic file manipulation are **creat, open, read, write, close, unlink**, and **trunc**. The **creat** system call, given a path name, creates an (empty) file (or truncates an existing one). An existing file is opened by the **open** system call, which takes a path name and a mode (such as read, write, or read-write) and returns a small integer, called a *file descriptor*. A file descriptor may then be passed to a **read** or **write** system call (along with a buffer address and the number of bytes to transfer) to perform data transfers to or from the file. A file is closed when its file descriptor is passed to the **close** system call. The **trunc** call reduces the length of a file to 0.

A file descriptor is an index into a small table of open files for this process. Descriptors start at 0 and seldom get higher than 6 or 7 for typical programs, depending on the maximum number of simultaneously open files.

Each **read** or **write** updates the current offset into the file, which is associated with the file-table entry and is used to determine the position in the file for the next **read** or **write**. The **lseek** system call allows the position to be reset explicitly. It also allows the creation of sparse files (files with "holes" in them). The **dup** and **dup2** system calls can be used to produce a new file descriptor that is a copy of an existing one. The **fcntl** system call can also do that, and in addition can examine or set various parameters of an open file. For example, it can make each succeeding **write** to an open file append to the end of that file. There is an additional system call, **ioctl**, for manipulating device parameters. It can set the baud rate of a serial port, or rewind a tape, for instance.

Information about the file (such as its size, protection modes, owner, and so on) can be obtained by the **stat** system call. Several system calls allow some of this information to be changed: **rename** (change file name), **chmod** (change the protection mode), and **chown** (change the owner and group). Many of these system calls have variants that apply to file descriptors instead of file names. The **link** system call makes a hard link for an existing file, creating a new name for an existing file. A link is removed by the **unlink** system call; if it is the last link, the file is deleted. The **symlink** system call makes a symbolic link.

Directories are made by the **mkdir** system call and are deleted by **rmdir**. The current directory is changed by **cd**.

Although it is possible to use the standard file calls on directories, it is inadvisable to do so, since directories have an internal structure that must be preserved. Instead, another set of system calls is provided to open a directory, to step through each file entry within the directory, to close the directory, and to perform other functions; these are **opendir**, **readdir**, **closedir**, and others.

Process Control

A *process* is a program in execution. Processes are identified by their *process identifier*, which is an integer. A new process is created by the **fork** system call. The new process consists of a copy of the address space of the original process (the same program and the same variables with the same values). Both processes (the parent and the child) continue execution at the instruction after the **fork** with one difference: The return code for the **fork** is zero for the new (child) process, whereas the (nonzero) process identifier of the child is returned to the parent.

Typically, the **execve** system call is used after a fork by one of the two processes to replace that process's virtual memory space with a new program. The **execve** system call loads a binary file into memory (destroying the memory image of the program containing the **execve** system call) and starts its execution.

A process may terminate by using the **exit** system call, and its parent process may wait for that event by using the **wait** system call. If the child process crashes, the system simulates the **exit** call. The **wait** system call provides the process ID of a terminated child so that the parent can tell which of possibly many children terminated. A second system call, **wait3**, is similar to **wait** but also allows the parent to collect performance statistics about the child. Between the time the child exits, and the time the parent completes one of the **wait** system calls, the child is *defunct*. A defunct process can do nothing, but exists merely so that the parent can collect its status information. If the parent process of a defunct process exits before a child, the defunct process is inherited by the *init* process (which in turn **waits** on it) and becomes a *zombie* process. A typical use of these facilities is shown in Figure 4-4.

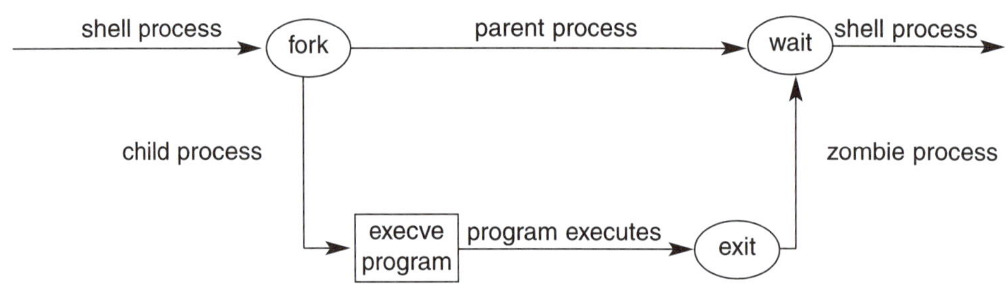

FIGURE 4-4 *A Shell Forks a Subprocess to Execute a Program*

The simplest form of communication between processes is by *pipes*, which may be created before the **fork**, and whose endpoints are then set up between the **fork** and the **execve**. A pipe is essentially a queue of bytes between two processes. The pipe is accessed by a file descriptor, like an ordinary file. One process writes into the pipe, and the other reads from the pipe. The size of the original pipe system was fixed by the system. With 4.3BSD, pipes are implemented on top of the socket system, which has variable-sized buffers. Reading from an empty pipe or writing into a full pipe causes the process to be blocked until the state of the pipe changes. Special arrangements are needed for a pipe to be placed between a parent and child (so only one is reading and one is writing).

All user processes are descendants of one original process, called *init*. Each terminal port available for interactive use has a *getty* process forked for it by *init*. The *getty* process initializes terminal line parameters and waits for a user's *login name*, which it passes through an **execve** as an argument to a *login* process. The *login* process collects the user's password, encrypts the password, and compares the result to an encrypted string taken from the file */etc/passwd*. If the comparison is successful, the user is allowed to log in. The *login* process executes a *shell*, or command interpreter, after setting the numeric *user identifier* of the process to that of the user logging in. (The shell and the user identifier are found in */etc/passwd* by the user's login name.) It is with this shell that the user ordinarily communicates for the rest of the login session; the shell itself forks subprocesses for the commands the user tells it to execute.

The user identifier is used by the kernel to determine the user's permissions for certain system calls, especially those involving file accesses. There is also a *group identifier*, which is used to provide similar privileges to a collection of users. In 4.3BSD a process may be in several groups simultaneously. The *login* process puts the shell in all the groups permitted to the user by the files */etc/passwd* and */etc/group*.

There are actually two user identifiers used by the kernel: the *effective user identifier* is the identifier used to determine file access permissions. If the file of a program being loaded by an **execve** has the **setuid** bit set in its inode, the effective user identifier of the process is set to the user identifier of the owner of the file, whereas the *real user identifier* is left as it was. This scheme allows certain processes to have more than ordinary privileges while still being executable by ordinary users. The **setuid** idea was patented by Dennis Ritchie (U.S. Patent 4,135,240) and is one of the distinctive features of UNIX. There is a similar **setgid** bit for groups. A process may determine its real and effective user identifier with the **getuid** and **geteuid** calls, respectively. The **getgid** and **getegid** calls determine the process identifier and group identifier, respectively. The rest of a process's groups may be found with the **getgroups** system call.

Signals

Signals are a facility for handling exceptional conditions similar to software interrupts. There are 20 different signals, each corresponding to a distinct condition. A signal may be generated by a keyboard interrupt, by an error in a process (such as a bad memory reference), or by a number of asynchronous events (such as timers or job-control signals from the shell). Almost any signal may also be generated by the **kill** system call.

The *interrupt* signal, SIGINT, is used to stop a command before that command completes. It is usually produced by the ^C character (ASCII 3). As of 4.2BSD, the important keyboard characters are defined by a table for each terminal and can be redefined easily. The *quit* signal, SIGQUIT, is usually produced by the ^bs character (ASCII 28). The *quit* signal both stops the currently executing program and dumps its current memory image to a file named *core* in the current directory. The core file can be used by debuggers. SIGILL is produced by an illegal instruction and SIGSEGV by an attempt to address memory outside of the legal virtual-memory space of a process.

Arrangements can be made either for most signals to be ignored (to have no effect), or for a routine in the user process (a signal handler) to be called. A signal handler may safely do one of two things before returning from catching a signal: call the **exit** system call, or modify a global variable. There is one signal (the *kill* signal, number 9, SIGKILL) that cannot be ignored or caught by a signal handler. SIGKILL is used, for example, to kill a runaway process that is ignoring other signals such as SIGINT or SIGQUIT.

Signals can be lost: If another signal of the same kind is sent before a previous signal has been accepted by the process to which it is directed, the first signal will be overwritten and only the last signal will be seen by the process. In other words, a call to the signal handler tells a process that there has been at least one occurance of the signal. Also, there is no relative priority among UNIX signals. If two different signals are sent to the same process at the same time, it is indeterminate which one the process will receive first.

Signals were originally intended to deal with exceptional events. As is true of the use of most other features in UNIX, however, signal use has steadily expanded. 4.1BSD introduced job control, which uses signals to start and stop subprocesses on demand. This facility allows one shell to control multiple processes: starting, stopping, and backgrounding them as the user wishes. 4.3BSD added the SIGWINCH signal, invented by Sun Microsystems, for informing a process that the window in which output is being displayed has changed size. Signals are also used to deliver urgent data from network connections.

Users also wanted more reliable signals, and a bug fix in an inherent race condition in the old signals implementation. Thus, 4.2BSD also brought with it a race-free, reliable, separately implemented signal capability. It allows individual signals to be blocked during critical sections, and has a new system call to let a process sleep until interrupted. It is similar to hardware-interrupt functionality. This capability is now part of the POSIX standard.

Process Groups

Groups of related processes frequently cooperate to accomplish a common task. For instance, processes may create, and communicate over, pipes. Such a set of processes is termed a *process group*, or a *job*. Signals may be sent to all processes in a group. A process usually inherits its process group from its parent, but the **setpgrp** system call allows a process to change its group.

Process groups are used by the C shell to control the operation of multiple jobs. Only one process group may use a terminal device for I/O at any time. This *foreground* job has the attention of the user on that terminal while all other nonattached jobs (*background* jobs) perform their function without user interaction. Access to the terminal is controlled by process group signals. Each job has a *controlling terminal* (again, inherited from its parent). If the process group of the controlling terminal matches the group of a process, that process is in the foreground, and is allowed to perform I/O. If a nonmatching (background) process attempts the same, a SIGTTIN or SIGTTOU signal is sent to its process group. This signal usually results in the process group freezing until it is foregrounded by the user, at which point it receives a SIGCONT signal, indicating that the process can perform the I/O. Similarly, a SIGSTOP may be sent to the foreground process group to freeze it.

Information Manipulation

System calls exist to set and return both an interval timer (**getitimer/setitimer**) and the current time (**gettimeofday/settimeofday**) in microseconds. In addition, processes can ask for their process identifier (**getpid**), their group identifier (**getgid**), the name of the machine on which they are executing (**gethostname**), and many other values.

Library Routines

The system-call interface to UNIX is supported and augmented by a large collection of library routines and header files. The header files provide the definition of complex data structures used in system calls. In addition, a large library of functions provides additional program support.

For example, the UNIX I/O system calls provide for the reading and writing of blocks of bytes. Some applications may want to read and write only 1 byte at a time. Although it would be possible to read and write 1 byte at a time, that would require a system call for each byte—a very high overhead. Instead, a set of standard library routines (the standard I/O package accessed through the header file *<stdio.h>*) provides another interface, which reads and writes several thousand bytes at a time using local buffers, and transfers between these buffers (in user memory) when I/O is desired. Formatted I/O is also supported by the standard I/O package.

Additional library support is provided for mathematical functions, network access, data conversion, and so on. The 4.3BSD kernel supports over 150 system calls; the C program library has over 300 library functions. Although the library functions eventually result in system calls where necessary (for example, the *getchar* library routine will result in a **read** system call if the file buffer is empty), it is generally unnecessary for the programmer to distinguish between the basic set of kernel system calls and the additional functions provided by library functions.

USER INTERFACE

Both the programmer and the user of a UNIX system deal mainly with the set of systems programs that have been written and are available for execution. These programs make the necessary system calls to support their function, but the system calls themselves are contained within the program and do not need to be obvious to the user.

The common systems programs can be grouped into several categories; most of them are file or directory oriented. For example, the systems programs to manipulate directories are *mkdir* to create a new directory, *rmdir* to remove a directory, *cd* to change the current directory to another, and *pwd* to print the absolute path name of the current (working) directory.

The *ls* program lists the names of the files in the current directory. Any of 18 options can ask that properties of the files be displayed also. For example, the *-l* option asks for a long listing, showing the file name, owner, protection, date and time of creation, and size. The *cp* program creates a new file that is a copy of an existing file. The *mv* program moves a file from one place to another in the directory tree. In most cases, this move simply requires a renaming of the file; if necessary, however, the file is copied to the new location and the old copy is deleted. A file is deleted by the *rm* program (which makes an **unlink** system call).

To display a file on the terminal, a user can run *cat*. The *cat* program takes a list of files and concatenates them, copying the result to the standard output, commonly the terminal. On a high-speed cathode-ray tube (CRT) display, of course, the file may speed by too fast to be read. The *more* program displays the file one screen at a time, pausing until the user types a character to continue to the next screen. The *head* program displays just the first few lines of a file; *tail* shows the last few lines.

These are the basic systems programs widely used in UNIX. In addition, there are a number of editors (*ed, sed, emacs, vi,* and so on), compilers (C, Pascal, FORTRAN, and so on), and text formatters (troff, TEX, scribe, and so on). There are also programs for sorting (*sort*) and comparing files (*cmp, diff*), looking for patterns (*grep, awk*), sending mail to other users (*mail*), and many other activities.

Shells and Commands

Both user-written and systems programs are normally executed by a command interpreter. The command interpreter in UNIX is a user process like any other. It is called a *shell*, as it surrounds the kernel of the operating system. Users can write their own shell, and there are, in fact, several shells in general use. The *Bourne shell*, written by Steve Bourne, is probably the most widely used—or, at least, it is the most widely available. The *C shell*, mostly the work of Bill Joy, a founder of Sun Microsystems, is the most popular on BSD systems. The Korn shell, by Dave Korn, has become popular because it combines the features of the Bourne shell and the C shell.

The common shells share much of their command-language syntax. UNIX is normally an interactive system. The shell indicates its readiness to accept another command by typing a prompt, and the user types a command on a single line. For instance, in the line:

%ls -l

the percent sign is the usual C shell prompt, and the *ls -l* (typed by the user) is the (long) list-directory command. Commands can take arguments, which the user types after the command name on the same line, separated by white space (spaces or tabs).

Although there are a few commands built into the shells (such as *cd*), a typical command is an executable binary object file. A list of several directories, the *search path*, is kept by the shell. For each command, each of the directories in the search path is searched, in order, for a file of the same name. If a file is found, it is loaded and executed. The search path can be set by the user. The directories */bin* and */usr/bin* are almost always in the search path, and a typical search path on a BSD system might be:

(./home/prof/avi/bin /usr/local/bin /usr/ucb /bin /usr/bin)

The *ls* command's object file is */bin/ls*, and the shell itself is */bin/sh* (the Bourne shell) or */bin/csh* (the C shell).

Execution of a command is done by a **fork** system call followed by an **execve** of the object file. The shell usually then does a **wait** to suspend its own execution until the command completes (Figure 4-4). There is a simple syntax (an ampersand [&] at the end of the command line) to indicate that the shell should *not* wait for the completion of the command. A command left running in this manner while the shell continues to interpret further commands is said to be a *background* command, or to be running in the background. Processes for which the shell *does* wait are said to run in the *foreground*.

The C shell in 4.3BSD systems provides a facility called *job control* (partially implemented in the kernel), as mentioned previously. Job control allows processes to be moved between the foreground and the background. The processes can be stopped and restarted on various conditions, such as a background job wanting input from the user's terminal. This scheme allows most of the control of processes provided by windowing or layering interfaces, but requires no special hardware. Job control is also useful in window systems, such as the X Window System developed at MIT. Each window is treated as a terminal, allowing multiple processes to be in the foreground (one per window) at any one time. Of course, background processes may exist on any of the windows. The Korn shell also supports job control, and it is likely that job control (and process groups) will be standard in future versions of UNIX.

Standard I/O

Processes can open files as they like, but most processes expect three file descriptors (numbers 0, 1, and 2) to be open when they start. These file descriptors are inherited across the **fork** (and possibly the **execve**) that created the process. They are known as *standard input* (0), *standard output* (1), and *standard error* (2). All three are frequently open to the user's terminal. Thus, the program can read what the user types by reading standard input, and the program can send output to the user's screen by writing to standard output. The standard-error file descriptor is also open for writing and is used for error output; standard output is used for ordinary output. Most programs can also accept a file (rather than a terminal) for standard input and standard output. The program does not care where its input is coming from and where its output is going. This is one of the elegant design features of UNIX.

The common shells have a simple syntax for changing what files are open for the standard I/O streams of a process. Changing a standard file is called *I/O redirection*. The syntax for I/O redirection is shown in Figure 4-5. In this example, the *ls* command produces a listing of the names of files in the current directory, the *pr* command formats that list into pages suitable for a printer, and the *lpr* command spools the formatted output to a printer, such as */dev/lp0*. The subsequent command forces all output and all error messages to be redirected to a file. Without the ampersand, error messages appear on the terminal.

Command	Meaning of command
% ls>filea	direct output of *ls* to *filea*
% pr<filea>fileb	input from *filea* and output to *fileb*
% lpr<fileb	input from *fileb*
% % make program>&errs	save both standard output and standard error in a file

FIGURE 4-5 *Standard I/O Direction*

Pipelines, Filters, and Shell Scripts

The first three commands of Figure 4-5 could have been coalesced into the one command:

% *ls* | *pr* | *lpr*

Each vertical bar tells the shell to arrange for the output of the preceding command to be passed as input to the following command. A pipe is used to carry the data from one process to the other. One process writes into one end of the pipe, and another process reads from the other end. In the example, the write end of one pipe would be set up by the shell to be the standard output of *ls*, and the read end of the pipe would be the standard input of *pr*; there would be another pipe between *pr* and *lpr*.

A command such as *pr* that passes its standard input to its standard output, performing some processing on it, is called a *filter*. Many UNIX commands can be used as filters. Complicated functions can be pieced together as pipelines of common commands. Also, common functions, such as output formatting, do not need to be built into numerous commands, because the output of almost any program can be piped through *pr* (or some other appropriate filter).

Both of the common UNIX shells are also programming languages, with shell variables and the usual higher-level programming-language control constructs (loops, conditionals). The execution of a command is analogous to a subroutine call. A file of shell commands, a *shell script*, can be executed like any other command, with the appropriate shell being invoked automatically to read it. *Shell programming* thus can be used to combine ordinary programs conveniently for sophisticated applications without the necessity of any programming in conventional languages.

This external user view is commonly thought of as the definition of UNIX, yet it is the most easily changed definition. Writing a new shell with a quite different syntax and semantics would greatly change the user view while not changing the kernel or even the programmer interface. Several menu-driven and iconic interfaces for UNIX now exist, and the X Window System is rapidly becoming a standard. The heart of UNIX is, of course, the kernel. This kernel is much more difficult to change than is the user interface, because all programs depend on the system calls that it provides to remain consistent. Of course, new system calls can be added to increase functionality, but programs must then be modified to use the new calls.

PROCESS MANAGEMENT

A major design problem for operating systems is the representation of processes. One substantial difference between UNIX and many other systems is the ease with which multiple processes can be created and manipulated. These processes are represented in UNIX by various control blocks. There are no system control blocks accessible in the virtual address space of a user process; control blocks associated with a process are stored in the kernel. The information in these control blocks is used by the kernel for process control and CPU scheduling.

Process Control Blocks

The most basic data structure associated with processes is the *process structure*. A process structure contains everything that the system needs to know about a process when the process is swapped out, such as its unique process identifier, scheduling information (such as the priority of the process), and pointers to other control blocks. There is an array of process structures whose length is defined at system linking time. The process structures of ready processes are kept linked together by the scheduler in a doubly linked list (the ready queue), and there are pointers from each process structure to the process's parent, to its youngest living child, and to various other relatives of interest, such as a list of processes sharing the same program code (text).

The *virtual address space* of a user process is divided into text (program code), data, and stack segments. The data and stack segments are always in the same address space, but may grow separately, and usually in opposite directions: most frequently, the stack grows down as the data grow up toward it. The text segment is sometimes (as on an Intel 8086 with separate instruction and data space) in an address space different from the data and stack, and is usually read-only. The debugger puts a text segment in read-write mode to be able to allow insertion of breakpoints.

Every process with sharable text (almost all, under 4.3BSD) has a pointer from its process structure to a *text structure*. The text structure records how many processes are using the text segment, including a pointer into a list of their process structures, and where the page table for the text segment can be found on disk when it is swapped. The text structure itself is always resident in main memory: an array of such structures is allocated at system link time. The text, data, and stack segments for the processes may be swapped. When the segments are swapped in, they are paged.

The *page tables* record information on the mapping from the process's virtual memory to physical memory. The process structure contains pointers to the page table, for use when the process is resident in main memory, or the address of the process on the swap device, when the process is swapped. There is no special separate page table for a shared text segment; every process sharing the text segment has entries for its pages in the process's page table.

Information about the process that is needed only when the process is resident (that is, not swapped out) is kept in the *user structure* (or *u structure*), rather than in the process structure. The *u* structure is mapped read-only into user virtual address space, so user processes can read its contents. It is writable by the kernel. On the VAX, a copy of the VAX PCB is kept here for saving the process's general registers, stack pointer, program counter, and page-table base registers when the process is not running. There is space to keep system-call parameters and return values. All user and group identifiers associated with the process (not just the effective user identifier kept in the process structure) are kept here. Signals, timers, and quotas have data structures here. Of more obvious relevance to the ordinary user, the current directory and the table of open files are maintained in the user structure.

Every process has both a user and a system phase. Most ordinary work is done in *user mode*, but, when a system call is made, it is performed in *system mode*. The system and user phases of a process never execute simultaneously. When a process is executing in system mode, a *kernel stack* for that process is used, rather than the user stack belonging to that process. The kernel stack for the process immediately follows the user structure: The kernel stack and the user structure together compose the *system data segment* for the process. The kernel has its own stack for use when it is not doing work on behalf of a process (for instance, for interrupt handling).

Figure 4-6 illustrates how the process structure is used to find the various parts of a process.

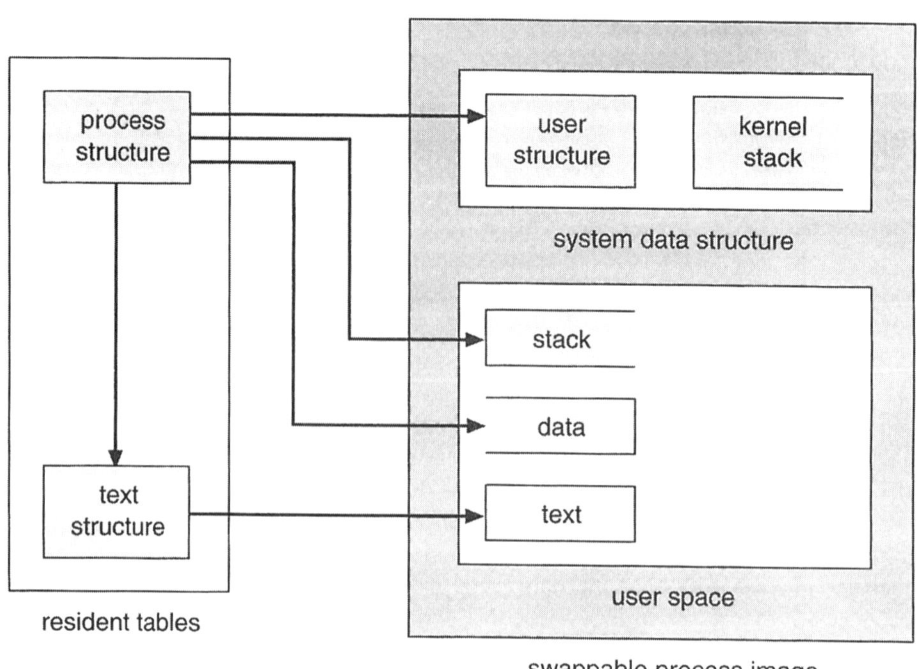

FIGURE 4-6 *Finding Parts of a Process Using the Process Structure*

The **fork** system call allocates a new process structure (with a new process identifier) for the child process, and copies the user structure. There is ordinarily no need for a new text structure, as the processes share their text; the appropriate counters and lists are merely updated. A new page table is constructed, and new main memory is allocated for the data and stack segments of the child process. The copying of the user structure preserves open file descriptors, user and group identifiers, signal handling, and most similar properties of a process.

The **vfork** system call does *not* copy the data and stack to the new process; rather, the new process simply shares the page table of the old one. A new user structure and a new process structure are still created. A common use of this system call is by a shell to execute a command and to wait for its completion. The parent process uses **vfork** to produce the child process. Because the child process wishes to use an **execve** immediately to change its virtual address space completely, there is no need for a complete copy of the parent process. Such data structures as are necessary for manipulating pipes may be kept in registers between the **vfork** and the **execve**. Files may be closed in one process without affecting the other process, since the kernel data structures involved depend on the user structure, which is not shared. The parent is suspended when it calls **vfork** until the child either calls **execve** or terminates, so that the parent will not change memory that the child needs.

When the parent process is large, **vfork** can produce substantial savings in system CPU time. However, it is a fairly dangerous system call, since any memory change occurs in both processes until the **execve** occurs. An alternative is to share all pages by duplicating the page table, but to mark the entries of both page tables as *copy-on-write*. The hardware protection bits are set to trap any attempt to write in these shared pages. If such a trap occurs, a new frame is allocated and the shared page is copied to the new frame. The page tables are adjusted to show that this page is no longer shared (and therefore no longer needs to be write-protected), and execution can resume.

An **execve** system call creates no new process or user structure; rather, the text and data of the process are replaced. Open files are preserved (although there is a way to specify that certain file descriptors are to be closed on an **execve**). Most signal-handling properties are preserved, but arrangements to call a specific user routine on a signal are canceled, for obvious reasons. The process identifier and most other properties of the process are unchanged.

CPU Scheduling

CPU scheduling in UNIX is designed to benefit interactive processes. Processes are given small CPU time slices by a priority algorithm that reduces to round-robin scheduling for CPU-bound jobs.

Every process has a *scheduling priority* associated with it; larger numbers indicate lower priority. Processes doing disk I/O or other important tasks have priorities less than "pzero" and cannot be killed by signals. Ordinary user processes have positive priorities and thus are all less likely to be run than are any system process, although user processes can set precedence over one another through the *nice* command.

The more CPU time a process accumulates, the lower (more positive) its priority becomes, and vice versa, so there is negative feedback in CPU scheduling and it is difficult for a single process to take all the CPU time. Process aging is employed to prevent starvation.

Older UNIX systems used a 1-second quantum for the round-robin scheduling. 4.3BSD reschedules processes every 0.1 second and recomputes priorities every second. The round-robin scheduling is accomplished by the *timeout* mechanism, which tells the clock interrupt driver to call a kernel subroutine after a specified interval; the subroutine to be called in this case causes the rescheduling and then resubmits a *timeout* to call itself again. The priority recomputation is also timed by a subroutine that resubmits a *timeout* for itself.

There is no preemption of one process by another in the kernel. A process may relinquish the CPU because it is waiting on I/O or because its time slice has expired. When a process chooses to relinquish the CPU, it goes to sleep on an *event*. The kernel primitive used for this purpose is called *sleep* (not to be confused with the user-level library routine of the same name). It takes an argument, which is by convention the address of a kernel data structure related to an *event* that the process wants to occur before that process is awakened. When the event occurs, the system process that knows about it calls *wakeup* with the address corresponding to the event, and *all* processes that had done a *sleep* on the same address are put in the ready queue to be run.

For example, a process waiting for disk I/O to complete will *sleep* on the address of the buffer header corresponding to the data being transferred. When the interrupt routine for the disk driver notes that the transfer is complete, it calls *wakeup* on the buffer header. The interrupt uses the kernel stack for whatever process happened to be running at the time, and the *wakeup* is done from that system process.

The process that actually does run is chosen by the scheduler. *Sleep* takes a second argument, which is the scheduling priority to be used for this purpose. This priority argument, if less than "pzero," also prevents the process from being awakened prematurely by some exceptional event, such as a *signal*.

When a signal is generated, it is left pending until the system half of the affected process next runs. This event usually happens soon, since the signal normally causes the process to be awakened if the process has been waiting for some other condition.

There is no memory associated with events, and the caller of the routine that does a *sleep* on an event must be prepared to deal with a premature return, including the possibility that the reason for waiting has vanished.

There are *race conditions* involved in the event mechanism. If a process decides (because of checking a flag in memory, for instance) to sleep on an event, and the event occurs before the process can execute the primitive that does the actual sleep on the event, the process sleeping may then sleep forever. We prevent this situation by raising the hardware processor priority during the critical section so that no interrupts can occur, and thus only the process desiring the event can run until it is sleeping. Hardware processor priority is used in this manner to protect critical regions throughout the kernel, and is the greatest obstacle to porting UNIX to multiple processor machines. However, this problem has not prevented such ports from being done repeatedly.

Many processes such as text editors are I/O bound and usually will be scheduled mainly on the basis of waiting for I/O. Experience suggests that the UNIX scheduler performs best with I/O-bound jobs, as can be observed when there are several CPU-bound jobs, such as text formatters or language interpreters, running.

What has been referred to here as *CPU scheduling* corresponds closely to *short-term scheduling*, although the negative-feedback property of the priority scheme provides some long-term scheduling in that it largely determines the long-term *job mix*. Medium-term scheduling is done by the swapping mechanism.

MEMORY MANAGEMENT

Much of UNIX's early development was done on a PDP-11. The PDP-11 has only eight segments in its virtual address space, and each of these are at most 8192 bytes. The larger machines, such as the PDP-11/70, allow separate instruction and address spaces, which effectively double the address space and number of segments, but this address space is still relatively small. In addition, the kernel was even more severely constrained due to dedication of one data segment to interrupt vectors, another to point at the per-process system data segment, and yet another for the UNIBUS (system I/O bus) registers. Further, on the smaller PDP-11s, total physical memory was limited to 256K. The total memory resources were insufficient to justify or support complex memory-management algorithms. Thus, UNIX swapped entire process memory images.

Swapping

Pre-3BSD UNIX systems use swapping exclusively to handle memory contention among processes: If there is too much contention, processes are swapped out until enough memory is available. Also, a few large processes can force many small processes out of memory, and a process larger than nonkernel main memory cannot be run at all. The system data segment (the *u* structure and kernel stack) and the user data segment (text [if nonsharable], data, and stack) are kept in contiguous main memory for swap-transfer efficiency, so external fragmentation of memory can be a serious problem.

Allocation of both main memory and swap space is done first-fit. When the size of a process's memory image increases (due to either stack expansion or data expansion), a new piece of memory big enough for the whole image is allocated. The memory image is copied, the old memory is freed, and the appropriate tables are updated. (An attempt is made in some systems to find memory contiguous to the end of the current piece, to avoid some copying.) If no single piece of main memory is large enough, the process is swapped out such that it will be swapped back in with the new size.

There is no need to swap out a sharable text segment, because it is read-only, and there is no need to read in a sharable text segment for a process when another instance is already in core. That is one of the main reasons for keeping track of sharable text segments: less swap traffic. The other reason is the reduced amount of main memory required for multiple processes using the same text segment.

Decisions regarding which processes to swap in or out are made by the *scheduler process* (also known as the *swapper*). The *scheduler* wakes up at least once every 4 seconds to check for processes to be swapped in or out. A process is more likely to be swapped out if it is idle, has been in main memory a long time, or is large; if no obvious candidates are found, other processes are picked by age. A process is more likely to be swapped in if it has been swapped out a long time, or is small. There are checks to prevent thrashing, basically by not letting a process be swapped out if it has not been in memory for a certain amount of time.

If jobs do not need to be swapped out, the process table is searched for a process deserving to be brought in (determined by how small the process is and how long it has been swapped out). If there is not enough memory available, processes are swapped out until there is.

In 4.3BSD, swap space is allocated in pieces that are multiples of a power of 2 and a minimum size (for example, 32 pages), up to a maximum that is determined by the size of the swap-space partition on the disk. If several logical disk partitions may be used for swapping, they should be the same size, for this reason. The several logical disk partitions should also be on separate disk arms to minimize disk seeks.

Many systems still use the swapping scheme just described. All Berkeley UNIX systems, on the other hand, depend primarily on paging for memory-contention management, and depend only secondarily on swapping. A scheme similar in outline to the traditional one is used to determine which processes get swapped, but the details differ and the influence of swapping is less.

Paging

Berkeley introduced paging to UNIX with 3BSD. VAX 4.2BSD is a demand-paged virtual-memory system. External fragmentation of memory is eliminated by paging. (There is, of course, internal fragmentation, but it is negligible with a reasonably small page size.) Swapping can be kept to a minimum because more jobs can be kept in main memory, because paging allows execution with only parts of each process in memory.

Demand paging is done in a straightforward manner. When a process needs a page and the page is not there, a page fault to the kernel occurs, a frame of main memory is allocated, and the proper disk page is read into the frame.

There are a few optimizations. If the page needed is still in the page table for the process, but has been marked invalid by the page-replacement process, it can be marked valid and used without any I/O transfer. Pages can similarly be retrieved from the list of free frames. When most processes are started, many of their pages are prepaged and are put on the free list for recovery by this mechanism. Arrangements may also be made for a process to have no prepaging on startup, but that is seldom done, as it results in more page-fault overhead, being closer to pure demand paging.

If the page has to be fetched from disk, it must be locked in memory for the duration of the transfer. This locking ensures that the page will not be selected for page replacement. Once the page is fetched and mapped properly, it must remain locked if raw physical I/O is being done on it.

The *page-replacement* algorithm is more interesting. The VAX architecture has no hardware memory page-reference bit. This lack of hardware support makes many memory-management algorithms, such as page-fault frequency, unusable. 4.2BSD uses a modification of the *second chance* (clock) algorithm. The map of all nonkernel main memory (the *core map* or *cmap*) is swept linearly and repeatedly by a software *clock hand*. When the clock hand reaches a given frame, if the frame is marked as in use by some software condition (for example, physical I/O is in progress using it), or the frame is already free, the frame is left untouched, and the clock hand sweeps to the next frame. Otherwise, the corresponding text or process page-table entry for this frame is located. If the entry is already invalid, the frame is added to the free list; otherwise, the page-table entry is made invalid but reclaimable (that is, if it does not get paged out by the next time it is wanted, it can just be made valid again).

4.3BSD Tahoe added support for systems which do implement the reference bit. On such systems, one pass of the clock hand turns the reference bit off, and a second pass places those pages whose reference bits remain off onto the free list for replacement. Of course, if the page is dirty (the VAX *does* have a dirty bit), it must first be written to disk before being added to the free list. Pageouts are done in clusters to improve performance.

There are checks to make sure that the number of valid data pages for a process does not fall too low, and to keep the paging device from being flooded with requests. There is also a mechanism by which a process may limit the amount of main memory it uses.

The LRU clock hand scheme is implemented in the *pagedaemon*, which is process 2 (remember that the *scheduler* is process 0, and *init* is process 1). This process spends most of its time sleeping, but a check is done several times per second (scheduled by a *timeout*) to see if action is necessary; if it is, process 2 is awakened. Whenever the number of free frames falls below a threshold, *lotsfree*, the *pagedaemon* is awakened; thus, if there is always a large amount of free memory, the *pagedaemon* imposes no load on the system, because it never runs.

The sweep of the clock hand each time the *pagedaemon* process is awakened (that is, the number of frames scanned, which is usually more than the number paged out), is determined both by the number of frames lacking to reach *lotsfree* and by the number of frames that the *scheduler* has determined are needed for various reasons (the more frames needed, the longer the sweep). If the number of frames free rises to *lotsfree* before the expected sweep is completed, the hand stops and the *pagedaemon* process sleeps. The parameters that determine the range of the clock-hand sweep are determined at system startup according to the amount of main memory, such that *pagedaemon* does not use more than 10 percent of all CPU time.

If the *scheduler* decides that the paging system is overloaded, processes will be swapped out whole until the overload is relieved. This swapping usually happens only if several conditions are met: load average is high, free memory has fallen below a low limit, *minfree*; and the average memory available over recent time is less than a desirable amount, *desfree*, where *lotsfree* > *desfree* > *minfree*. In other words, only a chronic shortage of memory with several processes trying to run will cause swapping, and even then free memory has to be extremely low at the moment. (An excessive paging rate or a need for memory by the kernel itself may also enter into the calculations, in rare cases.) Processes may be swapped by the *scheduler*, of course, for other reasons (such as simply for not running for a long time).

The parameter *lotsfree* is usually one-quarter of the memory in the map that the clock hand sweeps, and *desfree* and *minfree* are usually the same across different systems, but are limited to fractions of available memory.

Every process's text segment is by default shared and read-only. This scheme is practical with paging, because there is no external fragmentation, and the swap space gained by sharing more than offsets the negligible amount of overhead involved, as the kernel virtual space is large.

CPU scheduling, memory swapping, and paging interact: the lower the priority of a process, the more likely that its pages will be paged out and the more likely that it will be swapped in its entirety. The age preferences in choosing processes to swap guard against thrashing, but paging does so more effectively. Ideally, processes will not be swapped out unless they are idle, because each process will need only a small working set of pages in main memory at any one time, and the *pagedaemon* will reclaim unused pages for use by other processes.

The amount of memory the process will need is some fraction of that process's total virtual size, up to one-half if that process has been swapped out for a long time.

The VAX 512-byte hardware pages are too small for I/O efficiency, so they are clustered in groups of two so that all paging I/O is actually done in 1024-byte chunks. In other words, the effective page size is not necessarily identical to the hardware page size of the machine, although it must be a multiple of the hardware page size.

FILE SYSTEM

The UNIX file system supports two main objects: files and directories. Directories are just files with a special format, so the representation of a file is the basic UNIX concept.

Blocks and Fragments

Most of the file system is taken up by *data blocks*, which contain whatever the users have put in their files. Let us consider how these data blocks are stored on the disk.

The hardware disk sector is usually 512 bytes. A block size larger than 512 bytes is desirable for speed. However, because UNIX file systems usually contain a very large number of small files, much larger blocks would cause excessive internal fragmentation. That is why the earlier 4.1BSD file system was limited to a 1024-byte (1K) block.

The 4.2BSD solution is to use *two* block sizes for files which have no indirect blocks: all the blocks of a file are of a large *block* size (such as 8K), except the last. The last block is an appropriate multiple of a smaller *fragment* size (for example, 1024) to fill out the file. Thus, a file of size 18,000 bytes would have two 8K blocks and one 2K fragment (which would not be filled completely).

The *block* and *fragment* sizes are set during file-system creation according to the intended use of the file system: If many small files are expected, the fragment size should be small; if repeated transfers of large files are expected, the basic block size should be large. Implementation details force a maximum block-to-fragment ratio of 8:1, and a minimum block size of 4K, so typical choices are 4096:512 for the former case and 8192:1024 for the latter.

Suppose data are written to a file in transfer sizes of 1K bytes, and the block and fragment sizes of the file system are 4K and 512 bytes. The file system will allocate a 1K fragment to contain the data from the first transfer. The next transfer will cause a new 2K fragment to be allocated. The data from the original fragment must be copied into this new fragment, followed by the second 1K transfer. The allocation routines do attempt to find the required space on the disk immediately following the existing fragment so that no copying is necessary, but, if they cannot do so, up to seven copies may be required before the fragment becomes a block. Provisions have been made for programs to discover the block size for a file so that transfers of that size can be made, to avoid fragment recopying.

Inodes

A file is represented by an *inode*. An inode is a record that stores most of the information about a specific file on the disk. The name *inode* (pronounced *EYE node*) is derived from "index node" and was originally spelled "i-node"; the hyphen fell out of use over the years. The term is also sometimes spelled "I node."

The inode contains the user and group identifiers of the file, the times of the last file modification and access, a count of the number of hard links (directory entries) to the file, and the type of the file (plain file, directory, symbolic link, character device, block device, or socket). In addition, the inode contains 15 pointers to the disk blocks containing the data contents of the file. The first 12 of these pointers point to *direct blocks*; that is, they contain addresses of blocks that contain data of the file. Thus, the data for small files (no more than 12 blocks) can be referenced immediately, because a copy of the inode is kept in main memory while a file is open. If the block size is 4K, then up to 48K of data may be accessed directly from the inode.

The next three pointers in the inode point to *indirect blocks*. If the file is large enough to use indirect blocks, the indirect blocks are each of the major block size; the fragment size applies to only data blocks. The first indirect block pointer is the address of a *single indirect block*. The single indirect block is an index block, containing not data, but rather the addresses of blocks that do contain data. Then, there is a *double-indirect-block pointer*, the address of a block that contains the addresses of blocks that contain pointers to the actual data blocks. The last pointer would contain the address of a *triple indirect block*; however, there is no need for it. The minimum block size for a file system in 4.2BSD is 4K, so files with as many as 2^{32} bytes will use only double, not triple, indirection. That is, as each block pointer takes 4 bytes, we have 49,152 bytes accessible in direct blocks, 4,194,304 bytes accessible by a single indirection, and 4,294,967,296 bytes reachable through double indirection, for a total of 4,299,210,752 bytes, which is larger than 2^{32} bytes. The number 2^{32} is significant because the file offset in the file structure in main memory is kept in a 32-bit word. Files therefore cannot be larger than 2^{32} bytes. Since file pointers are signed integers (for seeking backward and forward in a file), the actual maximum file size is 2^{32-1} bytes. Two gigabytes is large enough for most purposes.

Directories

There is no distinction between plain files and directories at this level of implementation; directory contents are kept in data blocks, and directories are represented by an inode in the same way as plain files. Only the inode type field distinguishes between plain files and directories. Plain files are not assumed to have a structure, however, whereas directories have a specific structure. In Version 7, file names were limited to 14 characters, so directories were a list of 16-byte entries: 2 bytes for an inode number and 14 bytes for a file name.

In 4.2BSD, file names are of variable length, up to 255 bytes, so directory entries are also of variable length. Each entry contains first the length of the entry, then the file name and the inode number. This variable-length entry makes the directory management and search routines more complex, but greatly improves the ability of users to choose meaningful names for their files and directories, with no practical limit on the length of the name.

The first two names in every directory are "." and "..". New directory entries are added to the directory in the first space available, generally after the existing files. A linear search is used.

The user refers to a file by a path name, whereas the file system uses the inode as its definition of a file. Thus, the kernel has to map the supplied user path name to an inode. The directories are used for this mapping.

First, a starting directory is determined. If the first character of the path name is "/", the starting directory is the root directory. If the path name starts with any character other than a slash, the starting directory is the current directory of the current process. The starting directory is checked for proper file type and access permissions, and an error is returned if necessary. The inode of the starting directory is always available.

The next element of the path name, up to the next "/", or to the end of the path name, is a file name. The starting directory is searched for this name, and an error is returned if the name is not found. If there is yet another element in the path name, the current inode must refer to a directory, and an error is returned if it does not, or if access is denied. This directory is searched as was the previous one. This process continues until the end of the path name is reached and the desired inode is returned. This step-by-step process is needed because at any directory a mount point (or symbolic link, see below) may be encountered, causing the translation to move to a different directory structure for continuation.

Hard links are simply directory entries like any other. We handle symbolic links for the most part by starting the search over with the path name taken from the contents of the symbolic link. We prevent infinite loops by counting the number of symbolic links encountered during a path-name search and returning an error when a limit (eight) is exceeded.

Nondisk files (such as devices) do not have data blocks allocated on the disk. The kernel notices these file types (as indicated in the inode) and calls appropriate drivers to handle I/O for them.

Once the inode is found by, for instance, the **open** system call, a *file structure* is allocated to point to the inode. The file descriptor given to the user refers to this file structure. 4.3BSD added a *directory name cache* to hold recent directory-to-inode translations. This improvement greatly increased file system performance.

Mapping of a File Descriptor to an Inode

System calls that refer to open files indicate the file by passing a file descriptor as an argument. The file descriptor is used by the kernel to index a table of open files for the current process. Each entry of the table contains a pointer to a file structure. This file structure in turn points to the inode; see Figure 4-7. The open file table has a fixed length which is only settable at boot time. Therefore, there is a fixed limit on the number of concurrently open files in a system.

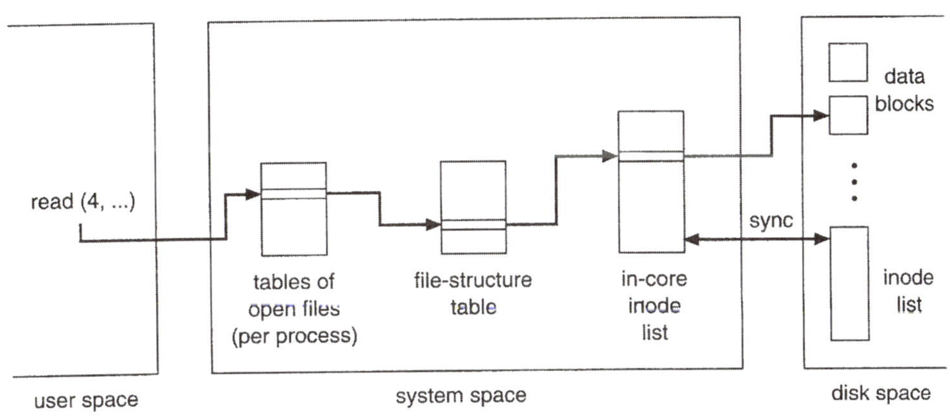

FIGURE 4-7 *File-System Control Blocks*

The **read** and **write** system calls do not take a position in the file as an argument. Rather, the kernel keeps a *file offset*, which is updated by an appropriate amount after each **read** or **write** according to the number of data actually transferred. The offset can be set directly by the **lseek** system call. If the file descriptor indexed an array of inode pointers instead of file pointers, this offset would have to be kept in the inode. Because more than one process may open the same file, and each such process needs its own offset for the file, keeping the offset in the inode is inappropriate. Thus, the file structure is used to contain the offset.

File structures are inherited by the child process after a **fork**, so several processes may share the *same* offset location for a file.

The *inode structure* pointed to by the file structure is an in-core copy of the inode on the disk. The in-core inode has a few extra fields, such as a reference count of how many file structures are pointing at it, and the file structure has a similar reference count for how many file descriptors refer to it. When a count becomes zero, the entry is no longer needed and may be reclaimed and reused.

Disk Structures

The file system that the user sees is supported by data on a mass storage device—usually, a disk. The user ordinarily knows of only one file system, but this one logical file system may actually consist of several *physical* file systems, each on a different device. Because device characteristics differ, each separate hardware device defines its own physical file system. In fact, it is generally desirable to partition large physical devices, such as disks, into multiple *logical* devices. Each logical device defines a physical file system. Figure 4-8 illustrates how a directory structure is partitioned into file systems, which are mapped onto logical devices, which are partitions of physical devices. The sizes and locations of these partitions were coded into device drivers in earlier systems, but are maintained on the disk by 4.3BSD.

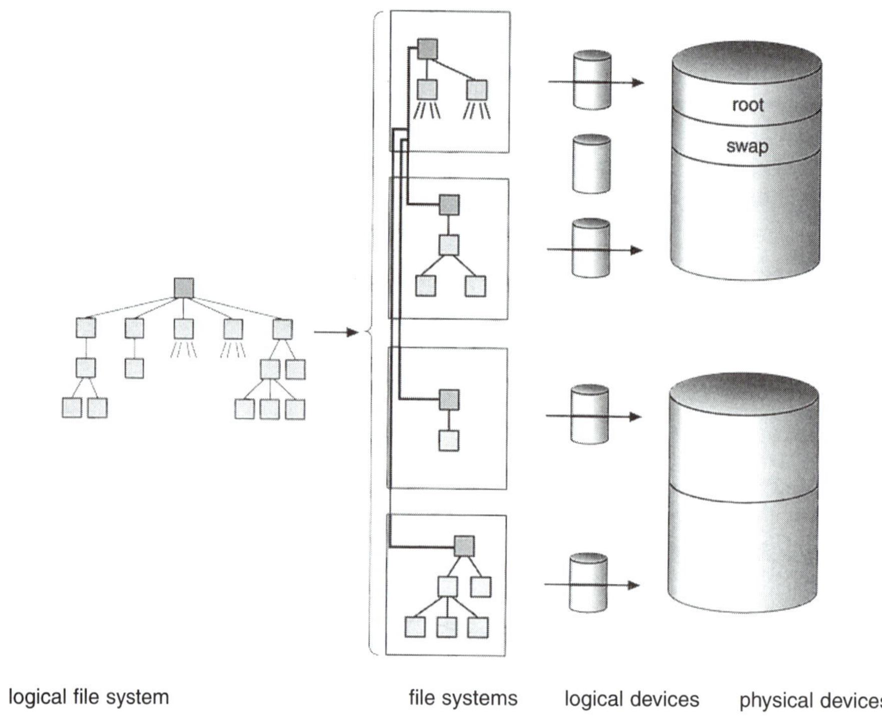

FIGURE 4-8 *Mapping of a Logical File System to Physical Devices*

Partitioning a physical device into multiple file systems has several benefits. Different file systems can support different uses. Although most partitions would be used by the file system, at least one will be necessary for a swap area for the virtual-memory software. Reliability is improved, because software damage is generally limited to only one file system. We can improve efficiency by varying the file-system parameters (such as the block and fragment sizes) for each partition. Also, separate file systems prevent one program from using all available space for a large file, because files cannot be split across file systems. Finally, disk backups are done per partition, and it is faster to search a backup tape for a file if the partition is smaller. Restoring the full partition from tape is also faster.

The actual number of file systems on a drive varies according to the size of the disk and the purpose of the computer system as a whole. One file system, the *root file system*, is always available. Other file systems may be *mounted*—that is, integrated into the directory hierarchy of the root file system.

A bit in the inode structure indicates that the inode has a file system mounted on it. A reference to this file causes the *mount table* to be searched to find the device number of the mounted device. The device number is used to find the inode of the root directory of the mounted file system, and that inode is used. Conversely, if a path-name element is ".." and the directory being searched is the root directory of a file system that is mounted, the mount table is searched to find the inode it is mounted on, and that inode is used.

Each file system is a separate system resource and represents a set of files. The first sector on the logical device is the *boot block*, possibly containing a primary bootstrap program, which may be used to call a secondary bootstrap program residing in the next 7.5K. A system needs only one partition containing boot-block data, but duplicates may be installed via privileged programs by the systems manager, to allow booting when the primary copy is damaged. The *superblock* contains static parameters of the file system. These parameters include the total size of the file system, the block and fragment sizes of the data blocks, and assorted parameters that affect allocation policies.

IMPLEMENTATIONS

The user interface to the file system is simple and well defined, allowing the implementation of the file system itself to be changed without significant effect on the user. The file system was changed between Version 6 and Version 7, and again between Version 7 and 4BSD. For Version 7, the size of inodes doubled, the maximum file and file-system sizes increased, and the details of free-list handling and superblock information changed. At that time also, *seek* (with a 16-bit offset) became *lseek* (with a 32-bit offset), to allow specification of offsets in larger files, but few other changes were visible outside the kernel.

In 4.0BSD, the size of blocks used in the file system was increased from 512 bytes to 1024 bytes. Although this increased size produced increased internal fragmentation on the disk, it doubled throughput, due mainly to the greater number of data accessed on each disk transfer. This idea was later adopted by System V, along with a number of other ideas, device drivers, and programs.

4.2BSD added the Berkeley Fast File System, which increased speed, and was accompanied by new features. Symbolic links required new system calls. Long file names necessitated the new directory system calls to traverse the now-complex internal directory structure. Finally, the **truncate** calls were added. The Fast File System was a success, and is now found in most implementations of UNIX. Its performance is made possible by its layout and allocation policies, which we discuss next.

LAYOUT AND ALLOCATION POLICIES

The kernel uses a *<logical device number, inode number>* pair to identify a file. The logical device number defines the file system involved. The inodes in the file system are numbered in sequence. In the Version 7 file system, all inodes are in an array immediately following a single superblock at the beginning of the logical device, with the data blocks following the inodes. The *inode number* is effectively just an index into this array.

With the Version 7 file system, a block of a file can be anywhere on the disk between the end of the inode array and the end of the file system. Free blocks are kept in a linked list in the superblock. Blocks are pushed onto the front of the free list, and are removed from the front as needed to serve new files or to extend existing files. Thus, the blocks of a file may be arbitrarily far from both the inode and one another. Furthermore, the more a file system of this kind is used, the more disorganized the blocks in a file become. We can reverse this process only by reinitializing and restoring the entire file system, which is not a convenient task to perform.

Another difficulty is that the reliability of the file system is suspect. For speed, the superblock of each mounted file system is kept in memory. Keeping the superblock in memory allows the kernel to access a superblock quickly, especially for using the free list. Every 30 seconds, the superblock is written to the disk, to keep the in-core and disk copies synchronized (by the update program, using the **sync** system call). However, it is not uncommon for system bugs or hardware failures to cause a system crash, which destroys the in-core superblock between updates to the disk. Then, the free list on disk does not reflect accurately the state of the disk; to reconstruct it, we must perform a lengthy examination of all blocks in the file system. Note that this problem still remains in the new file system.

The 4.2BSD file-system implementation is radically different from that of Version 7. This reimplementation was done primarily to improve efficiency and robustness, and most such changes are invisible outside the kernel. There were other changes introduced at the same time, such as symbolic links and long file names (up to 255 characters), that are visible at both the system-call and the user levels. Most of the changes required for these features were not in the kernel, however, but rather were in the programs that use them.

Space allocation is especially different. The major new concept in 4.3BSD is the *cylinder group*. The cylinder group was introduced to allow localization of the blocks in a file. Each cylinder group occupies one or more consecutive cylinders of the disk, so that disk accesses within the cylinder group require minimal disk head movement. Every cylinder group has a superblock, a cylinder block, an array of inodes, and some data blocks (Figure 4-9).

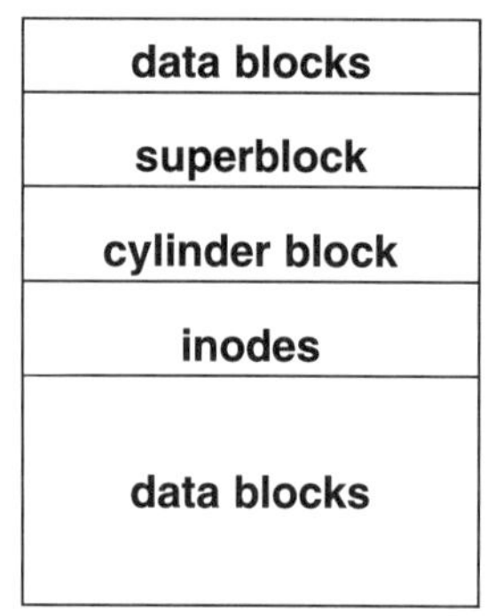

FIGURE 4-9 *4.3BSD Cylinder Group*

The superblock is identical in each cylinder group, so that it can be recovered from any one of them in the event of disk corruption. The *cylinder block* contains dynamic parameters of the particular cylinder group. These include a bit map of free data blocks and fragments, and a bit map of free inodes. Statistics on recent progress of the allocation strategies are also kept here.

The header information in a cylinder group (the superblock, the cylinder block, and the inodes) is not always at the beginning of the cylinder group. If it were, the header information for every cylinder group might be on the same disk platter; a single disk head crash could wipe out all of them. Therefore, each cylinder group has its header information at a different offset from the beginning of the group.

It is common for the directory-listing command *ls* to read all the inodes of every file in a directory, making it desirable for all such inodes to be close together on the disk. For this reason, the inode for a file is usually allocated from the same cylinder group as is the inode of the file's parent directory. Not everything can be localized, however, so an inode for a new directory is put in a *different* cylinder group from that of its parent directory. The cylinder group chosen for such a new directory inode is that with the greatest number of unused inodes.

To reduce disk head seeks involved in accessing the data blocks of a file, we allocate blocks from the same cylinder group as often as possible. Because a single file cannot be allowed to take up all the blocks in a cylinder group, a file exceeding a certain size (such as 2 megabytes) has further block allocation redirected to a different cylinder group, the new group being chosen from among those having more than average free space. If the file continues to grow, allocation is again redirected (at each megabyte) to yet another cylinder group. Thus, all the blocks of a small file are likely to be in the same cylinder group, and the number of long head seeks involved in accessing a large file is kept small.

There are two levels of disk-block-allocation routines. The global policy routines select a desired disk block according to the considerations already discussed. The local policy routines use the specific information recorded in the cylinder blocks to choose a block near the one requested. If the requested block is not in use, it is returned. Otherwise, the block rotationally closest to the one requested in the same cylinder, or a block in a different cylinder but in the same cylinder group, is returned. If there are no more blocks in the cylinder group, a quadratic rehash is done among all the other cylinder groups to find a block; if that fails, an exhaustive search is done. If enough free space (typically 10 percent) is left in the file system, blocks usually are found where desired, the quadratic rehash and exhaustive search are not used, and performance of the file system does not degrade with use.

Because of the increased efficiency of the Fast File System, typical disks are now utilized at 30 percent of their raw transfer capacity. This percentage is a marked improvement over that realized with the Version 7 file system, which used about 3 percent of the bandwidth.

4.3BSD Tahoe introduced the Fat Fast File System, which allows the number of inodes per cylinder group, the number of cylinders per cylinder group, and the number of distinguished rotational positions to be set when the file system is created. 4.3BSD used to set these parameters according to the disk hardware type.

I/O SYSTEM

One of the purposes of an operating system is to hide the peculiarities of specific hardware devices from the user. For example, the file system presents a simple consistent storage facility (the file) independent of the underlying disk hardware. In UNIX, the peculiarities of I/O devices are also hidden from the bulk of the kernel itself by the *I/O system*. The I/O system consists of a buffer caching system, general device driver code, and drivers for specific hardware devices. Only the device driver knows the peculiarities of a specific device. The major parts of the I/O system are diagrammed in Figure 4-10.

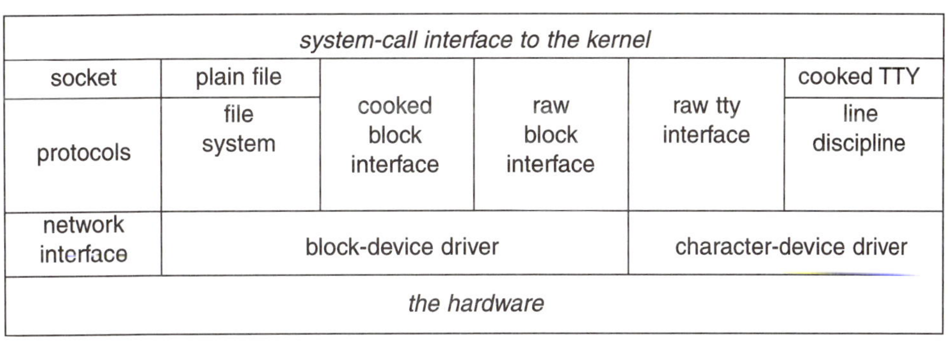

FIGURE 4-10 *4.3BSD Kernel I/O Structure*

There are three main kinds of I/O in 4.3BSD: block devices, character devices, and the *socket* interface. The socket interface, together with its protocols and network interfaces, will be treated in the section on sockets.

Block devices include disks and tapes. Their distinguishing characteristic is that they are directly addressable in a fixed block size—usually, 512 bytes. A block-device driver is required to isolate details of tracks, cylinders, and so on, from the rest of the kernel. Block devices are accessible directly through appropriate device special files (such as */dev/rp0*), but are more commonly accessed indirectly through the file system. In either case, transfers are buffered through the *block buffer cache*, which has a profound effect on efficiency.

Character devices include terminals and line printers, but also almost everything else (except network interfaces) that does not use the block buffer cache. For instance, */dev/mem* is an interface to physical main memory, and */dev/null* is a bottomless sink for data and an endless source of end-of-file markers. Some devices, such as high-speed graphics interfaces, may have their own buffers or may always do I/O directly into the user's data space; because they do not use the block buffer cache, they are classed as character devices.

Terminals and terminal-like devices use *C-lists*, which are buffers smaller than those of the block buffer cache.

Block devices and *character* devices are the two main device classes. Device drivers are accessed by one of two arrays of entry points. One array is for block devices; the other is for character devices. A device is distinguished by a class (block or character) and a *device number*. The device number consists of two parts. The *major device number* is used to index the array for character or block devices to find entries into the appropriate device driver. The *minor device number* is interpreted by the device driver as, for example, a logical disk partition or a terminal line.

A device driver is connected to the rest of the kernel only by the entry points recorded in the array for its class, and by its use of common buffering systems. This segregation is important for portability, and also for system configuration.

Block Buffer Cache

The block devices use a block buffer cache. The buffer cache consists of a number of buffer headers, each of which can point to a piece of physical memory, as well as to a device number and a block number on the device. The buffer headers for blocks not currently in use are kept in several linked lists, one each for:

- Buffers recently used, linked in LRU order (the LRU list)
- Buffers not recently used, or without valid contents (the AGE list)
- EMPTY buffers with no physical memory associated with them

The buffers in these lists are also hashed by device and block number for search efficiency.

When a block is wanted from a device (a read), the cache is searched. If the block is found, it is used, and no I/O transfer is necessary. If it is not found, a buffer is chosen from the AGE list, or the LRU list if AGE is empty. Then the device number and block number associated with it are updated, memory is found for it if necessary, and the new data are transferred into it from the device. If there are no empty buffers, the LRU buffer is written to its device (if it is modified) and the buffer is reused.

On a write, if the block in question is already in the buffer cache, the new data are put in the buffer (overwriting any previous data), the buffer header is marked to indicate the buffer has been modified, and no I/O is immediately necessary. The data will be written when the buffer is needed for other data. If the block is not found in the buffer cache, an empty buffer is chosen (as with a read) and a transfer is done to this buffer.

Writes are periodically forced for dirty buffer blocks to minimize potential file-system inconsistencies after a crash.

The number of data in a buffer in 4.3BSD is variable, up to a maximum over all file systems, usually 8K. The minimum size is the paging-cluster size, usually 1024 bytes. Buffers are page-cluster aligned, and any page cluster may be mapped into only one buffer at a time, just as any disk block may be mapped into only one buffer at a time. The EMPTY list holds buffer headers which are used if a physical memory block of 8K is split to hold multiple, smaller blocks. Headers are needed for these blocks and are retrieved from EMPTY.

The number of data in a buffer may grow as a user process writes more data following those already in the buffer. When this increase in the data occurs, a new buffer large enough to hold all the data is allocated, and the original data are copied into it, followed by the new data. If a buffer shrinks, a buffer is taken off the empty queue, excess pages are put in it, and that buffer is released to be written to disk.

Some devices, such as magnetic tapes, require blocks to be written in a certain order, so facilities are provided to force a synchronous write of buffers to these devices, in the correct order. Directory blocks are also written synchronously, to forestall crash inconsistencies. Consider the chaos that could occur if many changes were made to a directory, but the directory entries themselves were not updated.

The size of the buffer cache can have a profound effect on the performance of a system, because, if it is large enough, the percentage of cache hits can be high and the number of actual I/O transfers low.

There are some interesting interactions among the buffer cache, the file system, and the disk drivers. When data are written to a disk file, they are buffered in the cache, and the disk driver sorts its output queue according to disk address. These two actions allow the disk driver to minimize disk head seeks and to write data at times optimized for disk rotation. Unless synchronous writes are required, a process writing to disk simply writes into the buffer cache, and the system asynchronously writes the data to disk when convenient. The user process sees very fast writes. When data are read from a disk file, the block I/O system does some read-ahead; however, writes are much nearer to asynchronous than are reads. Thus, output to the disk through the file system is often faster than is input for large transfers, counter to intuition.

Raw Device Interfaces

Almost every block device also has a character interface, and these are called *raw device interfaces*. Such an interface differs from the *block interface* in that the block buffer cache is bypassed.

Each disk driver maintains a queue of pending transfers. Each record in the queue specifies whether it is a read or a write, a main memory address for the transfer (usually in 512-byte increments), a device address for the transfer (usually the address of a disk sector), and a transfer size (in sectors). It is simple to map the information from a block buffer to what is required for this queue.

It is almost as simple to map a piece of main memory corresponding to part of a user process's virtual address space. This mapping is what a raw disk interface, for instance, does. Unbuffered transfers directly to or from a user's virtual address space are thus allowed. The size of the transfer is limited by the physical devices, some of which require an even number of bytes.

The kernel accomplishes transfers for swapping and paging simply by putting the appropriate request on the queue for the appropriate device. No special swapping or paging device drive is needed.

The 4.2BSD file-system implementation was actually written and largely tested as a user process that used a raw disk interface, before the code was moved into the kernel. In an interesting about-face, the Mach operating system has no file system per se. File systems can be implemented as user-level tasks.

C-Lists

Terminal drivers use a character buffering system, which keeps small blocks of characters (usually 28 bytes) in linked lists. There are routines to enqueue and dequeue characters for such lists. Although all free character buffers are kept in a single free list, most device drivers that use them limit the number of characters that may be queued at one time for any given terminal line.

A **write** system call to a terminal enqueues characters on a list for the device. An initial transfer is started, and interrupts cause dequeuing of characters and further transfers.

Input is similarly interrupt driven. Terminal drivers typically support *two* input queues, however, and conversion from the first (raw queue) to the other (canonical queue) is triggered by the interrupt routine putting an end-of-line character on the raw queue. The process doing a read on the device is then awakened, and its system phase does the conversion; the characters thus put on the canonical queue are then available to be returned to the user process by the read.

It is also possible to have the device driver bypass the canonical queue and return characters directly from the raw queue. This mode of operation is known as *raw mode*. Full-screen editors, and other programs that need to react to every keystroke, use this mode.

INTERPROCESS COMMUNICATION

Many tasks can be accomplished in isolated processes, but many others require interprocess communication. Isolated computing systems have long served for many applications, but networking is increasingly important. With the increasing use of personal workstations, resource sharing is becoming more common. Interprocess communication has not traditionally been one of UNIX's strong points.

Most UNIX systems have not permitted *shared memory* because the PDP-11 hardware did not encourage it. System V does support a shared-memory facility, and one was planned for 4.2BSD, but was not implemented due to time constraints. Solaris 2 supports shared memory, as do many other current versions of UNIX. In any case, shared memory presents a problem in a networked environment, because network accesses can never be as fast as memory accesses on the local machine. Although we could, of course, pretend that memory was shared between two separate machines by copying data across a network transparently, the major benefit of shared memory (speed) would be lost.

SOCKETS

The *pipe* is the IPC mechanism most characteristic of UNIX. A pipe permits a reliable unidirectional byte stream between two processes. It is traditionally implemented as an ordinary file, with a few exceptions. It has no name in the file system, being created instead by the **pipe** system call. Its size is fixed, and when a process attempts to write to a full pipe, the process is suspended. Once all data previously written into the pipe have been read out, writing continues at the beginning of the file (pipes are not true circular buffers). One benefit of the small size (usually 4096 bytes) of pipes is that pipe data are seldom actually written to disk; they usually are kept in memory by the normal block buffer cache.

In 4.3BSD, pipes are implemented as a special case of the *socket* mechanism. The socket mechanism provides a general interface not only to facilities such as pipes, which are local to one machine, but also to networking facilities. Even on the same machine, a pipe can be used only by two processes related through use of the **fork** system call. The socket mechanism can be used by unrelated processes.

A socket is an endpoint of communication. A socket in use usually has an *address* bound to it. The nature of the address depends on the *communication domain* of the socket. A characteristic property of a domain is that processes communicating in the same domain use the same *address format*. A single socket can communicate in only one domain.

The three domains currently implemented in 4.3BSD are the UNIX domain (AF_UNIX), the Internet domain (AF_INET), and the XEROX Network Services (NS) domain (AF_NS). The address format of the UNIX domain is ordinary file-system path names, such as */alpha/beta/gamma*. Processes communicating in the Internet domain use DARPA Internet communications protocols (such as TCP/IP) and Internet addresses, which consist of a 32-bit host number and a 32-bit port number (representing a rendezvous point on the host).

There are several *socket types*, which represent classes of services. Each type may or may not be implemented in any communication domain. If a type is implemented in a given domain, it may be implemented by one or more protocols, which may be selected by the user:

- **Stream sockets:** These sockets provide reliable, duplex, sequenced data streams. No data are lost or duplicated in delivery, and there are no record boundaries. This type is supported in the Internet domain by the TCP protocol. In the UNIX domain, pipes are implemented as a pair of communicating stream sockets.
- **Sequenced packet sockets:** These sockets provide data streams like those of stream sockets, except that record boundaries are provided. This type is used in the XEROX AF_NS protocol.
- **Datagram sockets:** These sockets transfer messages of variable size in either direction. There is no guarantee that such messages will arrive in the same order

they were sent, or that they will be unduplicated, or that they will arrive at all, but the original message (record) size is preserved in any datagram that does arrive. This type is supported in the Internet domain by the UDP protocol.

- **Reliably delivered message sockets:** These sockets transfer messages that are guaranteed to arrive, and that otherwise are like the messages transferred using datagram sockets. This type is currently unsupported.
- **Raw sockets:** These sockets allow direct access by processes to the protocols that support the other socket types. The protocols accessible include not only the uppermost ones, but also lower-level protocols. For example, in the Internet domain, it is possible to reach TCP, IP beneath that, or an Ethernet protocol beneath that. This capability is useful for developing new protocols.

The socket facility has a set of system calls specific to it. The **socket** system call creates a socket. It takes as arguments specifications of the communication domain, the socket type, and the protocol to be used to support that type. The value returned by the call is a small integer called a *socket descriptor*, which is in the same name space as file descriptors. The socket descriptor indexes the array of open "files" in the *u* structure in the kernel, and has a file structure allocated for it. The 4.3BSD file structure may point to a *socket* structure instead of to an inode. In this case, certain socket information (such as the socket's type, message count, and the data in its input and output queues) is kept directly in the socket structure.

For another process to address a socket, the socket must have a name. A name is bound to a socket by the **bind** system call, which takes the socket descriptor, a pointer to the name, and the length of the name as a byte string. The contents and length of the byte string depend on the address format. The **connect** system call is used to initiate a connection. The arguments are syntactically the same as those for **bind**; the socket descriptor represents the local socket and the address is that of the foreign socket to which the attempt to connect is made.

Many processes that communicate using the socket IPC follow the *client-server model.* In this model, the *server* process provides a *service* to the *client* process. When the service is available, the server process listens on a well-known address, and the client process uses **connect**, as described previously, to reach the server.

A server process uses **socket** to create a socket and **bind** to bind the well-known address of its service to that socket. Then, it uses the **listen** system call to tell the kernel that it is ready to **accept** connections from clients, and to specify how many pending connections the kernel should queue until the server can service them. Finally, the server uses the **accept** system call to accept individual connections. Both **listen** and **accept** take as an argument the socket descriptor of the original socket. **Accept** returns a new socket descriptor corresponding to the new connection; the original socket descriptor is still open for further connections. The server usually uses **fork** to produce a new process after the **accept** to service the client while the original server process continues to listen for more connections.

There are also system calls for setting parameters of a connection and for returning the address of the foreign socket after an **accept**.

When a connection for a socket type such as a stream socket is established, the addresses of both endpoints are known and no further addressing information is needed to transfer data. The ordinary **read** and **write** system calls may then be used to transfer data.

The simplest way to terminate a connection and to destroy the associated socket is to use the **close** system call on its socket descriptor. We may also wish to terminate only one direction of communication of a duplex connection; the **shutdown** system call can be used for this purpose.

Some socket types, such as datagram sockets, do not support connections; instead, their sockets exchange datagrams that must be addressed individually. The system calls **sendto** and **recvfrom** are used for such connections. Both take as arguments a socket descriptor, a buffer pointer and the length, and an address-buffer pointer and length. The address buffer contains the address to send to for **sendto** and is filled in with the address of the datagram just received by **recvfrom**. The number of data actually transferred is returned by both system calls.

The **select** system call can be used to multiplex data transfers on several file descriptors and/or socket descriptors. It can even be used to allow one server process to listen for client connections for many services and to **fork** a process for each connection as the connection is made. The server does a **socket, bind**, and **listen** for each service, and then does a **select** on all the socket descriptors. When **select** indicates activity on a descriptor, the server does an **accept** on it and forks a process on the new descriptor returned by **accept**, leaving the parent process to do a **select** again.

Network Support

Almost all current UNIX systems support the UUCP network facilities, which are mostly used over dial-up telephone lines to support the UUCP mail network and the USENET news network. These are, however, rudimentary networking facilities, as they do not support even remote login, much less remote procedure call or distributed file systems. These facilities are also almost completely implemented as user processes, and are not part of the operating system proper.

4.3BSD supports the DARPA Internet protocols UDP, TCP, IP, and ICMP on a wide range of Ethernet, token-ring, and ARPANET interfaces. The framework in the kernel to support this is intended to facilitate the implementation of further protocols, and all protocols are accessible via the socket interface. The first version of the code was written by Rob Gurwitz of BBN as an add-on package for 4.1BSD.

The International Standards Organization's (ISO) Open System Interconnection (OSI) Reference Model for networking prescribes seven layers of network protocols and strict methods of communication between them. An implementation of a protocol may communicate only with a peer entity speaking the same protocol at the same layer, or with the protocol-protocol interface of a protocol in the layer immediately above or below in the same system. The ISO networking model is implemented in 4.3BSD Reno and 4.4BSD.

The 4.3BSD networking implementation, and to a certain extent the *socket* facility, is more oriented toward the ARPANET Reference Model (ARM). The ARPANET in its original form served as a proof of concept for many networking concepts, such as packet switching and protocol layering. The ARPANET was retired in 1988 because the hardware that supported it was no longer state of the art. Its successors, such as the NSFNET and the Internet, are even larger, and serve as a communications utility for researchers and as a testbed for Internet gateway research. The ARM predates the ISO model; the ISO model was in large part inspired by the ARPANET research.

Although the ISO model is often interpreted as requiring a limit of one protocol communicating per layer, the ARM allows several protocols in the same layer. There are only four protocol layers in the ARM, plus:

- **Process/Applications:** This layer subsumes the application, presentation, and session layers of the ISO model. Such user-level programs as the File Transfer Protocol (FTP) and Telnet (remote login) exist at this level.
- **Host-Host:** This layer corresponds to ISO's transport and the top part of its network layers. Both the Transmission Control Protocol (TCP) and the Internet Protocol (IP) are in this layer, with TCP on top of IP. TCP corresponds to an ISO transport protocol, and IP performs the addressing functions of the ISO network layer.
- **Network Interface:** This layer spans the lower part of the ISO network layer and all of the data-link layer. The protocols involved here depend on the physical network type. The ARPANET uses the IMP-Host protocols, whereas an Ethernet uses Ethernet protocols.
- **Network Hardware:** The ARM is primarily concerned with software, so there is no explicit network hardware layer; however, any actual network will have hardware corresponding to the ISO physical layer.

The networking framework in 4.3BSD is more generalized than is either the ISO model or the ARM, although it is most closely related to the ARM; see Figure 4-11.

ISO reference model	ARPANET reference model	4.2BSD layers	example layering
application	process applications	user programs and libraries	telnet
presentation			
session		sockets	sock_stream
transport	host–host	protocol	TCP
network data link			IP
hardware	network interface	network interfaces	Ethernet driver
	network hardware	network hardware	interlan controller

FIGURE 4-11 *Network Reference Models and Layering*

User processes communicate with network protocols (and thus with other processes on other machines) via the *socket* facility, which corresponds to the ISO Session layer, as it is responsible for setting up and controlling communications.

Sockets are supported by *protocols*—possibly by several, layered one on another. A protocol may provide services such as reliable delivery, suppression of duplicate transmissions, flow control, or addressing, depending on the socket type being supported and the services required by any higher protocols.

A protocol may communicate with another protocol or with the network interface that is appropriate for the network hardware. There is little restriction in the general framework on what protocols may communicate with what other protocols, or on how many protocols may be layered on top of one another. The user process may, by means of the raw socket type, directly access any layer of protocol from the uppermost used to support one of the other socket types, such as streams, down to a raw network interface. This capability is used by routing processes and also for new protocol development.

There tends to be one *network-interface* driver per network controller type. The network interface is responsible for handling characteristics specific to the local network being addressed. This arrangement ensures that the protocols using the interface do not need to be concerned with these characteristics.

The functions of the network interface depend largely on the *network hardware*, which is whatever is necessary for the network to which it is connected. Some networks may support reliable transmission at this level, but most do not. Some networks provide broadcast addressing, but many do not.

The socket facility and the networking framework use a common set of memory buffers, or *mbufs*. These are intermediate in size between the large buffers used by the block I/O system and the C-lists used by character devices. An *mbuf* is 128 bytes long, 112 bytes of which may be used for data; the rest is used for pointers to link the *mbuf* into queues and for indicators of how much of the data area is actually in use.

Data are ordinarily passed between layers (socket-protocol, protocol-protocol, or protocol-network interface) in *mbufs*. This ability to pass the buffers containing the data eliminates some data copying, but there is still frequently a need to remove or add protocol headers. It is also convenient and efficient for many purposes to be able to hold data that occupy an area the size of the memory-management page. Thus, it is possible for the data of an *mbuf* to reside not in the *mbuf* itself, but rather elsewhere in memory. There is an *mbufs* page table for this purpose, as well as a pool of pages dedicated to *mbuf* use.

SUMMARY

The early advantages of UNIX were that this system was written in a high-level language, was distributed in source form, and had provided powerful operating-system primitives on an inexpensive platform. These advantages led to UNIX's popularity at educational, research, and government institutions, and eventually in the commercial world. This popularity first produced many strains of UNIX with variant and improved facilities. Market pressures are currently leading to the consolidation of these versions. One of the most influential versions is 4.3BSD, developed at Berkeley for the VAX, and later ported to many other platforms.

UNIX provides a file system with tree-structured directories. Files are supported by the kernel as unstructured sequences of bytes. Direct access and sequential access are supported through system calls and library routines.

Files are stored as an array of fixed-size data blocks with perhaps a trailing fragment. The data blocks are found by pointers in the inode. Directory entries point to inodes. Disk space is allocated from cylinder groups to minimize head movement and to improve performance.

UNIX is a multiprogrammed system. Processes can easily create new processes with the **fork** system call. Processes can communicate with pipes or, more generally, sockets. They may be grouped into jobs that may be controlled with signals.

Processes are represented by two structures: the process structure and the user structure. CPU scheduling is a priority algorithm with dynamically computed priorities that reduces to round-robin scheduling in the extreme case.

4.3BSD memory management is swapping supported by paging. A *pagedaemon* process uses a modified second-chance page-replacement algorithm to keep enough free frames to support the executing processes.

Page and file I/O uses a block buffer cache to minimize the amount of actual I/O. Terminal devices use a separate character buffering system.

Networking support is one of the most important features in 4.3BSD. The socket concept provides the programming mechanism to access other processes, even across a network. Sockets provide an interface to several sets of protocols.

THE LINUX SYSTEM

BSD is just one of the UNIX-like systems. Linux is another UNIX-like system that has gained popularity in recent years. In this section, we look at the history and development of Linux, and cover the user and programmer interfaces that Linux presents—interfaces that owe a great deal to the UNIX tradition. We also discuss the internal methods by which Linux implements these interfaces. However, since Linux has been designed to run as many standard UNIX applications as possible, it has much in common with existing UNIX implementations. We do not duplicate the basic description of UNIX given in the previous section.

Linux is a rapidly evolving operating system. This section describes specifically the Linux 2.0 kernel.

HISTORY

Linux looks and feels much like any other UNIX system, and indeed UNIX compatibility has been a major design goal of the Linux project. However, Linux is much younger than most UNIX systems. Its development began in 1991, when a Finnish student, Linus Torvalds, wrote and christened a small but self-contained kernel for the 80386 processor, the first true 32-bit processor in Intel's range of PC-compatible CPUs.

Early in its development, Linux's source code was made available for free on the Internet. As a result, its history has been one of collaboration by many users from all around the world, corresponding almost exclusively over the Internet. From an initial kernel that partially implemented a small subset of the UNIX system services, Linux has grown to include evermore UNIX functionality.

In its early days, Linux development revolved largely around the central operating-system kernel—the core, privileged executive that manages all system resources and that interacts directly with the hardware. Much more than this kernel is needed to produce a full operating system, of course. It is useful to make the distinction between the Linux *kernel* and a Linux *system*: the kernel in Linux is an entirely original piece of software developed from scratch by the Linux community; the Linux system, as we know it today, includes a multitude of components, some written from scratch, others borrowed from other development projects or created in collaboration with other teams.

The basic Linux system is a standard environment for applications and for user programming, but it does not enforce any standard means of managing the available functionality as a whole. As Linux has matured, there has been a need for another layer of functionality on top of the Linux system. A Linux *distribution* includes all the standard components of the Linux system, plus a set of administrative tools to simplify the initial installation and subsequent upgrading of Linux, and to manage installation and deinstallation of other packages on the system. A modern distribution also typically includes tools for management of file systems, creation and management of user accounts, networking administration, and so on.

The Linux Kernel

The first Linux kernel released to the public was version 0.01, dated May 14th, 1991. It had no networking, ran on only 80386-compatible Intel processors and PC hardware, and had extremely limited device-driver support. The virtual-memory subsystem was also fairly basic, with no support for memory-mapped files; however, even this early incarnation supported shared pages with copy-on-write. The only file system supported was the Minix file system—the first Linux kernels were cross-developed on a Minix platform. However, the kernel did implement proper UNIX processes with protected address spaces.

It was not until March 14, 1994 that the next milestone version, Linux 1.0, was released. This release culminated 3 years of rapid development of the Linux kernel. Perhaps the single biggest new feature was networking: 1.0 included support for UNIX's standard TCP/IP networking protocols, as well as a BSD-compatible socket interface for networking programming. Device-driver support was added for running IP over an ethernet or (using PPP or SLIP protocols) over serial lines or modems.

The 1.0 kernel also included a new, much enhanced file system without the limitations of the original Minix file system, and supported a range of SCSI controllers for high-performance disk access. The virtual-memory subsystem was also extended to support paging to swap files and memory mapping of arbitrary files (but only read-only memory-mapping was implemented in 1.0).

A range of extra hardware support was also included in this release. Although still restricted to the Intel/PC platform, hardware support had grown to include floppy-disk and CD-ROM devices, as well as sound cards, a range of mice, and international keyboards. Floating-point emulation was also provided in the kernel for 80386 users who had no 80387 math coprocessor, and System V UNIX-style interprocess communication (IPC), including shared memory, semaphores, and message queues, was implemented. Simple support for dynamically loadable and unloadable kernel modules was also provided.

At this point, development started on the 1.1 kernel stream, but numerous bug-fix patches were released subsequently against 1.0. This pattern was adopted as the standard numbering convention for Linux kernels: Kernels with an odd minor-version number such as 1.1, 1.3, or 2.1 are development kernels; even-numbered minor-version numbers are stable, production kernels. Updates against the stable kernels are intended as only remedial versions, whereas the development kernels may include newer and relatively untested functionality.

In March 1995, the 1.2 kernel was released. This release did not represent nearly the same improvement in functionality as the 1.0 release, but it did include support for a much wider variety of hardware, including the new PCI hardware bus architecture. Another PC-specific feature—support for the 80386 CPU's virtual 8086 mode—was added to allow emulation of the DOS operating system for PC computers. The networking stack was updated to provide support for the IPX protocol, and a more complete IP implementation was provided that included accounting and firewalling functionality.

The 1.2 kernel also represented the final PC-only Linux kernel. The source distribution for Linux 1.2 included partially implemented support for Sparc, Alpha, and MIPS CPUs, but full integration of these other architectures did not begin until after the 1.2 stable kernel was released.

The Linux 1.2 release concentrated on wider hardware support and more complete implementations of existing functionality. Much new functionality was under development at the time, but integration of the new code into the main kernel source code had been deferred until after the stable 1.2 kernel had been released. As a result, the 1.3 development stream saw a great deal of new functionality added to the kernel.

This work was finally released as Linux 2.0 in June 1996. This release was given a major version-number increment on account of two major new capabilities: support for multiple architectures, including a fully 64-bit native Alpha port, and support for multiprocessor architectures. Linux distributions based on 2.0 are also available for the Motorola 68000-series processors and for Sun's Sparc systems. A derived version of Linux running on top of the Mach Microkernel also runs on PC and PowerMac systems.

The changes in 2.0 did not stop there. The memory-management code was substantially improved, to provide a unified cache for file-system data independent of the caching of block devices. As a result of this change, the kernel offered greatly increased file-system and virtual-memory performance. For the first time, file-system caching was extended to networked file systems, and writable memory-mapped regions also were supported.

The 2.0 kernel also included much improved TCP/IP performance, and a number of new networking protocols were added, including AppleTalk, AX.25 amateur radio networking, and ISDN support. The ability to mount remote Netware and SMB (Microsoft LanManager) network volumes was added.

Other major improvements in 2.0 were support for internal kernel threads, for handling dependencies between loadable modules, and for automatic loading of modules on demand. Dynamic configuration of the kernel at run time was much improved through a new, standardized configuration interface. Additional, unrelated new features included file-system quotas and POSIX-compatible real-time process-scheduling classes.

The Linux System

In many ways, the Linux kernel forms the core of the Linux project, but other components make up the complete Linux operating system. Whereas the Linux kernel is composed entirely of code written from scratch specifically for the Linux project, much of the supporting software which makes up the Linux system is not exclusive to Linux, but rather is common to a number of UNIX-like operating systems. In particular, Linux uses many tools developed as part of Berkeley's BSD operating system, MIT's X Window System, and the Free Software Foundation's GNU project.

This sharing of tools has worked in both directions. The main system libraries of Linux were originally started by the GNU project, but much effort was expended by the Linux community in improving the libraries to address omissions, inefficiencies, and bugs. Other components such as the GNU C compiler, **gcc**, were already of sufficiently high quality to be used directly in Linux. The networking-administration tools under Linux were derived from code first developed for 4.3BSD, but more recent BSD derivatives such as FreeBSD have borrowed code from Linux in return, such as the Intel floating-point-emulation math library and the PC sound-hardware device drivers.

The Linux system as a whole is maintained by a loose network of developers collaborating over the Internet, with small groups or individuals having responsibility for maintaining the integrity of specific components. A small number of public ftp (Internet file-transfer protocol) archive sites act as de facto standard repositories for these components. The *File System Hierarchy Standard* document is also maintained by the Linux community as a means of keeping compatibility across the various different system components. This standard specifies the overall layout of a standard Linux file system; it determines under which directory names configuration files, libraries, system binaries, and run-time data files should be stored.

Linux Distributions

In theory, anybody can install a Linux system by fetching the latest revisions of the necessary system components from the ftp sites and compiling them. In Linux's early days, this operation was often precisely the one that a Linux user had to carry out. As Linux has matured, however, various individuals and groups have attempted to make this job less painful, by providing a standard, precompiled set of packages for easy installation.

These collections, or *distributions*, include much more than just the basic Linux system. They typically include extra system-installation and management utilities, as well as precompiled and ready-to-install packages of many of the common UNIX tools, such as news servers, web browsers, text-processing and editing tools, and even games.

The first distributions managed these packages by simply providing a means of unpacking all the files into the appropriate places. One of the important contributions of modern distributions, however, is advanced package management. Today's Linux distributions include a package-tracking database that allows packages to be installed, upgraded, or removed painlessly.

In the early days of Linux, the SLS distribution was the first collection of Linux packages that was recognizable as a complete distribution. Although it could be installed as a single entity, SLS lacked the package-management tools now expected of Linux distributions. The *Slackware* distribution represented a great improvement in overall quality (despite also having poor package management); it is still one of the most widely installed distributions in the Linux community.

Since Slackware's release, a large number of commercial and noncommercial Linux distributions have become available. *Red Hat* and *Debian* are particularly popular distributions from a commercial Linux support company and from the free-software Linux community, respectively. Other commercially supported Linuxes include distributions from *Caldera, Craftworks*, and *WorkGroup Solutions*. A large Linux following in Germany has resulted in a number of dedicated German-language distributions, including versions from *SuSE* and *Unifix*. There are too many Linux distributions in current circulation for us to present an exhaustive list. The variety of distributions available does not prohibit compatibility across Linux distributions. The *RPM* package file format is used, or at least understood, by the majority of distributions, and commercial applications distributed in this format can be installed and run on any distribution that can accept RPM files.

Linux Licensing

The Linux kernel is distributed under the GNU General Public License (GPL), the terms of which are set out by the Free Software Foundation. Linux is not public-domain software: *Public domain* implies that the authors have waived copyright over the software, but copyright over Linux code is still held by the code's various authors. Linux is *free* software, however: It is free in the sense that people can copy it, modify it, use it in any manner they want, and give away their own copies without any restrictions.

The main implications of Linux's licensing terms are that anybody using Linux, or creating her own derivative of Linux (a legitimate exercise), cannot make the derived product proprietary. Software released under the GPL cannot be redistributed as a binary-only product. If you release software that includes any GPLed components, then, under the GPL, you must make source code available alongside any binary distributions. (This restriction does not prohibit making—or even selling—binary-only software distributions, as long as anybody who receives binaries is also given the opportunity to get source code too, for a reasonable distribution charge.)

DESIGN PRINCIPLES

In its overall design, Linux resembles any other traditional, nonmicrokernel UNIX implementation. It is a multiuser, multitasking system with a full set of UNIX-compatible tools. Linux's file system adheres to traditional UNIX semantics, and the standard UNIX networking model is fully implemented. The internal details of Linux's design have been heavily influenced by its history.

Although Linux runs on a wide variety of platforms, in its early days it was developed exclusively on PC architecture. A great deal of that early development was carried out by individual enthusiasts, rather than by well-funded development or research facilities, so from the start Linux attempted to squeeze as much functionality as possible from limited resources. Today, Linux can run happily on a multiprocessor machine with hundreds of megabytes of main memory and many gigabytes of disk space, but it is still capable of operating usefully in under 4 MB of RAM.

As PCs became more powerful and as memory and hard disks became cheaper, the original, minimalist Linux kernels grew to implement more UNIX functionality. Speed and efficiency are still important design goals, but much of the recent and current work on Linux has concentrated on a second major design goal: standardization. One of the prices paid for the diversity of UNIX implementations currently available is that source code written for one flavor may not necessarily compile or run correctly on another. Even when the same system calls are present on two different UNIX systems, they may not necessarily behave in exactly the same way. The POSIX standards are a set of specifications of different aspects of operating-system behavior. There are POSIX documents for common operating-system functionality and for extensions such as process threads and real-time operations. Linux is designed to be compliant with the relevant POSIX documents; at least two Linux distributions have achieved official POSIX certification.

Because it presents standard interfaces to both the programmer and the user, Linux should offer few surprises to anybody familiar with UNIX. We do not detail these interfaces under Linux. The sections on the programmer interface and user interface of 4.3BSD apply equally well to Linux. By default, however, the Linux programming interface adheres to SVR4 UNIX semantics, rather than to BSD behavior. A separate set of libraries is available to implement BSD semantics in places where the two behaviors are significantly different.

There are many other standards in the UNIX world, but full certification of Linux against them is sometimes slowed because they are often available only for a fee, and there is a substantial expense involved in certifying an operating system's compliance with most standards. However, supporting a wide base of applications is important for any operating system, so implementation of standards is a major goal for Linux development even if the implementation is not formally certified. In addition to the basic POSIX standard, Linux currently supports the POSIX threading extensions and a subset of the POSIX extensions for real-time process control.

Components of a Linux System

The Linux system is composed of three main bodies of code, in line with most traditional UNIX implementations:

- The **kernel** is responsible for maintaining all the important abstractions of the operating system, including such things as virtual memory and processes.
- The **system libraries** define a standard set of functions through which applications can interact with the kernel, and which implement much of the operating-system functionality that does not need the full privileges of kernel code.
- The **system utilities** are programs that perform individual, specialized management tasks. Some system utilities may be invoked just once to initialize and configure some aspect of the system; others (known as **daemons** in UNIX terminology) may run permanently, handling such tasks as responding to incoming network connections, accepting logon requests from terminals, or updating log files.

Figure 4-12 illustrates the various components that make up a full Linux system. The most important distinction here is between the kernel and everything else. All the kernel code executes in the processor's privileged mode with full access to all the physical resources of the computer. Linux refers to this privileged mode as *kernel mode*, equivalent to the monitor

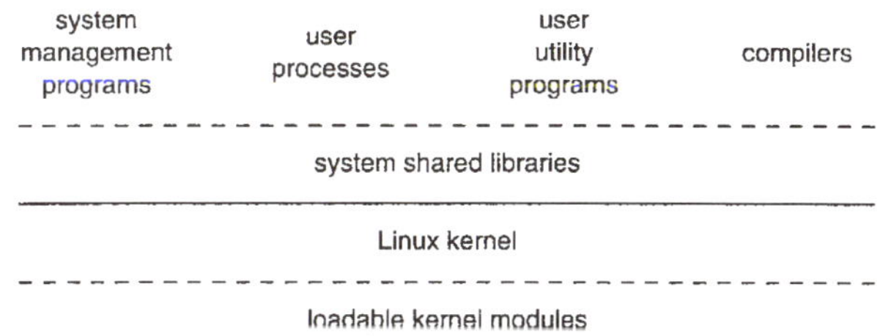

FIGURE 4-12 *Components of the Linux System*

mode. Under Linux, no user-mode code is built into the kernel. Any operating-system-support code that does not need to run in kernel mode is placed into the system libraries instead.

Although various modern operating systems have adopted a message-passing architecture for their kernel internals, Linux retains UNIX's historical model: The kernel is created as a single, monolithic binary. The main reason is to improve performance: Because all kernel code and data structures are kept in a single address space, no context switches are necessary when a process calls an operating-system function or when a hardware interrupt is delivered. Not only the core scheduling and virtual-memory code occupies this address space; *all* kernel code, including all device drivers, file systems and networking code, is present in the same single address space.

Just because all the kernel shares this same melting pot does not imply that there is no scope for modularity. In just the same way that user applications can load shared libraries at run time to pull in a needed piece of code, so the Linux kernel can load (and unload) modules dynamically at run time. The kernel does not necessarily need to know in advance which modules may be loaded—they are truly independent loadable components.

The Linux kernel forms the core of the Linux operating system. It provides all the functionality necessary to run processes, and it provides system services to give arbitrated and protected access to hardware resources. The kernel implements all the features that are required to qualify as an operating system. On its own, however, the operating system provided by the Linux kernel looks nothing like a UNIX system. It is missing many of the extra features of UNIX, and the features that it does provide are not necessarily provided in the format in which a UNIX application expects them to appear. The operating-system interface visible to running applications is not directly maintained by the kernel. Rather, applications make calls to the **system libraries**, which in turn call the operating-system services as necessary.

The system libraries provide many types of functionality. At the simplest level, they allow applications to make kernel system service requests. Making a system call involves transferring control from unprivileged user mode to privileged kernel mode; the details of this transfer vary from architecture to architecture. The libraries take care of collecting together the system-call arguments and, if necessary, arranging those arguments in the special form necessary to make the system call.

The libraries may also provide more complex versions of the basic system calls. For example, the C language's buffered file-handling functions are all implemented in the system libraries, providing more advanced control of file I/O than the basic kernel system calls provide. The libraries also provide routines that do not correspond to system calls at all, such as sorting algorithms, mathematical functions, and string-manipulation routines. All the functions that are necessary to support the running of UNIX or POSIX applications are implemented here in the system libraries.

Finally, the Linux system includes a wide variety of user-mode programs—both system utilities and user utilities. The system utilities include all the programs necessary to initialize the system, such as those to configure network devices or to load kernel modules. Continually running server programs also count as system utilities; such programs handle user login requests, incoming network connections, and the printer queues.

Not all the standard utilities serve key system-administration functions. The UNIX user environment contains a large number of standard utilities to do simple everyday tasks, such as listing directories, moving around and deleting files, or displaying the contents of a file. More complex utilities can perform text-processing functions, such as sorting textual data or performing pattern searches on input text. Together, these utilities form a standard toolset that users can expect to see on any UNIX system; although they do not perform any operating-system function, they are still an important part of the basic Linux system.

KERNEL MODULES

The Linux kernel has the ability to load and unload arbitrary sections of kernel code on demand. These loadable kernel modules run in privileged kernel mode, and as a consequence have full access to the entire hardware capabilities of the machine on which they run. In theory, there is no restriction on what a kernel module is allowed to do; typically, a module might implement a device driver, a file system, or a networking protocol.

There are several reasons why it is convenient to have kernel modules. Linux's source code is free, and so anybody wanting to write kernel code is able to compile a modified kernel and to reboot to load that new functionality, but recompiling, relinking, and reloading the entire kernel is a cumbersome cycle to undertake when you are developing a new driver. If you use kernel modules, you do not have to make a new kernel to test a new driver—the driver may be compiled on its own and loaded into the already-running kernel. Of course, once a new driver is written, it can be distributed as a module so that other users can benefit from it without having to rebuild their kernels.

This latter point has another implication. Because it is covered by the GPL license, the Linux kernel cannot be released with proprietary components added to it, unless those new components are also released under the GPL and the source code for them is made available on demand. The kernel's module interface allows third parties to write and distribute, on their own terms, device drivers or file systems that could not be distributed under the GPL.

Finally, kernel modules allow a Linux system to be set up with a standard, minimal kernel, without any extra device drivers built in. Any device drivers that the user needs can be either loaded explicitly by the system at startup, or loaded automatically by the system on demand and unloaded when not in use. For example, a CD-ROM driver might be loaded when a CD is mounted, and the driver unloaded again from memory when the CD is dismounted from the file system.

There are three components to the module support under Linux:

- The **module management** allows modules to be loaded into memory and to talk to the rest of the kernel.
- The **driver registration** allows modules to tell the rest of the kernel that a new driver has become available.
- A **conflict resolution** mechanism allows different device drivers to reserve hardware resources and to protect those resources from accidental use by another driver.

Module Management

Loading a module requires more than just loading its binary contents into kernel memory. The system must also make sure that any references that the module makes to kernel symbols or entry points get updated to point to the correct locations in the kernel's address space. Linux deals with this reference updating by splitting the job of module loading into two separate sections: the management of sections of module code in kernel memory, and the handling of symbols that modules are allowed to reference.

Linux maintains an internal symbol table in the kernel. This symbol table does not contain the full set of symbols defined in the kernel during the latter's compilation: rather, a symbol must be exported explicitly by the kernel. The set of exported symbols constitutes a well-defined interface by which a module may interact with the kernel.

Although exporting symbols from a kernel function requires an explicit request by the programmer, no special effort is needed to import those symbols into a module. A module writer just uses the standard external linkage of the C language: Any external symbols referenced by the module but not declared by it are simply marked as unresolved in the final module binary produced by the compiler. When a module is to be loaded into the kernel, a system utility first scans the module for these unresolved references. All symbols that still need to be resolved are looked up in the kernel's symbol table, and the correct addresses of those symbols in the currently running kernel are substituted into the module's code. Only then is the module passed to the kernel for loading. If the system utility cannot resolve any references in the module by looking them up in the kernel's symbol table, then the module is rejected.

The loading of the module is performed in two stages. First, the module-loader utility asks the kernel to reserve a continuous area of virtual kernel memory for the module. The kernel returns the address of the memory allocated, and the loader utility can use this address to relocate the module's machine code to the correct loading address. A second system call then passes the module, plus any symbol table that the new module wants to export, to the kernel. The module itself is now copied verbatim into the previously allocated space, and the kernel's symbol table is updated with the new symbols for possible use by other modules not yet loaded.

The final module-management component is the module requestor. The kernel defines a communication interface to which a module-management program can connect. With this connection established, the kernel will inform the management process whenever a process requests a device driver, file system, or network service that is not currently loaded, and will give the manager the opportunity to load that service. The original service request will complete once the module is loaded. The manager process regularly queries the kernel to see whether a dynamically loaded module is still in use, and unloads that module when it is no longer actively needed.

Driver Registration

Once a module is loaded, it remains no more than an isolated region of memory unless it lets the rest of the kernel know what new functionality it provides. The kernel maintains dynamic tables of all known drivers, and provides a set of routines to allow drivers to be added to or removed from these tables at any time. The kernel makes sure that it calls a module's startup routine when that module is loaded, and calls the module's cleanup routine before that module is unloaded: it is these routines that are responsible for registering the module's functionality.

There are many types of driver that a module may register. A single module may register drivers on any or all these types, and may register more than one driver if it wishes. For example, a device driver might want to register two separate mechanisms for accessing the device. Registration tables include the following items:

- **Device drivers.** These drivers include character devices (such as printers, terminals or mice), block devices (including all disk drives), and network interface devices.
- **File systems.** The file system may be anything that implements Linux's virtual-file-system calling routines. It might implement a format for storing files on a disk, but it might equally well be a network file system such as NFS, or a virtual file system whose contents are generated on demand, such as Linux's **proc** file system.
- **Network protocols.** A module may implement an entire networking protocol, such as IPX, or simply a new set of packet-filtering rules for a network firewall.
- **Binary format.** This format specifies a way of recognizing, and loading, a new type of executable file.

In addition, a module can register a new set of entries in the **sysctl** and **/proc** tables, to allow that module to be configured dynamically.

Conflict Resolution

Commercial UNIX implementations usually are sold to run on a vendor's own hardware. One advantage of a single-supplier solution is that the software vendor has a good idea about what hardware configurations are possible. IBM PC hardware, on the other hand, comes in a vast number of configurations, with large numbers of different possible drivers for devices such network cards, SCSI controllers, and video display adapters. The problem of managing the hardware configuration becomes more severe when modular device drivers are supported, since the currently active set of devices becomes dynamically variable.

Linux provides a central conflict-resolution mechanism to help arbitrate access to certain hardware resources. Its aims are as follows:

- To prevent modules from clashing over access to hardware resources
- To prevent *autoprobes* (device-driver probes to auto-detect device configuration) from interfering with existing device drivers
- To resolve conflicts among multiple drivers trying to access the same hardware; for example, the parallel printer driver and PLIP (parallel-line IP) network driver might both try to talk to the parallel printer port

To these ends, the kernel maintains lists of allocated hardware resources. The PC has only a limited number of possible I/O ports (addresses in its hardware I/O address space), interrupt lines, and DMA channels; when any device driver wants to access such a resource, it is expected to reserve the resource with the kernel database first. This requirement incidentally allows the system administrator to determine exactly which resources have been allocated by which driver at any given point.

A module is expected to use this mechanism to reserve in advance any hardware resources that it expects to use. If the reservation is rejected, because the resource is not present or is already in use, then it is up to the module to decide how to proceed. It may fail its initialization and request that it be unloaded if it cannot continue, or it may carry on, using alternative hardware resources.

PROCESS MANAGEMENT

A process is the basic context within which all user-requested activity is serviced within the operating system. To be compatible with other UNIX systems, Linux must necessarily use a process model similar to those of other UNIXes. There are a few key places where Linux does things a little differently, however. In this section, we review the traditional UNIX process model and introduce Linux's own threading model.

The Fork/Exec Process Model

The basic principle of UNIX process management is to separate out into two distinct operations: the creation of processes and the running of a new program. A new process is created by the **fork** system call, and a new program is run after a call to **execve**. These are two distinctly separate functions. A new process may be created with **fork** without a new program being run—the new subprocess simply continues to execute exactly the same program that the first, parent process was running. Equally, running a new program does not require that a new process is created first: any process may call **execve** at any time. The currently running program is immediately terminated, and the new program starts executing in the context of the existing process.

This model has the advantage of great simplicity. Rather than having to specify every detail of the environment of a new program in the system call that runs that program, new programs simply run in their existing environment. If a parent process wishes to modify the environment in which a new program is to be run, it can fork and then, still running the original program in a child process, make any system calls it requires to modify that child process before finally executing the new program.

Under UNIX, then, a process encompasses all the information that the operating system must maintain to track the context of a single execution of a single program. Under Linux, we can break down this context into a number of specific sections. Broadly, process properties fall into three groups: the process's identity, environment, and context.

PROCESS IDENTITY A process's identity consists mainly of the following items:

- **Process ID (PID).** Each process has a unique identifier. PIDs are used to specify processes to the operating system when an application makes a system call to signal, modify, or wait for another process. Additional identifiers associate the process with a process group (typically, a tree of processes **fork**ed by a single user command) and login session.
- **Credentials.** Each process must have an associated user ID and one or more group IDs that determine the process's rights to access system resources and files.
- **Personality.** Process personalities are not traditionally found on UNIX systems, but under Linux each process has an associated personality identifier that can modify slightly the semantics of certain system calls. Personalities are primarily used by emulation libraries to request that system calls be compatible with certain specific flavors of UNIX.

Most of these identifiers are under limited control of the process itself. The process's group and session identifiers can be changed if the process wants to start a new group or session. Its credentials can be changed, subject to appropriate security checks. However, the primary PID of a process is unchangeable and uniquely identifies that process until termination.

PROCESS ENVIRONMENT A process's environment is inherited from that process's parent, and is composed of two null-terminated vectors: the argument vector and the environment vector. The *argument vector* simply lists the command-line arguments used to invoke the running program, and conventionally starts with the name of the program itself. The *environment vector* is a list of "NAME=VALUE" pairs that associates named environment variables with arbitrary textual values. The environment is not held in kernel memory, but rather is stored in the process's own user-mode address space as the first datum at the top of the process's stack.

The argument and environment vectors are not altered when a new process is created: The new child process will inherit the same environment that its parent possesses. However, a completely new environment is set up when a new program is invoked. On calling **execve**, a process must supply the environment for the new program. These environment variables are passed by the kernel to the next program, replacing the process's current environment. The environment and command-line vectors are otherwise left alone by the kernel—their interpretation is left entirely to the user-mode libraries and applications.

The passing of environment variables from one process to the next, and the inheriting of these variables by a process's children, provide flexible ways to pass information to different components of the user-mode system software. A number of important environment variables have conventional meanings to related parts of the system software. For example, the TERM variable is set up to name the type of terminal connected to a user's login session, and many different programs use this variable to determine how to perform operations on the user's display such as moving the cursor around or scrolling a region of text. The LANG variable is used to determine in which language to display system messages for programs that have been programmed with multilingual support.

The important feature of the environment-variable mechanism is that it provides a customization of the operating system that can be set on a per-process basis, rather than being configured for the system as a whole. Users can choose their own languages or select their own preferred editors independent of one another.

PROCESS CONTEXT The process's identity and environment are usually properties that are set up when a process is created, and that are not changed until that process exits. A process may choose to change some aspects of its identity if it needs to do so, or may alter its environment. Process context, on the other hand, is the state of the running program at any one point in time; it changes constantly.

- **Scheduling context.** The most important part of the process context is its scheduling context: the information that the scheduler needs to suspend and restart the process. This information includes saved copies of all the process's registers. Floating-point registers are stored separately, and are restored only when needed, so that processes that do not use floating-point arithmetic do not incur the overhead of saving that state. The scheduling context also includes information about scheduling priority and about any outstanding signals waiting to be delivered to the process. A key part of the scheduling context is the process's kernel stack: a separate area of kernel memory reserved for use exclusively by kernel-mode code. Both system calls and interrupts that occur while the process is executing will use this stack.
- **Accounting.** The kernel maintains information about the resources currently being consumed by each process, and the total resources consumed by the process in its entire lifetime so far.
- **File table.** The file table is an array of pointers to kernel file structures. When making file I/O system calls, processes refer to files by their index into this table.
- **File-system context.** Whereas the file table lists the existing open files, the file-system context applies to requests to open new files. The current root and default directories to be used for new file searches are stored here.
- **Signal-handler table.** UNIX systems can deliver asynchronous signals to a process in response to various external events. The signal-handler table defines the routine in the process's address space to be called when specific signals arrive.
- **Virtual-memory context.** The virtual-memory context of a process describes the full contents of the latter's private address space.

Processes and Threads

Most modern operating systems support both processes and threads. Although the precise difference between the two terms often varies from implementation to implementation, we can define this main distinction: *Processes* represent the execution of single programs, whereas *threads* represent separate, concurrent execution contexts within a single process running a single program.

Any two separate processes will have their own independent address spaces, even if they are using shared memory to share some (but not all) of the contents of their virtual memory. In contrast, two threads within the same process will share *the same* address space (not just *similar* address spaces: any change to the virtual-memory layout made by one thread will be visible immediately to other threads in process, because there is in reality only one address space in which they are all running).

There are several different ways in which threads can be implemented. A thread may be implemented in the operating system's kernel as an object owned by a process, or it may be a fully independent entity. It may not be implemented in the kernel at all—threads may be implemented purely within application or library code with the help of kernel-supplied timer interruptions.

The Linux kernel deals with the difference between processes and threads simply: It uses exactly the same internal representation for each. A thread is simply a new process that happens to share the same address space as its parent. The distinction between a process and a thread is made only when a new thread is created, by the **clone** system call. Whereas **fork** creates a new process that has its own entirely new process context, **clone** creates a new process that has its own identity, but that is allowed to share the data structures of its parent.

This distinction can be accomplished because Linux does not hold all a process's context within the main process data structure; rather, it holds context within independent subcontexts. A process's file-system context, file-descriptor table, signal-handler table and virtual-memory context are held in separate data structures. The process data structure simply contains pointers to these other structures, so any number of processes can easily share one of these subcontexts by pointing to the same subcontexts as appropriate.

The **clone** system call accepts an argument that tells it which subcontexts to copy, and which to share, when it creates the new process. The new process always gets given a new identity and a new scheduling context; according to the arguments passed, however, it may either create new subcontext data structures initialized to be a copy of the parent's, or set up the new process to use the same subcontext data structure being used by the parent. The **fork** system call is nothing more than a special case of **clone** that copies all subcontexts, sharing none. Using **clone** gives an application fine-grained control over exactly what is shared between two threads.

The POSIX working groups have defined a programming interface, specified in the POSIX.1c standard, to allow applications to run multiple threads. The Linux system libraries support two separate mechanisms that implement this single standard in different ways. An application may choose to use either Linux's user-mode-based thread package or its kernel-based one. The user-mode thread library avoids the overhead of kernel scheduling and kernel system calls when threads interact, but is limited by the fact that all threads run in a single process. The kernel-supported thread library uses the **clone** system call to implement the same programming interface, but, since multiple scheduling contexts are created, it has the advantage of allowing an application to run threads on multiple processors at once on a multiprocessor system. It also allows multiple threads to be executing kernel system calls simultaneously.

SCHEDULING

Scheduling is the job of allocating CPU time to different tasks within an operating system. Normally, we think of scheduling as being the running and interrupting of processes, but there is another aspect of scheduling that is important to Linux, and that is the running of the various kernel tasks. Running kernel tasks encompasses both tasks that are requested by a running process and tasks that execute internally on behalf of a device driver.

KERNEL SYNCHRONIZATION

The way that the kernel schedules its own operations is fundamentally different from process scheduling. There are two ways in which a request for kernel-mode execution can occur. A running program may request an operating-system service, either explicitly via a system call, or implicitly—for example, when a page fault occurs. Alternatively, a device driver may deliver a hardware interrupt that causes the CPU to start executing a kernel-defined handler for that interrupt.

The problem posed to the kernel is that these various tasks may all try to access the same internal data structures. If one kernel task is in the middle of accessing some data structure when an interrupt service routine executes, then that service routine cannot access or modify the same data without risking data corruption. This fact relates to the idea of critical sections: portions of code that access shared data and that must not be allowed to execute concurrently.

As a result, kernel synchronization involves much more than just the scheduling of processes. A framework is required that will allow the kernel's critical sections to run without interruption by another critical section.

The first part of Linux's solution to this problem lies in making normal kernel code nonpreemptible. Usually, when a timer interrupt is received by the kernel, it invokes the process scheduler, potentially so that it can suspend execution of the currently running process and resume running another—one the natural time sharing of any UNIX system. However, when a timer interrupt is received while a process is executing a kernel-system service routine, the rescheduling does not take place immediately; rather, the kernel's **need_resched** flag is set to tell the kernel to run the scheduler after the system call has completed and control is about to be returned to user mode.

Once a piece of kernel code starts running, it can guarantee that it will be the only kernel code running until one of the following actions occurs:

- An interrupt
- A page fault
- A kernel-code call to the scheduler function itself

Interrupts are a problem only if they contain critical sections themselves. Timer interrupts never directly cause a process reschedule; they just request that a reschedule be performed later; so any incoming interrupts cannot affect the execution order of noninterrupt kernel code. Once the interrupt service is finished, execution will simply return to the same kernel code that was running when the interrupt was taken.

Page faults are a potential problem; if a kernel routine tries to read or write to user memory, it may incur a page fault that requires disk I/O to complete, and the running process will be suspended until the I/O completes. Similarly, if a system-call service routine calls the scheduler while it is in kernel mode, either explicitly by making a direct call to the scheduling code or implicitly by calling a function to wait for I/O to complete, then the process will be suspended and a reschedule will occur. When the process becomes runnable again, it will continue to execute in kernel mode, continuing at the instruction after the call to the scheduler.

Kernel code can thus make the assumptions that it will never be preempted by another process, and that no special care must be taken to protect critical sections. The only requirement is that critical sections do not contain references to user memory or waits for I/O completions.

The second technique that Linux uses to protect critical sections applies to critical sections that occur in interrupt service routines. The basic tool used to provide this functionality is the processor's interrupt-control hardware. By disabling interrupts during a critical section, the kernel guarantees that it can proceed without the risk of concurrent access of shared data structures.

There is a penalty for disabling interrupts. On most hardware architectures, interrupt enable and disable instructions are expensive. Furthermore, as long as interrupts remain disabled, all I/O is suspended, and any device waiting for servicing will have to wait until interrupts are reenabled, hurting performance. Linux's kernel uses a synchronization architecture that allows long critical sections to run without having interrupts disabled for the critical section's entire duration. This ability is especially useful in the networking code: An interrupt in a network device driver can signal the arrival of an entire network packet, which may result in a great deal of code being executed to disassemble, route, and forward that packet within the interrupt service routine.

Linux implements this architecture by separating interrupt service routines into two sections: the top half and bottom half. The *top half* is a normal interrupt service routine, and runs with recursive interrupts disabled (interrupts of a higher priority may interrupt the routine, but interrupts of the same or lower priority are disabled). The *bottom half* of a service routine is run, with all interrupts enabled, by a miniature scheduler that ensures that bottom halves never interrupt themselves. The bottom-half scheduler is invoked automatically whenever an interrupt service routine exits.

This separation means that any complex processing that has to be done in response to an interrupt can be completed by the kernel without the kernel worrying about being interrupted itself. If another interrupt occurs while a bottom half is executing, then that interrupt can request that the same bottom half executes, but the execution will be deferred until the currently running one completes. Each execution of the bottom half can be interrupted by a top half, but can never be interrupted by a similar bottom half.

The top half bottom half architecture is completed by a mechanism for disabling selected bottom halves while executing normal, foreground kernel code. The kernel can code critical sections easily using this system: Interrupt handlers can code their critical sections as bottom halves, and when the foreground kernel wants to enter a critical section, it can disable any relevant bottom halves to prevent any other critical sections from interrupting it. At the end of the critical section, the kernel can reenable the bottom halves and run any bottom-half tasks that have been queued by top-half interrupt service routines during the critical section.

Figure 4-13 summarizes the various levels of interrupt protection within the kernel. Each level may be interrupted by code running at a higher level, but will never be interrupted by code running at the same or a lower level (except for user-mode code, user processes can always be preempted by another process when a time-sharing scheduling interrupt occurs).

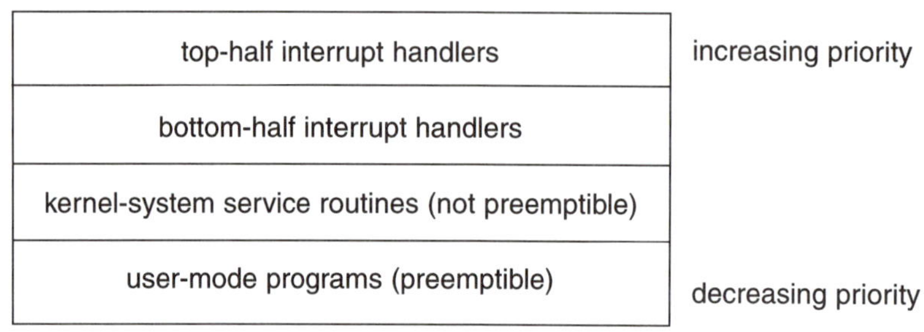

FIGURE 4-13 *Interrupt Protection Levels*

Process Scheduling

Once the kernel has reached a rescheduling point—either a rescheduling interrupt has occurred or a running kernel process has blocked waiting for some wakeup signal—it must decide what process to run next. Linux has two separate process-scheduling algorithms. One is a time-sharing algorithm for fair preemptive scheduling among multiple processes, and the other is designed for real-time tasks where absolute priorities are more important than fairness.

Part of every process's identity is a scheduling class, which defines which of these algorithms to apply to the process. The scheduling classes used by Linux are defined in the POSIX standard's extensions for real-time computing (POSIX.4, now known as POSIX.1b).

For time-sharing processes, Linux uses a prioritized, *credit-based* algorithm. Each process possesses a certain number of scheduling credits; when a new task must be chosen to run, the process with the most credits is selected. Every time that a timer interrupt occurs, the currently running process loses one credit; when its credits reach zero, it is suspended and another process is chosen.

If no runnable processes have any credits, then Linux performs a recrediting operation, adding credits to *every* process in the system (rather than to just the runnable ones), according to the following rule:

$$\text{credits} = \frac{\text{credits}}{2} + \text{priority}$$

This algorithm tends to mix two factors: the process's history and the process's priority. Half of the credits that a process still holds since the previous recrediting operation will be retained after the algorithm has been applied, retaining some history of the process's recent behavior. Processes that are running all the time tend to exhaust their credits rapidly, but processes that spend much of their time suspended can accumulate credits over multiple recreditings and will consequently end up with a higher credit count after a recredit. This crediting system automatically prioritizes interactive or I/O-bound processes, for which a rapid response time is important.

The use of a process priority in calculating new credits allows the priority of a process to be fine tuned. Background batch jobs can be given a low priority, and they will automatically receive fewer credits than interactive users' jobs, and will hence receive a smaller percentage of the CPU time than similar jobs with higher priorities. Linux uses this priority system to implement the standard UNIX *nice* process-priority mechanism.

Linux's real-time scheduling is simpler still. Linux implements the two real-time scheduling classes required by POSIX.1b: first in, first out (FIFO), and round-robin. In both cases, each process has a priority in addition to its scheduling class. In time-sharing scheduling, however, processes of different priorities can still complete with one another to some extent; in real-time scheduling, the scheduler always runs the process with the highest priority. Among processes of equal priority, it runs the process that has been waiting longest. The only difference between FIFO and round-robin scheduling is that FIFO processes continue to run until they either exit or block, whereas a round-robin process will be preempted after a while and will be moved to the end of the scheduling queue, so round-robin processes of equal priority will automatically time share among themselves.

Note that Linux's real-time scheduling is soft—not hard—real time. The scheduler offers strict guarantees about the relative priorities of real-time processes, but the kernel does not offer any guarantees about how quickly a real-time process will be scheduled once the latter becomes runnable. Remember that Linux kernel code cannot ever be preempted by user-mode code. If an interrupt arrives that wakes up a real-time process while the kernel is already executing a system call on behalf of another process, the real-time process will just have to wait until the currently running system call completes or blocks.

Symmetric Multiprocessing

The Linux 2.0 kernel was the first stable Linux kernel to support *symmetric multiprocessor (SMP)* hardware. Separate processes or threads can execute in parallel on separate processors. However, to preserve the nonpreemptible synchronization requirements of the kernel, the implementation of SMP in this kernel imposes the restriction that only one processor at a time can be executing kernel-mode code. SMP uses a single kernel spinlock to enforce this rule. This spinlock does not pose a problem for computation-bound tasks, but tasks that involve a lot of kernel activity can become seriously bottlenecked.

At the time of writing, one of the major projects in the Linux 2.1 development kernel is to make the SMP implementation more scalable, by splitting the single kernel spinlock into multiple locks that each protect only a small subset of the kernel's data structures against reentrance. Using such techniques, the latest development kernels do allow multiple processors to be executing kernel-mode code simultaneously.

MEMORY MANAGEMENT

There are two components to memory management under Linux. First, the physical memory-management system deals with allocating and freeing pages, groups of pages, and small blocks of memory. The second component handles virtual memory, which is memory mapped into the address space of running processes.

We describe these two components, and then examine the mechanisms by which the loadable components of a new program are brought into a process's virtual memory in response to an **exec** system call.

Management of Physical Memory

The primary physical memory manager in the Linux kernel is the page allocator. This allocator is responsible for allocating and freeing all physical pages, and is capable of allocating ranges of physically contiguous pages on request. The allocator uses a *buddy-heap* algorithm to keep track of available physical pages. A buddy-heap allocator pairs adjacent units of allocatable memory together; hence its name. Each allocatable memory region has an adjacent partner, or buddy, and whenever two allocated partner regions are both freed up, they are combined to form a larger region. That larger region also has a partner, with which it can combine to form still larger free regions. Alternatively, if a small memory request cannot be satisfied by allocation of an existing small free region, then a larger free region will be subdivided into two partners to satisfy the request. Separate linked lists are used to record the free memory regions of each allowable size; under Linux, the smallest size allocatable under this mechanism is a single physical page. Figure 4-14 shows an example of buddy-heap allocation: A 4 kilobytes region is being allocated, but the smallest available region is 16 kilobytes. The region is broken up recursively until a piece of the desired size is available.

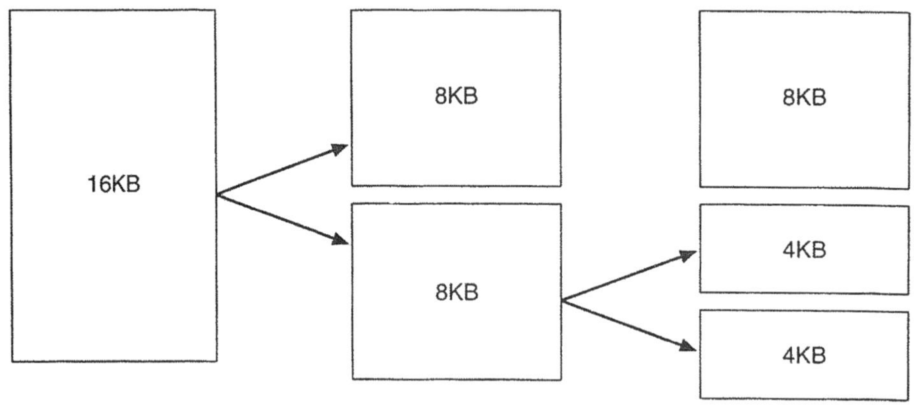

FIGURE 4-14 *Splitting of Memory in a Buddy Heap*

Ultimately, all memory allocations in the Linux kernel either occur statically, by drivers that reserve a contiguous area of memory during system boot time, or dynamically, by the page allocator, However, kernel functions do not necessarily have to use the basic allocator to reserve memory. Several specialized memory-management subsystems exist; they use the underlying page allocator to manage their own pool of memory. The most important memory subsystems are the virtual-memory system; the **kmalloc** variable-length allocator; and the kernel's two persistent data caches, the buffer cache and the page cache.

Many components of the Linux operating system need to allocate entire pages at will, but often smaller blocks of memory are required. The kernel provides an additional allocator for arbitrary-sized requests, where the size of a request is not necessarily known in advance and may be only a few bytes, rather than an entire page. Analogous to the C language's **malloc** function, this **kmalloc** service allocates entire pages on demand, but then splits them into smaller pieces. The kernel maintains a set of lists of pages in use by the **kmalloc** service, where all the pages on a given list have been split into pieces of a specific size. Allocating memory involves working out the appropriate list and either taking the first free piece available on the list or allocating a new page and splitting it up.

Both the page and **kmalloc** allocators are interrupt safe. A function that wants to allocate memory passes a request priority to the allocation function. Interrupt routines use an atomic priority that guarantees that the request is either satisfied or, if there is no more memory, failed immediately. In contrast, normal user processes that require a memory allocation will start attempting to find existing memory to free, and will stall until memory becomes available. The allocation priority can also be used for specifying that the memory is required for DMA, for use on architectures such as the PC where certain DMA requests are not supported on all pages of physical memory.

Memory regions claimed by the **kmalloc** system are allocated permanently until they are freed explicitly. The **kmalloc** system cannot relocate or reclaim these regions in response to memory shortages.

The other three main subsystems that do their own management of physical pages are closely related. These are the buffer cache, the page cache, and the virtual-memory system. The buffer cache is the kernel's main cache for block-oriented devices such as disk drives, and is the main mechanism through which I/O to these devices is performed. The page cache caches entire pages of file contents, and is not limited to block devices; it can also cache networked data, and is used both by the native Linux disk-based file systems and the NFS networked file system. The virtual-memory system manages the contents of each process's virtual address space.

These three systems interact closely with one another. Reading a page of data into the page cache requires going temporarily through the buffer cache; pages in the page cache can also be mapped into the virtual-memory system if a process has mapped a file into its address space. The kernel maintains a reference count on each page of physical memory, so that pages that are shared by two or more of these subsystems can be released when they are no longer in use anywhere.

Virtual Memory

The Linux virtual-memory system is responsible for maintaining the address space visible to each process. It creates pages of virtual memory on demand, and manages the loading of those pages from disk or their swapping back out to disk as required. Under Linux, the virtual-memory manager maintains two separate views of a process's address space: as a set of separate regions, and as a set of pages.

The first view of an address space is the logical view, describing instructions that the virtual-memory system has received concerning the layout of the address space. In this view, the address space consists of a set of nonoverlapping regions, each region representing a continuous, page-aligned subset of the address space. Each region is described internally by a single **vm_area_struct** structure, which defines the properties of the region, including the process's read, write, and execute permissions in the region, and information about any files associated with the region. The regions for each address space are linked into a balanced binary tree to allow fast lookup of the region corresponding to any virtual address.

The kernel also maintains a second, physical view of each address space. This view is stored in the hardware page tables for the process. The page-table entries determine the exact current location of each page of virtual memory, whether it is on disk or in physical memory. The physical view is managed by a set of routines that is invoked from the kernel's software-interrupt handlers whenever a process tries to access a page that is not currently present in the page tables. Each **vm_area_struct** in the address-space description contains a field that points to a table of functions that implement the key page-management functions for any given virtual-memory region. All requests to read or write an unavailable page are eventually dispatched to the appropriate handler in **vm_area_struct**'s table, so that the central memory-management routines do not have to know the details of managing each possible type of memory region.

VIRTUAL-MEMORY REGIONS Linux implements a number of different types of virtual-memory regions. The first property that characterizes a type of virtual memory is the backing store for the region: This store describes from where the pages for a region come. Most memory regions are backed either by a file, or by nothing. A region that is backed by nothing is the simplest type of virtual memory. Such a region represents *demand-zero* memory: When a process tries to read a page in such a region, it is simply given back a page of memory filled with zeros.

A region backed by a file acts as a viewport onto a section of that file: Whenever the process tries to access a page within that region, the page table is filled with the address of a page within the kernel's page cache corresponding to the appropriate offset in the file. The same page of physical memory is used both by the page cache and by the process's page tables, so any changes made to the file by the file system are immediately visible to any processes that have mapped that file into their address space. Any number of different processes can map the same region of the same file, and they will all end up using the same page of physical memory for the purpose.

A virtual-memory region is also defined by its reaction to writes. The mapping of a region into the process's address space can be either *private* or *shared*. If a process writes to a privately mapped region, then the pager detects that a copy-on-write is necessary to keep the changes local to the process. On the other hand, writes to a shared region result in the object mapped into that region being updated, so that the change will be visible immediately to any other process that is mapping that object.

LIFETIME OF A VIRTUAL ADDRESS SPACE There are exactly two situations where the kernel will create a new virtual address space: When a process runs a new program with the **exec** system call, and on creation of a new process by the **fork** system call. The first case is easy: When a new program is executed, the process is given a new, completely empty virtual address space. It is up to the routines for loading the program to populate the address space with virtual-memory regions.

In the second case, creating a new process with **fork** involves creating a complete copy of the existing process's virtual address space. The kernel copies the parent process's **vm-area-struct** descriptors, then creates a new set of page tables for the child. The parent's page tables are copied directly into the child's, with the reference count of each page covered being incremented; thus, after the fork, the parent and child share the same physical pages of memory in their address spaces.

A special case occurs when the copying operation reaches a virtual-memory region that is mapped privately. Any pages to which the parent process has written within such a region are private, and subsequent changes to these pages by either the parent or the child must not update the page in the other process's address space. When the page-table entries for such regions are copied, they are set to be read only and are marked for copy-on-write. As long as these pages are not modified by either process, the two processes share the same page of physical memory. However, if either process tries to modify a copy-on-write page, the reference count on the page is checked. If the page is still shared, then the process copies the page's contents to a brand new page of physical memory and uses its copy instead. This mechanism ensures that private data pages are shared between processes whenever possible; copies are made only when absolutely necessary.

SWAPPING AND PAGING An important task for a virtual-memory system is to relocate pages of memory from physical memory out to disk when that memory is needed. Early UNIX systems performed this relocation by swapping out the contents of entire processes at once, but modern UNIXes rely more on *paging*: the movement of individual pages of virtual memory between physical memory and disk. Linux does not implement whole-process swapping; it uses the newer paging mechanism exclusively.

The paging system can be divided into two sections. First, there is the *policy algorithm*, which decides which pages to write out to disk, and when to write them. Second, there is the *paging mechanism*, which carries out the transfer, and which pages data back into physical memory when they are needed again.

Linux's pageout policy uses a modified version of the standard clock (second-chance) algorithm. Under Linux, a multiple-pass clock is used, and every page has an *age* that is adjusted on each pass of the clock. The age is more precisely a measure of the page's youthfulness, or how much activity the page has seen recently. Frequently accessed pages will attain a higher age value, but the age of infrequently accessed pages will drop toward zero with each pass. This age valuing allows the pager to select pages to page out based on a least frequently used (LFU) policy.

The paging mechanism supports paging both to dedicated swap devices and partitions, and to normal files, although swapping to a file is significantly slower due to the extra overhead incurred by the file system. Blocks are allocated from the swap devices according to a bitmap of used blocks, which is maintained in physical memory at all times. The allocator uses a next-fit algorithm to try to write out pages to continuous runs of disk blocks for improved performance. The allocator records the fact that a page has been paged out to disk by using a feature of the page tables on modern processors: The page-table entry's page-not-present bit is set, allowing the rest of the page-table entry to be filled with an index identifying to where the page has been written.

KERNEL VIRTUAL MEMORY Linux reserves for its own internal use a constant, architecture-dependent region of the virtual address space of every process. The page-table entries that map to these kernel pages are marked as protected, so that the pages are not visible or modifiable when the processor is running in user mode. This kernel virtual-memory area contains two regions. The first section is a static area that contains page-table references to every available physical page of memory in the system, so that there is a simple translation from physical to virtual addresses when kernel code is run. The core of the kernel, plus all pages allocated by the normal page allocator, reside in this region.

The remainder of the kernel's reserved section of address space is not reserved for any specific purpose. Page-table entries in this address range can be modified by the kernel to point to any other areas of memory as desired. The kernel provides a pair of facilities that allow processes to use this virtual memory. The **vmalloc** function allocates an arbitrary number of physical pages of memory, and maps them into a single region of kernel virtual memory, allowing allocation of large contiguous memory chunks even if there are not sufficient adjacent free physical pages to satisfy the request. The **vremap** function maps a sequence of virtual addresses to point to an area of memory used by a device driver for memory-mapped I/O.

Execution and Loading of User Programs

The Linux kernel's execution of user programs is triggered by a call to the **exec** system call. This call commands the kernel to run a new program within the current process, completely overwriting the current execution context with the initial context of the new program. The first job of this system service is to verify that the calling process has permission rights to the file being executed. Once that matter has been checked, the kernel invokes a loader routine to start running the program. The loader does not necessarily load the contents of the program file into physical memory, but it does at least set up the mapping of the program into virtual memory.

There is no single routine in Linux for loading a new program. Instead, Linux maintains a table of possible loader functions, and it gives each such function the opportunity to try loading the given file when an **exec** system call is made. The initial reason for this loader table was that, between the release of the 1.0 and 1.2 kernels, the standard format for Linux's binary files was changed. Older Linux kernels understood the a.out format for binary files—a relatively simple format common on older UNIX systems. Newer Linux systems use the more modern ELF format, now supported by most current UNIX implementations. ELF has a number of advantages over a.out, including flexibility and extensibility: New sections can be added to an ELF binary (for example, to add extra debugging information), without the loader routines becoming confused. By allowing registration of multiple loader routines, Linux can easily support the ELF and a.out binary formats in a single running system.

We concentrate exclusively on the loading and running of ELF-format binaries. The procedure for loading a.out binaries is simpler, but is similar in operation.

MAPPING OF PROGRAMS INTO MEMORY The loading of a binary file into physical memory is not performed by the binary loader under Linux. Rather, the pages of the binary file are mapped into regions of virtual memory. Only when the program tries to access a given page will a page fault result in the loading of that page into physical memory.

It is the responsibility of the kernel's binary loader to set up the initial memory mapping. An ELF-format binary file consists of a header followed by several page-aligned sections. The ELF loader works by reading the header and mapping the sections of the file into separate regions of virtual memory.

Figure 4-15 shows the typical layout of memory regions set up by the ELF loader. In a reserved region at one end of the address space sits the kernel, in its own privileged region of virtual memory inaccessible to normal user-mode programs. The rest of virtual memory is available to applications, which can use the kernel's memory-mapping functions to create regions that map a portion of a file or that are available for application data.

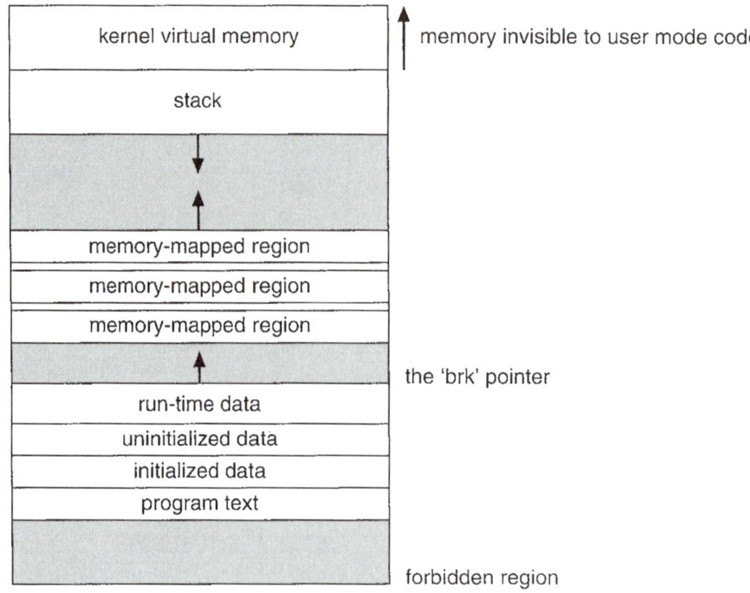

FIGURE 4-15 *Memory Layout for ELF Programs*

The loader's job is to set up the initial memory mapping to allow the execution of the program to start. The regions that need to be initialized include the stack and the program's text and data regions.

The stack is created at the top of the user-mode virtual memory; it grows downward toward lower-numbered addresses. It includes copies of the arguments and environment variables given to the program in the **exec** system call. The other regions are created near the bottom end of virtual memory. The sections of the binary file that contain program text or read-only data are mapped into memory as a write-protected region. Writable initialized data are mapped next; then any uninitialized data are mapped in as a private demand-zero region.

Directly beyond these fixed-sized regions is a variable-sized region that programs can expand as needed to hold data allocated at run time. Each process has a pointer, **brk**, which points to the current extent of this data region, and processes can extend or contract their **brk** region with a single system call.

Once these mappings have been set up, the loader initializes the process's program-counter register with the starting point recorded in the ELF header, and the process can be scheduled.

STATIC AND DYNAMIC LINKING Once the program has been loaded and has started running, all the necessary contents of the binary file have been loaded into the process's virtual address space. However, most programs also need to run functions from the system libraries, and these library functions also need to be loaded. In the simplest case, when a programmer builds an application, the necessary library functions are embedded directly in the program's executable binary file. Such a program is *statically* linked to its libraries, and statically linked executables can commence running as soon as they are loaded.

The main disadvantage of static linkage is that every program generated must contain copies of exactly the same common system library functions. It is much more efficient, in terms of both physical memory and disk-space usage, to load the system libraries into memory only once. *Dynamic* linking allows this single loading to happen.

Linux implements dynamic linking in user mode through a special linker library. Every dynamically linked program contains a small statically linked function that is called when the program starts. This static function just maps the link library into memory and runs the code that the function contains. The link library reads a list of the dynamic libraries required by the program and the names of the variables and functions needed from those libraries by reading the information contained in sections of the ELF binary. It then maps the libraries into the middle of virtual memory, and resolves the references to the symbols contained in those libraries. It does not matter exactly where in memory these shared libraries get mapped: They are compiled into position-independent code (PIC), which can run at any address in memory.

FILE SYSTEMS

Linux retains UNIX's standard file-system model. In UNIX, a file does not necessarily have to be an object stored on disk or fetched over a network from a remote file server. Rather, UNIX files can be anything capable of handling the input or output of a stream of data. Device drivers can appear as files, and interprocess-communication channels or network connections also look like files to the user.

The Linux kernel handles all these various different types of file by hiding the implementation details of any single file type behind a layer of software, the *virtual file system (VFS)*.

The Virtual File System

The Linux VFS is designed around object-oriented principles. It has two components: a set of definitions that define what a file object is allowed to look like, and a layer of software to manipulate those objects. The three main object types defined by the VFS are the *inode-object* and the *file-object* structures, which represent individual files, and the *file-system object*, which represents an entire file system.

For each of these three types of object, the VFS defines a set of operations that must be implemented by that structure. Every object of one of these types contains a pointer to a function table. The function table lists the addresses of the actual functions that implement those operations for that particular object. Thus, the VFS software layer can perform an operation on one of these objects by calling the appropriate function from that object's function table, without having to know in advance exactly with what kind of an object it is dealing. The VFS does not know, or care, whether an inode represents a networked file, a disk file, a network socket, or a directory file—the appropriate function for that file's *read data* operation will always be at the same place in its function table, and the VFS software layer will call that function without caring how the data are actually read.

The file-system object represents a connected set of files that forms a self-contained directory hierarchy. The operating-system kernel maintains a single file-system object for each disk device mounted as a file system and for each networked file system currently connected. The file system object's main responsibility is to give access to inodes. The VFS identifies every inode by a unique (file system-inode number) pair, and it finds the inode corresponding to a particular inode number by asking the file-system object to return the inode with that number.

The inode and file objects are the mechanisms used to access files. An inode object represents the file as a whole, and a file object represents a point of access to the data in the file. A process cannot access an inode's data contents without first obtaining a file object pointing to the inode. The file object keeps track of where in the file the process is currently reading or writing, to keep track of sequential file I/O. It also remembers whether the process asked for write permissions when the file was opened, and keeps track of the process's activity if necessary to perform adaptive read-ahead (fetching file data into memory in advance of the process requesting it, to improve performance).

File objects typically belong to a single process, but inode objects do not. Even once a file is no longer being used by any processes, its inode object may still be cached by the VFS to improve performance if the file is used again in the near future. All cached file data are linked onto a list in the file's inode object. The inode also maintains standard information about each file, such as the owner, size, and time most recently modified.

Directory files are dealt with slightly differently from other files. The UNIX programming interface defines a number of operations on directories, such as creating, deleting, and renaming a file in a directory. Unlike reading and writing data, for which a file must first be opened, the system calls for these directory operations do not require that the user open the files concerned. The VFS therefore defines these directory operations in the inode object, rather than in the file object.

The Linux ext2fs File System

The standard on-disk file system used by Linux is called *ext2fs*, for historical reasons. Linux was originally programmed with a Minix-compatible file system, to ease exchanging data with the Minix development system, but that file system was severely restricted by 14-character file-name limits and the maximum file-system size of 64 megabytes. The Minix file system was superseded by a new file system, which was christened the *extended file system, extfs*. A later redesign of this file system to improve performance and scalability and to add a few missing features led to the *second extended file system, ext2fs*.

ext2fs has much in common with the BSD Fast File System (ffs). It uses a similar mechanism for locating the data-blocks belonging to a specific file, storing data block pointers in indirect blocks throughout the file system with up to three levels of indirection. As they are in ffs, directory files are stored on disk just like normal files, although their contents are interpreted differently. Each block in a directory file consists of a linked list of entries, where each entry contains the length of the entry, the name of a file, and the inode number of the inode to which that entry refers.

The main differences between ext2fs and ffs concern the disk-allocation policies. In ffs, the disk is allocated to files in blocks of 8 kilobytes, with blocks being subdivided into fragments of 1 kilobyte to store small files or partially filled blocks at the end of a file. In contrast, ext2fs does not use fragments at all, but rather performs all its allocations in smaller units. The default block size on ext2fs is 1 kilobyte, although 2-kilobyte and 4-kilobyte blocks are also supported.

To maintain high performance, the operating system must try to perform I/Os in large chunks whenever possible, by *clustering* physically adjacent I/O requests. Clustering reduces the per-request overhead incurred by device drivers, disks, and disk-controller hardware. A 1 kilobyte I/O request size is too small to maintain good performance, so ext2fs uses allocation policies designed to place logically adjacent blocks of a file into physically adjacent blocks on disk, so that it can submit an I/O request for several disk blocks as a single operation.

The ext2fs allocation policy comes in two parts. As in ffs, an ext2fs file system is partitioned into multiple *block groups*. Ffs uses the similar concept of *cylinder groups*, where each group corresponds to a single cylinder of a physical disk. However, modern disk-drive technology packs sectors onto the disk at different densities, and thus with different cylinder sizes, depending on how far the disk head is from the center of the disk, so fixed-sized cylinder groups do not necessarily correspond to the disk's geometry.

When allocating a file, ext2fs must first select the block group for that file. For data blocks, it attempts to choose the same block group as that in which the file's inode has been allocated. For inode allocations, it selects the same block group as the file's parent directory, for nondirectory files. Directory files are not kept together, but rather are dispersed throughout the available block groups. These policies are designed to keep related information within the same block group, but also to spread out the disk load among the disk's block groups to reduce the fragmentation of any one area of the disk.

Within a block group, ext2fs tries to keep allocations physically contiguous if possible, reducing fragmentation if it can. It maintains a bitmap of all free blocks in a block group. When allocating the first blocks for a new file, it starts searching for a free block from the beginning of the block group; when extending a file, it continues the search from the block most recently allocated to the file. The search is performed in two stages. First, it searches for an entire free byte in the bitmap; if it fails to find one, it looks for any free bit. The search for free bytes aims to allocate disk space in chunks of at least eight blocks where possible.

Once a free block has been identified, the search is extended backward until an allocated block is encountered. When a free byte is found in the bitmap, this backward extend prevents ext2fs from leaving a hole between the most recently allocated block in the previous nonzero byte and the zero byte found. Once the next block to be allocated has been thus found by either bit or byte search, ext2fs, extends the allocation forward for up to eight blocks and *preallocates* these extra blocks to the file. This preallocation helps to reduce fragmentation during interleaved writes to separate files, and also reduces the CPU cost of disk allocation by allocating multiple blocks simultaneously. The preallocated blocks are returned to the free-space bitmap when the file is closed.

Figure 4-16 illustrates the allocation policies. Each row represents a sequence of set and unset bits in an allocation bitmap, representing used and free blocks on disk. In the first case, if we can find any free blocks sufficiently near the start of the search, then we allocate them no matter how fragmented they may be. The fragmentation is partially compensated for by the fact that the blocks are close together and can probably all be read without any disk seeks being incurred, and allocating them all to one file is better in the long run than is allocating isolated blocks to separate files once large free areas become scarce on disk. In the second case, we have not immediately found a free block close by, so we search forward for an entire free byte in the bitmap. If we allocated that byte as a whole, we would end up creating a fragmented area of free space before it, so before allocating we back up to make this allocation flush with the allocation preceding it, and then we allocate forward to satisfy the default allocation of eight blocks.

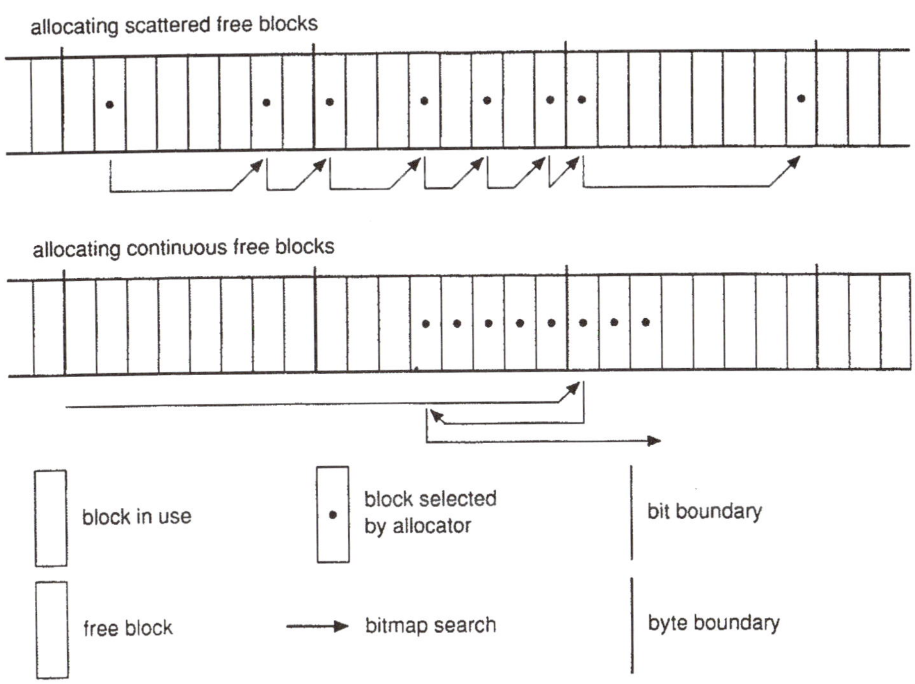

FIGURE 4-16 *Ext2fs Block-Alloction Policies*

THE LINUX PROC FILE SYSTEM

The Linux VFS is sufficiently flexible that it is possible to implement a file system that does not store data persistently at all, but rather simply provides an interface to some other functionality. The Linux *process file system*, known as the **proc** file system, is an example of a file system whose contents are not actually stored anywhere, but are rather computed on demand according to user file I/O requests.

A **proc** file system is not unique to Linux. SVR4 UNIX introduced a **proc** file system as an efficient interface to the kernel's process debugging support: Each subdirectory of the file system corresponded not to a directory on any disk, but rather to an active process on the current system. A listing of the file system reveals one directory per process, with the directory name being the ASCII decimal representation of the process's unique process identifier (PID).

Linux implements such a **proc** file system, but extends it greatly by adding a number of extra directories and text files under the file-system's root directory. These new entries correspond to various statistics about the kernel and the associated loaded drivers. The **proc** file system provides a way for programs to access this information as plain text files, which the standard UNIX user environment provides powerful tools to process. For example, in the past, the traditional UNIX **ps** command for listing the states of all running processes has been implemented as a privileged process that read the process state directly from the kernel's virtual memory. Under Linux, this command is implemented as an entirely unprivileged program that simply parses and formats the information from **proc**.

The **proc** file system must implement two things: a directory structure, and the file contents within. Given that a UNIX file system is defined as a set of file and directory inodes identified by their inode numbers, the **proc** file system must define a unique and persistent inode number for each directory and the associated files. Once such a mapping exists, it can use this inode number to identify just what operation is required when a user tries to read from a particular file inode or to perform a lookup in a particular directory inode. When data are read from one of these files, the **proc** file system will collect the appropriate information, format it into textual form, and place it into the requesting process's read buffer.

The mapping from inode number to information type splits the inode number into two fields. In Linux, a PID is 16 bits, but an inode number is 32 bits. The top 16 bits of the inode number are interpreted as a PID, and the remaining bits define what type of information is being requested about that process.

A PID of zero is not valid, so a zero PID field in the inode number is taken to mean that this inode contains global—rather than process-specific—information. Separate global files exist in **proc** to report information such as the kernel version, free memory, performance statistics, and drivers currently running.

Not all the inode numbers in this range are reserved: The kernel can allocate new **proc** inode mappings dynamically, maintaining a bitmap of allocated inode numbers. It also maintains a tree data structure of registered global **proc** file-system entries: Each entry contains the file's inode number, file name, access permissions, and the special functions used to generate the file's contents. Drivers can register and deregister entries in this tree at any time, and a special section of the tree (appearing under the **/proc/sys** directory) is reserved for kernel variables. Files under this tree are dealt with by a set of common handlers that allow both reading and writing of these variables, so a system administrator can tune the value of kernel parameters simply by writing the new desired values out in ASCII decimal to the appropriate file.

To allow efficient access to these variables from within applications, the **/proc/sys** subtree is made available through a special system call, **sysctl**, which reads and writes the same variables in binary, rather than in text, without the overhead of the file system. **sysctl** is not an extra facility; it simply reads the **proc** dynamic entry tree to decide to which variables the application is referring.

INPUT AND OUTPUT

To the user, the I/O system in Linux looks much like it does in any UNIX. That is, to the extent possible, all device drivers appear as normal files. A user can open an access channel to a device in the same way as she can open any other file—devices can appear as objects within the file system. The system administrator can create special files within a file system that contain references to a specific device driver, and a user opening such a file will be able to read from and write to the device referenced. By using the normal file-protection system, which determines who can access which file, the administrator can set access permissions for each device.

Linux splits all devices into three classes: *block devices, character devices*, and *network devices*. Figure 4-17 illustrates the overall structure of the device-driver system. Block devices include all devices that allow random access to completely independent, fixed-sized blocks of data, including hard disks, floppy disks, and CD-ROMs. Block devices are typically used to store file systems, but direct access to a block device is also allowed so that programs can create and repair the file system that the device contains. Applications can also access these block devices directly if they wish; for example, a database application may prefer to perform its own, fine-tuned laying out of data onto the disk, rather than using the general-purpose file system.

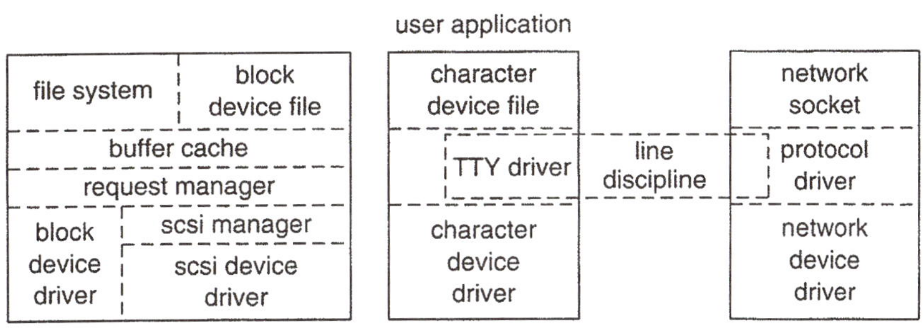

FIGURE 4-17 *Device-Driver Block Structure*

Character devices include most other devices, with the main exception of network devices. Character devices do not need to support all the functionality of regular files. For example, a loudspeaker device would allow data to be written to it, but would not support reading of data back from it. Similarly, seeking to a certain position in the file might be supported for a magnetic-tape device, but would make no sense to a pointing device such as a mouse.

Network devices are dealt with differently from block and character devices. Users cannot directly transfer data to network devices, but must instead communicate indirectly by opening a connection to the kernel's networking subsystem.

Block Devices

Block devices provide the main interface to all disk devices in a system. Performance is particularly important for disks, and the block-device system must provide functionality to ensure that disk access is as fast as possible. This functionality is achieved through the use of two system components: the *block buffer cache* and the *request manager*.

THE BLOCK BUFFER CACHE The Linux block buffer cache serves two main purposes. It acts as both a pool of buffers for active I/O, and a cache for completed I/O. The buffer cache consists of two parts. First, there are the buffers themselves: a dynamically sized set of pages allocated directly from the kernel's main memory pool. Each page is split up into a number of equally sized buffers. Second, there is a set of corresponding buffer descriptors, the **buffer_heads**—one for each buffer in the cache.

The **buffer_heads** contain all the information that the kernel maintains about the buffers. The primary information is the buffer's identity. Each buffer is identified by a 3-tuple: the block device to which the buffer belongs, the offset of the data within that block device, and the size of the buffer. Buffers are also held on a number of lists. There are separate lists for clean, dirty, and locked buffers, plus a list of free buffers. Buffers enter the free list by being placed there either by a file system (for example, when a file is deleted), or by a **refill_freelist** function, which is called whenever the kernel needs more buffers. The kernel fills the free list by expanding the pool of buffers or by recycling existing buffers, according to whether sufficient free memory is available. Finally, each buffer not on the free list is indexed by a hash function on its device and block number, and is linked onto a corresponding hash lookup list.

The kernel's buffer management automatically deals with the writing of dirty buffers back to disk. Two background daemons assist. One simply wakes up at a regular interval and requests that all data be written back to disk if it has been dirty for longer than a certain interval. The other is a kernel thread that is awakened whenever the **refill_freelist** function finds that too high a proportion of the buffer cache is dirty.

THE REQUEST MANAGER The request manager is the layer of software that manages the reading and writing of buffer contents to and from a block device driver. The request system revolves around a function, **ll_rw_block**, which performs low-level read and write of block devices. This function takes a list of **buffer_head** buffer descriptors and a read-write flag as its argument, and sets the I/O in progress for all those buffers. It does not wait for that I/O to complete.

Outstanding I/O requests are recorded in **request** structures. A **request** represents an outstanding I/O request for the read or write of a contiguous range of sectors on a single block device. Since more than one buffer may be involved in the transfer, the **request** contains a pointer to the first in a linked list of **buffer_heads** to be used for the transfer.

A separate list of requests is kept for each block device driver, and these requests are scheduled according to a unidirectional elevator (C-SCAN) algorithm, which exploits the order in which requests are inserted and removed from the per-device lists. The request lists are maintained in sorted order of increasing starting-sector number. When a request is accepted for processing by a block device driver, it is not removed from the list. It is removed only after the I/O is complete, at which point the driver continues with the next request in the list, even if new requests have been inserted into the list before the active request.

As new I/O requests are made, the request manager attempts to merge requests in the per-device lists. Passing a single, large request, instead of many smaller requests, is often much more efficient in terms of the overhead of the underlying devices. All the **buffer_heads** in such an aggregate request are locked as soon as the initial I/O request is made. As the request is processed by a device driver, the individual **buffer_heads** constituting the aggregate request are unlocked one at a time; there is no need for a process waiting on one buffer to wait for all the other buffers in the request to become unlocked, too. This factor is particularly important because it ensures that read-ahead can be performed efficiently.

One final feature of the request manager is that I/O requests can be made that bypass the buffer cache entirely. The low-level page I/O function, **brw_page**, creates a set of temporary **buffer_heads** to label the contents of a page of memory for the purpose of submitting I/O requests to the request manager. However, these temporary **buffer_heads** are not linked into the buffer cache, and once the final buffer on the page has completed its I/O, the entire page is unlocked and the **buffer_heads** discarded.

This cache-bypassing mechanism is used in the kernel whenever the caller is doing independent caching of data, or whenever the data are known to be no longer cachable. The page cache fills its pages in this way, to avoid unnecessary caching of the same data in both the page cache and the buffer cache. The virtual-memory system also bypasses the cache when performing I/O to swap devices.

Character Devices

A character device driver can be almost any device driver that does not offer random access to fixed blocks of data. Any character device drivers registered to the Linux kernel must also register a set of functions that implements the various file I/O operations that the driver can handle. The kernel performs almost no preprocessing of a file read or write request to a character device, but rather simply passes on the request to the device in question, and lets the device deal with the request.

The main exception to this rule is the special subset of character device drivers that implement terminal devices. The kernel maintains a standard interface to these drivers by means of a set of **tty_struct** structures. Each of these structures provides buffering and flow control on the data stream from the terminal device and feeds those data to a line discipline.

A *line discipline* is an interpreter for the information from the terminal device. The most common line discipline is the *tty* discipline, which glues the terminal's data stream onto the standard input and output streams of a user's running processes, allowing those processes to communicate directly with the user's terminal. This job is complicated by the fact that more than one such process may be running simultaneously, and the *tty* line discipline is responsible for attaching and detaching the terminal's input and output from the various processes connected to it as those processes are suspended or are awakened by the user.

Other line disciplines also are implemented that have nothing to do with I/O to a user process. The PPP and SLIP networking protocols are ways of encoding a networking connection over a terminal device such as a serial line. These protocols are implemented under Linux as drivers that at one end appear to the terminal system as line disciplines, and at the other end appear to the networking system as a network device driver. After one of these line disciplines has been enabled on a terminal device, any data appearing on that terminal will be routed directly to the appropriate network device driver.

INTERPROCESS COMMUNICATION

UNIX provides a rich environment for allowing processes to communicate with each other. Communication may be just a matter of letting another process know that some event has occurred, or it may involve transferring data from one process to another.

SYNCHRONIZATION AND SIGNALS

The standard UNIX mechanism for informing a process that an event has occurred is the *signal*. Signals can be sent from any process to any other (with restrictions on signals sent to processes owned by another user), but there is only a limited number of signals available and they cannot carry information: Only the fact that a signal occurred is available to a process. Signals do not need to be generated by another process. The kernel also generates signals internally; for example, it can send a signal to a server process when data arrive on a network channel, to a parent process when a child terminates, or when a timer expires.

Internally, the Linux kernel does not use signals to communicate with processes which are running in kernel mode: If a kernel-mode process is expecting an event to occur, it will not normally use signals to receive notification of that event. Rather, communication about incoming asynchronous events within the kernel is performed through the use of scheduling states and **wait_queue** structures. These mechanisms allow kernel-mode processes to inform one another about relevant events, and also allow events to be generated by device drivers or by the networking system. Whenever a process wants to wait for some event to complete, it places itself on a **wait_queue** associated with that event and tells the scheduler that it is no longer eligible for execution. Once the event has completed, it will wake up every process on the **wait_queue.** This procedure allows multiple processes to wait for a single event. For example, if several processes are trying to read a file from a disk, then they will all be awakened once the data have been read into memory successfully.

Although signals have always been the main mechanism for communicating asynchronous events among processes, Linux also implements the semaphore mechanism of System V UNIX. A process can wait on a semaphore as easily as it can wait for a signal, but semaphores have the advantages that large numbers of semaphores can be shared among multiple independent processes, and that operations on multiple semaphores can be performed atomically. Internally, the standard Linux **wait_queue** mechanism is used to synchronize processes communicating with semaphores.

Passing of Data Among Processes

Linux offers several mechanisms for passing data among rocesses. The standard UNIX **pipe** mechanism allows a child process to inherit a communication channel to its parent; data written to one end of the pipe can be read at the other. Under Linux, pipes appear as just another type of inode to virtual-file-system software, and each pipe has a pair of **wait_queues** to synchronize the reader and writer. UNIX also defines a set of networking facilities that can be used to send streams of data to both local and remote processes.

Two other methods of sharing data among processes are also available. First, shared memory offers an extremely fast way to communicate large or small numbers of data; any data written by one process to a shared memory region can be read immediately by any other process that has mapped that region into its address space. The main disadvantage of shared memory is that, on its own, it offers no synchronization: A process can neither ask the operating system whether a piece of shared memory has been written to, nor suspend execution until such a write occurs. Shared memory becomes particularly powerful when used in conjunction with another interprocess-communication mechanism to provide that missing synchronization.

A shared memory region in Linux is a persistent object that can be created or deleted by processes. Such an object is treated as though it were a small independent address space: The Linux paging algorithms can page out to disk shared memory pages, just as they can page out a process's data pages. The shared memory object acts as a backing store for shared memory regions, just as a file can act as a backing store for a memory-mapped memory region. When a file is mapped into a virtual-address-space region, then any page faults that occur cause the appropriate page of the file to be mapped into virtual memory. Similarly, shared memory mappings direct page faults to map in pages from a persistent shared memory object. Also just as for files, shared memory objects remember their contents even if no processes are currently mapping them into virtual memory.

NETWORK STRUCTURE

Networking is a key area of functionality for Linux. Not only does it support the standard Internet protocols used for most UNIX-to-UNIX communications, but also it implements a number of protocols native to other, non-UNIX operating systems. In particular, since Linux was originally implemented primarily on PCs, rather than on large workstations or on server class systems, it supports many of the protocols typically used on PC networks, such as AppleTalk and IPX.

Internally, networking in the Linux kernel is implemented by three layers of software:

- The socket interface
- Protocol drivers
- Network device drivers

User applications perform all networking requests through the socket interface. This interface is designed to look like the BSD4.3 socket layer, so that any programs designed to make use of Berkeley sockets will run on Linux without any source-code changes. One of the important features of the BSD socket interface is that it is sufficiently general purpose to represent network addresses for a wide range of different networking protocols. This single interface is used in Linux to access not only those protocols implemented on standard BSD systems, but rather, all the protocols supported by the system.

The next layer of software is the protocol stack, which is similar in organization to BSD's own framework. Whenever any networking data arrive at this layer, either from an application's socket or from a network device driver, the data are expected to have been tagged with an identifier specifying which network protocol they contain. Protocols can communicate with one another if they desire; for example, within the Internet protocol set, there are separate protocols to manage routing, error reporting, and reliable retransmission of lost data.

The protocol layer may rewrite packets, create new packets, split or reassemble packets into fragments, or simply discard incoming data. Ultimately, once it has finished processing a set of packets, it passes them on, either up to the socket interface if the data are destined for a local connection or downward to a device driver if the packet needs to be transmitted remotely. It is up to the protocol layer to decide to which socket or device to send the packet.

All communication between the layers of the networking stack is performed by passing of single **skbuff** structures. An **skbuff** contains a set of pointers into a single continuous area of memory, representing a buffer inside which network packets can be constructed. The valid data in an **skbuff** does not need to start at the beginning of the **skbuff**'s buffer, and do not need to run to the end: The networking code can add data to or trim data from either end of the packet, as long as the result still fits into the **skbuff**. This capacity is especially important on modern microprocessors where improvements in CPU speed have far outstripped the performance of main memory: the **skbuff** architecture allows flexibility in manipulating packet headers and checksums while avoiding any unnecessary data copying.

The most important set of protocols in the Linux networking system is the Internet protocol (IP) suite. This suite comprises a number of separate protocols. The IP implements routing between different hosts anywhere on the network. On top of the routing protocol are built the UDP, TCP, and ICMP protocols. The UDP protocol carries arbitrary individual datagrams between hosts, whereas TCP implements reliable connections between hosts with guaranteed in-order delivery of packets and automatic retransmission of lost data. ICMP is used to carry various error and status messages between hosts.

Packets (**skbuffs**) arriving at the networking stack's protocol software are expected to be already tagged with an internal identifier indicating to which protocol the packet is relevant. Different networking device drivers encode the protocol type in different ways over their communications media, so identifying the protocol for incoming data must be done in the device driver. The device driver uses a hash table of known networking-protocol identifiers to look up the appropriate protocol, and passes the packet to that protocol. New protocols can be added to the hash table as kernel-loadable modules.

Incoming IP packets are delivered to the IP driver. The job of this layer is to perform routing: It decides where the packet is destined and forwards the packet to the appropriate internal protocol driver to be delivered locally, or injects it back into a selected network device driver queue to be forwarded to another host. It performs the routing decision using two tables: the persistent forwarding information base (FIB), and a cache of recent routing decisions. The FIB holds routing-configuration information and can specify routes based either on a specific destination address or on a wildcard representing multiple destinations. The FIB is organized as a set of hash tables indexed by destination address; the tables representing the most specific routes are always searched first. Successful lookups from this table are added to the route-caching table, which caches routes only by specific destination; no wildcards are stored in the cache, so lookups can be made more quickly. An entry in the route cache expires after a fixed period with no hits.

At various stages, the IP software passes packets to a separate section of code for *firewall management*: selective filtering of packets according to arbitrary criteria, usually for security purposes. The firewall manager maintains a number of separate *firewall chains*, and allows an **skbuff** to be matched against any chain. Separate chains are reserved for separate purposes: one is used for forwarded packets, one for packets being input to this host, and one for data generated at this host. Each chain is held as an ordered list of rules, where a rule specifies one of a number of possible firewall-decision functions plus some arbitrary data to match against.

Two other functions performed by the IP driver are disassembly and reassembly of large packets. If an outgoing packet is too large to be queued to a device, it is simply split up into smaller *fragments*, which are all queued to the driver. At the receiving host, these fragments must be reassembled. The IP driver maintains an **ipfrag** object for each fragment awaiting reassembly, and a **ipq** for each datagram being assembled. Incoming fragments are matched against each known **ipq**. If a match is found, the fragment is added to it; otherwise, a new

ipq is created. Once the final fragment has arrived for a **ipq**, a completely new **skbuff** is constructed to hold the new packet, and this packet is passed back into the IP driver.

Packets that are matched by the IP as destined for this host are passed on to one of the other protocol drivers. The UDP and TCP protocols share a means of associating packets with source and destination sockets: Each connected pair of sockets is uniquely identified by its source and destination addresses and by the source and destination *port* numbers. The socket lists are linked onto hash tables keyed on these four address-port values for socket lookup on incoming packets. The TCP protocol has to deal with unreliable connections, so it maintains ordered lists of unacknowledged outgoing packets to retransmit after a timeout, and of incoming out-of-order packets to be presented to the socket when the missing data have arrived.

SECURITY

Linux's security model is closely related to typical UNIX security mechanisms. The security issues can be classified in two groups:

- **Authentication.** Making sure that nobody can access the system without first proving that she has entry rights
- **Access control.** Providing a mechanism for checking whether a user has the right to access a certain object, and preventing access to objects as required

AUTHENTICATION

Authentication in UNIX has typically been performed through the use of a publicly readable password file. A user's password is combined with a random "salt" value and the result is encoded with a one-way transformation function and is stored in the password file. The use of the one-way function means that it is not possible to deduce the original password from the password file except by trial and error. When a user presents a password to the system, it is recombined with the salt value stored in the password file and is passed through the same one-way transformation. If the result matches the contents of the password file, then the password is accepted.

Historically, UNIX implementations of this mechanism have had several problems. Passwords were often limited to eight characters, and the number of possible salt values was so low that an attacker could easily combine a dictionary of commonly used passwords with every possible salt value and have a good chance of matching one or more passwords in the password file, gaining unauthorized access to any accounts compromised as a result. Extensions to the password mechanism have been introduced that keep the encrypted password secret in a non-publicly-readable file, that allow longer passwords, or that use more secure methods of encoding the password. Other authentication mechanisms have been introduced to limit the times during which a user is permitted to connect to the system or to distribute authentication information to all the related systems in a network.

A new security mechanism has been developed by a number of UNIX vendors to address these issues. The *pluggable authentication modules (PAM)* system is based on a shared library that can be used by any system component that needs to authenticate users. An implementation of this system is available under Linux. PAM allows authentication modules to be loaded on demand as specified in a systemwide configuration file. If a new authentication mechanism is added at a later date, it can be added to the configuration file and all system components will immediately be able to take advantage of it. PAM modules can specify authentication methods, account restrictions, session-setup functions, or password-changing functions (so that, when users change their passwords, all the necessary authentication mechanisms can be updated at once).

Access Control

Access control under UNIX systems, including Linux, is performed through the use of unique numeric identifiers. A user identifier *(uid)* identifies a single user or a single set of access rights. A group identifier *(gid)* is an extra identifier that can be used to identify rights belonging to more than one user.

Access control is applied to various objects in the system. Every file available in the system is protected by the standard access-control mechanism. In addition, other shared objects, such as shared memory sections and semaphores, employ the same access system.

Every object in a UNIX system that is under user and group access control has a single uid and a single gid associated with it. User processes also have a single uid, but they may have more than one gid. If a process's uid matches the uid of an object, then the process has *user* or *owner* rights to that object; otherwise, if any of the process's gids match the object's gid, then *group* rights are conferred; otherwise, the process has *world* rights to the object.

Linux performs access control by assigning objects a *protection mask*, which specifies which access modes—read, write, or execute—are to be granted to processes with owner, group, or world access. Thus, the owner of an object might have full read, write, and execute access to a file; other users in a certain group might be given read access but denied write access; and everybody else might be given no access at all.

The only exception is the privileged **root** uid. A process with this special uid is granted automatic access to any object in the system, bypassing normal access checks. Such processes are also granted permission to perform privileged operations such as reading any physical memory or opening reserved network sockets. This mechanism allows the kernel to prevent normal users from accessing these resources: most of the kernel's key internal resources are implicitly owned by this root uid.

Linux implements the standard UNIX **setuid** mechanism. This mechanism allows a program to run with privileges different from those of the user running the program: for example, the **lpr** program (which submits a job onto a print queue) has access to the system's print queues even if the user running that program does not. The UNIX implementation of **setuid** distinguishes between a process's *real* and *effective* uid: The real uid is that of the user running the program, but the effective uid is that of the file's owner.

Under Linux, this mechanism is augmented in two ways. First, Linux implements the POSIX specification's *saved user-id* mechanism, which allows a process to drop and reaquire its effective uid repeatedly; for security reasons, a program may want to perform most of its operations in a safe mode, waiving the privileges granted by its **setuid** status, but may wish to perform selected operations with all its privileges. Standard UNIX implementations achieve this capacity only by swapping the real and effective uids; the previous effective uid is remembered but the program's real uid does not always correspond to the uid of the user running the program. Saved uids allow a process to set its effective uid to its real uid and then back to the previous value of its effective uid, without having to modify the real uid at any time.

The second enhancement provided by Linux is the addition of a process characteristic that grants just a subset of the rights of the effective uid. The *fsuid* and *fsgid* process properties are used when access rights are granted to files, and are set every time the effective uid or gid are set. However, the fsuid and fsgid can be set independently of the effective ids, allowing a process to access files on behalf of another user without taking on the identity of that other user in any other way. Specifically, server processes can use this mechanism to serve files to a certain user without the process becoming vulnerable to being killed or suspended by that user.

Linux provides another mechanism that has become common in modern UNIXes for flexible passing of rights from one program to another. When a local network socket has been set up between any two processes on the system, either of those processes may send to the other process a file descriptor for one of its open files; the other process receives a duplicate file descriptor for the same file. This mechanism allows a client to pass access to a single file selectively to some server process, without granting that process any other privileges. For example, it is no longer necessary for a print server to be able to read all the files of a user who submits a new print job; the print client could simply pass the server file descriptors for any files to be printed, denying the server access to any of the user's other files.

SUMMARY

Linux is a modern, free operating systein based on UNIX standards. It has been designed to run efficiently and reliably on common PC hardware; it also runs on a variety of other platforms. It provides a programming interface and user interface compatible with standard UNIX systems, and can run a large number of UNIX applications, including an increasing number of commercially supported applications.

Linux has not evolved in a vacuum. A complete Linux system includes many components that were developed ipdependently of Linux. The core Linux operating-system kernel is entirely original, but it allows much existing free UNIX software to run, resulting in an entire UNIX-compatible operating system free from proprietary code.

The Linux kernel is implemented as a traditional monolithic kernel for performance reasons, but is modular enough in design to allow most drivers to be dynamically loaded and unloaded at run time.

Linux is a multiuser system, providing protection between processes and running multiple processes according to a time-sharing scheduler. Newly created processes can share selective parts of their execution environment with their parent processes, allowing multithreaded programming. Interprocess communication is supported by both System V mechanisms—message queues, semaphores, and shared memory—and BSD's socket interface. Multiple networking protocols can be accessed simultaneously through the socket interface.

To the user, the file system appears as a hierarchical directory tree that obeys UNIX semantics. Internally, Linux uses an abstraction layer to manage multiple different file systems. Device-oriented, networked, and virtual file systems are supported. Device-oriented file systems access disk storage through two caches: data are cached in the page cache that is unified with the virtual memory system, and metadata are cached in the buffer cache—a separate cache indexed by physical disk block.

The memory-management system uses page sharing and copy-on-write to minimize the duplication of data shared by different processes. Pages are loaded on demand when they are first referenced, and are paged back out to backing store according to an LFU algorithm if physical memory needs to be reclaimed.

EXERCISES

- Linux runs on a variety of hardware platforms. What steps must the Linux developers take to ensure that the system is portable to different processors and memory-management architectures, to minimize the amount of architecture-specific kernel code?
- Dynamically loadable kernel modules give flexibility. When drivers are added to a system, but do they have disadvantages too? Under what circumstances would a kernel be compiled into a single binary file, and when would it be better to keep it split into modules? Explain your answer.
- Multithreading is a commonly used programming technique. Describe three different ways that threads could be implemented. Explain how these ways compare to the Linux clone mechanism. When might each alternative mechanism be better or worse than using clones?
- What are the extra costs incurred by the creation and scheduling of a process, as compared to the cost of a cloned thread?

- The Linux scheduler implements soft real-time scheduling. What features are missing that are necessary for some real-time programming tasks? How might they be added to the kernel?
- The Linux kernel does not allow paging out of kernel memory. What effect does this restriction have on the kernel's design? What are two advantages and two disadvantages of this design decision?
- In Linux, shared libraries perform many operations central to the operating system. What is the advantage of keeping this functionality out of the kernel? Are there any drawbacks? Explain your answer.
- What are three advantages of dynamic (shared) linkage of libraries compared to static linkage? What are two cases where static linkage is preferable?
- Compare the use of networking sockets with the use of shared memory as a mechanism for communicating data between processes on a single computer. What are the advantages of each method? When might each be preferred?
- UNIX systems used to use disk-layout optimizations based on the rotation position of disk data, but modern implementations, including Linux, simply optimize for sequential data access. Why do they do so? Of what hardware characteristics does sequential access take advantage? Why is rotational optimization no longer so useful?
- The Linux source code is freely and widely available over the Internet or from CD-ROM vendors. What are three implications of this availability for the security of the Linux system?

BIBLIOGRAPHICAL NOTES

The Linux system is a product of the Internet; as a result, most of the available documentation on Linux is available in some form on the Internet. The following key sites reference most of the useful information available:

- The Linux Cross-Reference Pages at http://lxr.linux.no/ maintain current listings of the Linux kernel, browsable via the Web and fully cross-referenced.
- Linux-HQ at http://www.linuxhq.com/ hosts a large amount of information relating to the Linux 2.0 and Linux 2.1 kernels. This site also includes links to the home pages of most Linux distributions, as well as archives of the major mailing lists.
- The Linux Documentation Project at http://sunsite.unc.edu/linux/ lists many books on Linux that are available in source format as part of the Linux Documentation Project. The project also hosts the Linux How-To guides: a series of hints and tips relating to aspects of Linux.
- The Kernel Hackers' Guide is an Internet-based guide to kernel internals in general. This constantly expanding site is located at http://www.redhat.com:8080/HyperNews/get/khg.html.

In addition, there are many mailing lists devoted to Linux. The most important are maintained by a mailing-list manager that can be reached at the email address **majordomo@vger.rutgers.edu.** Send e-mail to this address with the single line "help" in the mail's body for information on how to access the list server and to subscribe to any lists.

The one book that currently describes the internal details of the Linux kernel—*Linux Kernel Internals* by Beck et al. 1996—deals with only Linux 1.2.13. For further reading on UNIX in general, a good place to start is Vahalia's *Unix Internals: The New Frontiers* (Vahalia 1996).

Finally, the Linux system itself can be obtained over the Internet. Complete Linux distributions can be obtained from the home sites of the companies concerned, and the Linux community also maintains archives of current system components at several places on the Internet. The most important are these:

- ftp://tsx-11.mit.edu/pub/linux/
- ftp://sunsite.unc.edu/pub/Linux/
- ftp://linux.kernel.org/pub/linux/

SECTION 5

WINDOWS NT

The Microsoft Windows NT operating system is a 32-bit preemptive multitasking operating system for modern microprocessors. NT is portable to a variety of processor architectures. One or more versions of NT have been ported to Intel 386 and higher, MIPS R4000, DEC Alpha, and the PowerPC. Key goals for the system are portability, security, Portable Operating System Interface (POSIX) or IEEE Std. 1003.1 compliance, multiprocessor support, extensibility, international support, and compatibility with MS-DOS and MS-Windows applications. NT uses a micro-kernel architecture (like Mach), so enhancements can be made to one part of the operating system without greatly affecting other parts of the system. NT (through version 4) is not a multiuser operating system.

The two versions of NT are Windows NT Workstation and Windows NT Server. They use the same kernel and operating-system code, but NT Server is configured for client-server applications and can act as an application server on NetWare and Microsoft LANs. Version 4.0 of NT Server incorporates Internet web-server software and the Windows 95 user interface. In 1996, more NT Server licenses were sold than all versions of UNIX licenses.

HISTORY

In the mid-1980s, Microsoft and IBM cooperated to develop the OS/2 operating system, which was written in assembly language for single-processor Intel 80286 systems. In 1988, Microsoft decided to make a fresh start, and to develop a "new technology" (NT) portable operating system that supported both the OS/2 and POSIX application programming interfaces (APIs). In October of 1988, Dave Cutler, the architect of the DEC VAX/VMS operating system, was hired and given the charter of building this new operating system. Originally, NT was supposed to use the OS/2 API as its native environment, but during development NT was changed to use the 32-bit Windows API or Win32 API, reflecting the popularity of Windows 3.0. The first versions of NT were Windows NT 3.1 and Windows NT 3.1 Advanced Server. (At that time, 16-bit Windows was at Version 3.1.) In Version 4.0, NT adopted the Windows 95 user interface and incorporated Internet web-server and browser software. In addition, some user interface routines and graphics code were moved into the kernel to improve performance with the side effect of decreased system reliability.

DESIGN PRINCIPLES

The design goals that Microsoft has stated for NT include extensibility, portability, reliability, compatibility, performance, and international support.

Extensibility is an important property of any operating system that hopes to keep up with advancements in computing technology. So that changes are facilitated over time, NT is implemented using a layered architecture. The NT executive, which runs in kernel or protected mode, provides the basic system services. On top of the executive, several server subsystems operate in user mode. Among these are *environmental subsystems* that emulate different operating systems. Thus, programs written for MS-DOS, Microsoft Windows, and POSIX can all run on NT in the appropriate environment. Because of the modular structure, additional environmental subsystems can be added without affecting the executive. In addition, NT uses loadable drivers in the I/O system, so that new file systems, new kinds of I/O devices, and new kinds of networking can be added while the system is running. NT utilizes a client-server model like the Mach operating system, and supports distributed processing by remote procedure calls (RPCs) as defined by the Open Software Foundation.

An operating system is *portable* if it can be moved from one hardware architecture to another with relatively few changes. NT is designed to be portable. As is true of UNIX, the majority of the system is written in C and C++. All processor-dependent code is isolated in a dynamic link library (DLL), called the *hardware abstraction layer (HAL)*. A DLL is a file that gets mapped into a process's address space such that any functions in the DLL appear as if they are part of the process. The upper layers of NT depend on HAL, rather than on the underlying hardware, and that helps NT to be portable. The HAL manipulates hardware directly, isolating the rest of NT from hardware differences among the platforms on which it runs.

Reliability is the ability to handle error conditions, including the ability of the operating system to protect itself and its users from defective or malicious software. NT is designed to resist defects and attacks by using hardware protection for virtual memory, and software protection mechanisms for operating-system resources. Also, NT comes with a file system, called the native NT file system (NTFS), that recovers automatically from many kinds of file system errors after a system crash. NT Version 3.51 has a C-2 security classification from the U.S. government, which signifies a moderate level of protection from defective software and malicious attacks.

NT provides source-level *compatibility* to applications that follow the IEEE 1003.1 (POSIX) standard. Thus, they can be compiled to run on NT without changing the source code.

In addition, NT can run the executable binaries for many programs compiled for Intel X86 running MS-DOS, 16-bit Windows, OS/2, Lan Manager, and 32-bit Windows. It does so via two mechanisms. First, versions of NT for non-Intel processors provide X86 instruction-set emulation in software. Second, the system calls for MS-DOS, 32-bit Windows, and so on are handled by the environmental subsystems mentioned earlier. These environmental subsystems support a variety of file systems, including the MS-DOS FAT file system, the OS/2 HPFS file system, the ISO9660 CD file system, and NTFS. NT's binary compatibility, however, is not perfect. In MS-DOS, for example, applications can access hardware ports directly. For reliability and security, NT prohibits such access.

NT is designed to afford good *performance*. The subsystems that comprise NT can communicate with one another efficiently by a local-procedure-call facility that provides high-performance message passing. Except for the kernel, threads in the subsystems of NT can be preempted by higher-priority threads. Thus the system can respond quickly to external events. In addition, NT is designed for symmetrical multiprocessing: On a multiprocessor computer, several threads can run at the same time. The current scalability of NT is limited, compared to UNIX. As of 1997 it supported systems with up to eight CPUs, while Solaris ran on systems with up to 64 processors.

NT is also designed for *international* use. It provides support for different locales via the national language support (NLS) API. NLS API provides specialized routines to format dates, time, and money in accordance with various national customs. String comparisons are specialized to account for varying character sets. UNICODE is NT's native character code, although NT supports ANSI characters by converting them to UNICODE characters before manipulating them (8-bit to 16-bit conversion).

SYSTEM COMPONENTS

The architecture of NT is a layered system of modules. Figure 5-1 shows the architecture of NT Version 4. The main layers are the hardware abstraction layer, the kernel and the executive that run in protected mode, and a large collection of subsystems that run in user mode. The user-mode subsystems are in two categories. The environmental subsystems emulate different operating systems; the protection subsystems provide security functions. One of the chief advantages of this type of architecture is that interactions between modules can be kept simple. The remainder of this chapter describes these layers and subsystems.

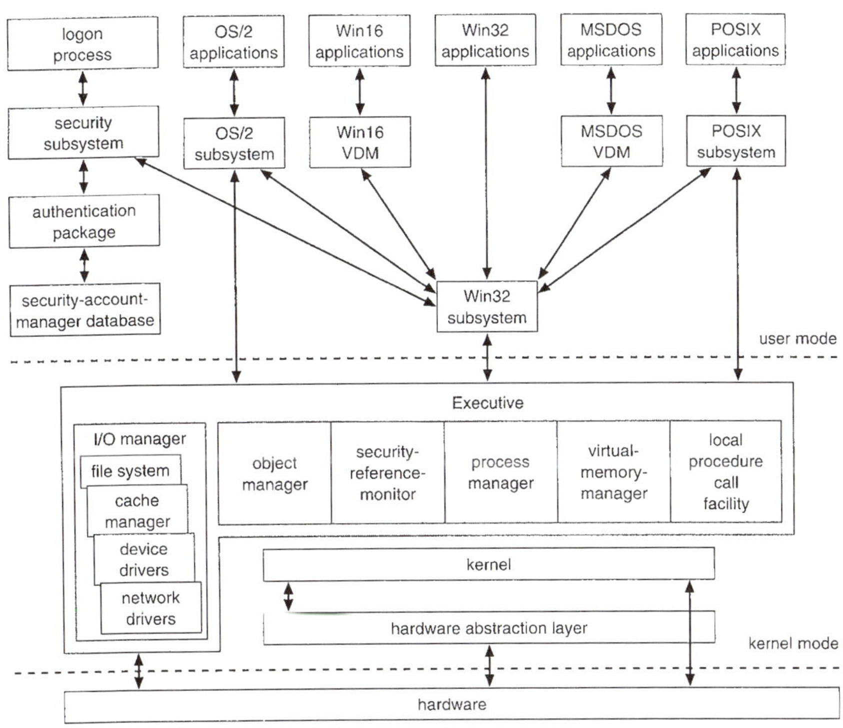

FIGURE 5-1 *Windows NT Block Diagram*

Hardware Abstraction Layer

HAL is a layer of software that hides hardware differences from upper levels of the operating system, to help make NT portable. HAL exports a virtual-machine interface that is used by the kernel, the executive, and the device drivers. One advantage of this approach is that only a single version of each device driver is needed—it can run on all hardware platforms without porting the driver code. HAL also provides the support for symmetric multiprocessing. For performance reasons, I/O drivers (and graphics drivers in NT 4.0) may access the hardware directly.

Kernel

The kernel of NT provides the foundation for the executive and the subsystems. The kernel is never paged out of memory, and its execution is never preempted. It has four main responsibilities: thread scheduling, interrupt and exception handling, low-level processor synchronization, and recovery after a power failure.

The kernel is object oriented. An *object type* in NT is a system-defined data type that has a set of attributes (data values) and a set of methods (i.e., functions or operations). An *object* is just an instance of a particular object type. The kernel performs its job by using a set of kernel objects whose attributes store the kernel data, and whose methods perform the kernel activities.

The kernel uses two sets of objects. The first set of objects are the *dispatcher objects*. These control dispatching and synchronization in the system. Examples of these objects are events, mutants, mutexes, semaphores, threads, and timers. The *event object* is used to record an event occurrence and to synchronize the latter with some action. The *mutant* provides kernel-mode or user-mode mutual exclusion with the notion of ownership. The *mutex*, which is available in only kernel mode, provides deadlock-free mutual exclusion. A *semaphore object* acts as a counter or gate to control the number of threads that access some resource. The *thread object* is the entity that is run by the kernel and is associated with a *process object*. *Timer objects* are used to keep track of the time and to signal "time outs" when operations take too long and need to be interrupted.

The second set of kernel objects comprises the *control objects*. These objects include asynchronous procedure calls, interrupts, power notify, power status, process, and profile objects. The *asynchronous procedure call* is used to break into an executing thread and to call a procedure. The *interrupt object* binds an interrupt service routine to an interrupt source. The *power notify object* is used to call a specified routine automatically after a power failure, and the *power status object* is used to check whether the power has failed. A *process object* represents the virtual address space and control information necessary to execute the set of threads associated with a process. Finally, the *profile object* is used to measure the amount of time used by a block of code.

As do many modern operating systems, NT has the notions of processes and threads for executable code. The *process* has a virtual-memory address space, and information such as a base priority and an affinity for one or more processors. Each process has one or more *threads*, which are the units of execution dispatched by the kernel. Each thread has its own state, including a priority, processor affinity, and accounting information.

The six possible thread states are ready, standby, running, waiting, transition, and terminated. *Ready* means waiting to run. The highest-priority ready thread is moved to the *standby* state, which means that it will be the next thread to run. In a multiprocessor system, one thread is kept in the standby state for each processor. A thread is *running* when it is executing on a processor. It will run until it is preempted by a higher-priority thread, until it terminates, until its time quantum ends, or until it calls a blocking system call, such as for I/O. A thread is in the *waiting* state when it is waiting for a signal such as an I/O completion. A new thread is in the *transition* state while it is waiting for the resources necessary for execution. A thread enters the *terminated* state when it finishes execution.

The dispatcher uses a 32-level priority scheme to determine the order of thread execution. Priorities are divided into two classes: the *real-time class* contains threads with priorities ranging from 16 to 31, and the *variable class* contains threads having priorities from 0 to 15. The dispatcher uses a queue for each scheduling priority, and traverses the set of queues from highest to lowest until it finds a thread that is ready to run. If a thread has a particular processor affinity but that processor is not available, the dispatcher will skip past it, and will continue looking for a thread that is ready to run. If no ready thread is found, the dispatcher will execute a special thread called the *idle thread*.

When a thread's time quantum runs out, the thread is interrupted, and if the thread is in the variable-priority class its priority is lowered. The priority is never lowered below the base priority, however. Lowering the thread's priority tends to limit the CPU consumption of compute-bound threads. When a variable-priority thread is released from a wait operation, the dispatcher boosts its priority. The amount of the boost depends on for what it was waiting. A thread that was waiting for keyboard I/O would get a large priority increase, whereas a thread waiting for a disk operation would get a moderate one. This strategy tends to give good response times to interactive threads that are using the mouse and windows, and enables

I/O-bound threads to keep the I/O devices busy, while permitting compute-bound threads to use spare CPU cycles in the background. This strategy is used by several time-sharing operating systems, including UNIX. Additionally, the current window that the user is interacting with also receives a priority boost to enhance its response time.

Scheduling can occur when a thread enters the ready or wait state, when a thread terminates, or when an application changes a thread's priority or processor affinity. If a higher-priority real-time thread becomes ready while a lower-priority thread is running, the lower-priority thread will be preempted. This preemption gives a real-time thread preferential access to the CPU when the thread needs such access. NT is not a hard real-time operating system, however, because it does not guarantee that a real-time thread will start to execute within any particular time limit.

The kernel also provides trap handling for exceptions and interrupts that are generated by hardware or software. NT defines several architecture-independent exceptions, including memory-access violation, integer overflow, floating-point overflow or underflow, integer divide by zero, floating-point divide by zero, illegal instruction, data misalignment, privileged instruction, page read error, guard-page violation, paging file quota exceeded, debugger breakpoint, and debugger single step.

Exceptions that are simple can be handled by the trap handler; others are handled by the kernel's *exception dispatcher*. The exception dispatcher creates an exception record that contains the reason for the exception, and that finds an exception handler that can deal with the exception.

When an exception occurs in kernel mode, the exception dispatcher simply calls a routine to locate the exception handler. If no handler is found, a fatal system error occurs and the user is left with the infamous "blue screen of death" that signifies system failure.

Exception handling is more complex for user-mode processes, because an environmental subsystem (such as the POSIX system) can set up a debugger port and an exception port for every process that it creates. If a debugger port is registered, the exception handler sends the exception to the debugger. If the debugger port is not found or does not handle that exception, the dispatcher then attempts to find an appropriate exception handler. If a handler is not found, the debugger is called again so that it can catch the error for debugging. If a debugger is not running, a message is then sent to the process's exception port to give the environmental subsystem a chance to translate the exception. For example, the POSIX environment translates NT exception messages into POSIX signals before sending them to the thread that caused the exception. Finally, if nothing else works, the kernel simply terminates the process containing the thread that caused the exception.

The interrupt dispatcher in the kernel handles interrupts by calling either an interrupt service routine (such as in a device driver) or an internal kernel routine. The interrupt is represented by an interrupt object that contains all the information needed to handle the interrupt. Using an interrupt object makes it easy to associate interrupt service routines with an interrupt without having to access the interrupt hardware directly.

Various processor architectures, such as Intel or DEC Alpha, have different types and numbers of interrupts. For portability, the interrupt dispatcher maps the hardware interrupts into a standard set. The interrupts are prioritized and are serviced in priority order. There are 32 interrupt levels (IRQLs) in NT. Eight are reserved for the use of the kernel; the other 24 represent hardware interrupts via the HAL. The NT interrupts are defined in Figure 5-2.

The kernel uses an *interrupt dispatch table* to bind each interrupt level to a service routine. In a multiprocessor computer, NT keeps a separate interrupt dispatch table for each processor, and each processor's IRQL can be set independently to mask out interrupts. All interrupts that occur at a level equal to or less than the IRQL of a processor get blocked until the IRQL is lowered by a kernel-level thread. NT takes advantage of this property to use software interrupts to perform system functions. For instance, the kernel uses software interrupts to start a thread dispatch, to handle timers, and to support asynchronous operations.

The kernel uses the dispatch interrupt to control thread context switching. When the kernel is running, it raises the IRQL on the processor to a level above the dispatch level. When

Interrupt levels	Types of interrupts
31	machine check or bus error
30	power fail
29	interprocessor notification (request another processor to act; e.g., dispatch a process or update the TLB)
28	clock (used to keep track of time)
12–27	traditional PC IRQ hardware interrupts
4–11	dispatch and deferred procedure call (by the kernel)
3	software debugger
0–2	software interrupts (used by device drivers)

FIGURE 5-2 *NT Interrupts*

the kernel determines that a thread dispatch is required, the kernel generates a dispatch interrupt, but this interrupt is blocked until the kernel finishes what it is doing and lowers the IRQL. At that point, the dispatch interrupt can be serviced, so the dispatcher chooses a thread to run.

When the kernel decides that some system function should be executed eventually, but not immediately, it queues a *deferred procedure call (DPC)* object that contains the address of the function to be executed, and generates a DPC interrupt. When the IRQL of the processor drops low enough, the DPC objects are executed. The IRQL of the DPC interrupt is typically higher than that of user threads, so DPCs will interrupt the execution of user threads. To avoid problems, DPCs are restricted to be fairly simple. They cannot modify a thread's memory; create, acquire or wait on objects; call system services; or generate page faults.

The *asynchronous procedure call (APC)* mechanism is similar to the DPC mechanism, but for more general use. The APC mechanism enables threads to set up a procedure call that will happen out of the blue at some future time. For instance, many system services accept a user-mode routine as a parameter. Instead of calling a synchronous system call that will block the thread until the system call completes, a user thread can call an asynchronous system call and supply an APC. The user thread will continue running. When the system service finishes, the user thread will be interrupted to run the APC spontaneously.

An APC can be queued on either a system thread or a user thread, although a user-mode APC will be executed only if the thread has declared itself to be *alertable*. An APC is more powerful than a DPC, in that it can acquire and wait on objects, cause page faults, and call system services. Since an APC executes in the address space of the target thread, the NT executive uses APCs extensively for I/O processing.

NT can run on symmetric multiprocessor machines, so the kernel must prevent two of its threads from modifying a shared data structure at the same time. The kernel uses spin locks that reside in global memory to achieve multiprocessor mutual exclusion. Because all activity on a processor stops when a thread is attempting to acquire a spin lock, a thread that holds a spin lock is not preempted, so it can finish and release the lock as quickly as possible.

A power-fail interrupt, which has the second highest priority, notifies the operating system whenever a power loss is detected. The *power notify object* provides a way for a device driver to register a routine that will be called upon power restoration and ensures that devices get set to the proper state upon recovery. For battery backed up systems the *power status object* is useful to determine the power status. A driver examines the power status object to determine whether or not the power has failed before it begins a critical operation. If the driver determines that power has not failed, it raises the IRQL of its processor to powerfail, performs the operation and resets the IRQL. This sequence of actions blocks the powerfail interrupt until after the critical operation completes.

Executive

The NT executive provides a set of services that all environmental subsystems can use. The services are in the following groups: object manager, virtual-memory manager, process manager, local procedure call facility, I/O manager, and security reference monitor.

OBJECT MANAGER As an object-oriented system NT uses objects for all its services and entities. Examples of objects are directory objects, symbolic link objects, semaphore objects, event objects, process and thread objects, port objects, and file objects. The job of the object manager is to supervise the use of all objects. When a thread wants to use an object, it calls the object manager's **open** method to get a *handle* to the object. Handles are a standardized interface to all kinds of objects. Like a file handle, an object handle is an identifier unique to a process that gives the ability to access and manipulate a system resource.

Since the object manager is the only entity that can generate an object handle, it is the natural place to check security. For instance, the object manager checks whether a process has the right to access an object when the process tries to open that object. The object manager can also enforce quotas, such as the maximum amount of memory that a process may allocate.

The object manager can also keep track of which processes are using each object. Each object header contains a count of the number of processes that have handles to that object. When the counter goes to zero, the object is deleted from the name space if it is a temporary object name. Since NT itself often uses pointers (instead of handles) to access objects, the object manager also maintains a reference count which it increments when NT gains access to an object, and decrements the count when the object is no longer needed. When the reference count of a temporary object goes to zero, the object is deleted from memory. Permanent objects represent physical entities, such as disk drives, and are not deleted when the reference count and the open handle counter go to zero.

The objects are manipulated by a standard set of methods—namely **create, open, close, delete, query name, parse,** and **security**. The final three need explanation:

- **query name** is called when a thread has a handle to an object, but wants to know the object's name.
- **parse** is used by the object manager to search for an object given the object's name.
- **security** is called when a process opens or changes the protection of an object.

NAMING OBJECTS The NT executive allows any object to be given a name. The name space is global, so one process may create a named object, and a second process can then open a handle to the object and share it with the first process. A process opening a named object can ask for the search to be either case sensitive or case insensitive.

A name can be either permanent or temporary. A permanent name represents an entity, such as a disk drive, that remains even if no process is accessing it. A temporary name exists only while some process holds a handle to that object.

Although the name space is not directly visible across a network, the object manager's **parse** method is used to help access a named object on another system. When a process attempts to open an object that resides on a remote computer, the object manager calls the parse method, which then calls a network redirector to find the object.

Object names are structured like file path names in MS-DOS and UNIX. Directories are represented by a *directory object* that contains the names of all the objects in that directory. The object name space can grow by the addition of *object domains*, which are self-contained sets of objects. Examples of *object domains* are floppy disks and hard drives. It is easy to see how the name space gets extended when a floppy disk is added to the system—the floppy has its own name space that is grafted onto the existing name space.

UNIX file systems have *symbolic links*, so multiple nicknames or aliases can refer to the same file. Similarly, NT implements a *symbolic link object*. One way that NT uses symbolic links is to map drive names to the standard MS-DOS drive letters. The drive letters are just symbolic links that may be remapped to suit the user's preferences.

A process gets an object handle by creating an object, by opening an existing one, by receiving a duplicated handle from another process, or by inheriting a handle from a parent process. This is similar to the way a UNIX process can get a file descriptor. These handles are all stored in the process's *object table*. An entry in the object table contains the object's access rights and states whether the handle should be inherited by child processes. When a process terminates, NT automatically closes all the process's open handles.

When a user is authenticated by the log in process, an access-token object is attached to the user's process. The access token contains information such as the security ID, group IDs, privileges, primary group, and default access control list. These attributes determine which services and objects can be used.

In NT, each object is protected by an *access-control list*. This list contains the security ids and the set of access rights granted to each one. When a process attempts to access an object, the system compares the security ID in the process's access token with the object's access control list to determine whether access should be permitted. This check is done only when an object is opened, so internal NT services that use pointers rather than opening a handle to an object bypass the access check.

Generally, the creator of the object determines the access-control list for that object. If none is supplied explicitly, one may be inherited from the creator object, or a default list may be obtained from the user's access token object.

One field in the access token controls auditing of the object. Operations that are being audited get logged to the system's audit log with an identification of the user. The audit field can watch this log to discover attempts to break into the system or to access protected objects.

VIRTUAL-MEMORY MANAGER The virtual-memory portion of the NT executive is the *virtual-memory (VM) manager*. The design of the VM manager assumes that the underlying hardware supports virtual-to-physical mapping, a paging mechanism, transparent cache coherence on multiprocessor systems, and allows multiple page-table entries to map to the same page frame. The VM manager in NT uses a page-based management scheme with a page size of 4 KB. Pages of data that are assigned to a process but are not in physical memory are stored in the *paging file* on disk.

The VM manager uses 32-bit addresses, so each process has a 4 GB virtual address space. The upper 2 GB is identical for all processes, and is used by NT in kernel mode. The lower 2 GB is distinct for every process, and is accessible by both user- and kernel-mode threads.

The NT VM manager uses a two-step process to allocate memory. The first step *reserves* a portion of the process's address space. The second step *commits* the allocation by assigning space in the NT paging file. NT can limit the amount of paging file space that a process consumes by enforcing a quota on committed memory. A process can uncommit memory that it is no longer using to free up its paging quota. Since memory is represented by objects, when one process (the *parent*) creates a second process (the *child*), the parent can maintain the ability to access the virtual memory of the child. That is how environmental subsystems can manage the memory of their client processes. For performance, the VM manager allows a privileged process to lock selected pages in physical memory, thus ensuring that the pages will not be swapped out to the paging file.

Two processes can share memory by getting handles to the same memory object, but this approach can be inefficient since the entire memory space of that object would need to be committed before either process could access that object. NT provides an alternative called a *section object* to represent a block of shared memory. After getting a handle to a section object, a process can map only the needed portion of the memory. This portion is called a *view*. The view mechanism also enables a process to access an object that is too large to fit into the process's paging file quota. The system can use the view to walk through the address space of the object, one piece at a time.

A process can control the use of a shared-memory section object in many ways. The maximum size of a section can be bounded. The section can be backed by disk space in either the system paging file or by a regular file (called a *memory-mapped* file). A section can be

based, meaning that the section appears at the same virtual address for all processes that access it. The memory protection of pages in the section can be set to read only, read-write, execute only, guard page, and copy on write. A guard page raises an exception if accessed; the exception can be used (for example) to check whether a faulty program iterates beyond the end of an array. The copy-on-write mechanism allows the VM manager to save memory. When two processes want independent copies of an object, the VM manager places only one shared copy into physical memory, but the VM manager sets the copy-on-write property on that region of memory. If one of the processes tries to modify data in a copy-on-write page, the VM manager first makes a private copy of the page for that process to use.

The virtual address translation in NT uses several data structures. Each process has a *page directory* that contains 1024 *page-directory entries* of size 4 bytes. Typically the page directory is private, but it could be shared among processes if the environment required it. Each page-directory entry points to a *page table* that contains 1024 *page-table entries (PTEs)* of size 4 bytes. Each PTE points to a 4-KB *page frame* in physical memory. The total size of all the page tables for a process is 4 MB, so the VM manager will swap out these tables to disk when necessary. See Figure 5-3 for a diagram of this structure.

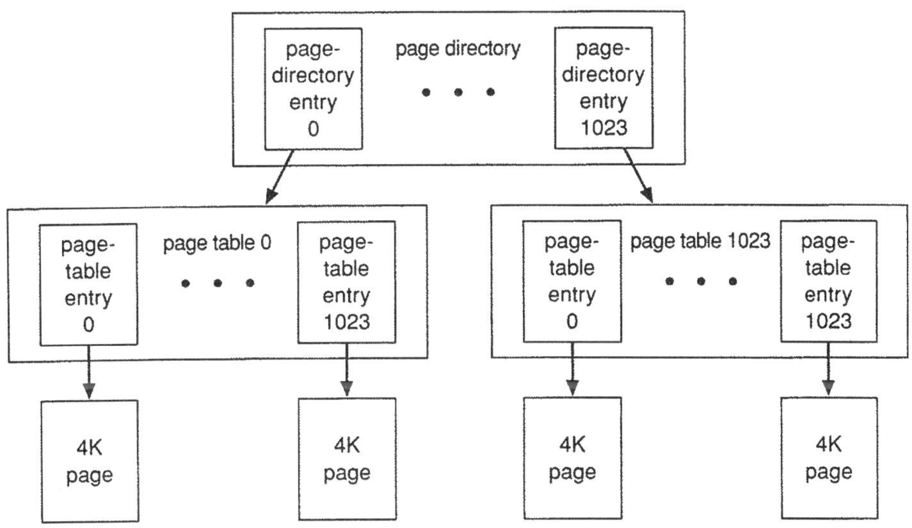

FIGURE 5-3 *Virtual-Memory Layout*

A 10-bit integer can represent all the values from 0 to 1023. Thus, a 10-bit integer can select any entry in the page directory, or in a page table. This property is used when a virtual-address pointer is translated to a byte address in physical memory. A 32-bit virtual-memory address is split into three integers, as shown in Figure 5-4. The first 10 bits of the virtual address are used as a subscript in the page directory. This address selects one page-directory entry, which points to a page table. The next 10 bits of the virtual address are used to select a PTE from that page table. The PTE points to a page frame in physical memory. The remaining 12

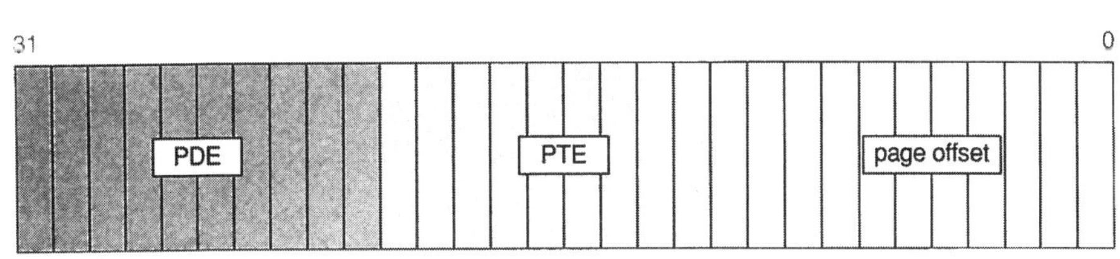

FIGURE 5-4 *Virtual-to-Physical Address Translation*

bits of the virtual address point to a specific byte in that page frame. A pointer to that specific byte in physical memory is made by concatenating 20 bits from the PTE with the lower 12 bits from the virtual address. Thus, the 32-bit PTE has 12 bits left over; these bits are used to describe the page. The first 5 bits specify the page protection, such as **PAGE_READONLY** or **PAGE_READWRITE**. The next 4 bits specify which paging file backs the page of memory. The final 3 bits specify the state of the page in memory.

A page can be in one of six states: valid, zeroed, free, standby, modified, and bad. A *valid* page is in use by an active process. A *free* page is a page that is not referenced in a PTE. A *zeroed* page is a free page that has been zeroed out and is ready for immediate use. A *standby* page has been removed from the working set of a process. A *modified* page has been written to, but not yet flushed to disk. The final page type is the *bad* page; it is unusable because a hardware error has been detected.

The actual structure of the PTE is shown in Figure 5-5. The PTE contains 5 bits for page protection, 20 bits for page frame address, 4 bits to select a paging file, and 3 bits that describe the page state. If the page is not in memory, the 20 bits of page frame address hold an offset into the paging file, instead. Since executable code and memory-mapped files already have a copy on disk, they do not need space in a paging file. If one of these pages is not in physical memory, the PTE structure is as follows. The most significant bit is used to specify the page protection, the next 28 bits are used to index into a system data structure that indicates a file and offset within the file for the page, and the lower 3 bits specify the page state.

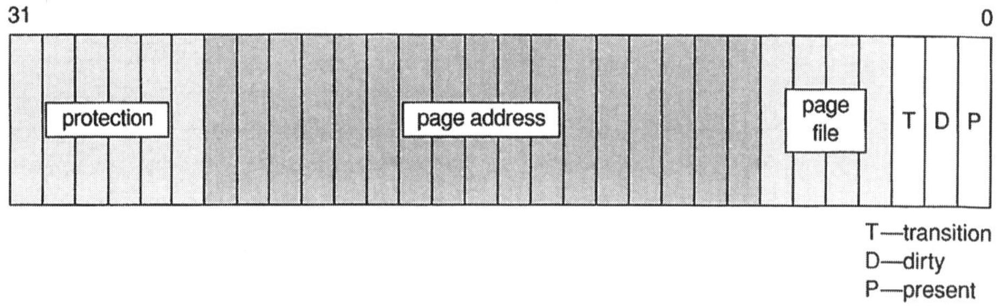

FIGURE 5-5 *Standard Page-Table Entry*

It is difficult to share a page between processes if every process has its own set of page tables, because each process will have its own PTE for the page frame. When a shared page is faulted in to physical memory, the physical address will have to be stored in the PTEs belonging to each process sharing the page. The protection bits and page state bits in these PTEs will all need to be set and updated consistently. To avoid these problems, NT uses an indirection. For every page that is shared, the process has a PTE that points to a *prototype page-table entry*, rather than to the page frame. The prototype PTE contains the page-frame address and the protection and state bits. Thus, the VM manager has to update only the one prototype PTE for the page, rather than one in each process sharing the page.

The VM manager keeps track of all pages of physical memory in a *page-frame database*. There is one entry for every page frame. The entry points to the PTE that points to the page frame, so the VM manager can maintain the state of the page. Page frames are linked to form (for instance) the list of zeroed pages, and the list of free pages.

When a page fault occurs, the VM manager faults in the missing page, placing that page into the first frame on the free list. But it does not stop there. Research shows that the memory referencing of a thread tends to have a property termed *locality*: When a page is used, it is likely that adjacent pages will be referenced in the near future. (Think of iterating over an array, or fetching sequential instructions that form the executable code for a thread.) Because of locality, when the VM manager faults in a page, it also faults in a few adjacent pages. This adjacent faulting tends to reduce the total number of page faults.

If no page frames are available on the free list, NT uses a per-process FIFO replacement policy to take pages from processes that are using more than their minimum working-set size. NT monitors the page faulting of each process that is at its minimum working-set size, and adjusts the working-set size accordingly. In particular, when a process is started under NT, it is assigned a default working set size of 30 pages. NT periodically tests this size by stealing a valid page from the process. If the process continues executing without generating a page fault for the stolen page, the working-set of the process is reduced by 1, and the page is added to the list of free pages.

PROCESS MANAGER The NT process manager provides services for creating, deleting, and using threads and processes. It has no knowledge about parent-child relationships or process hierarchies—those refinements are left to the particular environmental subsystem that owns the process.

An example of process creation in the Win32 environment is as follows. When a Win32 application calls **CreateProcess**, a message is sent to the Win32 subsystem, which calls the process manager to create a process. The process manager calls the object manager to create a process object, and then returns the object handle to Win32. Win32 calls the process manager again to create a thread for the process, and finally Win32 returns handles to the new process and thread.

LOCAL-PROCEDURE-CALL FACILITY The local-procedure-call (LPC) facility is used to pass requests and results between client and server processes within a single machine. In particular, it is used to request services from the various NT subsystems. It is similar in many respects to the remote-procedure-call (RPC) mechanisms that are used by many operating systems for distributed processing across networks, but LPC is optimized for use within one NT system.

LPC is a message-passing mechanism. The server process publishes a globally visible connection-port object. When a client wants services from a subsystem, it opens a handle to the subsystem's connection-port object, and then sends a connection request to that port. The server creates a channel and returns a handle to the client. The channel consists of a pair of private communication ports: one for client-to-server messages, and the other for server-to-client messages. Communication channels support a callback mechanism, so the client and server can accept requests when they would normally be expecting a reply.

When an LPC channel is created, one of three types of message-passing techniques must be specified. The first type is suitable for small (up to 256-byte) messages. In this case, the port's message queue is used as intermediate storage, and the messages are copied from one process to the other. The second type is for larger messages. In this case, a shared-memory section object is created for the channel. Messages sent through the port's message queue contain a pointer and size information that refer to the section object. Thus the need to copy large messages is avoided: The sender places data into the shared section, and the receiver can view them directly.

The third method of LPC message passing, called *quick LPC*, is used by graphical display portions of the Win32 subsystem. When a client asks for a connection that will use quick LPC, the server sets up three objects: a dedicated server thread to handle requests, a 64-KB section object, and an event-pair object. An *event-pair object* is a synchronization object that is used by the Win32 subsystem to provide notification when the client thread has copied a message to the Win32 server, or vice versa. LPC messages are passed in the section object, and synchronization is performed by the event-pair object. The section object eliminates message copying, since it represents a region of shared memory. Using the event-pair object for synchronization eliminates the overhead of using the port object to pass messages containing pointers and lengths. The dedicated server thread eliminates the overhead of determining which client thread is calling the server, since there is one server thread per client thread. Also, the kernel gives scheduling preference to these dedicated server threads to improve performance further. The drawback is that quick LPC uses more resources than do the other two methods, so the Win32 subsystem uses quick LPC for only the window-manager and graphics-device interfaces.

I/O MANAGER The I/O manager is responsible for file systems, cache management, device drivers, and network drivers. It keeps track of which installable file systems are loaded, and manages buffers for I/O requests. It works with the VM manager to provide memory-mapped file I/O, and controls the NT cache manager, which handles caching for the entire I/O system. The I/O manager supports both synchronous and asynchronous operations, provides timeouts for drivers, and has mechanisms for one driver to call another.

The I/O manager converts the requests that it receives into a standard form called an *I/O request packet (IRP)*. It then forwards the IRP to the correct driver for processing. When the operation is finished, the I/O manager receives the IRP from the driver that most recently performed an operation, and completes the request.

In many operating systems, caching is done by the file system. NT provides a centralized caching facility, instead. The cache manager provides cache services for all components under the control of the I/O manager, and works closely with the VM manager. The size of the cache changes dynamically, according to how much free memory is available in the system. Recall that the upper 2 GB of a process's address space is the system area; it is identical for all processes. The VM manager allocates up to one-half of this space to the system cache. The cache manager maps files into this address space, and uses the capabilities of the VM manager to handle file I/O.

The cache is divided into blocks of 256 KB. Each cache block can hold a view (i.e., a memory-mapped region) of a file. Each cache block is described by a *virtual-address control block (VACB)* that stores the virtual address and file offset for that view, and also the number of processes that are using the view. The VACBs reside in a single array that is maintained by the cache manager.

For each open file, the cache manager maintains a separate VACB index array. This array has an element for each 256-KB chunk of the file; so, for instance, a 2-MB file would have an 8-entry VACB index array. An entry in the VACB index array points to the VACB if that portion of the file is in the cache; it is null otherwise.

When a user-level read request is received by the I/O manager, it sends an IRP to the cache manager (unless the request specifically asks for a noncached read). The cache manager calculates which entry of that file's VACB index array corresponds to the byte offset of the request. The entry either points to the view in the cache, or is null. If it is null, the cache manager allocates a cache block (and the corresponding entry in the VACB array), and maps the view into that cache block. The cache manager then attempts to copy data from the mapped file to the caller's buffer. If the copy succeeds, the operation is completed. If the copy fails, it does so because of a page fault, which causes the VM manager to send a noncached read request to the I/O manager. The I/O manager asks the appropriate device driver to read the data, and returns the data to the VM manager, which loads the data into the cache. The data, now in the cache, are copied to the caller's buffer, and the I/O request completes. Figure 5-6 shows how this operation proceeds.

A kernel-level read operation is similar, except that the data can be accessed directly from the cache, rather than being copied to a buffer in user space. To use file-system *metadata*, or data structures that describe the file system, the kernel uses the cache manager's mapping interface to read the metadata. To modify the metadata, the file system uses the cache manager's pinning interface. *Pinning* a page locks the page into a physical-memory page frame, so the VM manager cannot move or swap out the page. After updating the metadata, the file system asks the cache manager to unpin the page. Since the page has been modified, it is marked dirty, so the VM manager will flush the page to disk.

To improve performance, the cache manager keeps a small history of read requests, and attempts to predict future requests. If the cache manager can find a pattern in the previous three requests, such as sequential access forward or backward, it can prefetch data into the cache before the next request is submitted by the application. Then, the application may find

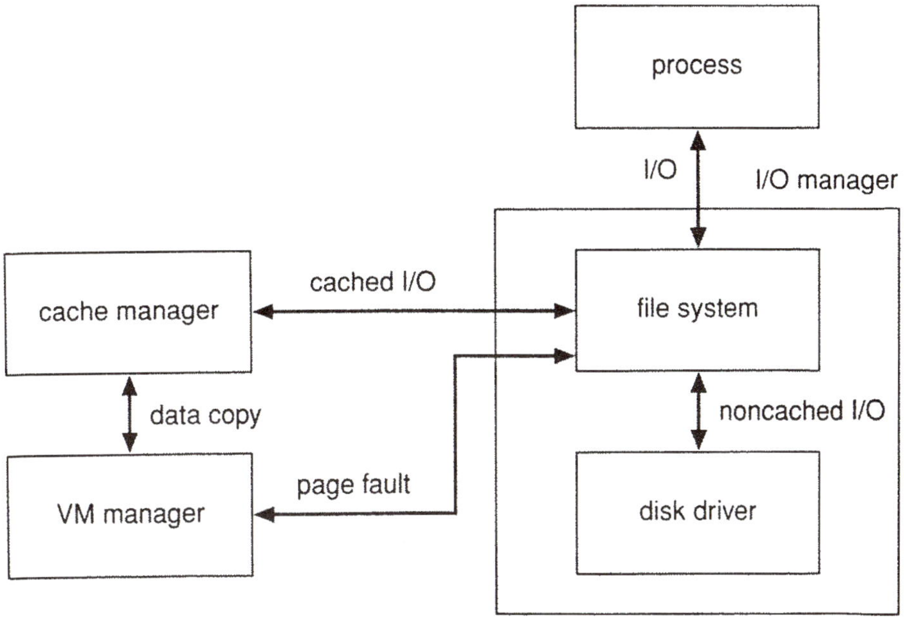

FIGURE 5-6 *File I/O*

its data already in the cache, and may not need to wait for disk I/O. The Win32 API **OpenFile** and **CreateFile** functions can be passed by the **FILE_FLAG_SEQUENTIAL_SCAN** flag, which is a hint to the cache manager to try to prefetch 192 KB ahead of the thread's requests. Typically, NT performs I/O operations in chunks of 64 KB or 16 pages, thus this readahead is three times the normal amount.

The cache manager is also responsible for telling the VM manager to flush the contents of the cache. The cache manager's default behavior is write-back caching. The cache manager accumulates writes for 4 to 5 seconds, and then the writer thread wakes up. When write-through caching is needed, a process can set a flag when opening the file, or the process can call an explicit cache-flush function when needed.

A fast-writing process could potentially fill all the free cache pages before the cache-writer thread has a chance to wake up and to flush the pages to disk. To prevent a process from flooding the system in this way, when the amount of free cache memory gets low, the cache manager temporarily blocks processes that attempt to write data, and wakes the cache-writer thread to flush pages to disk. If the fast-writing process is actually a network redirector for a network file system, blocking it for too long could cause network transfers to time out and be retransmitted. This retransmission would waste network bandwidth. To prevent this waste, network redirectors can tell the cache manager not to let a large backlog of writes accumulate in the cache.

Because a network file system needs to move data between a disk and the network interface, the cache manager also provides a DMA interface to move the data directly. Moving data directly avoids copying data through an intermediate buffer.

SECURITY REFERENCE MANAGER The object-oriented nature of NT enables the use of a uniform mechanism to perform run-time access validation and audit checks for every entity in the system. Whenever a process opens a handle to an object, the security reference monitor checks the process's security token and the object's access-control list to see whether the process has the necessary rights.

ENVIRONMENTAL SUBSYSTEMS

Environmental subsystems are user-mode processes layered over the native NT executive services to enable NT to run programs developed for other operating systems, including 16-bit Windows, MS-DOS , POSIX, and character-based applications for 16-bit OS/2. Each environmental subsystem provides one API or application environment.

NT uses the Win32 subsystem as the main operating environment, and Win32 is used to start all processes. When an application is executed, the Win32 subsystem calls the VM manager to load the application's executable code. The memory manager returns a status to Win32 that tells what kind of executable it is. If it is not a native Win32 executable, the Win32 environment checks whether the appropriate environmental subsystem is running; if the subsystem is not running, it is started as a user-mode process. Then, Win32 creates a process to run the application, and passes control to the environmental subsystem.

The environmental subsystem uses the NT local-procedure call facility to get kernel services for the process. This utilization helps NT to be robust, because the parameters passed to a system call can be checked for correctness before the actual kernel routine is invoked. NT prohibits applications from mixing API routines from different environments. For instance, a Win32 application cannot call a POSIX routine.

Since each subsystem is run as a separate user-mode process, a crash in one has no effect on the others. The exception is Win32, which provides all the keyboard, mouse, and graphical display capabilities. If it fails, the system is effectively disabled.

Win32 categorizes applications as either graphical or character based, where a character-based application is one that thinks that interactive output goes to an 80 by 24 ASCII display. Win32 transforms the output of a character-based application to a graphical representation in a window. This transformation is easy: Whenever an output routine is called, the environmental subsystem calls a Win32 routine to display the text. Since the Win32 environment performs this function for all character-based windows, it can transfer screen text between windows via the clipboard. This transformation works for MS-DOS applications, as well as for POSIX command-line applications.

MS-DOS ENVIRONMENT

MS-DOS does not have the complexity of the other NT environmental subsystems. It is provided by a Win32 application called the *virtual dos machine (VDM)*. Since the VDM is just a user-mode process, it is paged and dispatched like any other NT thread. The VDM has an *instruction-execution unit* to execute or emulate Intel 486 instructions. It also provides routines to emulate the MS-DOS ROM BIOS and "int 21" software-interrupt services, and has virtual device drivers for the screen, keyboard, and communication ports. The VDM is based on the MS-DOS 5.0 source code and gives the application at least 620 KB of memory.

The NT command shell is a program that creates a window that looks like an MS-DOS environment. It can run both 16-bit and 32-bit executables. When an MS-DOS application is run, the command shell starts a VDM process to execute the program.

If NT is running on an X86 processor, MS-DOS graphical applications run in full-screen mode, and character applications can run full screen or in a window. If NT is running on a different processor architecture, all MS-DOS applications run in windows. Some MS-DOS applications access the disk hardware directly, but they fail to run on NT because disk access is privileged to protect the file system. In general, MS-DOS applications that directly access hardware will fail to operate under NT.

Since MS-DOS is not a multitasking environment, some applications have been written that hog the CPU—for instance, by using busy loops to cause time delays or pauses in execution. The priority mechanism in the NT dispatcher detects such delays and automatically throttles the CPU consumption (and causes the offending application to operate incorrectly).

16-Bit Windows Environment

The Win16 execution environment is provided by a VDM that incorporates additional software called *Windows on Windows* that provides the Windows 3.1 kernel routines and stub routines for window manager and GDI functions. The stub routines call the appropriate Win32 subroutines, converting or *thunking* 16-bit addresses into 32-bit ones. Applications that rely on the internal structure of the 16-bit window manager or GDI may not work, because Windows on Windows does not really implement the 16-bit API.

Windows on Windows can multitask with other processes on NT, but it resembles Windows 3.1 in many ways. Only one Win16 application can run at a time, all applications are single threaded and reside in the same address space, and they all share the same input queue. These features imply that an application that stops receiving input will block all the other Win16 applications, just like in Windows 3.x, and one Win16 application can crash other Win16 applications by corrupting the address space.

Win32 Environment

The main subsystem in NT is the Win32 subsystem. It runs Win32 applications, and manages all keyboard, mouse, and screen I/O. Since it is the controlling environment, it is designed to be extremely robust. Several features of Win32 contribute to this robustness. Unlike the Win16 environment, each Win32 process has its own input queue. The window manager dispatches all input on the system to the appropriate process's input queue, so a failed process will not block input to other processes. The NT kernel also provides preemptive multitasking, which enables the user to terminate applications that have failed or are no longer needed. Win32 also validates all objects before using them, to prevent crashes that could otherwise occur if an application tried to use an invalid or wrong handle. The Win32 subsystem verifies the type of the object to which a handle points before using that object. The reference counts kept by the object manager prevent objects from being deleted while they are still being used, and prevents their use after they have been deleted.

POSIX Subsystem

The POSIX subsystem is designed to run POSIX applications following the POSIX.1 standard, which is based on the UNIX model. POSIX applications can be started by the Win32 subsystem or by another POSIX application. POSIX applications use the POSIX subsystem server **PSXSS.EXE**, the POSIX dynamic link library **PSXDLL.DLL**, and the POSIX console session manager **POSIX.EXE**.

Although the POSIX standard does not specify printing, POSIX applications can use printers transparently via the NT redirection mechanism. POSIX applications have access to any file system on the NT system; the POSIX environment enforces UNIX-like permissions on directory trees. Several Win32 facilities are not supported by the POSIX subsystem, including memory-mapped files, networking, graphics, and dynamic data exchange.

OS/2 Subsystem

While NT was originally intended to provide a robust OS/2 operating environment, the success of Microsoft Windows led to a change, during the early development of NT, for the Windows environment to become the default. Consequently NT provides only limited facilities in the OS/2 environmental subsystem. OS/2 1.x character-based applications can run on only NT on Intel X86 computers. Real-mode OS/2 applications can run on all platforms by using the MS-DOS environment. Bound applications, which are applications that have dual code for both MS-DOS and OS/2, run in the OS/2 environment unless the OS/2 environment is disabled.

Logon and Security Subsystems

Before a user can access objects on NT, the user must be authenticated by the log-on subsystem. To be authenticated, a user must have an account and provide the password for that account.

The security subsystem generates access tokens to represent users on the system. It calls an *authentication package* to perform authentication using information from the log-on subsystem or network server. Typically, the authentication package simply looks up the account information in a local database and checks to see that the password is correct. The security subsystem then generates the access token for the user ID containing the appropriate privileges, quota limits and group ids. Whenever the user attempts to access an object in the system, such as by opening a handle to the object, the access token is passed to the security reference monitor, which checks privileges and quotas.

FILE SYSTEM

Historically, MS-DOS systems have used the *file-allocation table (FAT)* file system. The 16-bit FAT file system has several shortcomings, including internal fragmentation, a size limitation of 2 GB, and a lack of access protection for files. The 32-bit FAT file system has solved the size and fragmentation problems, but the performance and features are still weak by comparison with modern file systems. The NTFS is much better. It was designed with many features in mind, including data recovery, security, fault tolerance, large files and file systems, multiple data streams, UNICODE names, and file compression. For compatibility, NT provides support for the FAT and OS/2 HPFS file systems.

Internal Layout

The fundamental entity in NTFS is a *volume*. A volume is created by the NT disk administrator utility, and is based on a logical disk partition. The volume may occupy a portion of a disk, may occupy an entire disk, or may span across several disks. In NTFS, all *metadata*—such as information about the volume—are stored in a regular file.

NTFS does not deal with individual sectors of a disk, but instead uses *clusters* as the unit of disk allocation. A cluster is a number of disk sectors that is a power of 2. The cluster size is configured when an NTFS file system is formatted. The default cluster size is the sector size for volumes up to 512 MB, 1 KB for volumes up to 1 GB, 2 KB for volumes up to 2 GB, and 4 KB for larger volumes. This cluster size is much smaller than that for the 16-bit FAT file system, and the small size reduces the amount of internal fragmentation. As an example, consider a 1.6 GB disk with 16,000 files. If you use a FAT-16 file system, 400 MB may be lost to internal fragmentation because the cluster size is 32 KB. Under NTFS, only 17 MB would be lost when storing the same files.

NTFS uses *logical cluster numbers (LCNs)* as disk addresses. It assigns them by numbering clusters from the beginning of the disk to the end. Using this scheme, the system can calculate a physical disk offset (in bytes) by multiplying the LCN by the cluster size.

A file in NTFS is not a simple byte stream, as it is in MS-DOS or UNIX; rather, it is a structured object consisting of *attributes*. Each attribute of a file is an independent byte stream that can be created, deleted, read, and written. Some attributes are standard for all files, including the file name (or names, if the file has aliases), the creation time, and the security descriptor that specifies access control. Other attributes are specific to certain kinds of files. For instance, Macintosh files have two data attributes: the resource fork and the data fork. A directory has attributes that implement an index for the file names in the directory. Most traditional data files have an *unnamed* data attribute that contains all that file's data. It is clear from this discussion that some attributes are small, and others are large.

Every file in NTFS is described by one or more records in an array stored in a special file called the *master file table (MFT)*. The size of a record is determined when the file system is created; it ranges from 1 to 4 KB. Small attributes are stored in the MFT record itself, and are called *resident* attributes. Large attributes, such as the unnamed bulk data, called *nonresident* attributes, are stored in one or more contiguous *extents* on the disk, and a pointer to each extent is stored in the MFT record. For a tiny file, even the data attribute may fit inside the MFT record. If a file has many attributes, or if it is highly fragmented and therefore many pointers are needed to point to all the fragments, one record in the MFT might not be large enough. In this case, the file is described by a record called the *base file record*, which contains pointers to overflow records that hold the additional pointers and attributes.

Each file in an NTFS volume has a unique ID called a *file reference*. The file reference is a 64-bit quantity that consists of a 48-bit file number and a 16-bit sequence number. The file number is the record number (i.e., the array slot) in the MFT that describes the file. The sequence number is incremented every time that an MFT entry is reused. This incrementation enables NTFS to perform internal consistency checks, such as catching a stale reference to a deleted file after the MFT entry has been reused for a new file.

As in MS-DOS and UNIX, the NTFS name space is organized as a hierarchy of directories. Each directory uses a data structure called a *B+ tree* to store an index of the file names in that directory. A B+ tree is used because it eliminates the cost of reorganizing the tree and has the property that the length of every path from the root of the tree to a leaf is the same. The *index root* of a directory contains the top level of the B+ tree. For a large directory, this top level contains pointers to disk extents that hold the remainder of the tree. Each entry in the directory contains the name and file reference of the file, and also a copy of the update timestamp and file size taken from the file's resident attributes in the MFT. Copies of this information are stored in the directory, so it is efficient to generate a directory listing—all the file names, sizes, and update times are available from the directory itself, so there is no need to gather these attributes from the MFT entries for each of the files.

The NTFS volume's metadata are all stored in files. The first file is the MFT. The second file, which is used during recovery if the MFT is damaged, contains a copy of the first 16 entries of the MFT. The next few files are also special. They are called the log file, volume file, attribute-definition table, root directory, bitmap file, boot file, and bad-cluster file. The *log file* records all metadata updates to the file system. The *volume file* contains the name of the volume, the version of NTFS that formatted the volume, and a bit that tells whether the volume may have been corrupted and needs to be checked for consistency. The *attribute-definition table* indicates which attribute types are used in the volume, and what operations can be performed on each of them. The *root directory* is the top level directory in the file-system hierarchy. The *bitmap file* indicates which clusters on a volume are allocated to files, and which are free. The *boot file* contains the startup code for NT and must be located at a particular disk address so that it can be found easily by a simple ROM bootstrap loader. The boot file also contains the physical address of the MFT. Finally, the *bad-cluster file* keeps track of any bad areas on the volume which NTFS uses for error recovery.

Recovery

In many simple file systems, a power failure at the wrong time can damage the file-system data structures so severely that the entire volume is scrambled. Many versions of UNIX store redundant metadata on the disk, and recover from crashes using the **fsck** program to check all the file-system data structures, and to restore them forcibly to a consistent state. Restoring them often involves deleting damaged files and freeing data clusters that had been written with user data but have not been properly recorded in the file system's metadata structures. This checking can be a slow process, and can lose significant amounts of data.

NTFS takes a different approach to file-system robustness. In NTFS, all file-system data-structure updates are performed inside *transactions*. Before a data structure is altered, the transaction writes a log record that contains redo and undo information; after the data structure has been changed, a commit record is written to the log to signify that the transaction succeeded. After a crash, the system can restore the file-system data structures to a consistent state by processing the log records, first redoing the operations for committed transactions, then undoing the operations for transactions that did not commit successfully before the crash. Periodically (usually every 5 seconds), a checkpoint record is written to the log. The system does not need log records prior to the checkpoint to recover from a crash, so they can be discarded. The first time that an NTFS volume is accessed after system startup, NTFS automatically performs file-system recovery.

This scheme does not guarantee that all the user-file contents are correct after a crash; it ensures only that the file-system data structures (the metadata files) are undamaged and reflect some consistent state prior to the crash. It would be possible to extend the transaction scheme to cover user files, but the overhead would impair the file-system performance.

The log is stored in the third metadata file at the beginning of the volume. It is created with a fixed maximum size when the file system is formatted. It has two sections: the *logging area*, which is a circular queue of log records, and the *restart area*, which holds context information, such as the position in the logging area where NTFS should start reading during a recovery. In fact, the restart area holds two copies of its information, so recovery is still possible if one copy is damaged during the crash.

The logging functionality is provided by the NT *log-file service*. In addition to writing the log records and performing recovery actions, the log-file service keeps track of the free space in the log file. If the free space gets too low, the log-file service queues pending transactions, and NTFS halts all new I/O operations. After the in-progress operations complete, NTFS calls the cache manager to flush all data, then resets the log file and performs the queued transactions.

Security

Security of an NTFS volume is derived from the NT object model. Each file object has a security-descriptor attribute stored in its MFT record. This attribute contains the access token of the owner of the file, and an access-control list that states the access privileges that are granted to each user that has access to the file.

Volume Management and Fault Tolerance

FtDisk is the fault-tolerant disk driver for NT. When installed, it provides several ways to combine multiple disk drives into one logical volume, to improve performance, capacity, or reliability.

One way to combine multiple disks is to concatenate them logically to form a large logical volume, as shown in Figure 5-7. In NT, this logical volume is called a *volume set*, which can consist of up to 32 physical partitions. A volume set that contains an NTFS volume can be extended without the data already stored in the file system being disturbed. The bitmap metadata on the NTFS volume are simply extended to cover the newly added space. NTFS continues to use the same LCN mechanism that it uses for a single physical disk, and the **FtDisk** driver supplies the mapping from a logical volume offset to the offset on one particular disk.

Another way to combine multiple physical partitions is to interleave their blocks in round-robin fashion to form what is called a *stripe set*, as shown in Figure 5-8. This scheme is also called *RAID level 0*, or *disk striping*. **FtDisk** uses a stripe size of 64 KB: The first 64 KB of the logical volume are stored in the first physical partition, the second 64 KB of the logical volume are stored in the second physical partition, and so on, until each partition has contributed 64 KB of space. Then, the allocation wraps around to the first disk, allocating the second 64 KB block. A stripe set forms one large logical volume, but the physical layout can improve the I/O bandwidth, because, for a large I/O, all the disks can transfer data in parallel.

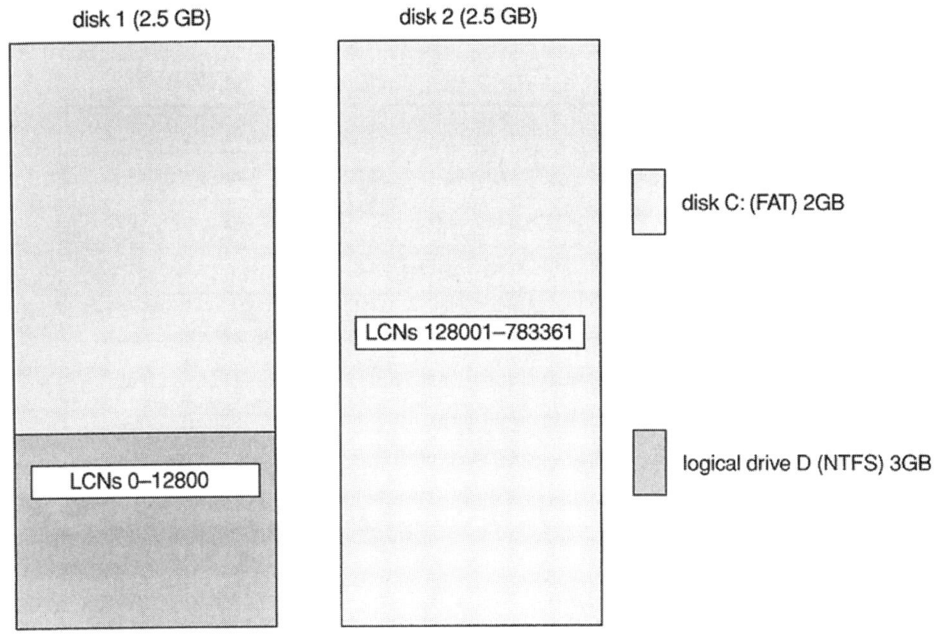

FIGURE 5-7 *Volume Set in Two Drives*

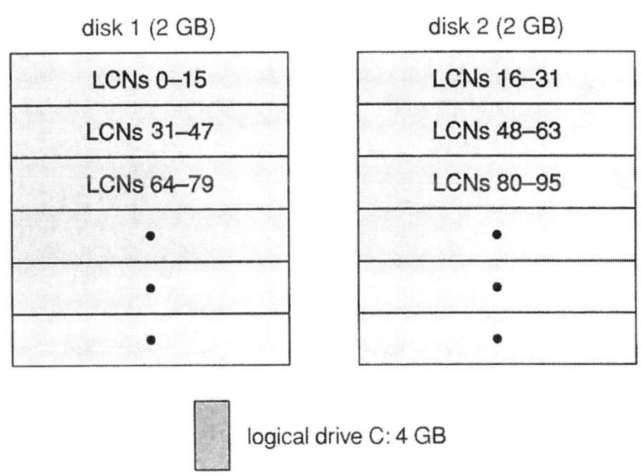

FIGURE 5-8 *Stripe Set on Two Drives*

A variation of this idea is the *stripe set with parity*, which is shown in Figure 5-9. This scheme is also called RAID level 5. If the stripe set has eight disks, then for each seven data stripes, on seven separate disks, there will be a parity stripe on the eighth disk. The parity stripe contains the byte-wise **exclusive or** of the data stripes. If any one of the eight stripes is destroyed, the system can reconstruct the data by calculating the **exclusive or** of the remaining seven. This ability to reconstruct data makes the disk array much less likely to lose data in case of a disk failure. Notice that an update to one data stripe also requires recalculation of the parity stripe. Seven concurrent writes to seven different data stripes thus would also require seven parity stripes to be updated. If the parity stripes were all on the same disk, that disk could have seven times the I/O load of the data disks. To avoid creating this bottleneck, we spread the parity stripes over all the disks, such as by assigning them round-robin. To build a stripe set with parity, we need a minimum of three equal-sized partitions located on three separate disks.

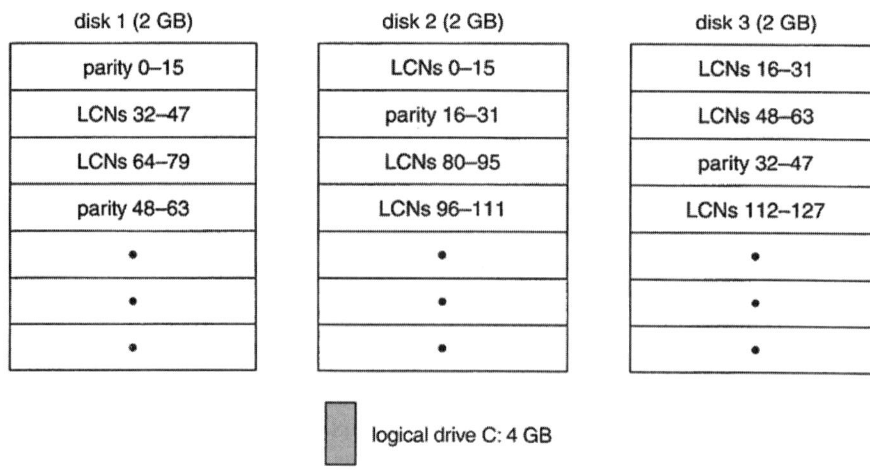

FIGURE 5-9 *Stripe Set with Parity on Three Drives*

An even more robust scheme is called *disk mirroring* or *RAID level 1*; it is depicted in Figure 5-10. A *mirror set* comprises two equal-sized partitions on two disks, such that their data contents are identical. When an application writes data to a mirror set, **FtDisk** writes the data to both partitions. If one partition fails, **FtDisk** has another copy safely stored on the mirror. Mirror sets can also improve the performance, because read requests can be split between the two mirrors, giving each mirror half of the workload. To protect against the failure of a disk controller, we can attach the two disks of a mirror set to two separate disk controllers. This arrangement is called a *duplex set*.

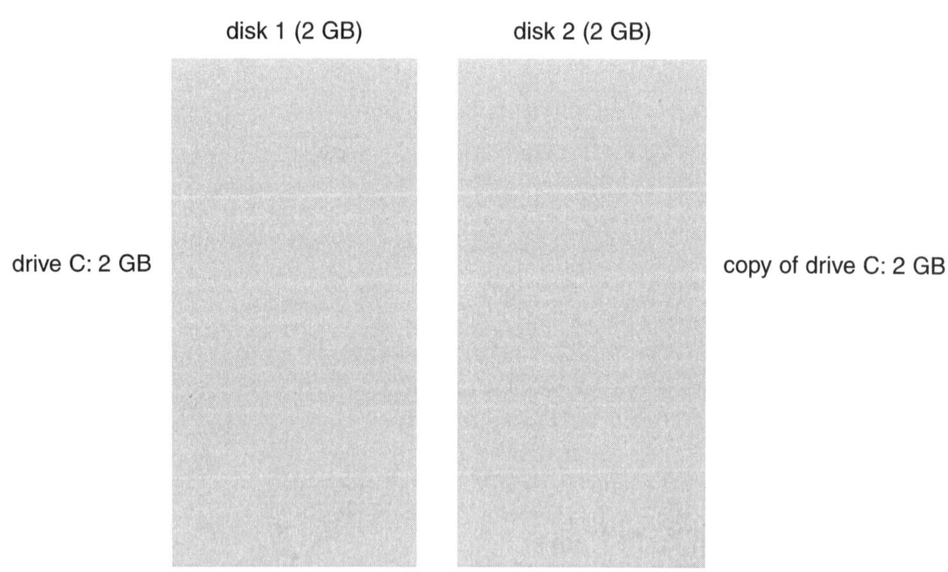

FIGURE 5-10 *Mirror Set on Two Drives*

To deal with disk sectors that go bad, **FtDisk** uses a hardware technique called *sector sparing*, and NTFS uses a software technique called *cluster remapping*. Sector sparing is a hardware capability provided by many disk drives. When a disk drive is formatted, it creates a map from logical block numbers to good sectors on the disk. It also leaves extra sectors unmapped, as spares. If a sector fails, **FtDisk** will instruct the disk drive to substitute a spare.

Cluster remapping is a software technique performed by the file system. If a disk block goes bad, NTFS will substitute a different, unallocated block by changing any affected pointers in the MFT. NTFS also makes a note that the bad block should never be allocated to any file.

When a disk block goes bad, the usual outcome is a data loss. But sector sparing or cluster remapping can be combined with fault-tolerant volumes such as stripe sets to mask the failure of a disk block. If a read fails, the system reconstructs the missing data by reading the mirror or by calculating the **exclusive or** parity in a stripe set with parity. The reconstructed data are stored into a new location that is obtained by sector sparing or cluster remapping.

COMPRESSION

NTFS can perform data compression on individual files or on all data files in a directory. To compress a file, NTFS divides the file's data into *compression units*, which are blocks of 16 contiguous clusters. When each compression unit is written, a data-compression algorithm is applied. If the result fits into fewer than 16 clusters, the compressed version is stored. When reading, NTFS can determine whether data have been compressed, because in this case the length of the stored compression unit is less than 16 clusters. To improve performance when reading contiguous compression units, NTFS prefetches and decompresses ahead of the application requests.

For *sparse* files or files that mostly contain zeros, NTFS uses another technique to save space. Clusters that contain all zeros are not actually allocated or stored on disk. Instead, gaps are left in the sequence of virtual-cluster numbers stored in the MFT entry for the file. When reading a file, if it finds a gap in the virtual-cluster numbers, NTFS just zero-fills that portion of the caller's buffer. This technique is also used by UNIX.

NETWORKING

NT supports both peer-to-peer and client-server networking. It also has facilities for network management. The networking components in NT provide data transport, interprocess communication, file sharing across a network, and the ability to send print jobs to remote printers.

NT supports many protocols that are used in computer networking. We discuss the distributed-processing mechanisms of NT. A *redirector* in NT is an object that provides a uniform interface for files, whether they are local or remote. A *domain* is a group of NT server machines that share a common security policy and user database. Finally, NT has mechanisms for *name resolution* that enable one computer to look up the address of another computer, given that computer's name.

To describe networking in NT, we will refer to two of the internal networking interfaces, called the *Network Device Interface Specification (NDIS)* and the *Transport Driver Interface (TDI)*. The NDIS interface was developed in 1989 by Microsoft and 3Com to separate network adapters from the transport protocols so that either could be changed without affecting the other. NDIS resides at the interface between the data link control and media access control layers in the OSI model and enables many protocols to operate over many different network adapters. In terms of the OSI model, the TDI is the interface between the transport layer (layer 4) and the session layer (layer 5). This interface enables any session-layer component to use any available transport mechanism. (Similar reasoning led to the *streams* mechanism in UNIX.) The TDI supports both connection-based and connectionless transport, and has functions to send any type of data.

PROTOCOLS

NT implements transport protocols as drivers. These drivers can be loaded and unloaded from the system dynamically, although in practice the system typically has to be rebooted after a change. NT comes with several networking protocols.

The *server message-block (SMB)* protocol was first introduced in MS-DOS 3.1. The protocol is used to send I/O requests over the network. The SMB protocol has four message types. The **Session control** messages are commands that start and end a redirector connection to a shared resource at the server. The **File** messages are used by a redirector to access files at the server. The **Printer** messages are used to send data to a remote print queue and to receive back status information, and the **Message** message is used to communicate with another workstation.

The *Network Basic Input/Output System (NetBIOS)* is a hardware-abstraction interface for networks, analogous to the BIOS hardware-abstraction interface devised for PCs running MS-DOS . NetBIOS was developed in the early 1980s, and has become a standard network-programming interface. NetBIOS is used to establish logical names on the network, to establish logical connections or *sessions* between two logical names on the network, and to support reliable data transfer for a session via either NetBIOS or SMB requests.

The *NetBIOS Extended User Interface (NetBEUI)* was introduced by IBM in 1985 as a simple, efficient networking protocol for up to 254 machines. It is the default protocol for Windows 95 peer networking and for Windows for Workgroups. NT uses NetBEUI when it wants to share resources with these networks. Among the limitations of NetBEUI are that it uses the actual name of a computer as the address, and it does not support routing.

The TCP/IP protocol suite that is used on the Internet has become the *de facto* standard networking infrastructure, and is widely supported. Windows NT uses TCP/IP to connect to a wide variety of operating systems and hardware platforms. The NT TCP/IP package includes the simple network-management protocol (SNMP), dynamic host-configuration protocol (DHCP), Windows Internet name service (WINS), and NetBIOS support.

The *point-to-point tunneling protocol (PPTP)* is a new protocol provided by Windows NT 4.0 to communicate between remote-access server modules running on NT machines that are connected over the Internet. The remote-access servers can encrypt data sent over the connection, and they support multiprotocol virtual private networks over the Internet.

The Novell NetWare protocols (IPX datagram service on the SPX transport layer) are widely used for PC local-area networks. The NT NWLink protocol connects the NetBIOS to NetWare networks. In combination with a redirector such as Microsoft's Client Service for Netware or Novell's NetWare Client for Windows NT, this protocol enables an NT client to connect to a NetWare server.

The *data-link control (DLC) protocol* is used to access IBM mainframes and HP printers that are connected directly to the network. It is not otherwise used by NT systems.

The *AppleTalk protocol* was designed as a low-cost connection by Apple so that Macintosh computers could share files. NT systems can share files and printers with Macintosh computers via AppleTalk if an NT server on the network is running the Windows NT Services for Macintosh package.

Distributed-Processing Mechanisms

Although NT is not a distributed operating system, it does support distributed applications. Mechanisms that support distributed processing on NT include NetBIOS, *named pipes* and *mailslots*, windows sockets, remote procedure calls (RPC), and network dynamic data exchange (NetDDE).

In NT, NetBIOS applications can communicate over the network using NetBEUI, NWLink, or TCP/IP.

Named pipes are a connection-oriented messaging mechanism. Named pipes were originally developed as a high-level interface to NetBIOS connections over the network. A process can also use named pipes to communicate with other processes on the same machine. Since named pipes are accessed through the file-system interface, the security mechanisms used for file objects also apply to named pipes.

The name of a named pipe has a format called the *uniform naming convention (UNC)*. An UNC name looks like a typical remote file name. The format of a UNC name is **\\server_name\share_name\x\y\z**, where the **server_name** identifies a server on the network; a **share_name** identifies any resource that is made available to network users, such as directories, files, named pipes and printers; and the **\x\y\z** part is a normal file path name.

Mailslots are a connectionless messaging mechanism. Mailslots are unreliable, in that a message sent to a mailslot may be lost before the intended recipient receives it. Mailslots are used for broadcast applications, such as for finding components on the network. Mailslots are also used by the NT Computer Browser service.

Winsock is the windows sockets API. Winsock is a session-layer interface that is largely compatible with UNIX sockets, with some windows extensions. It provides a standardized interface to many transport protocols that may have different addressing schemes, so that any Winsock application can run on any Winsock-compliant protocol stack.

A *remote procedure call (RPC)* is a client-server mechanism that enables an application on one machine to make a procedure call to code on another machine. The client calls a local procedure—a *stub routine*—that packs its arguments into a message and sends them across the network to a particular server process. The client-side stub routine then blocks. Meanwhile, the server unpacks the message, calls the procedure, packs the return results into a message, and sends them back to the client stub. The client stub unblocks, receives the message, unpacks the results of the RPC, and returns them to the caller. This packing of arguments is sometimes called *marshaling.*

The NT RPC mechanism follows the widely used distributed-computing environment standard for RPC messages, so programs written to use NT RPCs are highly portable. The RPC standard is detailed. It hides many of the architectural differences between computers, such as the sizes of binary numbers and the order of bytes and bits in computer words, by specifying standard data formats for RPC messages.

NT can send RPC messages using NetBIOS, or Winsock on TCP/IP networks, or named pipes on Lan Manager networks. The LPC facility, discussed earlier, is similar, except that the messages are passed between two processes running on the same computer.

It is tedious and error-prone to write the code to marshal and transmit arguments in the standard format, to unmarshal and execute the remote procedure, to marshal and send the return results, and to unmarshal and return them to the caller. But much of this code can be generated automatically from a simple description of the arguments and return results.

NT provides the *Microsoft Interface Definition Language* to describe the remote procedure names, arguments, and results. The compiler for this language generates header files that declare the stubs for the remote procedures, and the data types for the argument and return-value messages. It also generates source code for the stub routines used at the client side, and for an unmarshaller and dispatcher at the server side. When the application is linked, the stub routines are included. When the application executes the RPC stub, the generated code handles the rest.

Dynamic Data Exchange (DDE) is a mechanism for interprocess communication that was developed for Microsoft Windows. NT has an extension called *Network DDE* that can be used over a network. It communicates over a pair of one-way pipes.

Redirectors and Servers

In NT, an application can use the NT I/O API to access files from a remote computer as though they were local, provided that the remote computer is running an MS-NET server, such as is provided by NT or Windows for Workgroups. A *redirector* is the client-side object that forwards I/O requests to remote files, where they are satisfied by a *server*. For performance and security, the redirectors and servers run in kernel mode.

In more detail, access to a remote file occurs as follows:

- The application calls the I/O manager to request that a file be opened with a file name in the standard UNC format.
- The I/O manager builds an I/O request packet.
- The I/O manager recognizes that the access is for a remote file, and calls a driver called a multiple universal-naming-convention provider (MUP).
- The MUP sends the I/O request packet asynchronously to all registered redirectors.

- A redirector that can satisfy the request responds to the MUP. To avoid asking all the redirectors the same question in the future, the MUP uses a cache to remember which redirector can handle this file.
- The redirector sends the network request to the remote system.
- The remote-system network drivers receive the request and pass it to the server driver.
- The server driver hands the request to the proper local file-system driver.
- The proper device driver is called to access the data.
- The results are returned to the server driver, which sends the data back to the requesting redirector. The redirector then returns the data to the calling application via the I/O manager.

A similar process occurs for applications that use the Win32 network API, rather than the UNC services, but a module called a multiprovider router is used, instead of a MUP.

For portability, redirectors and servers use the TDI API for network transport. The requests themselves are expressed in a higher-level protocol, which by default is the SMB protocol. The list of redirectors is maintained in the system registry database.

Domains

Many networked environments have natural groups of users, such as students in a computer laboratory at school, or employees in one department in a business. Frequently we want all the members of the group to be able to access shared resources on the computers in the group. To manage the global access rights within such groups, NT uses the concept of a domain. (This term has no relation to the Domain Name System that maps Internet host names to IP addresses.) Specifically, an *NT domain* is a group of NT workstations and servers that share a common security policy and user database. One server in the domain acts as the primary domain controller that maintains the security databases for the domain. Other servers in the domain can act as backup domain controllers, and can also authenticate log-in requests. The workstations in the domain trust the primary domain controller to give correct information about the access rights of each user (via the user's access token). All users retain the ability to restrict access to their own workstations, no matter what any domain controller may say.

Because a business may have many departments, and a school has many classes, it is often necessary to manage multiple domains within a single organization. NT provides four domain models to do so. In the *single-domain model*, each domain is isolated from the others. In the *master-domain model*, one designated master domain is trusted by all the other domains. It maintains a global user account database, and provides authentication services to the other domains. This model provides centralized administration of multiple domains. A master domain can support up to 40,000 users. The *multiple-master-domain model* is designed for large organizations. It has more than one master domain, and all the masters trust one another. This trust enables a user who has an account in one master domain to access resources of another master domain—the master that has an account for the user can certify the user's privileges. In the *multiple-trust model*, there is no master domain. All domains manage their own users, but they also all trust one another.

So, if a user in domain A tried to access a resource in domain B, the interaction between domain B and the user would be as follows. In the single-domain model, domain B would say "I do not know anything about you. Go away." In the master-domain model, B would say "Let me ask the master whether you have permission." In the multiple-master-domain model, B would say "Let me ask my master whether any of the other masters say you have permission." In the multiple-trust model, B would say "Let me ask around to see whether any domain says you have permission."

Name Resolution in TCP/IP Networks

On an IP network, *name resolution* is the process of converting a computer name to an IP address, such as resolving **www.bell-labs.com** to **135.104.1.14**. NT provides several methods of name resolution, including Windows Internet Name Service (WINS), broadcast name resolution, domain name system (DNS), a hosts file, and an LMHOSTS file. Most of these methods are used by many operating systems, so we describe only WINS here.

Under WINS, two or more WINS servers maintain a dynamic database of name-to-IP address bindings, and client software to query the servers. At least two servers are used, so that the WINS service can survive a server failure, and so that the name resolution workload can be spread over multiple machines.

WINS uses the dynamic host-configuration protocol (DHCP). DHCP updates address configurations automatically in the WINS database, without user or administrator intervention, as follows. When a DHCP client starts up, it broadcasts a **discover** message. Each DHCP server that receives the message replies with an **offer** message that contains an IP address and configuration information for the client. The client then chooses one of the configurations and sends a **request** message to the selected DHCP server. The DHCP server responds with the IP address and configuration information it gave previously, and with a *lease* for that address. The lease gives the client the right to use that IP address for a specified period of time. When the lease time is half expired, the client will attempt to renew the lease for that address. If the lease is not renewed, the client must get a new one.

PROGRAMMER INTERFACE

The Win32 API is the fundamental interface to the capabilities of NT. This section describes five main aspects of the Win32 API: the use of kernel objects, sharing objects between processes, process management, inter-process communication, and memory management.

ACCESS TO KERNEL OBJECTS

The NT kernel provides many services that application programs can use. Application programs obtain these services by manipulating kernel objects. A process gains access to a kernel object named **XXX** by calling the **CreateXXX** function to open a *handle* to **XXX**. This handle is unique to that process. Depending on which object is being opened, if the **create** function fails, it may return 0, or it may return a special constant named **INVALID_HANDLE_VALUE**. A process can close any handle by calling the **CloseHandle** function, and the system may delete the object if the count of processes using the object drops to 0.

SHARING OBJECTS NT provides three ways to share objects between processes. The first way is for a child process to inherit a handle to the object. When the parent calls the **CreateXXX** function, the parent supplies a **SECURITIES_ATTRIBUTES** structure with the **bInheritHandle** field set to **TRUE**. This field creates an inheritable handle. Then, the child process can be created, passing a value of **TRUE** to the **CreateProcess** function's **bInheritHandle** argument. Figure 5-11 shows a code sample that creates a semaphore handle that is inherited by a child process.

```
...
SECURITY_ATTRIBUTES sa;
sa.nlength = sizeof(sa);
sa.lpSecurityDescriptor = NULL;
sa.bInheritHandle = TRUE;
Handle a_semaphore = CreateSemaphore(&sa,1,1,NULL);
char command_line[132];
ostrstream ostring(command_line,sizeof(command_line));
ostring << a_semaphore << ends;
CreateProcess("another_process.exe",command_line,NULL,NULL,TRUE, ... );
...
```

FIGURE 5-11 *Code for a Child to Share an Object by Inheriting a Handle*

Assuming that the child process knows which handles are shared, the parent and child can achieve interprocess communication through the shared objects. In the example in Figure 5-11, the child process would get the value of the handle from the first command-line argument, and could then share the semaphore with the parent process.

The second way to share objects is for one process to give the object a name when that object is created, and for the second process to open that name. This method has two drawbacks. One is that NT does not provide a way to check whether an object with the chosen name already exists. A second drawback is that the object namespace is global, without regard to the object type. For instance, two applications may create an object named "pipe" when two distinct (and possibly different) objects are desired.

The advantage of named objects is that unrelated processes can readily share them. The first process would call one of the **CreateXXX** functions and supply a name in the **lpszName** parameter. The second process can get a handle to share this object by calling **OpenXXX** (or **CreateXXX**) with the same name, as shown in the example of Figure 5-12.

```
// process A
...
Handle a_semaphore = CreateSemaphore(NULL,1,1,"MySEM1");
...
// process B
...
Handle b_semaphore = OpenSemaphore(SEMAPHORE_ALL_ACCESS,FALSE,
    "MySEM1");
...
```

FIGURE 5-12 *Code for Sharing an Object by Name Lookup*

The third way to share objects is via the **DuplicateHandle** function. This method requires some other method of interprocess communication to pass the duplicated handle. Given a handle to a process, and the value of a handle within that process, a second process can get a handle to the same object, and thus share it. An example of this method is shown in Figure 5-13.

```
...
// process A wants to give process B access to a semaphore
// process A
Handle a_semaphore = CreateSemaphore(NULL,1,1,NULL);
// send the value of the semaphore to process B
// using a message or shared memory
...
// process B
Handle process_a = OpenProcess(PROCESS_ALL_ACCESS,FALSE,
    process_id_of_A);
Handle b_semaphore; DuplicateHandle(process_a,a_semaphore,
    GetCurrentProcess(),&b_semaphore,
    0,FALSE,DUPLICATE_SAME_ACCESS);
// use b_semaphore to access the semaphore
...
```

FIGURE 5-13 *Code for Sharing an Object by Passing a Handle*

Process Management

In NT, a *process* is an executing instance of an application, and a *thread* is a unit of code that can be scheduled by the operating system. Thus, a process contains one or more threads. A process is started when some other process calls the **CreateProcess** routine. This routine loads any dynamic link libraries that are used by the process, and creates a *primary thread*. Additional threads can be created by the **CreateThread** function. Each thread is created with its own stack, which defaults to one MB unless specified otherwise in an argument to **CreateThread**. Because some C run-time functions maintain state in static variables, such as **errno**, a multi-thread application needs to guard against unsynchronized access. The wrapper function **beginthreadex** provides appropriate synchronization.

Every dynamic link library or executable file that is loaded into the address space of a process is identified by an *instance handle*. The value of the instance handle is actually the virtual address where the file is loaded. An application can get the handle to a module in its address space by passing the name of the module to **GetModuleHandle**. If NULL is passed as the name, the base address of the process is returned. The lowest 64 KB of the address space is not used, so a faulty program that tries to dereference a NULL pointer will get an access violation.

Priorities in the Win32 environment are based on the NT scheduling model, but not all priority values may be chosen. Win32 uses four priority classes: **IDLE_PRIORITY_CLASS** (priority level 4), **NORMAL_PRIORITY_CLASS** (level 8), **HIGH_PRIORITY_CLASS** (level 13) and **REALTIME_PRIORITY_CLASS** (level 24). Processes are typically members of the **NORMAL_PRIORITY_CLASS** unless the parent of the process was of the **IDLE_PRIORITY_CLASS**, or another class was specified when **CreateProcess** was called. The priority class of a process can be changed with the **SetPriorityClass** function, or by an argument being passed to the **START** command. For example, the command **START/REALTIME cbserver.exe** would run the cbserver program in the **REALTIME_PRIORITY_CLASS**. Note that only users with the *increase scheduling priority* privilege can move a process into the **REALTIME_PRIORITY_CLASS**. Administrators and Power Users have this privilege by default.

When a user is running an interactive program, the system needs to provide especially good performance for that process. For this reason, NT has a special scheduling rule for processes in the **NORMAL_PRIORITY_CLASS**. NT distinguishes between the *foreground process* that is currently selected on the screen, and the *background processes* that are not currently selected. When a process moves into the foreground, NT increases the scheduling quantum by some factor—typically by 3. (This factor can be changed via the performance option in the system section of the control panel). This increase gives the foreground process three times longer to run before a timesharing preemption occurs.

A thread starts with an initial priority determined by its class, but the priority can be altered by the **SetThreadPriority** function. This function takes an argument that specifies a priority relative to the base priority of its class:

- THREAD_PRIORITY_LOWEST: base—2
- THREAD_PRIORITY_BELOW_NORMAL: base—1
- THREAD_PRIORITY_NORMAL: base 0
- THREAD_PRIORITY_ABOVE_NORMAL: base + 1
- THREAD_PRIORITY_HIGHEST: base + 2

Two other designations are also used to adjust the priority. Recall that the kernel has two priority classes: 16-31 for the real-time class, and 0-15 for the variable-priority class. **THREAD_PRIORITY_IDLE** sets the priority to 16 for real-time threads, and to 1 for variable-priority threads. **THREAD_PRIORITY_TIME_CRITICAL** sets the priority to 31 for real-time threads, and to 15 for variable-priority threads

The kernel adjusts the priority of a thread dynamically depending on whether the thread is I/O bound or CPU bound. The Win32 API provides a method to disable this adjustment, via **SetProcessPriorityBoost** and **SetThreadPriorityBoost** functions.

A thread can be created in a *suspended* state: The thread will not execute until another thread makes it eligible via the **ResumeThread** function. The **SuspendThread** function does the opposite. These functions set a counter, so if a thread is suspended twice, it must be resumed twice before it can run.

To synchronize the concurrent access to shared objects by threads, the kernel provides synchronization objects, such as semaphores and mutexes. In addition, threads can synchronize by using the **WaitForSingleObject** or **WaitForMultipleObjects** functions. Another method of synchronization in the Win32 API is the *critical section*. A critical section is a synchronized region of code that can be executed by only one thread at a time. A thread establishes a critical section by calling **InitializeCriticalSection**. The application must call **EnterCriticalSection** before the critical section, and **LeaveCriticalSection** after exiting the critical section. These two routines guarantee that, if multiple threads attempt to enter the critical section concurrently, only one thread at a time will be permitted to proceed, and the others will wait in the **EnterCriticalSection** routine. The critical-section mechanism is slightly faster than the kernel-synchronization objects.

A *fiber* is user-mode code that gets scheduled according to a user-defined scheduling algorithm. A process may have multiple fibers in it, just as it can have multiple threads. A major difference between threads and fibers is that threads can execute concurrently, but only one fiber at a time is permitted to execute, even on multiprocessor hardware. This mechanism is included in NT to facilitate the porting of those legacy UNIX applications that were written for a fiber-execution model.

The system creates a fiber by calling either **ConvertThreadToFiber** or **CreateFiber**. The primary difference between these functions is that **CreateFiber** does not begin executing the fiber that was created. To do that the application must call **SwitchToFiber**. The application can terminate a fiber by calling **DeleteFiber**.

Interprocess Communication

One way that Win32 applications can have interprocess communication is by sharing kernel objects. Another way is by passing messages, which is particularly popular for Windows GUI applications.

One thread can send a message to another thread or to a window by calling **PostMessage, PostThreadMessage, SendMessage, SendThreadMessage**, or **SendMessageCallback**. The difference between posting a message and sending a message is that the post routines are asynchronous: They return immediately, and the calling thread does not know when the message is actually delivered. The send routines are synchronous—they block the caller until the message has been delivered and processed.

In addition to sending a message, a thread can also send data with the message. Since processes have separate address spaces, the data must be copied. The system copies them by calling **SendMessage** to send a message of type **WM_COPYDATA** with a **COPYDATASTRUCT** data structure that contains the length and address of the data to be transferred. When the message is sent, NT copies the data to a new block of memory and gives the virtual address of the new block to the receiving process.

Unlike the 16-bit windows environment, every Win32 thread has its own input queue from which the thread receives messages. (All input is received via messages.) This structure is more reliable than the shared input queue of 16-bit windows, because, with separate queues, one stuck application cannot block input to the other applications. If a Win32 application does not call **GetMessage** to handle events on its input queue, the queue will fill up, and after about 5 seconds the system will mark the application as "Not Responding."

Memory Management

The Win32 API provides several ways for an application to use memory: virtual memory, memory-mapped files, heaps, and thread-local storage.

An application calls **VirtualAlloc** to reserve or commit virtual memory, and **VirtualFree** to decommit or release the memory. These functions enable the application to specify the virtual address at which the memory is allocated. They operate on multiples of the memory pagesize, and the starting address of an allocated region must be greater than 0 x 10,000. Examples of these functions appear in Figure 5-14.

```
...
// allocate 16 MB at the top of our address space
void *buf = VirtualAlloc(0,0×1000000,MEM_RESERVE | MEM_TOP_DOWN,
    PAGE_READWRITE);
// commit the upper 8 MB of the allocated space
VirtualAlloc(buf + 0×800000,0×800000,MEM_COMMIT,PAGE_READWRITE);
// do some stuff with it
// decommit
VirtualFree(buf + 0×800000,0×800000,MEM_DECOMMIT);
// release all the allocated address space
VirtualFree(buf,0,MEM_RELEASE);
...
```

FIGURE 5-14 *Code Fragments for Allocating Vitual Memory*

A process may lock some of its committed pages into physical memory by calling **VirtualLock**. The maximum number of pages that a process can lock is 30, unless the process first calls **SetProcessWorkingSetSize** to increase the minimum working set size.

Another way for an application to use memory is by memory mapping a file into its address space. Memory mapping is also a convenient way for two processes to share memory—both processes map the same file into their virtual memory. Memory mapping is a multistage process, as you can see in the example of Figure 5-15.

```
...
// open the file and create it if it does not exist
HANDLE hfile = CreateFile("somefile",GENERIC_READ | GENERIC_WRITE,
    FILE_SHARE_READ | FILE_SHARE_WRITE,NULL,OPEN_ALWAYS,
    FILE_ATTRIBUTE_NORMAL,
    NULL);
// create the file mapping 8 MB in size
HANDLE hmap = CreateFileMapping(hfile,PAGE_READWRITE,
    SEC_COMMIT,0,0×800000,"SHM_1");
// get a view to the space mapped
void *buf = MapViewOfFile(hmap,FILE_MAP_ALL_ACCESS,0,0,0×800000);
// do some stuff with it
// unmap the file
UnmapViewOfFile(buf);
CloseHandle(hmap);
CloseHandle(hfile); ...
```

FIGURE 5-15 *Code Fragments for Memory Mapping of a File*

If a process wants to map some address space just to share a memory region with another process, no file is needed. The process can call **CreateFileMapping** with a file handle of 0xffffffff and a particular size. The resulting file-mapping object can be shared by inheritance, by name lookup, or by duplication.

A *heap* in the Win32 environment is just a region of reserved address space. When a Win32 process is initialized, it is created with a 1-MB *default heap*. Since many Win32 functions use the default heap, access to the heap is synchronized to protect the heap's space-allocation data structures from being damaged by concurrent updates by multiple threads. Win32 provides several heap-management functions so that a process can allocate and manage a private heap. These functions are **HeapCreate, HeapAlloc, HeapRealloc, HeapSize, HeapFree**, and **HeapDestroy**. The Win32 API also provides the **HeapLock** and **HeapUnlock** functions to enable a thread to gain exclusive access to a heap. Unlike **VirtualLock**, these functions perform only synchronization; they do not lock pages into physical memory.

Functions that rely on global or static data typically fail to work properly in a multithreaded environment. For instance, the C runtime function **strtok** uses a static variable to keep track of its current position while parsing a string. For two concurrent threads to execute **strtok** correctly, they need separate "current position" variables. The thread-local storage mechanism allocates global storage on a per-thread basis. The thread-local storage mechanism provides both dynamic and static methods of creating thread-local storage. The dynamic method is illustrated by the example in Figure 5-16.

```
// reserve a slot for a variable
DWORD var_index = TlsAlloc();
// set it to some value
TlsSetValue(var_index,10);
// get the value back
int var = TlsGetValue(var_index);
// release the index
TlsFree(var_index);
```

FIGURE 5-16 *Code for Dynamic Thread-Local Storage*

To use a thread-local static variable, so that every thread has its own private copy, the application would declare the variable as follows:

_declspec(thread) DWORD cur_pos = 0;

SUMMARY

Microsoft designed NT to be an extensible, portable operating system, able to take advantage of new techniques and hardware. NT supports multiple operating environments and symmetric multiprocessing. The use of kernel objects to provide basic services, and the support for client-server computing, enable NT to support a wide variety of application environments. For instance, NT can run programs compiled for MS-DOS, Win16, Windows 95, NT, and POSIX. It provides virtual memory, integrated caching, and preemptive scheduling. NT supports a security model stronger than those of previous Microsoft operating systems, and includes internationalization features. NT runs on a wide variety of computers, so users can choose and upgrade hardware to match their budgets and performance requirements, without needing to alter the applications that they run.

REFERENCES

Anderson, T., Bershad, B., Lazowska, E., and Levy, H., "Thread Management for Shared-Memory Multiprocessors." In Tucker, A., ed. *The Computer Science and Engineering Handbook.* Boca Raton, FL: CRC Press, 1997.

Anderson, T., Bershad, B., Lazowska, E., and Levy, H., "Scheduler Activations: Effective Kernel Support for the User-Level management of Parellelism." *ACM Transactions on Computer Systems,* February 1992

Anderson, T., Bershad, B., Lazowska, E., and Levy, H. "The Performance Implications of Thread Management Alternatives for Shared-Memory Multiprocessors." *IEEE Transactions on Computers,* December 1989.

Borg, A., Kessler, R., and Wall, D. "Generation and Analysis of Very Long Address Traces." *Proceedings of the 17th Annual International Symposium on Computer Architecture,* May 1990.

Carr, R. *Virtual Memory Management.* Ann Arbor, MI: UMI Research Press, 1984.

Corbato, F., Merwin-Daggett, M., and Dealey, R. "An Experimental Time-Sharing System." *Proceedings of the 1962 Spring Joint Computer Conference,* 1962.

Denning, P., Buzen, J., Dennis, J., Gaines, R., Hansen, P., Lynch, W., and Organick, E. "Operating Systems." In Arden, B., ed. *What Can Be Automated?* Cambridge, MA: MIT Press, 1980.

Feitelson, D., and Rudolph, L. "Distributed Hierarchical Control for Parallel Processing." *Computer,* May 1990.

Flynn, M. "Computer Organizations and Their Effectiveness." *IEEE Transactions on Computers,* September 1972.

Foster, I. "Automatic Generation of Self-Scheduled Programs." *IEEE Transactions on Parallel and Distributed Systems,* January 1991.

Gehringer, E., Siewiorek, D., and Segall, Z. *Parallel Processing: The Cm* Experience.* Bedford, MA: Digital Press, 1987.

Grosshans, D. *File Systems: Design and Implementation.* Englewood Cliffs, NJ: Prentice Hall, 1986.

Hennessey, J., and Patterson, D. *Computer Architecture: A Quantiative approach.* San Mateo, CA: Morgan Kaufmann, 1990.

Hoare, C. *Communicating Sequential Processes.* Englewood Cliffs, NJ: Prentice Hall, 1985.

Huck, J., and Hays, J. "Architectural Support for Translation Table Management in Large Address Space Machines." *Proceedings of the 20th Annual International Symposium on Computer Architecture,* May 1993.

Johnson, R. *MVS Concepts and Facilities.* New York: McGraw-Hill, 1989.

Katzan, H., and Tharayil, D. *Invitation to MVS: Logic and Debugging.* New York: Petrocelli, 1984.

Kessler, R., and Hill, M. "Page Placement Algorithms for Large Real-Indexed Caches." *ACM Transactions on Computer Systems,* November 1992.

Khalidi, Y., Talluri, M., Williams, D., and Nelson, M. "Virtual Memory Support for Multiple Page Sizes." *Proceedings, Fourth Workshop on Workstation Operating Systems,* October 1993.

Leban, J., and Arnold, J. *IBM I/O Architecture and Virtual Storage Concepts: System /370-Mode and 370-XA-Mode Processors.* New York: Wiley, 1984.

Letwin, G. *Inside OS/2.* Redmond, WA: Microsoft Press, 1988.

Leutenegger, S., and Vernon, M. "The Performance of Multiprogrammed Multiprocessor Scheduling Policies." *Proceedings, Conference on Measurement and Modeling of Computer Systems,* May 1990.

Lister, A., and Eager, R. *Fundamentals of Operating Systems.* New York: Springer-Verlag, 1993.

Livadas, P. *File Structures: Theory and Practice.* Englewood Cliffs, NJ: Prentice Hall, 1990.

Maekawa, M., Oldehoeft, A., and Oldehoeft, R. *Operating Systems: Advanced Concepts.* Menlo Park, CA: Benjamin Cummings, 1987.

Paans, R. *A Close Look at MVS Systems: Mechanisms, Performance, and Security.* New York: Elsevier, 1986.

Pasad, N. *Architecture and Implementation of Large Scale IBM Computer Systems.* Wellesley, MA: Q.E.D., 1981.

Pinkert, J., and Wear, L. *Operating Systems: Concepts, Policies, and Mechanisms.* Englewood Cliffs, NJ: Prentice Hall, 1989.

Plambeck, K. "Concepts of Enterprise Systems Architecture." *IBM Systems Journal,* No. 1, 1989.

Rashid, R., et al. "Machine-Independent Virtual Memory Management for Paged Uniprocessor and Multiprocessor Architectures." *IEEE Transactions on Computers,* August 1988.

Stallings, W. *Computer Organization and Architecture, Fourth Edition.* Upper Saddle River, NJ: Prentice Hall, 1996.

Talluri, M., Kong, S., Hill, M., and Patterson, D. "Tradeoffs in Supporting Two Page Sizes." *Proceedings of the 19th Annual International Symposium on Computer Architecture,* May 1992.

Tevanian, A., et al. "Mach Threads and the UNIX Kernel: The Battle for Control." *Proceedings, Summer 1987 USENIX Conference,* June 1987.

Turner, R. *Operating Systems: Design and Implementations.* New York: Macmillan, 1986.

Vahalia, U. *UNIX Internals: The New Frontiers.* Upper Saddle River, NJ: Prentice Hall, 1996.

Weizer, N. "A History of Operating Systems." *Datamation,* January 1981.

Wiederhold, G. *File Organization for Database Design.* New York: McGraw-Hill, 1987

Woodbury, P., et al. "Shared Memory Multiprocessors: The Right Approach to Parallel Processing." *Proceedings, COMPCON Spring'89,* March 1989.

INDEX

A

access control, 83, 85, 92–93, 208–209, 222, 230, 235
access method, 85, 129, 139–141
access rights, 81, 95–96, 209, 222, 238
address space, 17–18, 20, 25, 29, 31–33, 37, 39, 45, 53–54, 58, 61–62, 64, 67–68, 73, 97, 107, 109, 128–139, 153, 159–162, 173, 180, 184–185, 187–189, 193, 195–198, 206, 216, 218, 220, 222, 226, 229, 241–244
addressing, 16, 20, 22, 33, 107, 128, 136, 175–177, 237
application programming interface, 65
architecture, 3, 20, 23, 35, 39, 66–67, 73, 75, 77, 81, 84, 96–97, 107, 109–110, 127–129, 134, 136, 141, 164, 180, 182, 184, 191, 207, 215–217, 228
ARPAnet, 176
asynchronous procedure call (APC), 220
authentication, 208, 230, 238

B

base address, 19, 37, 241
basic file system, 84–85
basic I/O supervisor, 85
batch processing, 7, 12
Bell Laboratories, 145–148
block, 7, 18, 23, 26, 30, 33, 37, 42, 50–56, 61, 63–67, 74, 76–78, 84–85, 87, 90–92, 97, 103, 113, 128, 130–133, 138, 140–141, 156, 159, 165–174, 177–178, 181, 186, 193–196, 200–201, 203–204, 210, 217–218, 220, 222, 226–227, 229, 232, 234–235, 237, 242
block-oriented devices, 194
blocked state, 55, 64

C

cache coherence, 68, 222
cache manager, 226–227, 232
cache memory, 68, 227
central processing unit (CPU), 77
certification, 183
change mode (CHM), 53
chorus, 148
circular buffer, 42
cleaning policy, 40, 43
client, 96, 113–116, 175–176, 209–210, 215–216, 222, 225, 236–237, 239, 244
cluster(s), 42, 66–67, 72, 96, 148, 164–165, 172, 200, 230–231, 234–235
communications architecture, 81, 96–97, 141
computer systems, 7, 29, 66, 75–77, 82, 146–147
concurrent, 65, 68, 73, 103–104, 112–113, 117, 119–120, 127, 130, 139, 167, 189–191, 233, 242, 244
condition codes, 51–52
context switch, 23, 97, 184, 219
control and status registers, 51–52
control objects, 218
critical section, 134, 155, 162, 190–192, 242
CTSS, 14–15, 50, 145

D

data, 4–5, 8–10, 14–18, 22, 26, 30–32, 35–36, 44–47, 49–51, 53–54, 56, 58, 61–64, 66, 75–79, 81–85, 87, 91, 95–97, 102–103, 106, 108–111, 113, 115–122, 128, 130, 133, 136, 140–141, 145, 149, 153, 155–156, 158–178, 181, 184, 189–191, 193–208, 210–211, 218–220, 222–227, 229–238, 242, 244
database, 82–83, 96, 109, 148, 181–182, 187, 203, 224, 230, 235, 238–239
deadline scheduling, 72
deadlock, 44, 46–47, 68, 96–97, 134, 218
dedicated processor assignment, 74
Defense Advanced Research Projects Agency (DARPA), 146
Delete_One, 83
demand cleaning, 43–44
demand paging, 29, 146, 148–149, 163–164
device driver, 84, 105, 147, 149, 168–169, 171–173, 181, 184–187, 190–191, 197, 199–200, 202, 204–207, 217, 219–220, 226, 238
direct access, 7, 27, 141, 175, 178, 203
direct memory access (DMA), 76–77
directory files, 95, 200
disabled interrupts, 191
dispatcher objects, 218
distributed data processing (DDP), 96
distributed operating system, 96–97, 105–107, 115, 117, 180, 228, 236
distributed processing, 73, 96, 107, 216, 225, 236
DOS, *see* distributed operating system
dynamic link libraries (DLLs), 103
dynamic partitioning, 19, 26
dynamic relocation, 21, 37
dynamic scheduling, 74

E

EFLAGS register, 52
Ethernet, 175–176, 180
exit state, 55
external fragmentation, 18, 21, 28, 32, 37, 163–164

F

fetch cycle, 55
fetch policy, 40–41, 43
fields, 51, 82–83, 87, 90–91, 138, 141
file allocation, 82, 85, 87
file directories, 85, 91
file management, 49, 62, 76, 82–86, 91, 96
file management system, 49, 82–85, 91, 96
file organization, 82, 85, 87–92
file sharing, 95, 109, 235
file systems, 85, 87, 109–110, 147, 165, 168, 172–173, 176, 179, 181, 184–186, 195, 199, 203, 210, 216, 221, 226, 230–231
file tables, 49, 52
file transfer protocol (FTP), 176
files, 3–5, 49, 51, 54, 59–60, 62, 76, 81–85, 87, 90–93, 95–96, 103, 111, 120–122, 133, 149–153, 155–158, 160–161, 165–169, 171, 175, 178, 180–184, 186, 188–189, 195–197, 199–203, 206, 209–210, 224, 226, 229–232, 235–237, 243
First In First Out (FIFO), 40, 193
fixed-allocation policy, 43
fixes, 6, 109, 147, 150
flags, 51

FORTRAN, 8–9, 33, 35, 153, 157
frame locking, 41
free list, 164, 169, 173, 203–204, 224–225
functionally specialized processors, 72

G

gang scheduling, 74
granularity, 73

H

hardware, 3–7, 9–10, 12, 16–17, 19–27, 29–30, 32–35, 40–41, 43, 46, 56, 66, 68–69, 76, 80–81, 102–110, 117, 128–130, 136–137, 141, 145, 148, 150, 152, 158, 161–162, 164–165, 168–169, 171, 174, 176–177, 179–180, 184–187, 190–191, 193, 195, 200, 210–211, 216–217, 219, 222, 224, 228, 234, 236, 242, 244

I

I/O buffering, 75
I/O channel, 77, 128, 130
I/O devices, 3–4, 9–10, 49, 54, 59, 67, 75, 77, 80, 97, 128–129, 149, 171, 216, 219
I/O function, 75–77, 80, 204
I/O interrupt, 26, 55, 107
I/O management, 53, 74, 139
I/O manager, 221, 226, 237–238
I/O modules, 77, 79
I/O operations, 42, 80–81, 84, 130, 139, 204, 227, 232
I/O processor, 72, 77
I/O scheduling, 69, 85
I/O tables, 49
IBM, 7, 14, 29, 31, 39, 110, 127–128, 134–136, 147, 186, 215, 236
IBSYS, 7
index register, 137
indexed file, 87, 91
indexed sequential file, 87, 90–91
inheritance, 244
inodes, 165, 169–171, 178, 199, 202
Insert_One, 83
instruction cycle, 55, 78
internal fragmentation, 21, 25, 28, 30, 37, 163, 165, 169, 230
internet protocol (IP), 176, 207
interprocess communication (IPC), 180
interrupt, 9, 12, 14, 26, 45, 51, 53–56, 58, 64, 72, 76–79, 81, 107, 110, 117, 129–130, 132, 140–141, 150, 155, 160–162, 173, 184, 187, 189–194, 217–220
interrupt-driven I/O, 76

J

jacketing, 65
job control language (JCL), 8, 14
jobs, 7–8, 11–13, 15, 71, 74, 127–130, 133, 156, 161–163, 178, 192–193, 235

K

kernel, 5, 15, 41, 53, 55, 57–59, 61–65, 67–68, 131, 145–147, 149–167, 169–173, 175–176, 178–197, 199, 202–206, 209–212, 215–220, 222, 225–226, 228–229, 237, 239, 241–242, 244
kernel threads, 181, 216
kernel-level threads (KLTs), 63
key field, 90–91

L

linking, 7, 52, 105–106, 122, 129, 159, 198
load control, 40, 44
load sharing, 74
loading, 7, 19, 56, 117, 133, 181, 185–186, 195–198
log file, 90, 231–232
logical address, 18, 20–23, 25–26, 29, 32–33, 35, 37–39
logical I/O, 80–81, 85
long-term scheduling, 37, 69–71, 162
long-term storage, 17, 82
loosely coupled multiprocessor, 72

M

Mach, 42, 60–61, 147–148, 173, 180, 215–216
main memory, 4–5, 7–10, 12, 14–19, 22–23, 26–28, 30–32, 39, 41–44, 47, 49–50, 52, 55, 59, 62, 67–70, 72–73, 76–77, 79–80, 85, 90, 92, 97, 128, 130, 132–134, 138, 140, 159–161, 163–166, 171, 173, 182, 203, 207
master/slave, 67
medium-term scheduling, 69–70, 72, 162
memory fault, 39, 55
memory management, 12, 15, 18, 26, 32, 35, 39–41, 44, 49–53, 69, 72, 103, 117, 134–135, 137, 148, 150, 162, 178, 193, 239, 243
memory partitioning, 18
memory protection, 9, 16–17, 24, 109, 223
memory sharing, 107
memory tables, 49–50, 52
message, 9, 63, 67, 72, 102–104, 111–112, 115, 117–120, 128, 141, 158, 174–175, 180, 184, 207, 210, 216, 219, 225, 235–237, 239, 242
message passing, 216, 225
methods, 18, 23, 85, 140–141, 176, 179, 206, 208, 218, 221, 225, 238–239, 244
MFT, 231–232, 235
microkernel, 59, 180
mode switch, 54–56, 58, 64–65, 97
monitor, 5, 7–11, 14–15, 47, 59, 105, 109, 112, 116, 130, 183, 221, 225, 227, 230
MS-DOS, 40, 60, 102, 106–107, 109–110, 215–216, 221, 228–231, 235–236, 244
multics, 37–38, 145
Multiple Instruction Single Data (MISD) stream, 66
multiprocessing, 59, 62, 64, 66, 73, 102, 108, 128, 193, 216–217, 244
multiprocessor, 59, 62, 66–69, 72–74, 108, 138, 180, 182, 190, 193, 215–216, 218–220, 222, 242
multiprocessor scheduling, 72
multiprogramming, 10–16, 18–19, 27, 40, 44, 50, 64, 67–69, 71–73, 80, 127, 145
multiprogramming utilization histogram, 13
multitasking, 11, 73, 102–104, 110–113, 117–118, 182, 215, 228–229
multithreading, 60, 65, 68, 210
mutual exclusion, 68, 96, 133–134, 218, 220

N

network drivers, 226, 238
network operating system, 96–97
networking, 107–108, 110, 146–148, 150, 174, 176–182, 184–186, 191, 203, 205–207, 210–211, 216, 229, 235–236
nucleus, 5

O

objects, 31, 33, 101–102, 114–116, 120, 165, 199, 202, 206, 208–209, 218, 220–222, 225, 229–230, 236, 239–240, 242, 244
operating system, 1, 3–7, 9–19, 21–23, 25–29, 31–33, 35, 37, 39–69, 71–77, 79–85, 87, 89, 91, 93, 95–97, 101–110, 112, 127–131, 134, 137, 145–148, 150, 152, 157, 159, 171, 173, 176, 179–181, 183–184, 187–190, 194, 200, 206, 210–211, 215–217, 219–220, 225–226, 228, 236, 239, 241, 244
operating system control structures, 48
overhead, 10, 13, 17, 19, 22, 37, 40–43, 56, 64–65, 90, 156, 164–165, 189–190, 196, 200, 202, 204, 225, 232

P

page fault, 30, 40–41, 43–44, 163, 190–191, 197, 206, 220, 224–226
paging, 6, 18–29, 32–33, 35–37, 39–40, 42, 69, 82, 146, 148–149, 163–165, 173, 178, 180, 196, 206, 211, 219, 222, 224
passwords, 208
pathname, 94–95
peer, 176, 236
physical address, 21–24, 26, 33, 35, 37, 39, 92, 109, 224, 231
physical layer, 176
pile, 87, 89–90
pipes, 108, 154, 174, 206, 236–237
placement policy, 40–41
POSIX subsystem, 229
preallocation, 201
precleaning policy, 43
prepaging, 40, 164
priorities, 76, 129, 138–139, 161, 178, 192–193, 218, 241
privileged instructions, 9
process attributes, 50
process control, 16, 23, 49–56, 61, 131–132, 147, 151, 153, 159, 183
process control block, 23, 50–56, 61, 131
process control information, 16, 51–52, 54

process control structures, 49, 132
process creation, 43, 45, 53, 61, 225
process description, 44, 48
process description and control, 44
process identification, 51–52, 54
process location, 49
process sharing, 160, 224
process spawning, 63
process states, 44
process switch, 40, 53–56, 58, 65, 73, 97
process tables, 49–50, 52
process termination, 45–46
processes, 10, 15–17, 19, 22, 25–27, 29–30, 32, 35–36, 39–40, 43–49, 51–55, 57–63, 65, 67–74, 76, 80, 92, 97, 102, 107–109, 128–129, 131, 149, 153–165, 167, 174–178, 180, 183–184, 187–190, 192–199, 202, 205–206, 209–211, 218–219, 221–229, 236–237, 239–243
processor, 5, 7–19, 24, 26–28, 32, 43–45, 47–48, 51–59, 61–64, 66–69, 71–72, 74, 76–80, 97, 102–104, 108, 112, 120, 128, 130, 132, 134, 138–141, 162, 179, 183, 191, 193, 197, 215, 217–220, 228
processor registers, 51–52, 55, 61
processor state information, 51–52, 54–56
program status word (PSW), 52–53
programmed I/O, 76–77, 79
programming, 3, 8, 16, 18, 26, 31, 40, 44, 65–66, 101, 105, 107, 109, 111, 114–115, 118, 122, 148, 150, 159, 178–180, 183, 190, 200, 210–211, 215
protocols, 101, 146–147, 171, 174–178, 180–181, 186, 205–208, 210, 235–237

R

RAID, 232–234
ready state, 26, 55, 63–65
real memory, 27, 41, 129–130, 136–138
real-time scheduling, 72, 138, 193, 211
real-time task, 192
records, 10, 59, 80–83, 85, 87, 89–91, 96, 133, 141, 159, 196, 231–232
reference monitor, 221, 227, 230
register context, 62–63
relocation, 15–17, 21, 37, 118, 196
remote procedure call, 108, 176, 216, 236–237
rendezvous, 174
replacement policy, 40–43, 138, 225
resident monitor, 8, 11, 14–15
resident set management, 40–42
resource fork, 230
Retrieve_All, 83
Retrieve_Few, 83
Retrieve_Next, 83
Retrieve_One, 83
Retrieve_Previous, 83
running state, 54–56, 63–64

S

schedule, 40, 48, 57, 59, 62, 64–65, 68–69, 71–72, 74, 91, 129, 190, 198, 242
scheduling, 7–8, 12, 37, 51, 53–54, 62–74, 76, 81, 85, 97, 117, 127, 138–139, 149–150, 159, 161–162, 165, 178, 184, 189–193, 205, 210–211, 217–219, 225, 241–242, 244
secondary memory, 17–18, 29, 40, 42–43, 49–50, 55, 85, 97
security, 82, 107–110, 147, 188, 207–209, 211, 215–217, 221–222, 227, 230, 232, 235–238, 244
segment, 9, 26, 28–29, 31–39, 49–51, 53, 55, 69, 109, 120, 134, 136–138, 159–160, 162–164
segmentation, 17–19, 26–29, 31–35, 37–40, 82, 134
semaphore(s), 180, 205, 209–210, 218, 221, 239–240, 242
sequential access, 141, 178, 211, 226
sequential file, 87, 90–92, 94, 199
sequential processing, 83
serial processing, 7
server, 62, 96, 102, 106, 175–176, 181, 184, 199, 205–206, 209–211, 215–216, 225, 229–230, 235–239
setup time, 7–8
shared memory, 49, 66–67, 107, 146, 174, 180, 189, 206, 209–211, 222, 225
shared memory multiprocessor, 66–67
shell, 128–129, 145, 147, 149, 154–159, 161, 228
short-term scheduling, 69–70, 72, 162
simple batch systems, 7
simultaneous access, 95–96
Single Instruction Multiple Data (SIMD) stream, 66
Single Instruction Single Data (SISD) stream, 66
software, 3, 5, 7, 16–17, 32, 40–41, 43, 53, 56–57, 59, 67, 76, 81, 83–84, 96, 101–102, 105, 107–108, 111, 127, 141, 146–148, 155, 164, 168, 176, 179, 181–182, 186, 188, 199, 204, 206–207, 210, 215–217, 219, 229, 234–235, 239
Solaris, 60, 66, 97, 174, 216
spin lock, 134, 220
stack, 16, 31–33, 49–52, 54–55, 57–58, 61–64, 120, 131, 150, 159–163, 180, 188–189, 197–198, 206–207, 237, 241
stack pointer, 51, 120, 160
starvation, 161
swapping, 16, 23, 27, 29, 43–44, 47–49, 53, 62, 70, 72, 80, 149, 162–165, 173, 178, 195–196, 209
synchronization, 53, 66, 68, 73, 129, 190–191, 193, 205–206, 217–218, 225, 241–242, 244
system interconnection, 176
system interrupts, 54
system stack, 50, 54, 57
system structure, 80

T

tasks, 4, 35, 56, 77, 103, 108, 111, 127–134, 136, 138, 150, 161, 173–174, 183–184, 190, 192–193, 211
TCP/IP, 97, 146–147, 174–176, 180–181, 236–238
TELNET, 176
thrashing, 27, 29, 44, 163, 165
thread switch, 64–65, 73, 97
threads, 59–68, 73–74, 97, 109, 131, 136, 181, 183, 189–190, 193, 210, 216, 218–220, 222, 225, 241–242, 244
tightly coupled multiprocessing, 73, 128
time sharing, 13–15, 190
time-sharing systems, 12
timer, 9, 104, 119, 156, 189–192, 205, 218
transport layer, 235–236
trap, 25, 33, 35, 39, 54–55, 58, 65, 150, 161, 219

U

uniprocessor scheduling, 69
uniprogramming utilization histogram, 12
unit of dispatching, 59–60, 130
unit of resource ownership, 59–60
UNIX, 6, 40, 44, 52, 60–61, 101–102, 107, 128, 143, 145–153, 155–159, 161–163, 165, 167, 169, 171, 173–191, 193, 195–197, 199–203, 205–212, 215–216, 219, 221–222, 229–231, 235, 237, 242
Update_One, 83
user data, 50, 149, 163, 231
user program, 5, 8–9, 11, 13, 22, 33, 36, 45, 50, 53, 58–59, 71, 132, 139–141
user-level threads (ULTs), 63
user-visible registers, 51–52

V

variable-allocation policy, 43
variables, 32–33, 35, 49, 61, 120, 131, 153, 159, 188, 198, 202, 241, 244
virtual address, 19, 23–24, 59–60, 109, 127–128, 134, 136–137, 159–162, 173, 195–198, 218, 222–224, 226, 241–243
virtual memory, 18–19, 26–31, 40, 42, 47, 49–51, 55, 72, 76, 82, 107, 109, 127–128, 130, 132, 136, 141, 146–148, 154, 160, 183, 189, 193, 195–199, 202, 206, 210, 216, 222, 243–244
virtual memory manager, 109

W

Windows, 6, 44, 52, 60, 65, 101–123, 147, 158, 213, 215–219, 221, 223, 225, 227–229, 231, 233, 235–237, 239, 241–244
Windows NT, 52, 60, 65, 101–103, 106–111, 113, 147, 213, 215, 217, 219, 221, 223, 225, 227, 229, 231, 233, 235–237, 239, 241, 243
working directory, 95, 157